SPIRITUAL PILGRIM

SPIRITUAL PILGRIM

A Reassessment of the Life of the

Countess of Huntingdon

EDWIN WELCH

CARDIFF
UNIVERSITY OF WALES PRESS

© Edwin Welch, 1995

Reprinted, 2013

All rights reserved. No part of this book may be reproduced in any material form (including photocopying or storing it in any medium by electronic means and whether or not transiently or incidentally to some other use of this publication) without the written permission of the copyright owner except in accordance with the provisions of the Copyright, Designs and Patents Act 1988. Applications for the copyright owner's written permission to reproduce any part of this publication should be addressed to The University of Wales Press, 10 Columbus Walk, Brigantine Place, Cardiff CF10 4UP.

www.uwp.co.uk

British Library Cataloguing-in-Publication Data
A catalogue record for this book is available from the British Library.

ISBN 978-1-7831-6002-0

Printed and bound by CPI Group (UK) Ltd, Croydon, CR0 4YY

*In memory
of
Eleanor Cottrill
who first introduced me to the Countess*

Contents

List of Illustrations	viii
Acknowledgements	ix
List of Abbreviations	xiii
Shirley Family Pedigree	xv
Hastings Family Pedigree	xvi
Introduction	1
1 Childhood and Youth	7
2 Marriage	21
3 Conversion	37
4 Widowhood	56
5 Family and Friends	73
6 Freedom	93
7 The College at Trefeca	111
8 The Bethesda Orphan House	131
9 Secession	148
10 Bethesda Again	162
11 The College and the Apostolic Society	176
12 The Connexion	190
Appendix: Seymour's *Life and Times*	211
Note on Sources	215
Manuscript Sources	218
Index	225

Illustrations

1. Lord and Lady Huntingdon with their children, *c.* 1744.
2. Donnington House before it was rebuilt.
3. Monument to Theophilus, Earl of Huntingdon, in Ashby de la Zouch parish church.
4. Map of southern Georgia, *c.* 1752, showing Bethesda.
5. Portrait of Lady Huntingdon by J. Russell.
6. Map of Trefeca taken from the Talgarth tithe map, 1842.
7. Trefeca College, 1768.
8. Spa Fields Chapel and House.

Acknowledgements

Although the research for writing this life began only in 1986, the preparation for it may be considered to have started almost twenty-five years before, when I first began to list the many papers which had been found at Cheshunt College. Inevitably I have incurred debts to many people, some whose names I never knew and others whose names I confess I have forgotten, for information about Lady Huntingdon and records relating to her life. A full list of everyone who should be thanked would take up a great portion of this book. The work of some has been acknowledged in footnotes. Here I thank institutions rather than persons, naming only those whose work was not affiliated with any organization, or whose efforts on my behalf have far exceeded their official duties.

The following archives, libraries and other organizations have provided access to or copies of records and manuscripts, and often given very helpful advice:

Aberystwyth, National Library of Wales
Bedford, County Record Office
Belfast, Public Record Office of Northern Ireland
Birmingham University Library
Bristol, City Record Office
Bristol, The New Room
Bristol University Library
Cambridge, Westminster College, Cheshunt College Foundation archives
Cardiff, Glamorgan Record Office
Cardiff, St Fagans Museum
Chelmsford, Essex Record Office
Ely, Countess's Church
Fulneck (West Yorks.), Moravian Church archives
Gloucester, County Record Office
Hull, University Library
Leeds District Archives
Leicester, County Record Office
Lewes, East Sussex Record Office
London, Dept of Western MSS, British Library
London, Dr Williams's Library
London, Congregational Library (at DWL)

London, New College Library (at DWL)
London, Friends House Library
London, Greater London Record Office
London, Guildhall Library
London, Hoare's Bank archives
London, House of Lords Record Office
London, Lambeth Palace Library
London, Moravian Church House Library
London, Public Record Office
London, SPCK archives
Manchester, John Rylands University Library
Manchester, Methodist Archives Centre (at JRL)
Matlock, Derbyshire Record Office
Olney (Bucks.), Cowper and Newton Museum
Oxford, Rhodes House Library
Rayleigh (Essex), Countess of Huntingdon's Connexion archives
Stafford, County Record Office
Warwick, County Record Office
York, Borthwick Institute of Historical Research

Athens (Georgia), University of Georgia Library
Atlanta (Georgia), Emory University Library
Atlanta (Georgia), Georgia Dept of Archives
Carlisle (Pennsylvania), Dickinson College Library
Durham (North Carolina), Duke University Library
Madison (New Jersey), Methodist Archives, Drew University Library
Nashville (Tennessee), The Upper Room
New Haven, Yale University Library
New York, Columbia University Library
New York, Pierpont Morgan Library
San Marino (California), Huntington Library
Santa Barbara, University of California Library
Savannah (Georgia), Georgia Historical Society
Washington (DC), Library of Congress
Washington (DC), National Archives

Australia, Sydney, Mitchell Library
Germany, Herrnhut, Moravian Archives
Ireland, Dublin, National Library of Ireland

I also thank the following owners of manuscripts, who have supplied me with copies and assisted in various other ways:

P. Conlan, Esq., of Kent
Lord Granard of Castle Forbes (Ireland)
J. P. Heard, Esq., of Arlington (Virginia)
G. D. H. Wheler, Esq., of Ledston (Yorks.)

Acknowledgements

I am indebted to all those owners and custodians of archives and manuscripts who have given permission to reproduce quotations from them.

These institutions have provided information and assistance:

    Edinburgh, National Library of Scotland
    Edinburgh, Scottish Record Office
    Glasgow, University Library
    Guildford, Surrey Record Office
    Hertford, Hertfordshire Record Office
    Kendal, Cumbria Record Office
    London, Business Archives Council
    London, Historical Manuscripts Commission
    Northampton, Northamptonshire Record Office
    Winchester, Hampshire Record Office

The following libraries have assisted with access to printed books:

    Chicago, Newberry Library, which granted me a fellowship
    Chicago, University of Chicago Library
    Yellowknife (NWT, Canada), Court Library
    Yellowknife (NWT, Canada), Government Library

The individuals whose help I specially acknowledge include:

- The owners or custodians of Law's library at King's Cliffe, College Farm at Trefeca and Trefeca College, for access to those places;
- The Historical Society of the Presbyterian Church of Wales, which gave permission for me to see and quote from Howell Harris's diaries;
- Ms Genie Brown, who brought the Dallas MSS to my attention and has since helped in many ways;
- The Revd Dr David Cornick, Director of Cheshunt College Foundation;
- Mr Arwyn Lloyd Hughes of the National Museum of Wales;
- The Revd Dr Stephen Mayor, former Director of Cheshunt College Foundation, who initiated the proposal to publish a new biography, and helped in many ways;
- The late Revd Jack Newport, the last President of Cheshunt College, the staff and the governors of Cheshunt College, for years of hospitality and assistance in writing and publishing this book;
- Dr Mary Robertson of the Huntington Library who has done everything possible to make the Hastings papers available to me;
- Dr Boyd Schlenther of University College, Aberystwyth, for information about records in the National Library and elsewhere;
- The Revd Norman Smith of Chidham (Sussex) for copies of the Chichester church records;
- Mr and Mrs Staplehurst of Rayleigh for their hospitality and for access to the Connexion archives;

Dr Kate Thompson, formerly the Leicestershire County Archivist, who has patiently helped me over many years;

Professor W. R. Ward, who supplied me with advance information from his edition of John Wesley's journals and helped in other ways;

Dr Peter Willis of Newcastle upon Tyne, who has helped me with sources;

My daughters, who have acted as unpaid research assistants.

Above all I am particularly indebted to the Newberry Library trustees for a fellowship which enabled me to make intensive use of their resources. Without their help it would have been impossible to search the printed sources. I am grateful to my wife who has read the book twice in draft and carried out innumerable pieces of research on my behalf, and, finally, to Dr Geoffrey Nuttall who has very patiently read, helped, criticized and urged me on. This book could never have been written without his support. I can only hope that he, and everyone else concerned, will not be disappointed with the result.

Abbreviations

BL	British Library, Dept of Western MSS, London
Cheshunt archives	Archives of Cheshunt College Foundation, Westminster College, Cambridge
Cong. Lib.	Congregational Library, Dr Williams's Library, London
DWL	Doctor Williams's Library, London
Drew Univ.	Methodist Archives Centre, Drew University, Madison, NJ
GLRO	Greater London Record Office, London
Hastings Wheler Letters	[G. H. Wheler], *Hastings Wheler Family Letters*, 1 (London, 1929); 2 (Wakefield, 1935)
HMC	Reports of the Royal Commission on Historical Manuscripts
Hunt. Lib.	Huntington Library, San Marino, CA
JRL	John Rylands University Library, Manchester
Lamb. Pal. Lib.	Lambeth Palace Library, London
Meth. Archives	Methodist Archives Centre, John Rylands University Library
NLI	National Library of Ireland, Dublin
NLW	National Library of Wales, Aberystwyth
PRO	Public Record Office, London
PRONI	Public Record Office of Northern Ireland, Belfast
SMU	Bridwell Library, Southern Methodist University, Dallas, TX
Stemmata Shirleiana	E. P. Shirley, *Stemmata Shirleiana* (London, 1841, 2nd edn., 1873)
RO	Record Office (preceded by name of county or city)
Two Calv. Meth. Chapels	E. Welch (ed.), *Two Calvinistic Methodist Chapels, 1743–1811* (London Record Society, 1975)

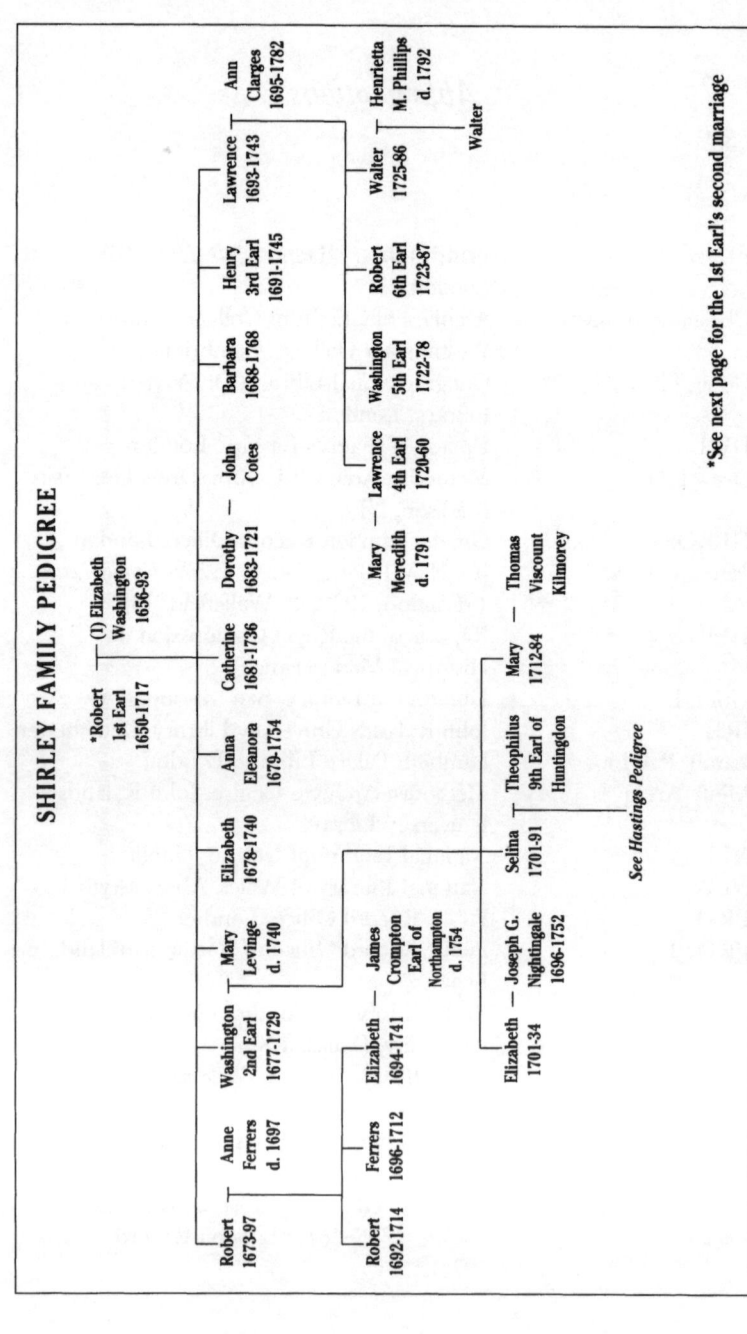

SHIRLEY FAMILY PEDIGREE

(continued)

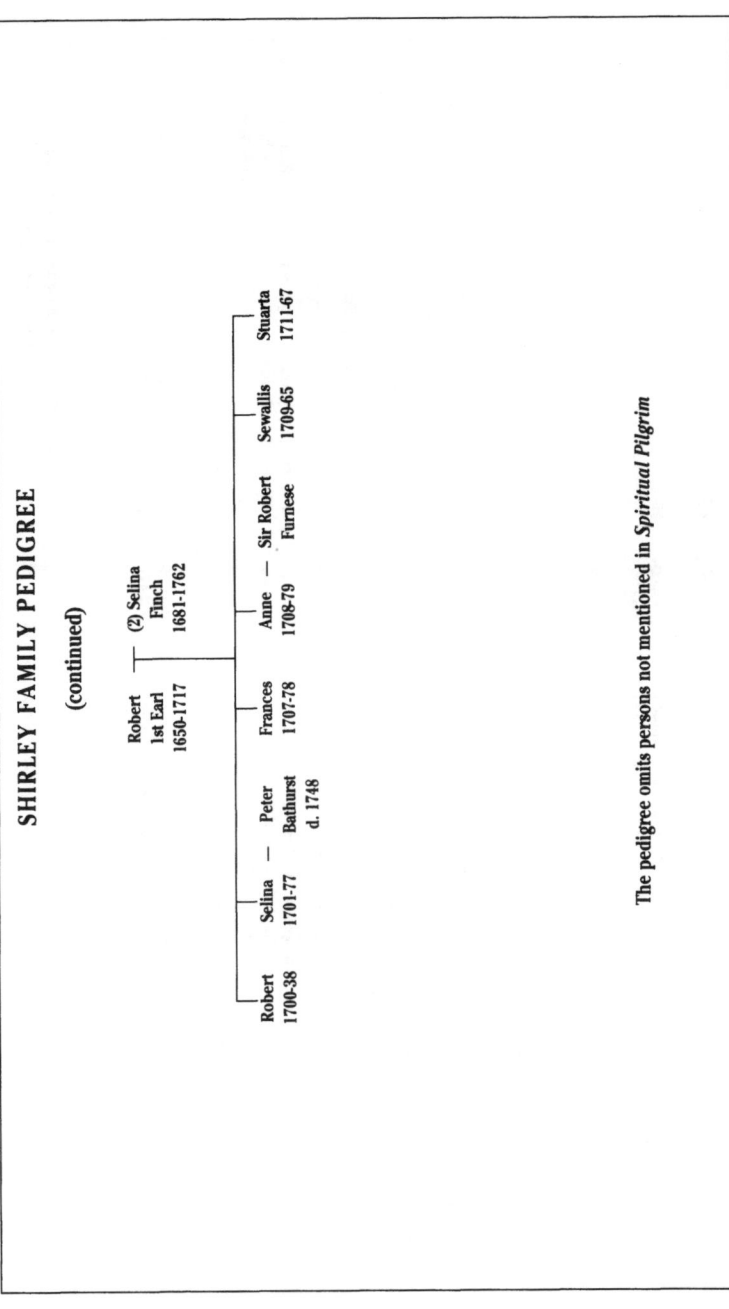

The pedigree omits persons not mentioned in *Spiritual Pilgrim*

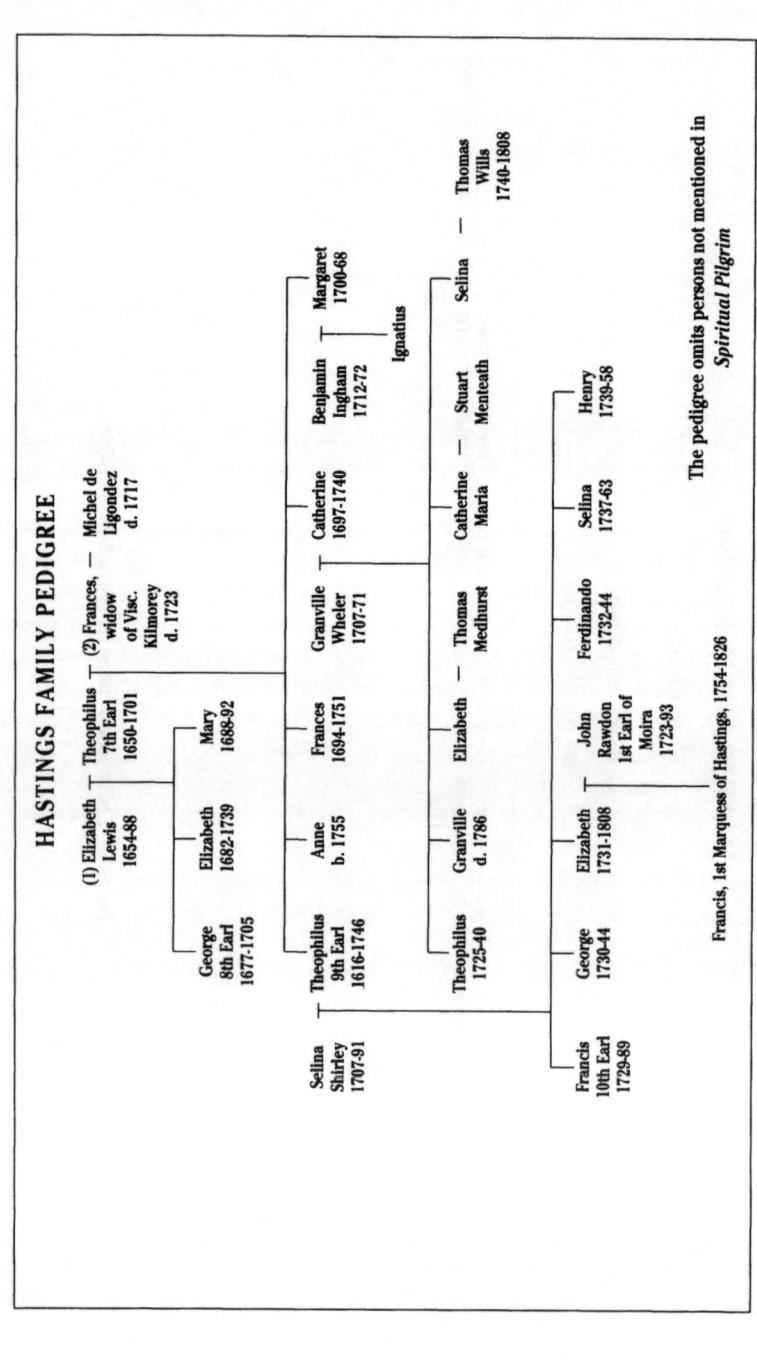

Introduction

The lives of eighteenth-century Methodists suffered in varying degrees from the attentions of nineteenth-century hagiographers. It is almost impossible to discover from the earlier lives of Howell Harris why he separated from the other Welsh Calvinists.[1] In early histories of Methodism John Wesley's wife gets a brief mention as a monomaniac, since it was clearly impossible to avoid any mention of her.[2] The writers of such biographies were also somewhat hindered by the attempts of descendants to conceal episodes which they thought demeaning. Letters, diaries and autobiographical writings were unavailable. The journal of Thomas Haweis, one of Lady Huntingdon's trustees, was suppressed by his son, an Anglican clergyman who disapproved of his father's preference for evangelical dissenters rather than his fellow Anglicans.[3] Various other examples could be cited. The Revd Edwin Sidney published a number of biographies, two about his noble patron's kinsmen (Sir Richard and Rowland Hill), in which no hint of scandal or misbehaviour is mentioned. Sidney is one of the better writers since he had access to manuscript sources and transcribed them accurately. Others hagiographers were quite willing to alter a manuscript source to suit their intention of describing their subject as a perfect human.

No one has suffered more from this treatment than the principal female Methodist of the period, Selina Countess of Huntingdon. She has been described as one brought up to riches and opulence, but when she was born her parents were living on a soldier's pay and the charity of her mother's relations. Her noble rank has been emphasized, but until she was ten she was the second daughter of the penniless younger son of a peer.

---

[1] E.g. John Bulmer, *Memoirs of the Life and Religious Labours of Howell Harris* (Haverfordwest, 1824) says only that he endeavoured to suppress 'a spirit of levity, pride, and unwatchfulness' (p. 46).
[2] Abel Stevens, *History of the Life and Times of John Wesley* (London, 1864), 283.
[3] *The Autobiography of William Jay* (London, 1974), 479.

When she finally achieved the courtesy title of Lady Selina Shirley, her father was entangled in so many lawsuits that he was unable to pay the dowries of his three daughters, except by granting mortgages on the family estates. By that time too her parents had separated. She remained with her father, while her mother went abroad with her younger sister. After Lady Selina's marriage to Lord Huntingdon and her conversion, her evangelism was severely curtailed for many years by the need to care for her husband, her children and the family estates. Her contribution to the first Methodist awakening was small (and not very successful). She was only to become important in the Methodist movement during the second revival in the 1760s, when her work was unhampered by other commitments. She directed her attentions towards the same people as the Wesleys and Whitefield, and not to the peerage as her biographers have claimed. Her efforts to convert the rich and noble were confined to a brief period in the fifties and (as she herself admitted) had little effect.[4] Very few of her chapels were established in fashionable watering places, and only that at Bath attracted a crowd of patricians who admired the music rather than the sermons.

For all these misrepresentations Lady Huntingdon herself must be assigned part of the blame. Throughout her life she tried to avoid publicity. She did not keep a journal or diary as so many of her Methodist contemporaries did. Except for the last decade of her life little was published which bore her name. In her will she requested her executors would 'not encourage, but will, so far as they can, prevent any publication of my life, or in any other way concerning me, nor publish, nor permit any of my letters, private correspondence, or other papers to be published'.[5] It was in the same spirit that she requested that her funeral should be as modest as possible and no monument should be erected over her grave. Her executors respected these provisions. The sole indication of her grave in the church at Ashby de la Zouch is the monument which she raised to her husband. Except for a pamphlet describing her last days written by Thomas Haweis, her wishes were respected and no biography appeared until forty-eight years after her death. During that long interval most of her correspondence had disappeared into various muniment rooms, and all those who had known her, even in her later life, were dead. I have summarized my reasons for rejecting A. C. H. Seymour's *Life and Times of Selina Countess of Huntingdon* in the Appendix. It is so unreliable that none of its statements can be accepted as evidence unless supported by indepen-

[4] Lord Granard's MSS, Lady H. to Lord Moira, 10 April 1759.
[5] Cheshunt, C 16/3.

dent sources. Seymour's attempts to produce the biography of a saint have disguised the true character of a woman who triumphed over her disabilities to establish a college and a connexion.

In writing this biography I have been mindful of C. V. Wedgwood's advice to read the original sources before looking at any later printed works on the subject.[6] Much of Lady Huntingdon's correspondence has survived, though it has been very widely scattered during the last two centuries. Her own letters, which are also to be found in many parts of the world, are difficult to read. To the end of her life she found spelling and capitalization difficult. Her punctuation was almost non-existent, and only Howell Harris amongst the Methodists exceeds her in illegibility. At times of grief she was unable to express her feelings in writing. Only one account of the death of a member of her family has been found. It is for her daughter Lady Selina in 1763, and, like that for Fanny Cowper in 1742, was only prepared for circulation to their many friends. We have no account of the death of her husband whom she adored, or her children who were much loved by her. Yet she was not indifferent to them or to her fellow Methodists. Her letters enquiring after John Wesley's illnesses even after they had separated for ever show her concern.

Although Lady Huntingdon's letters are evidence that her formal education was very limited, and although she rarely quotes from books, yet there is evidence that she read widely in later life. Some seventy books from her library are still to be found at Cheshunt College, and they indicate her wide range of interests. They include works by Moravians, Quakers and the French Pietists, works on gardening, elocution and medicine. Her name appears in various subscription lists for books which interested her.[7] In addition, throughout her life she arranged for the publication of works by William Law and puritan divines. Some of the students at her college have recorded that she read and expounded the Bible to them. Others have left evidence of her ability to encourage conversions.

But perhaps the most surprising information about Lady Huntingdon which is revealed by her correspondence is her energy and ability. Until the last few years of her life she employed neither amanuensis nor secretary, yet her correspondence was voluminous. After her marriage she gradually took over the management of her husband's affairs – first by suggestions and later by conducting the correspondence herself. Some

---

[6] C. V. Wedgwood, *History and Hope* (London, 1987), 15.

[7] Dr Peter Wallis of Newcastle upon Tyne has supplied me with information about Lady H's subscriptions from the Book Subscriptions Lists project.

resented the interference of a woman, even in matters which concerned the Shirley family, while others soon found it more convenient to write directly to her about estate and financial matters. All this was excellent experience because her husband died intestate in 1746, leaving her with the responsibility for his estates and their children. Her improvement of the estates led her eldest son to leave his mother in charge after he reached his majority. She took a great interest in building, and organized an extension to his house at Donnington Park in which to house the treasures which he brought back from the Grand Tour. Her successful attempts to collect his rents which had remained unpaid for years and other changes seem to have been responsible for riots in Leicestershire and Derbyshire. She had them suppressed by calling on the local magistrates to read the Riot Act and request military aid.

Her ability to organize was responsible for George Whitefield's bequest of his Orphan House at Bethesda in Georgia. It was a very difficult task to organize an institution with various problems so many miles across the Atlantic. She tackled it with her usual energy, and was only defeated by the outbreak of war in the colonies; but for that she may well have carried out her intention of visiting Bethesda in person. As her chapels increased in number, and especially after her secession in 1782, the task of finding ministers and students to supply them all required her constant vigilance and frequent letters. In this she was usually successful, and there are few examples of her chapels being closed for lack of a preacher. Although she built and paid for her first few chapels, she soon realized the importance of local contributions, and by 1773 she was setting out the terms on which she would contribute to the erection of a chapel in Dublin.[8] Even on her deathbed she was concerned about the supply of ministers for the Spa Fields chapel, and almost her last act was an attempt to pay the departing minister his stipend.

Her married life was punctuated by illnesses, probably the result of continuous childbearing, and after her husband's death she continued to complain of ill-health. However her later illnesses often coincided with periods of depression and were probably more psychosomatic than the earlier ones. At the age of fifty-eight she was still able to outwalk her younger companions: 'Dear Lady Ann [Erskine] had such a drive, but I walked over the sea, She and Hannah [Scutt] wadeing through after me and finding me safe on land when they arriv'd after infinite difficultys. This is enough to frighten you all.'[9] She had built her first chapel at the age

[8] Cong. Lib., II a 17/25.
[9] SMU, Hunt. 63, Lady H. to Mrs Wadsworth, 16 January 1776.

of fifty-three, and planned her college at Trefeca when she was sixty. At sixty-three she took responsibility for Bethesda, and at seventy-five formed her own Connexion. Until she was eighty she continued to travel extensively in southern England and Wales to supervise her chapels and students.

Thomas Haweis in his somewhat fulsome description of Lady Huntingdon was compelled to admit that she was not a saint: 'But it may be said, was she a perfect character? No. This is not the lot of mortals on this side the grave. When the moon walketh in her brightness, her shadows are most visible.'[10] He went on to list her defects as a 'temper warm and sanguine'. She was too hasty in her conclusions and sometimes injudicious in her choice of ministers. If she lived in our times, it might be thought necessary to add to these her ownership of slaves, her use of snuff, and even her drinking wine and spirits,[11] but all these were still socially acceptable in the eighteenth century. Slavery was a problem which could only be solved by an international agreement. She considered slavery in a Christian establishment preferable to freedom without religion. Snuff was considered the height of fashion. John Wesley thought tea-drinking unhealthy (but the Countess drank tea too) and recommended small beer.[12] These matters must be included in any honest biography. As Thomas Haweis wrote on the same subject, 'I am the historian of truth, as far as I know it.'

I have chosen to describe Lady Huntingdon's life as a spiritual pilgrimage because this seems to me to sum up her slow progress towards the foundation of a separate religious denomination. Even before she became a Methodist in 1739 she was searching for a religious movement with which she could identify herself. Because of the nature of eighteenth-century Methodism, conversion did not immediately satisfy her. In 1748 she found Whitefield's Calvinism more acceptable than John Wesley's Arminianism. She took a great interest in the Society of Friends although there is no evidence that she considered joining it. She undoubtedly thought seriously of asking to be admitted to the Moravian Church. The only Protestant denomination which did not attract her attention was possibly the Baptists, although evidence of this may be forthcoming in the future. It was not until the middle of the century that she finally settled on

[10] T. Haweis, *An Impartial and Succinct History . . . of the Christian Church* (London, 1800), 253.
[11] Leics. RO, 14D32/6, 12, Henry Hastings to Lady H., 8 Oct. 1745; T. Aveling, *Memorials of the Clayton Family* (London, 1867), 22.
[12] See H. D. Rack, *Reaonable Enthusiast* (London, 1989), 442, 443 for John Wesley's views of tobacco and alcohol.

the Anglican form of Calvinistic Methodism. A former Trefeca student, the Revd W. F. Platt, preaching a funeral sermon on her death, described her pilgrimage: 'this discovery [of the truth] was like the rising of the sun, which rose by degrees upon her precious soul, till within these twenty years past when she saw it in its meridian splendour.'[13] Her opinions, even after she had decided to remain in the Church of England, were ecumenical, as were those of Howell Harris and George Whitefield. When events forced her to leave the Anglican Church in 1782, she did so with reluctance. Although her spiritual pilgrimage ended there, her lifework did not.

---

[13] W. F. Platt, *The Waiting Christian* (Bristol, 1791), 6.

1

Childhood and Youth

About 1724 when Theophilus the ninth Earl of Huntingdon was travelling in France, his elder half-sister, Lady Betty Hastings, sent him a letter with all the English gossip she could collect. Some of this came from his sisters and related to his native county, Leicestershire: 'I had a letter the other day from Lady Frances, both she and Lady Ann are well and meet with the Civility and regard they deserve from everyone; Lord Ferris's Daughters are now come into the neighbourhood.'[1] In this anonymous fashion, Lady Selina Shirley, second daughter of Earl Ferrers[2] and the future wife of Theophilus, Earl of Huntingdon, makes her first appearance in contemporary records. Her early life, in contrast to the vast quantity of records about her life after she married, is very poorly documented. We do not have a record of her place and date of birth, though the former was traditionally said to be at Astwell in Northamptonshire, and the latter can be deduced from later records. We do not know when or where she was baptized. Neither can we be certain where or how she lived during her first seventeen years, although some deductions can be made from the circumstantial evidence. The reason for this obscurity can be found in the history of the Shirley family during the eighteenth century.

Her grandfather was Sir Robert Shirley. He had succeeded to the family's estates and baronetcy in 1669 when his nephew died. The family had always supported the Crown and he continued the tradition.[3] In 1677 Charles II had revived the title of Baron Ferrers in his favour 'without any

---

[1] Hunt. Lib., HA 4723. An extract of this letter is printed in *HMC Hastings 3*, p.1.
[2] She should not be confused with her aunt, Lady Selina Shirley, who was born in 1701.
[3] His ancestor, another Sir Robert, had rebuilt the chapel on the family estate of Staunton Harold after his predecessors had allowed it to fall into decay (see PRO, SP 16 535, 26). The well-known inscription over the chapel door was added after the Restoration (N. Pevsner, *The Buildings of England: Leicestershire and Rutland* (London, 1960), 238). See also A. C. Lacy, 'Sir Robert Shirley', *Trans. Leics. Arch. and Hist. Soc.*, 58 (1982–3), 25–35.

interposition or money given either to mistress or to minister'.[4] However his opposition to the king's Roman Catholicism caused him to desert James II in 1688. He was one of the peers who conducted Princess Anne to Nottingham when she fled her father's court, and he remained her favourite until she died.[5] In August 1711 she became godmother to his last daughter, who was named Stewarta in her honour.[6] Only a month later he was created the first Earl Ferrers and Viscount Tamworth. Before the Queen's death he attended the House of Lords regularly, and took an active part in its debates.[7] After the Queen's death he was believed to favour the restoration of James III.[8] This, together with old age, may account for his withdrawal from politics after the accession of George I.

His first wife was Elizabeth, the daughter and heiress of Lawrence Washington of Wiltshire, to whom he had been married in 1671 when he was twenty and she only fifteen. Before her death in 1693 she had brought him five sons and five daughters.[9] Only one of their daughters married – Dorothy, to John Cotes of Lichfield in 1700. Three of the Earl's sons married – the eldest, Robert, to a cousin Anne Ferrers, the second, Washington, to Mary Levinge, and the youngest, Lawrence, to Anne Clarges. Six years after his first wife's death, and at a time when his first grandchildren were born, the Earl married again. His bride was Selina Finch, the daughter of a London merchant, who was said to have brought him no property or marriage portion. By his second wife he had four sons and five daughters. The estates which he had accumulated would have been sufficient for the maintenance of all his children, but he diverted as much as possible to his second wife and her children. The Shirley estates which he inherited from his nephew were extensive. The two principal family mansions were Staunton Harold in Leicestershire, inherited from the Stauntons in the fifteenth century, and Chartley in Staffordshire from the estate of the last Earl of Essex in the seventeenth. Around each he owned extensive property. In Leicestershire there were other properties near Melton and at Coleorton.[10] He owned lands in Staffordshire, southern Derbyshire and southern Nottinghamshire. There were outlying properties at Ettington in Warwickshire, which was the original home of

---

[4] G. E. C[okayne], *The Complete Peerage*, vol.6, p.606, from which most of the information in these paragraphs is derived.
[5] *Stemmata Shirleiana* (1873), 165.
[6] *HMC, Portland 4*, pp.608, 612.
[7] J. J. Cartwright, *The Wentworth Papers* (London, 1883), 159, 239.
[8] D. Szechi, *Jacobitism and Tory Politics* (Edinburgh, 1984), 62, 71-2.
[9] For the family pedigree see *Stemmata Shirleiana*.
[10] Hunt. Lib., HA Legal, box 19, 10, Chancery proceedings, n. d.

the Shirleys, and at Astwell in Northamptonshire, both of which included smaller family mansions. In addition to his first wife's property in Wiltshire, he had inherited a share of the Earl of Essex's Irish lands in County Monaghan. These were divided between Shirley and the Hertford family in 1692.[11]

The Earl's eldest son, another Robert, died in 1697, but left a son, also Robert, who became Viscount Tamworth in 1711 and was heir to his grandfather's titles and estates. He unfortunately died of smallpox in 1714, leaving his uncle Washington as heir to the earldom.[12] Washington, like most of his brothers and sisters, had already quarrelled with his father, who now set out to disinherit him of everything but the title. The traditional cause of the breach was Washington's marriage in 1704. His wife Mary was the daughter of Sir Richard Levinge of Parwich in Derbyshire, and a neighbour of the Shirleys.[13] Being only a second son, Richard Levinge had become a lawyer – which may already have been a family tradition. In 1690 he went to Ireland and became Solicitor General with a seat in the Irish Commons. In 1692 he was elected Speaker of the Irish House of Commons. After holding and losing several offices, he was appointed Lord Chief Justice of the Irish Common Pleas in 1720.[14] He was generally reckoned a cautious or moderate man: Swift described him as 'the most timorous man alive.'[15] It is difficult to see why Earl Ferrers objected to the marriage of a younger son with Levinge's daughter. Earl Ferrers had no objection to the legal profession as such: his son Lawrence was admitted to the Bar in 1716.[16] There is evidence from the Earl's will that he was very concerned about his children's marriages, but it does not appear that his second wife did anything to fan the flames.

By 1714 three of Washington's sisters were also in disgrace. Elizabeth, the eldest daughter, had taken refuge in London with Lady Ann Courtney, and her younger brother Lawrence wrote at her father's request to say that if she left the care of her relation Lord Abingdon and turned off

---

[11] E. P. Shirley, *Some Account of the Territory or Dominion of Farney* (London, 1845), 136–8. A note of the division of the estates can be found at the Warws. R.O., CR 2131 15.

[12] The baronry passed to the first Earl's granddaughter Elizabeth and, by her marriage, to the Townshend family.

[13] Levinge family pedigrees can be found in Derbys. RO, Daniel Drakeyne's book of pedigrees, and Hunt. Lib., HA, Genealogy, box 3, 5. Neither is complete.

[14] For Sir Richard Levinge see F. A. Inderwick, *A Calendar of the Inner Temple Records*, 3 (London, 1901), 131; F. E. Ball, *The Judges in Ireland* (London, 1926), 93, 94; J. Swift, *A Short Character of Thomas Earl of Wharton* (1710); J. A. Froude, *The English in Ireland* (London, 1872), 270.

[15] H. Williams (ed.), *The Correspondence of Jonathan Swift* (Oxford, 1963), vol.1, p.202.

[16] R. A. Roberts (ed.), *A Calendar of the Inner Temple Records*, 4 (London, 1933), 23.

'the French woman' she might return home to Twickenham.[17] Two of her sisters, Barbara and Anna Eleanora were living with their married sister Dorothy at Lichfield. The former wrote, 'I do not care what my father thinks... my father has already showed his ill will to me, as much as he can.'[18] Washington had taken refuge in Ireland with his wife's family. He had been an ensign in the Coldstream Guards under the colonelcy of General John Cutts. Cutts was Deputy to Lord Ormonde, the Lord Lieutenant of Ireland, so Washington resigned his ensigncy a year after his marriage and sought employment in one of the new regiments which Lord Cutts was raising in Ireland. Lord Abingdon, his 'cousin' and the protector of his sister, Elizabeth, had already recommended him to Ormonde in February 1704/5.[19] Cutts wrote from Dublin to Ormonde in London a year later to remind him that Washington had been promised a company in a new regiment.[20] In March 1706 Sir Richard Levinge was pressing the claims of his son-in-law, and Cutts had found a suitable regiment.[21] Within a month Washington had received 'Coll: Stannix's company'.[22] Returning to England, probably to join his wife, Washington was saved from the wreck of the *Fox* man of war in Holyhead Bay, but, so far as can be discovered, Washington spent the next ten years in Ireland.[23] In 1713 he was elected a member of the Irish Parliament by the corporation of Fore, a small town in Co. Westmeath.[24] This Parliament met only from the end of November until Christmas Eve 1713, when it was prorogued, and was then dissolved by the death of Queen Anne in 1714, and Washington did not stand for election again.

Washington Shirley and his wife had three daughters and no sons. Neither the date of his marriage nor that of the birth of the three daughters was entered in the Shirley family records.[25] Nor have the official entries been traced in any parish register. This in a family so conscious of its ancestry shows how angry the first Earl was with his son.

[17] Montagu Bertie, second Earl of Abingdon, called Washington Shirley his cousin, but the relationship seems somewhat distant.
[18] *HMC, 11th Rep., pt 4* (London, 1887), 228.
[19] *HMC, Ormonde MSS, 8,* p.137.
[20] NLI, Ormonde MSS, vol.168, 61, Cutts to Ormonde, 13 February 705 6. Abstract printed in *Ormonde*, op. cit., 219.
[21] *Ormonde*, op. cit., 225, quoting NLI; Ormonde MSS, vol.168, 197.
[22] NLI, Ormonde MSS, vol.168, 545, Cutts to Ormonde, 9 May 1706; Ormonde MSS., op. cit., 230, 237.
[23] Ormonde MSS. op. cit., 254.
[24] *Journal of the House of Commons of Ireland* (Dublin, 1795), vol.2, pp.741, 743; J. L. McCracken, *The Irish Parliament in the 18th Century* (Dublin, 1971), 4.
[25] E. P. Shirley in *Stemmata Shirleiana* refers frequently to the Staunton parish register. However Staunton Harold was part of the parish of Breedon on the Hill, and the register he

Washington's first daughter Elizabeth, named after his mother, was born about 1704, and probably in England. The second daughter Selina, who took his stepmother's name, was born on 13 August 1707. Although the authorities differ between 12 and 13, the latter is certainly correct, because after the introduction of the Gregorian calendar in 1752 she celebrated her birthday on 24 August, eleven days later.[26] The historian of Northamptonshire, who gives the correct date, also says that she was born at Astwell House on the Shirleys' Northamptonshire estates. This is the more probable because Washington's nephew Robert, and not his father, occupied this estate at that time. As late as 1906 visitors to the house (now Astwell Castle) were shown the room in which she was born, but this can no longer be identified by the owners.[27] The third daughter Mary, named after her mother, was born in Dublin on 25 September 1712. Despite the compliment paid in the names of his first two daughters his father was not reconciled to Washington. Elizabeth married Joseph Gascoigne Nightingale of Enfield in 1725. She died nine years later, leaving a son who erected an impressive monument to his parents in Westminster Abbey. Selina, the subject of this biography, married Theophilus, Earl of Huntingdon, in 1728. Mary married Thomas Viscount Kilmorey in 1730, after her father's death.[28]

There is an indication in later evidence that Washington's family spent part of the time in Ireland on the Shirley family estates at Carrickmacross in Co. Monaghan. Two inhabitants of the town giving evidence in 1735 stated that they knew Washington and his daughters Mary and Selina.[29] Their life cannot have been very comfortable at Carrickmacross. In 1641 the castle had been rendered uninhabitable, and the parish church destroyed. A house for the use of the family was not built there until about 1750.[30] They may also have spent some time in Dublin, where the youngest daughter was born and from where Washington addressed

quotes from was clearly a family record only. This volume has since disappeared, being neither in the Leics. RO nor in Earl Ferrers's possession. I am indebted to the County Archivist and Earl Ferrers for this information. The earlier Shirley Great Pedigree roll is in the Leics. RO.

[26] Cheshunt archives, C 1/1, p.104; G.E.C., op. cit. (vol.6, p.661) is incorrect.

[27] G. Baker, *The History and Antiquities of Northamptonshire* (London, 1822), 40; W. Dry, *Northamptonshire: Little Guide* (London, 1906), 251; Warws. RO, CR 2131 19. Astwell is extra-parochial and I am indebted to Patrick King, sometime County Archivist, for checking the two registers of the neighbouring parishes of Wappenham and Syresham for me.

[28] *Stemmata Shirleiana* (1841), 147–51.

[29] PRONI, D 1351 A 4, depositions in Chancery, 9 December 1735. Neither Washington's wife nor Elizabeth was mentioned because they were not involved in the suit.

[30] S. Lewis, *Topographical Dictionary of Ireland* (London, 1837), vol.1, p.275; Shirley, *Farney*, 145.

a letter to his father, in which he unsuccessfully sought a reconciliation.[31]

During the last few years of his life the Earl settled his Irish estates on the eldest son of his second marriage. All the unentailed English estates he conveyed to trustees. The Leicestershire and Warwickshire estates were to benefit his wife, and their eldest surviving son after her death. The Leicestershire, Derbyshire and Nottinghamshire estates were also to provide annuities for their younger children. The Northamptonshire estates were already charged by an earlier trust with capital sums for Washington's children, and the Wiltshire estates were reserved for the younger children of his first marriage.[32] Having disposed in this manner of as much of the family estates as he could, Earl Robert made his will on 25 November 1717.[33] His body was to be buried in the family chapel at Staunton Harold, and a monument, modelled on that of the Duke of Beaufort in St George's chapel at Windsor, to be erected there. The funeral was a grand one with about fifty mourners headed by the Earl of Chesterfield, but not one of his children was present.[34] He instructed his executors, the three trustees, to sell his house in Pall Mall for the benefit of his widow. The house which he owned at Twickenham was for his wife's use during her lifetime and then to go to the eldest surviving son of his second marriage. His Countess was also allowed all the fittings and furniture there as well as a selection of jewels and coaches. Each of his unmarried daughters, except Lady Barbara, was given a dowry of £5,000, but if any daughters of the second marriage married without their mother's consent they were to forfeit half of it to the others. Washington and his sister Barbara, was given £20 for mourning 'and no more'. Of the two other surviving sons by his first marriage Henry was given an annuity of £100 out of the Derbyshire and Nottinghamshire estates, and Lawrence £100 for mourning, since he was already provided for. The Earl anticipated an attempt to upset this arrangement of the estates. If any children of his first marriage attempted to overturn his will the executors were to pay his widow £1,000 a year until the lawsuit ended. In addition all the legal costs of his wife and children in any action brought against them were to be paid out of the Staffordshire estates. Washington took no

[31] Hunt. Lib., HA 10844, letter of Washington to Lord Ferrers, dated 5 July 1707. This letter appears to refer to the death of Washington's nephew, Ferrers Shirley, which happened in Oxford in October 1712 (*Stemmata Shirleiana* (1841), p. 136).
[32] Leics. RO, 26D53 1897 and 190, legal summaries produced in the subsequent lawsuits; E. P. Shirley, *Lower Eatington* (London, 1869), 22.
[33] PRO, PROB 11/562; Prerogative Court of Canterbury register of wills.
[34] The list of mourners is in Warws. RO CR 2131/16, p. 27.

legal action when the Earl died at Bath on Christmas day of 1717. Instead he seized possession of all his father's property, except the Wiltshire estates, and left the widow and her children to seek their legal remedy. For the Irish estates he made use of his father-in-law, who hired an agent to seize the Carrickmacross property.[35] Washington also changed the provision for the dowry of his three daughters, charging it on the other estates in the Midlands. The executors vainly endeavoured to get all the rents paid to them and to see the estate account books.[36] In addition, although he allowed his father to be buried in Staunton church, Washington later refused permission for the large monument to be erected there. His half-brother George later placed it in Ettington church with an inscription giving the reason.[37]

It was in this way that the lawsuits and other disputes which were to dog the Shirley family for the next hundred years or more began. Washington reached an agreement with his niece, Lady Elizabeth Compton, and her husband over their claim on the estate, but failed to keep full possession of the lands.[38] When the Chancery suit brought against him was partly successful in 1725 he carried his appeal to the House of Lords. He alleged that a settlement on the eldest son of the family had disappeared together with a number of other important documents, and tried to prove their validity by letters of his mother and the family lawyer. He was able to establish that his father had revoked the entail on several of the estates between 1710 and 1717 in an attempt to disinherit him. In Chancery proceedings between 1719 and 1724 Washington concentrated on trying to get access to the missing settlement and allied deeds, while the Countess, on her own behalf and that of her children, and the executors said that they had made every deed they had available to Sir Richard Levinge. Although a compromise agreement between the parties was reached in the Lords in March 1725/6, it did not settle all the problems.[39] After Washington's death his three daughters and their husbands were sued by most of the other members of the family, and Lady Huntingdon's dowry was not finally settled until 1810 almost twenty years after her death.[40]

[35] Hunt. Lib., HA 15190, letter of Levinge to anon., 26 February 1717 18.
[36] Hunt. Lib., HAF, box 70, 22; HAM, box 70, 25, attornment of Ettington tenants, 1717, 1719; HA 4584, trustees to Mr Clark, 25 January 1717 8; Warws. RO, CR 2131 16, letters of 25 January 1717 8 and 20 November 1718.
[37] This is in the church, now only a ruin, at Lower Ettington and near the Hall.
[38] BL, Add MS 6689, pp.922–33.
[39] Warws. RO, CR 2131/19; BL, Add. MS 36148, fo. 125; *House of Lords Journals*, vol.22, pp.584–613.
[40] Hunt. Lib., HA Personal Papers box 34, 31, papers about marriage settlement, 13 October 1810.

In later life Lady Huntingdon seems not to have talked of her childhood and adolescence. Her reaction to these family quarrels can only be surmised from her later behaviour. We have only two fragments of reminiscence which were preserved by Thomas Haweis to prove her early piety:

> In very early infancy, when only nine years old, the sight of a corpse about her own age conveying to the grave, engaged her to attend the burial. There the first impressions of deep seriousness about an eternal world laid hold on her conscience: and with many tears, she cried earnestly to God on the spot, that whenever he should be pleased to take her away, he would deliver her from all her fears, and give her a happy departure. She often afterwards visited the grave, and always preserved a lively sense of the affecting scene.[41]

The other anecdote is even more vague, that 'even during her juvenile days' she retired to a closet for prayer, pouring out 'all her little troubles'. Her troubles cannot all have been little. The family were comparatively poor while living in Ireland. Her father had his army pay, and possibly a small income from Carrickmacross.[42] After he had inherited the title a contemporary wrote of him, 'He keeps as hospitable a house and entertains as nobly as any Peer of the Realm. His Lordship has experienced *both* fortunes, and was no more depressed by adversity than he is elevated with prosperity.'[43] Since his income in 'prosperity' was seriously limited by the expense of various lawsuits, and he was unable to raise the capital for his daughters' dowries, his income in 'adversity' must have been very small indeed. It is to this that we can attribute Lady Huntingdon's great care in financial matters throughout her life. Even though her husband was a very wealthy man she always tried to avoid every unnecessary expense. In widowhood her income was considerably more than £1,000 a year, but she spent nothing on luxuries.

Her upbringing in rural Ireland may also explain her lack of a formal education. In an age when female education was undoubtedly improving for the middle and upper classes, the Countess's letters display a curious mixture of poor spelling, little punctuation, and poor arrangement, together with considerable knowledge. Later evidence shows that she was better at speaking than writing. Most of those she led to conversion were convinced by meeting with her, and her opponents sometimes declined to

---

[41] T. Haweis, *An Impartial and Succinct History* 3, (London, 1800) vol.3, pp.239, 240. Toplady, a better reporter, has preserved no anecdotes of her youth.

[42] Coal was mined at Carrickmacross (as well as Coleorton in Leics.) and this may have provided some income and a reason for living there (Lewis, *Topographical Dictionary* vol.1, p.275.

[43] Quoted in G.E.C., op. cit., vol.6, p.611.

meet her face to face. She was also the child of a divided family. At some time after the birth of her younger sister Mary in 1712, her parents separated. Mary was taken abroad by her mother and lived in France and Italy.[44] Selina, and Elizabeth until her marriage, stayed with their father. The few surviving letters which she received from her parents in later life suggest that she was much closer to her father than her mother. He addresses her as 'Dear Linny', or

> Dear Child, I have sent this Messenger to enquire how you gott home, and hope noe one has suffered. I must desire if you, and my Lord, think proper that you would lend me my wife's letter ... she wrote me one not long since, but I believe this is not of that stile, for it was of such a sort, that I never can forgett, or forgive ...[45]

On the other hand her mother addresses her as 'Madam' and refers to receiving letters from 'Dear Lady Mary and one from Lady Huntingdon'.[46] The cause of their separation is unknown, but there is a hint that the problem was financial. In June 1726 she complained of the difficulties of getting her allowance from her husband.[47] In August 1729, soon after Washington's death, her mother wrote to Lady Huntingdon about the impending Chancery suit against her and her sisters, the executrices,

> ... nor is it possible you can with any sort of Justice Complain of my design to File a Bill, when 'tis evident by the whole of my proceeding that I sought all Imaginable means to prevent it and therefore it cannot be imput'd to me as a point of Inclination since every circumstance of my Conduct proves it to be the effect of the last necessity ...[48]

In a later letter her mother complained of her youngest daughter who 'wrote my woman word that she must not expect her wages without going to Law for them and that Campai my other servant was to meet with the same treatment ...'[49] Lady Huntingdon shared the Shirley family's failing of 'a choleric temper', but she controlled it more effectively than most of her family.

The Hastings family, into which Washington Shirley's daughter was to marry, in many ways resembled her own. They were neighbours, living in

---

[44] Cf. W. S. Lewis (ed.), *Horace Walpole's Correspondence with Sir Horace Mann*, 4 (Yale, 1960), 298: Mary 'lived in France with Lady Ferrers her mother a great part of her younger days.'

[45] Hunt. Lib., HA 10847, Lord Ferrers to Lady H., 11 June 1728.

[46] Hunt. Lib., HA 182, Lady Ferrers to Lady Mary Shirley, 22 February [1730]; HA 184, Lady F. to Lady H., 19 November 1730.

[47] Hunt. Lib., HA 179, Lady F. to Mr Shenton, 17 June [1726].

[48] Hunt. Lib., HA 180, Lady F. to Lady H., 26 August 1729.

[49] Hunt. Lib., HA 184, Lady F. to Lady H., 19 November 1730.

that part of north-west Leicestershire which looks to Ashby de la Zouch as its centre. Both had a long line of noble ancestors who had served their monarchs in various capacities. Both, in the seventeenth century, had supported the Crown throughout all the troubles,[50] and the heads of both families were suspected of being Jacobites at the beginning of the next century. Both fathers married twice and quarrelled with their heirs from the first marriage. Here, however, the resemblance ceases. The Earl of Huntingdon made no attempt to disinherit his heir, though he deprived him of an immediate independent income because of his own financial difficulties. The children of both marriages of Lord Huntingdon did not quarrel, but lived together in amity. None of the Hastings could be accused of 'a choleric temper', and some could be described as lethargic. The monumental inscription which Selina, Dowager Countess erected to her husband's memory expresses this in a more tactful fashion – 'Despairing to do National Good, He mingled as little as his Rank permitted in National affairs.'[51] From the turmoil of her own family Selina Shirley was to pass into the tranquillity of her husband's.

The sixth Earl, Theophilus, inherited the title in 1656, at the age of five. As an adult he was very loyal to both Charles II and James II. In 1683 he purchased the office of Captain of the Gentlemen Pensioners for £4000 – a payment which later caused the family considerable financial embarrassment when he lost the position.[52] He was present at Charles II's deathbed and continued to serve James II.[53] After the Revolution he was, as a prominent Jacobite, excluded from the Act of Indemnity and deprived of all his offices.[54] He was twice imprisoned for his politics, but was apparently treated well by the government, probably because he was prepared to compromise at the urging of his wife. On the second occasion of his imprisonment, his son wrote to his sister to reassure her that 'there was no danger at all.'[55]

In February 1671/2 Theophilus had married Elizabeth, the daughter of Sir John Lewis, Bt. She was an heiress selected for him by his mother.

[50] M. Bennett, 'Henry Hastings and the Flying Army', *Trans. Leics. Arch. & Hist. Soc.*, 56 (1980–1), 62–70; F. W. Hensman, 'Henry Hastings and the Great Civil War', in Dryden (ed.), *Memorials of Old Leicestershire*, (London, 1911), 201–27.

[51] *Stemmata Shirleiana* (1841), 150. The inscription is on his monument in the south aisle of Ashby de la Zouch parish church.

[52] The Huntington Library has a box of records relating to his administration of the Gentlemen Pensioners.

[53] For much of this information see G.E.C., op. cit., vol. 6, pp.659–60.

[54] Act 2 Wm & Mary, sess. 2, c. 13. Cf *Albion*, 18 (1986), 209, where it is wrongly stated that the Earl was a Roman Catholic.

[55] *Hastings Wheler Letters*, 1, p.20; letter of George H. to Lady Elizabeth, 21 May 1692.

From 1672 to 1677 they had lived quietly at the family home of Donnington Park in Leicestershire (Ashby Castle having been slighted in the Civil Wars), and restored the family fortune.[56] By his first wife Theophilus had two sons and two daughters, but only the second son, George and the first daughter, Elizabeth, survived him. His first wife died in childbirth in December 1688, and in May 1690 he remarried.[57] By Frances, the widow of Viscount Kilmorey, he had two sons and four daughters. Writing considerably later, one of his daughters thought that the Earl's quarrel with his son George was political.[58] However, the true reason for the lawsuit which George launched against his father was more financial than political. The loss of the office of Captain of the Gentlemen Pensioners had reduced the amount available for the maintenance and education of his children.[59] At the end of 1696 his eldest son was without any support from his father.[60] On 14 December, he had petitioned the House of Lords for permission to sue his father in order to obtain access to the family's deeds of settlement and to recover any income to which he might be entitled.[61] The Lords suggested that both parties should go to arbitration rather than resort to Chancery, but the arbitrators failed to reach agreement. The outcome of the dispute is unknown, but it cannot have divided father and son completely, and the Earl sought a suitable heiress for his son to marry with George's complete approval. The match was broken off because the lady proved to possess no more than £16,000.[62]

The children of the first marriage were very close. George referred to his two sisters as 'My dearest dear Betty and Mary'. Mary died in 1692, but he continued to write letters to Elizabeth filled with the fashionable gossip, good advice and a concern for her happiness. When their father died in London on 30 May 1701 the new Earl wrote a letter of consolation to his sister Elizabeth, and his first concern was to provide for her.[63] Their mother, and her sister Lady Scarsdale, had jointly inherited the reversion of the property of their father, Sir John Lewis, the Ledston estate in Yorkshire. The new Earl had inherited both sisters' shares and settled it all on Lady Elizabeth on condition that she did not claim a share of her

---

[56] Hunt. Lib., HA Genealogy, box 1, 32, autobiography of the seventh Earl.
[57] J. L. Chester, *The Registers of the ... Abbey of St Peter, Westminster* (London, 1876), 30.
[58] *Hastings Wheler Letters*, 1, p.13.
[59] See Leeds RO, LD 230, 231 for details of the financial difficulties.
[60] *Hastings Wheler Letters*, 1, p.24.
[61] *Journals of the House of Lords*, vol.16, p.38a.
[62] *Hastings Wheler Letters*, 1, pp.22, 23.
[63] Ibid., 34.

father's estate.[64] It was a magnificent gift which she valued at £3,000 a year and it is not surprising that she had many suitors.[65] Steele published two commendations of her in the *Tatler*.[66] Given the ferocity of Steele's attack on two of Lady Betty's friends, Mary Astell and Elizabeth Elstob, this is praise indeed. In May 1702 the Earl began a friendly Chancery suit with his stepmother, who acted on behalf of her six children. It was intended to secure provision for the younger children of the second marriage.[67] Even before his appeal had been heard George had returned to his regiment in the Low Countries and spent the summer there. He did not return to London until the end of 1704, and died there the following February of a 'malignant fever'.[68]

The next Earl was the elder son of the second marriage, another Theophilus, who was only eight years old. By his half-brother's will, made on the day he died, Theophilus inherited all the family estates in Leicestershire and Derbyshire.[69] They included considerable property in the market towns of Loughborough and Ashby de la Zouch, lands in the villages around Ashby and Castle Donnington, and various charges on the counties of Leicester, Cambridge and Huntingdon. The latter had not always been collected regularly, and tenants also seem to have been allowed to get into arrears with their rents.[70] The new Earl, his brother Ferdinando, and their sisters Anne, Frances, Catherine and Margaret lived with their mother for a few years. However, in October 1704 she married a French prisoner of war, the Chevalier Michel de Ligondez of Auvergne, thereby losing custody of her children. Lady Betty, the executrix of the will, then made a home for them at Ledston. Another friendly Chancery action was brought in 1707. The infant Earl of Huntingdon by Viscount Kilmorey, his half-brother by their mother's first marriage, brought an action against their mother and her husband. Dr Geary, archdeacon of Buckingham and a Leicestershire incumbent, became his guardian, and a Master in Chancery was appointed to prepare a report on the financial arrangements in November 1707. Another similar suit for a

[64] Ibid., 15, 16, statement by Lady Betty.
[65] Ibid., 38, 39; J. J. Cartwright, *The Wentworth Papers* (London, 1883), 55; *HMC, Rutland MSS*, 2, p.186.
[66] G. S. Aitken (ed.), *The Tatler* (London, 1898), vol.1, p.395 (no.49). The other description is no. 42 (p.342). Both were printed in 1709.
[67] Leeds RO, LD 230, 231.
[68] *Antiquaries Journal*, vol.22, 1942, p.180 and Le Neve's *Monumenta Anglicana*, vol.1, 1717 pp.75, 76. He was buried in St James Westminster and a monument was erected by his sister.
[69] Hunt. Lib., HAP, box 26, 30, copy of PCC will, 22 February 1704/5.
[70] The Huntington Library has a very large collection of manor court records, rent rolls and other records for these estates.

formal accounting was brought in 1710, but the final account in 1717, when the Earl came of age, has not been found.[71]

The children of the second marriage seem to have stayed with different members of their extended family at different times, but spent much of their time with their half-sister Lady Betty.[72] From Ledston she arranged for Theophilus to go to Christ Church, Oxford, where Martin Benson, later to be bishop of Gloucester, was his tutor.[73] Benson remained a friend of the young Earl and when the latter left Oxford without taking a degree in 1715 wrote him long and gossipy letters.[74] In 1724 the Earl went on the Grand Tour, visiting France, Italy and Spain. This was possibly the most notable thing in his life, since Spain was then a country rarely visited by Englishmen, and it was commented on in his obituary and on his memorial, to the amusement of subsequent generations.[75] While he was abroad, a proposal of marriage with his sister Catherine was made by Granville Wheler, and Lady Betty acted as head of the family in his absence. Wheler, who with his family was later to play an important part in the life of the Hastings, was the only son of Sir George Wheler, a canon of Durham and rector of Houghton le Spring. He was an eligible husband with an estate at Otterden in Kent.[76] Having disposed of one of his sisters in marriage, Lady Betty and the other sisters turned to matchmaking for the Earl himself. Her letter does not name the lady on whom they had fixed since she had already been discussed with the Earl.[77] Although she had two sisters and no brothers (like the future Countess), it was not Selina Shirley who was their first choice. Nothing came of their matchmaking at this time, but a year later the sisters were successful in marrying him to their friend Selina Shirley. After her father had succeeded to the title and

[71] Hunt. Lib., HA Legal, box 18, 6 gives the month of the marriage – which is wrongly given in G.E.C., op. cit., vol. 6, p.660; Hunt. Lib., HA Legal, box 18, 6; box 18, 7.

[72] *Hastings Wheler Letters*, 2, pp. 27–35.

[73] *HMC., Portland MSS* 7, p.87. Christ Church then received more than half the nobility entering Oxford. This may be the explanation of its popularity (J. Cannon, *Aristocratic Century* (Cambridge, 1984), 50).

[74] Hunt. Lib., HA 690, Benson to the Earl, 21 March 1714/5; Leics. RO, 14D32/14, 78, Benson to the Earl, 14 April 1716.

[75] C. B. Andrews (ed.), *The Torrington Diaries*, 2 (London, 1935), 70 – 'a pompous inscription... saying that he not *only* visited France and Italy, but *even* Spain; as may be said of me, that I not *only* visited Nottinghamshire and Derbyshire, but *even* Leicestershire'; *Gentleman's Magazine*, 11 (1741), 667.

[76] J. C. Cox, *Little Guide: Kent* (London, 1927), 223; *HMC, Hastings*, 3, p.2. The original letter has not been traced. Granville Wheler's letter to the Earl from Ledston on 21 November 1724 is Hunt. Lib., HA 13243. Wheler was interested in science and experimented with electricity.

[77] Hunt. Lib., HA 4725, Lady Betty to the Earl, 5 July 1727.

moved into the house at Staunton Harold it was inevitable that the two should meet. Earl Ferrers was invited to visit Donnington Park to hunt, and Selina was invited to Ashby Place to stay with his sisters.[78] Three affectionate letters written by Lady Frances Hastings to 'Dear Lady Liney' have survived.[79] On 3 June 1728 the Earl and Selina were married in the church at Staunton Harold.[80] Lady Betty did not attend but wrote to the bride to wish her 'all true happiness and felicity'.[81] For eighteen years the new Countess of Huntingdon was to enjoy that happiness in her married life.

---

[78] Leics. RO, 14D32/ 14, 35, J. Corbin to Lord H., 8 November 1731. They probably hunted the deer in the Park. For Ashby Place, which was erected about 1724 in the north courtyard of the castle and demolished in 1830, see T. H. Fosbrooke, *Ashby de la Zouch Castle* (Lincoln, 1914), 26; *Trans. Leics. Arch. Soc.*, 17 (1932–3), 203; T. L. Jones, *Ashby de la Zouch Castle* (London, 1953), 11.

[79] They are in Cheshunt archives, E 1/1, 1 (22 May 1727); E 1/1, 2 (4 May 1728); E 1/1, 3 (n.d.).

[80] Leics. RO, Breedon parish register, DE 2478/3 gives 3 May as the date of the wedding, but *Stemmata Shirleiana* (1841), 148n. and the letters of congratulation agree on 3 June as the correct date.

[81] Leics. RO, 14D32/8A, 10, Lady Betty to Lady Huntingdon, Ledston, 3 June [1728].

2

Marriage

We do not know whether the marriage of Lady Selina was arranged or was a love-match, but all the available evidence points to the latter. Her dowry was only £15,000, less than that rejected as inadequate by the eighth Earl of Huntingdon in 1696, and there was considerable doubt about her father's abilty to pay it.[1] Her father was unable to raise the cash and was obliged to give mortgages on the family estates to his two sons-in-law, but his ownership of some of these mortgaged estates was being challenged in Chancery. The Earl's mother had died in 1723, and although Lady Betty and his sisters had indulged in matchmaking it is unlikely that the choice of a bride was not his own. But the best evidence for a love-match are the letters which were to pass between the Earl and his Countess during every temporary separation. While at Bath for the waters she wrote to him by every post and expected a reply equally often. Those of her letters which have survived constantly express her deep affection and her longing to see him again. His letters to her are missing, but the mere fact of his writing so often is sufficiently expressive of the love of one who was usually so indifferent a correspondent.[2]

Letters of congratulation on their marriage came from friends and relations, both before and after the ceremony. Her uncle, Lawrence Shirley, although immersed in the family lawsuits, found time to congratulate the Earl. Her sister-in-law, Lady Catherine Wheler, was happy with the match.[3] Mrs Felicia Rant, Sir Richard Levinge's sister in law, wrote from Norfolk, requesting a marriage 'faover' and probably got one

---

[1] A copy of the marriage settlement is in Leics. RO, 26D53/ 805.
[2] Very few letters written by the Earl have survived. On many occasions his wife wrote on his behalf.
[3] Leics. RO, 14D32/ 14, 72, Guise to Lord Huntingdon, 3 June [1728]. I have not identified this relationship. It seems unlikely that it was Dr John Guyse (1680–1762) who later wrote the *Practical Expositor*. Leics. RO, DE 23/ 1/ 1421, L. Shirley to Lord H., 4 June 1728; 14D31/ 10, 1, C. Wheler to Lady H., 9 June 1728. Other letters of congratulation are DE 23/ 1, 1422 and 1423.

since Washington's daughters hoped for legacies when she died.[4] Selina's mother wrote from Paris to congratulate Lord Huntingdon before the marriage, but complained that she had not been told of the match by her husband.[5] She did not attend the ceremony.

During the next ten years the Earl and his bride had seven children. The eldest, Francis, born on 13 March 1728/9, succeeded to his father's title in 1746. The second son, George, was born on 29 March 1730. He and a third son, Ferdinando, born on 23 January 1731/2, both died in 1744. Between these two sons came Elizabeth, their first daughter and the Countess's only child to survive her, born on 23 March 1730/1. She married Lord Rawdon, later Earl of Moira, as his third wife, and carried the title of Baron Hastings into that family.[6] A second daughter, Selina, born in June 1735 died almost immediately, and the next child, born on 3 December 1737, was also named Selina. The last child, Henry, was born on 12 December 1739, and died in 1758. All the children, except Elizabeth, died unmarried. The births were probably difficult if the letters at the time and Lady Huntingdon's visits to Bath can be relied upon. Even shortly before the birth of her eldest son her health was indifferent, and her father wrote from London seven days before the birth 'under a great concern' for her.[7]

The Countess's first recorded visit to Bath for her health was about 9 February 1731/2, soon after the birth of Ferdinando. This had been agreed even before his birth, according to letters which have survived. The Countess was pleased on her arrival to find both her sister-in-law, Lady Frances Hastings and brother-in-law, J. G. Nightingale, to comfort her in 'the most stupid place I ever yet saw'. The Earl did not accompany her to Bath on this or subsequent occasions, and it is for this reason that we have a series of love-letters which she wrote to him:

---

[4] Leics. RO, 14D32/ 14, 11, Mrs Rant to Lady Selina, 22 April 1728; Hunt. Lib., HA 10399, Mrs Rant to Lady H., 8 June 1728; Leics. RO, 14D32/ 28, 3, Lord F. to Lady H., 20 December 1728; Hunt. Lib., HAP box 29, 7, will of F. Rant, 27 September 1728.

[5] Leics. RO, DE 23/ 1/ 1420, Lady F. to Lord H., 27 April [1728] NS.

[6] The Hastings estates were divided between an illegitimate son of Francis and his sister Lady Moira. The title of Earl, however, went to another branch of the family – see H. N. Bell, *The Huntingdon Peerage* (London, 1820). Elizabeth was related to Lord Rawdon, as his mother and her grandmother were daughters of Sir Richard Levinge. It is for this reason that some early Rawdon records can be found in the Hastings papers (e.g. Hunt. Lib., HA 15189).

[7] Leics. RO, 14D32/ 28, 5, Lord Ferrers to Lady H., 6 March 1728/9; Hunt. Lib., HA 5828, Lady Margaret to Lord H., 27 December 1731, quoted in *HMC Hastings*, 3, p. 8.

Saturday Post brought me my Dearest Lordships most tender and affectionate Letter which almost overcame me with Joy to find my absence from you had not rendered me less fortunate in that esteem which is more valuable than any satisfaction I have on earth ... I know that writing to be a great Punishment to you ...[8]

In her letters she tried to amuse the Earl with the gossip from Bath giving him the latest news of Walpole's 'dirty work' and details of the pregnancy of the Prince of Wales's mistress.[9] She also urged him to economize and promised to reduce her own expenses as far as possible.[10] But her chief concern was a desire to return home as soon as possible: 'I Cannot without tears of Gratitude read over that Part of your letter ware you tell me it is the last time we shall be Parted.'[11] Every post saw letters pass between Bath and Donnington Park. Lady Betty was surprised that the Earl could 'so farr overcome his avertion to writing', but sometimes he employed a deputy for the task.[12] The Countess wrote to him giving advice on estate and financial matters, but in domestic arrangements she expected to have a free hand and closely supervised the household even while in Bath.[13] Neither did she forget her children on future absences sending 'some Play things' for 'her little angels'.[14]

It was during her first visit to Bath that Lady Frances had persuaded her to consult Dr George Cheyne. He was to prove a close friend to the Countess and her husband until his death in 1743. He had studied medicine at Edinburgh, and moved to Bath where he become famous for his cures. In 1720 he published a treatise on gout, recommending vegetarianism and the Bath waters.[15] He diagnosed the stone or gravel as Lady Huntingdon's complaint and recommended the Bristol waters rather

---

[8] Drew Univ., Hunt. A 1, Lady H. to Lord H., 14 February 1731/2.
[9] For Anne Vane see Lord Hervey's *Memoirs*. She was his mistress as well as the Prince of Wales's. Lady Huntingdon reported anecdotes about her from time to time.
[10] The Earl kept an account at Hoare's Bank. Drew Univ., Hunt. A2, Lady H. to Lord H., 16 February 1731/2.
[11] Drew Univ., Hunt. A3, Lady H. to Lord H., 19 February 1731/2. Part of this letter is printed in *HMC, Hastings*, 3, p. 10.
[12] Leics. RO, 14D32/ 8A, 21, Lady Betty to Lady H., 18 March 1731/2.
[13] Leics. RO, 14D32/ 24, 2, Lady H. to Lord H., 5 March 1731/2.
[14] Leics. RO, 14D32/ 24, 3 Lady H. to Lord H., 6 March 1731/2; Drew Univ., Hunt. A 7, Lady H. to Lord H., 8 March 1731/2. The box was too heavy and the toys did not reach Donnington until 13 March (Leics. RO, 14D32/ 24, 4).
[15] For Cheyne see C. F. Mullett (ed.), *The Letters of Dr George Cheyne to the Countess of Huntingdon* (Hunt. Lib., 1940), v–xxiv; A. Guerrini, 'The Tory Newtonians', *Journal of British Studies*, 25 (1986), 288–309; G. S. Rousseau, 'Mysticism and Millenarianism', in R. H. Popkin (ed.), *Millenarianism and Messianism in English Literature and Thought* (Leiden, 1988), 81–126.

than those at Bath, together with a purge.[16] Cheyne also suggested exercise, so she had hired a horse and chaise, finding this the cheapest way of exercising.[17] By the end of March she was bored with 'dull' Bath and had decided that her health was sufficiently restored to make the 'long wisht for hour' quite close, but her doctor and friends thought otherwise.[18] However the Countess's will proved the stronger, and she returned home, promising to continue to drink the waters.[19] In a last letter almost incoherent with pleasure she wrote of seeing him in three hours instead of three days.[20] She begged the Earl not to come to meet his 'old Goody', but to send Kendall to show them the way from Burton-on-Trent. She was still not completely well, and Dr Cheyne continued to advise her by letter.[21]

It was at this time that the Countess began to be interested in medicine herself and to experiment with or recommend various cures. She may have been encouraged in this by Lady Betty, who recommended 'Pyrmont waters' for the Countess and other prescriptions for her sisters.[22] The Earl's sisters, Margaret, Anne and Frances, now spent much of their time at Ledston, and medical advice passed between Ledston and Donnington Park. The Countess now began to doctor her 'poor Neighbours' in Leicestershire. Dr Cheyne sent his prescriptions to her Leicestershire physician, and confined his direct advice to dietary matters, and suggested she should go to Scarborough for the waters there.[23] Many of the Countess's problems were gynaecological. In January 1733/4 Dr Cheyne wrote to her regretting that her 'modesty and reservedness' had prevented him from completing the cure, and suggesting an early return to Bath so that she might drink and bathe in Bristol water.[24] She arrived there the

---

[16] Mullett, op. cit., 2. Mullett dates this undated letter (in the Hunt. Lib.) as *c.* 1730, but it appears to follow immediately before the next letter, which is dated 3 June 1732. It cannot be as early as 1730.

[17] Leics. RO, 14D32/ 24, 4, Lady H. to Lord H., 13 March 1731/2.

[18] Drew Univ., Hunt. A 19, postscript to letter of Lady H. to Lord H., 29 [March] 1732.

[19] Hunt. Lib., HA 905, Dr Bostock to Lord H., 6 April 1732; Drew Univ., Hunt. A 15, Lady H. to Lord H., 8 April 1732.

[20] Drew Univ., Hunt. A 18, Lady H. to Lord H., 17 April 1732.

[21] Mullett, op. cit., 3–12.

[22] Leics. RO, 14D32/ 8A, 22, Lady Betty to Lady H., 3 July 1732. Pyrmont water came from Bad Pyrmont, a spa in Germany.

[23] Mullett, op. cit., 16–21. It is not known when she went to Scarborough Leics. RO, 14D32/ 8a, 14, Lady Betty to Lady H., n.d.), but see Hunt. Lib., HA 5831, Lady Margaret to Lady H., 21 September 1733.

[24] Mullett, op. cit., 32, 33. Unlike some physicians Cheyne did not recommend Bath waters for all complaints.

next month, but by the end of August she had moved to London and Enfield. By that time Dr Cheyne was able to assure the Earl that 'if she be suffered to go on in the Method of Dyet and Medicins I have put her, that in time she [will] be as Healthy Chearfull and Active as any Lady in England and Had she not bin put in this Method and Regimen she must have Dy'd Miserably of a Cancer in her Bowels.'[25]

The reason for her long absence from Leicestershire at this time was a plan to provide the family with a house in London and another in the adjacent country. The Earl leased 2 Savile Row from William Kent, the architect, from 1734 until 1740. The negotiations took some time, but it was the Countess who made all the arrangements.[26]

> I ... Could not be at rest till I had seen our house here and our landlord to who in these different kinds are most delightfull, but the former is I think beyond any thing I ever saw for it is not only the house of all others in tast and beauty, but upon examining it one of the most Convenient in the wide world ... Mr Kent has spent the evening with me and is going out of hand to prepare the draught of the whole inside of your library ... all other parts he and I shall settle monday or tuesday.[27]

The Earl was most concerned about his library, but his wife wanted to display her 'old China' in the morning room. She praised the view and 'the prettyest water Closets I ever saw'. Her energy was prodigious as she moved between the house in Savile Row and another at Enfield Chase. The Chase was the property of the Crown as part of the Duchy of Lancaster, but the Duke of Chandos had purchased the remainder of the grant of offices there in 1714 and had appointed Lord Huntingdon as keeper of the East Bailey. This was an honorary position and until 1734 the Earl seems to have taken no interest in it. However Enfield Chase, like Windsor, had become a desirable place for a summer home far from the heat and dust of London, and Lady Huntingdon remodelled the Lodge there to provide a retreat from Savile Row.[28] She arrived in London on Wednesday, 28 August, to consult Mr Kent, went on to Enfield on the

[25] Leics. RO, 14D32/ 14, 58.
[26] P. Willis, 'William Kent's Letters in the Huntington Library, California', *Architectural History*, 29 (1986), 158–67; Leics. RO, 14D32/ 27, 3 and 4, John Wright to Lord H., 9 July 1734, and to Lady H., 25 July 1734.
[27] Drew Univ., Hunt. A 20, Lady H. to Lord H., 29 [August] 1734. William Kent (1684–1748) was celebrated as a sculptor, architect and iandscape gardener. He designed the monument to the Earl of Huntingdon in Ashby de la Zouch parish church.
[28] The date of the Earl's appointment is not to be found in the records of the Duchy of Lancaster, which was responsible for the property. I am indebted to Mr R. A. Smith of the Duchy Office for this information. Lord Chatham occupied the South Lodge (G. H. Hodson and E. Ford, *A History of Enfield* (Enfield, 1873), 46, 48.

Friday, and hoped to be back in Town by Monday or Tuesday, 'for I believe no Gally slave has worked harder'. She had arranged to meet the contractor at Enfield at nine o'clock, and all the workmen were to be there by noon. Her intention was to have a small farm on the seventy-three acres which the Earl leased there.[29] Progress was slower than she wished, and a week later she was back in Enfield: 'I have been in the most violent spirits ever since I Came here and hurried the workmen to such a degree that I believe the[y] wish my absence almost as much as I do myself...'[30] On a second visit to Enfield she was too tired to return to London, and stayed there

> as I thought my being there might hasten the workmen and I find it did so. Before I left it was quite in a state of security, all the sashes being put up, but I thought the danger so infinitely great even of fire that I was glad to leve the house with as few as possable shaveinge being up to one knees in every Corner of the house and an insistant knocking that I thought would drive me wild.[31]

She returned again when the furniture arrived and was happy to tell her husband that she could buy all she needed then much cheaper than it would be at Christmas. The final result was a house and farm which she enjoyed, and which others admired.[32] However the Earl found himself in the Duchy of Lancaster court accused of encroachments, cutting down trees without authority and making bricks from the local clay. The Countess's building activities are not specifically mentioned in the records but they undoubtedly contributed to a lawsuit which continued for several years.[33]

How far all these activities and a deeper involvement in the social life of London appealed to the Earl we cannot tell, but his wife's innate caution and economy were overcome by the wish that he should play a larger part in society. A few letters reveal that he had bought a racehorse which he kept at Newmarket, and that he was importing dogs as well as his tobacco from France.[34] The family spent the winter of 1735/6 in town when it was reported that the Countess 'looks pale and thin but very clear her lips red

[29] Hunt. Lib., HAM box 66, 22, particulars of lands rented at Enfield Chase, n.d.
[30] Drew Univ., Hunt. A 21, Lady H. to Lord H., 6 September 1734, quoted in *HMC, Hastings*, 3, p. 19.
[31] Drew Univ., Hunt. A 107, Lady H. to Lord H., n.d.
[32] *Hastings Wheler Letters*, 2, p. 118.
[33] Hunt. Lib., HA Legal, box 20, 9 is a copy of the court's decree in 1743. Hunt. Lib., HA 12712–16 (John Stillingfleet to Lord H., 1735–7) describe some of the court proceedings. PRO, DL 41/96, 6 is a bundle of legal papers of the Duchy including several relating to this suit dated 1736.
[34] Leics. RO, DE 12/1, 1426, Lord Gower to Lord H., 16 November 1734; 14D32/27, 2, J. Wright to Lord H., 24 February 1732/3.

and not a bit yellow. Her spirits are excellent and she always finds benefit by exercise of which she uses a good deal.'³⁵ Despite having a town house, the Earl neglected his parliamentary duties, giving his proxies first to Lord Strafford and later to Lord Chesterfield.³⁶ The name of Lady Huntingdon, but not that of her husband, now begins to appear in the fashionable gossip of the time. In January 1737/8 she gave a christening party for her daughter Selina. Lady Strafford wrote: 'I was yesterday at Lady Huntingdon's christening; we first had a dinner of five then seven. The godfathere was Lord Batman, and the godmother Lady K. Wheler (but Mrs Walkinshaw stood for her) so there was but six at dinner.'³⁷ The Earl and Countess attended more social functions, including the races at Nottingham. In 1739 her dress for the Prince's birthday inspired a long description:

> Her petticoat was black velvet embroidered with chenille, the pattern a large stone vase filled with ramping flowers that spread almost over a breadth of the petticoat from the bottom to the top; between each vase of flowers was a pattern of gold shells, and foliage embossed and most heavily rich; the gown was white satin embroidered also with chenille mixt with gold ornaments, no vases on the sleeve, but two or three on the tail.³⁸

Soon after this came the well-known attack on the gallery of the House of Lords by a group of noble ladies, which included the Countess, described by Lady Mary Wortley Montagu.³⁹ The Lords had decided that the gallery should be reserved for members of the Commons during the debate on the convention of El Pardo, but the ladies laid siege to the gallery from nine in the morning until after five in the afternoon. They successfully kept the MPs out, and finally gained entrance themselves by convincing the Lord Chancellor by their silence that they had abandoned the siege. This most lively escapade of Lady Huntingdon was also to be her last.

The round of social activity did not prevent Lady Huntingdon from

³⁵ *Hastings Wheler Letters*, 2, p. 122.
³⁶ BL, Add. MS 31142, fos. 31, 57, Lord H. to Lord [Strafford], 15 January 1731/2 and 13 January 1732/3; Leics. RO, 14D32/ 20, 1 and 2, Chesterfield to Lord H., 13 December 1740, and 25 November 1742; *RMC, Hastings 3*, p. 9.
³⁷ J.J. Cartwright, op. cit., 535. Lady Catherine Wheler was her sister-in-law, and Lord Bateman was a friend of the Earl and Countess.
³⁸ Hunt. Lib., HA, Lady Kilmorey to Lady H., 18 June 1739; Lady Llanover (ed.), *Autobiography and Correspondence of Mrs Delany*, 1 (London, 1861), 28. 'Ramping flowers' are climbing plants.
³⁹ R. Halsband (ed.), *The Complete Letters of Lady Mary Wortley Montagu*, 2 (Oxford, 1966), 136. The convention had aroused considerable opposition, and the vote on it in the Commons was only carried by a small majority.

caring for her children and her home. Her eldest son, Francis, was sent to school in London; the second, George, went to Leeds, where he was close to Ledston and able to visit his aunts from time to time. Letters passed between the sons and their mother as frequently as they could be persuaded to write.[40] While Francis was at Mr Fountain's school at Marylebone, his brother Ferdinando was sent to join him. Writing to her 'Dear Frank', she complains that he said 'nothing of your Brother Firdy', but allows the matron Mrs La Place to give Frank a shilling and Firdy sixpence for a treat. She made careful provision for their clothes, telling Frank to order a winter suit and allowing him to choose the colour, though she 'would have it quite plaine'.[41] She agreed that Frank should go to a play, but hoped that he would not catch cold.[42] She recommended him to read Josephus' *History of the Jews*, which must have been hard reading for a boy of ten, but also promised him 'Mr Janeways tokens for Children'. Her sons expected her letters, even though they did not always answer them, and Frank 'reproved' her when she failed to write.[43] About 1737 Frank went to Westminster School, where he was visited by his father's old tutor, Martin Benson (now bishop of Gloucester): 'I was last night to see Lord Hastings, whom I found very cheerful and left so too. I talked with Mr Bourne about giving to the Masters. He thought 3 guineas to Dr Nicol, 2 to Mr Johnson, and one to the Usher under who he should be placed should be sufficient.'[44] Westminster School was at the height of its popularity with sons of the nobility at this time – even more popular than Eton.

George boarded at Leeds Grammar School under the Revd Thomas Barnard. This school appears to have been chosen for its proximity to Ledston, and because Barnard was a favourite of Lady Betty.[45] In the summer of 1739, when he returned from Donnington Park to Ledston with his aunt, he wrote a typical schoolboy letter to his mother:

> The pleasure of driving my aunt Anne back to Ledston in the chair contributed much to drying up the tears I shed at parting with you and my dear papa and

[40] Most of the school letters are not dated.
[41] Drew Univ., Hunt. A 88, Lady H. to Frank, [28 September 1739].
[42] Drew Univ., Hunt. A 84, Lady H. to son, 19 March 1745.
[43] Drew Univ., Hunt. A 94, Lady H. to Frank, 24 [? 1739]. The Revd James Janeway wrote his very popular *Tokens for Children* in 1671.
[44] Hunt. Lib., HA 693, Benson to Lord H., 18 April 1737. Westminster School was then at the height of its popularity under Dr John Nicoll. J. Cannon, *Aristocratic Century* (Cambridge, 1984), 40; L. E. Tanner, *Westminster School* (London, 1934), 23.
[45] For the school see E. Wilson (ed.), *Leeds Grammar School Admission Books* (Leeds, 1906), xxiv; T. Barnard, *An Historical Character ... of the Right Honourable the Lady Elisabeth Hastings* (Leeds, 1742).

my dear brothers and sisters. Aunt Betty's health is much the same as when you left her. She is very good to me and tells me I behave myself well. I hope to continue to do so and if possible better.[46]

Later, probably in 1740, George was also sent to school in London when his mother promised him a horse if he attended to his books.[47]

Since her daughters spent much of their time with their parents we do not have so many letters either from or to them, but both Lady Elizabeth and Lady Selina received a good education, probably from a tutor who was kept for the younger children. The former was noted for her intelligence and knowledge in later life.[48] The tutor was recommended by Dr Cheyne in 1734 as one who could teach English well and knew Latin, Greek, Hebrew, Italian and French, could 'Cast accounts', and instruct the children in the 'right principals of religion'. Being tired of the drudgery of teaching school he was willing to go to Donnington Park for £15 a year.[49]

There was also the burden of legal business. Lady Huntingdon's father was a sick man when she married. In November 1728 he wrote to her that he was detained in town by 'a violent Cold'. He was no better in December, suffering from gout and 'lameness in my Knee' and had not left his house for five weeks. He was unable to attend the christening of his grandchild in April, having now 'soe violent a Cold and Ascma' that he might go to Bath instead of Staunton Harold.[50] To his daughter he wrote on 12 April: 'It is a concern to me I cannot come down to the Cristining, for I am not only in a very ill state of health but I have an affair with your Mother to settle that prevents me.'[51] Two days later he died in his house in Clarges Street, leaving his 'affair' with the Countess Ferrers unsettled. In his will he appointed his three daughters his executrices, which immediately plunged them and their husbands into the midst of the Shirley lawsuits.[52] The will was proved by the two elder daughters (Mary did not marry Lord Kilmorey until the following year) on 9 July. He made provision for the marriage portions of all three, since no money had yet

---

[46] *Hastings Wheler Letters*, vol. 2, p. 116. The letter is there dated 13 July 1734, when George was only four. The reference to Lady Betty's health dates it as 1739.

[47] Drew Univ., Meth. Archives, A 91, Lady H. to son, n.d.

[48] Mrs Delany, op. cit., vol. 2, pp. 208, 552; C. Maxwell, *The Stranger in Ireland* (London, 1954), 227.

[49] Drew Univ., Meth. Archives, A 107, Lady H. to Lord H., n.d. [31 August 1734].

[50] Leics. RO, 14D32/ 28. 1, Lord Ferrers to Lady H., 16 November 1728; 14D32/ 28, 2, Lord Ferrers to Lord H., 14 December 1728; 14D32/ 28, 6, Lord Ferrers to Lord H., 11 April 1729.

[51] Leics. RO, 124D32/ 28, 7, Lord Ferrers to Lady H., 12 April 1729.

[52] The Earl's will is PRO, PROB 11/ 631.

been received by Mr Nightingale and Lord Huntingdon. All his debts were to be paid from his personal estate and the sale of his houses in London and Richmond, but any debts claimed by his stepmother or her children under the provisions of any deed were not to be paid – 'itt being my opinion that the same were not honourably obtained'. The will contains no mention of his wife, and in her place he appointed two guardians for his unmarried daughter.

The legal disputes which involved the Countess can be conveniently divided into five groups. The two oldest were those brought by Selina Countess Dowager on behalf of herself and her children to recover the rights she claimed under the deeds and will made by her husband. Although Washington had taken possession of both the English and Irish estates, two separate suits were brought, one presumably in the Irish Court of Chancery and the other in the English.[53] Washington had also been sued by his brothers and sisters, the children of Countess Elizabeth, who believed that additional provision had been made for them.[54] By 1730 the other Countess Dowager, Lady Huntingdon's mother, was suing her daughters and their husbands for maintenance out of the Shirley estates. Finally the new Earl, Washington's brother Henry, was considered insane and the next brother, Lawrence, obtained a commission of lunacy against him. In October 1730 Henry succeeded in convincing Chancery of his sanity and took possession of the estates.[55] However this was only a temporary improvement, and Lawrence soon took over the administration and lawsuits again. Each of these lawsuits led almost inevitably to counter-suits.

The case concerning the English estates began in 1719. Washington had claimed that the property was entailed on the eldest surviving son and impugned the authenticity of the deeds executed by his father.[56] In February 1724/5 the Countess Dowager obtained a decree for all the arrears and a receiver of the rents was appointed. Washington appealed against this decision to the House of Lords, but it was settled by an agreement between the Earl and the Countess that the Warwickshire and

---

[53] As the early records of the Irish Chancery were destroyed, there is very little evidence surviving for this period (see Hunt. Lib. HA Legal, box 19, 14 for an Irish Chancery writ). Later the suit was apparently transferred to London.

[54] Leics. RO, 26D53/ 1897, Chancery petition, n.d. [1721–5].

[55] Warws. RO, CR 2131, 16 (4), Lord Ferrers to Mr Conduitt, 22 October 1730. At that time he took his seat in the Lords. The *House of Lords Journals*, vol. 23, p. 591b and vol. 26, p. 570a, are incorrect about this. See also ibid., vol. 23, pp. 635–40.

[56] For this lawsuit see Leics. RO, 26D53/ 1897 and 1908, and 2 *English Reports*, 958–65.

Irish estates should be transferred to Mr Robert Shirley.⁵⁷ However, before this could be fully implemented Washington died, and then an accusation of forgery was brought against him.⁵⁸ It does not appear that any decision was ever reached on this. A further complication after the Earl's death was the embezzlement of some of the Irish rents by his agent, who had fled the country.⁵⁹

Lawrence Shirley having taken possession of the family property on behalf of his brother Henry, there were disputes about the division of the personal estate. Lawrence was very angry that Lady Huntingdon had 'sent for the Earl of Essex's picture and the night peice out of the Gallery', but eventually he reached agreement with the husbands of the executrices about the disposal of the late Earl's personal goods.⁶⁰ Both he and the executrices were then sued by the Countess Dowager Selina for the arrears of the annuities together with interest. Difficulties now arose because Lawrence Shirley owed money to the estate, but was unable or unwilling to pay it to the executrices. Lord Kilmorey spent a considerable time trying to persuade his two brothers-in-law to act in concert with him over this. Mr Nightingale was willing to do so, but as usual Lord Huntingdon delayed giving instructions to his lawyer, and it was not until 1737 that another settlement was reached.⁶¹ Since legal fees had by now seriously encumbered the estates, the Countess Dowager only obtained a mortgage and the right to cut and sell timber. She then petitioned the Lords for leave to bring in a private Bill to settle the Shirley estates, and all the other members of the family, including Washington's three daughters, launched counter-petitions.⁶² The Irish estates passed under the control of George, the second son of Countess Selina, by agreement with Lawrence.⁶³

Washington's three daughters now believed that they could make good a claim to the Chartley property. Lady Betty Hastings did not approve of this, and it is uncertain whether the three daughters took any legal

⁵⁷ See *Lords' Journals*, vol. 22, pp. 584–613.
⁵⁸ 24 *English Reports*, 976, 977; 25 *English Reports*, 456; 94 *English Reports*, 716, 717; Warws. RO, CR 2131, 16 (2, 3), L. Shirley to Edw. Conduitt, 21 October 1729 and 20 June 1730.
⁵⁹ H. Williams (ed.), *The Correspondence of Jonathan Swift*, 3 (Oxford, 1963), 340.
⁶⁰ Hunt. Lib., HA 10817, L. Shirley to Mr Conduitt, 24 April 1729; HA 10818, L. Shirley to Lady H, 17 December 1729; HAP, box 30, 6, agreement of L. Shirley, n.d. Warws. RO, CR 2131, 16, L. Shirley to Mr Conduitt, 21 October 1729, and 27 December 1729.
⁶¹ Leics. RO, 14D32/ 7, 4 and 5, Lord Kilmorey to Lady H., 8 and 22 June; Hunt. Lib., HA 9572 and 9573, Lord K. to Lord H., n.d.
⁶² *Lords' Journals*, vol. 23, pp. 523–33.
⁶³ PRONI, D 3531/A/ 5, 2 and 3, copies of letters, 20 November and 24 December 1729 and 28 May 1730.

action.⁶⁴ There was however a claim and a counter-claim for the rents of the Irish estates during Washington's lifetime between the Countess Dowager Selina and all her children, and Lawrence Shirley, all his children, Lord and Lady Huntingdon, Lord and Lady Kilmorey and the executors of Earl Robert.⁶⁵ Lady Huntingdon took the initiative in this case and annoyed her brother-in-law, Lord Kilmorey, who wrote an indignant letter to Lord Huntingdon about such interference.⁶⁶

Nothing seems to have happened with the Countess Dowager Mary's claim against her three daughters. She wrote a series of petulant letters to them for the next two years. She had returned to England to claim her rights against her husband's estates. On the eve of returning to France at the end of March 1729 she complained that he had not paid the bill of her doctor, the wages of her servants and 'some other triffling Debts'. She also complained that she had placed a banknote for £100 in Lady Betty Nightingale's hands 'to pay whatever I should have occasion to send for in my absence, and tho: she sent me very few things yet 'tis certain she never paid for any one of them.' She claimed that her daughters' failure to provide for her meant that she had no bed to lie on, or a farthing to buy food.⁶⁷ A draft reply by Lady Huntingdon must date from this period. It begins with an apology for writing a direct reply to a message sent through her younger sister:

> your Lady ship I am informed has made a firm resolution of [filing] a bill in Chancery against us which I reflect on with Great Concern that your Children must defend any cause against you, and that to [o] without knowing for what, for I yet am, I Can affirm to your Ladyship, wholy Ignorant of what debts or Contracts there is against you.⁶⁸

From France Lady Ferrers went on with her brother to Italy, and both were taken ill at Rome. She wrote to her youngest daughter about their symptoms in February, but did not mention the lawsuit. Instead she complained of not being consulted about Lady Mary's forthcoming marriage: 'Tho: I do not personally know Lord Killmorey yet I have no sort of objection to his Character or Family and if you think his fortune sufficient to your expectation there can be no reason for me to disapprove.'⁶⁹

⁶⁴ Hunt. Lib., HA 4730, Lady Betty to Lady H., 29 June [1729].
⁶⁵ PRONI, D3531/ A/ 2 and 4, depositions taken at Carrickmacross, 29 December 1735.
⁶⁶ Hunt. Lib., HA 9569, Lord Kilmorey to Lord H., 26 June 1739.
⁶⁷ Hunt. Lib., HA 10830, Lady Ferrers to [Lady H.], 26 August 1729.
⁶⁸ Leics. RO, 14D32/ 8, 10, undated draft.
⁶⁹ Hunt. Lib., HA 10832, Lady Ferrers to Lady Mary Shirley, 22 February 1729/30.

That summer Countess Ferrers and her brother returned to London by way of Turin and Lyons, and in November Lady Huntingdon received a letter from her mother in which she cast off all her children.[70] She seems to have kept her word, and when Lady Strafford met her in November 1730 she wrote to Lady Huntingdon that 'we had a great deal of discourse about Travelling but she did not name any of her own famely and your Ladyship may be sure I wou'd not begin.'[71]

Ten years later she made her will. Only her favourite daughter Mary was mentioned, being given 'my Diamond Cross and Coulant with the Quilt and Pillows which were her Grandmothers'.[72] She died in Paris on 26 January 1739/40, and Lady Huntingdon received two accounts of her last days. One correspondent found her 'in the hands of a Quack from whom she had great hopes', persuaded her to receive the sacrament and make her will. The other sent an affecting account of her deathbed and the news that her fortune was too small to pay the few small legacies in her will.[73] It is pleasant to record that her two surviving daughters paid the legacies and arranged for her to be buried beside her mother in Bath Abbey as she had wished. Lady Huntingdon took the initiative in this, and Lady Kilmorey sent her the cross 'as much fitter ornament for you whose Conduct on this occasion has so justly deserved it'.[74]

It was Lady Betty Hastings who played the part of a mother, not only to her half-sisters, but also to the Countess. They visited each other occasionally as well as conducting an extensive correspondence.[75] Twenty-five years older than Lady Huntingdon, Lady Betty became the model for her. She was a good businesswoman, taking great interest in the management of the estates which she had inherited.[76] Few of her business papers have survived, but the records of her bank account with Hoare's show her efficiency.[77] They also record some of her benevolence – gifts of money to

[70] Hunt. Lib., HA 10833 and 10834, Lady Ferrers to Lady H., 6 June and 19 November 1730.
[71] Hunt. Lib., HA 13197, Lady Strafford to Lady H., 19 November 1730.
[72] PRO, PROB 11/708. A coulant was a ring for a purse or similar object. Hunt. Lib., HA 8276, S. Levinge to Lord H., 28 February 1739/40.
[73] Leics. RO, 14D32/ 14, 40, Shadwell to Lady H., 30 April [1741]; Leics. RO, 14D32/ 14, 44, Knight to Lady H., 15 March 1740/1; 14D32/ 14, 22, Sam. Levinge to Lady H., 7 February 1739/40. He adds, 'I have lost my best help and friend.'
[74] Leics. RO, 14D32/ 7, 3, Lady Kilmorey to Lady H., 22 March 1740/1.
[75] Leics. RO, 14D32/ 8A, 4, Lady Betty to Lady H., 13 April, n.y.
[76] J. Hunter (ed.), *The Diary of Ralph Thoresby*, 2 (London, 1830), 302, 303. For modern lives of Lady Betty see M. G. Jones, 'Lady Elizabeth Hastings', *Church Quarterly Review* (December 1939) and C. E. Medhurst, *The Life and Work of Lady Elizabeth Hastings* (London, 1914).
[77] E.g. Hoare's Bank, ledger J, fo. 65 (1726–7).

help Mary Astell with her projects and to 'the Maid that was discharged from the Hospital to bear her expences into the Country'.[78] She made similar gifts to all the relations she could discover.[79] For the children of her brother-in-law, Granville Wheler, she bought lottery tickets and got her banker to check 'the Chances 9 times'.[80] She made donations to the Society for the Propagation of the Gospel and the Society for Promoting Christian Knowledge each year. The Church of England received her support. Prayers were held at Ledston Hall four times a day.[81] Lady Betty was also a scholar. She subscribed to Thoresby's *Vicaria Leodiensis* and to Elizabeth Elstob's *English-Saxon Homily*, and the catalogue of her books, which she bequeathed to her nephew George Hastings, runs to many pages.[82] Her interest in education led her to establish schools and provide scholarships at the universities. George Whitefield the Methodist, and other students at Oxford, benefited from her benevolence.[83] In her will she was to make elaborate provision for the improvement of education in the north of England with a charity which still continues to serve the same purpose.

Lady Huntingdon consciously imitated her sister-in-law. As early as 5 March 1728/9 she was buying Bibles and Books of Common Prayer for distribution, and a few years later was enquiring the cost of a 'Set of Communion plate'.[84] In July 1729 she sent ten guineas to the SPCK, which the enthusiastic secretary, Henry Newman, thought was an annual

---

[78] Hoare's Bank, ledger K, fo. 304 and ledger L, fo. 174. For Mary Astell and her educational projects see R. Perry, *The Celebrated Mary Astell* (Chicago, 1986).

[79] For the identity of her various relations see her will (Borthwick Institute, LE/ F 4).

[80] Hoare's Bank, ledger K, fo. 304 (1731).

[81] Rhodes House Lib., USPG Archives, *Annual Reports*, 1730–5; SPCK Archives, FT 9/ 5, treasurer's cash book, 1720–41; M. Clement (ed.), *Correspondence and Minutes of the SPCK relating to Wales* (Cardiff, 1952), 151. For Phillips and the SPCK see T. Shankland, 'The Charity School Movement in Wales', *Trans. of Hon. Soc. of Cymmrodorion* (1904–5), 74–216, and for Henry Hastings see W. O. B. Allen and E. McClure, *Two Hundred Years* (London, 1898), p. 132.

[82] S. Lewis, *Topographical Dictionary of England*, 3 (London, 1842); 49; Leics. RO, 14D32/ 8A, 8 and 42, Lady Betty to Lady H., 3 May, and Lady Betty to anon., 7 April 1726; 14D32/ 11, 3. Hunt. Lib., HA 4732, Lady Betty to Lord H., 26 June n.y.; C. L. S. Linnell, *The Diaries of Thomas Wilson, D.D.* (London, 1964), 40; Hunter, op. cit., vol. 2, p. 313; Hunt. Lib., HA Inv. box 2, 28. Elstob's book and several others from this library are now in the Cheshunt College library. For Elizabeth Elstob see D. M. Stenton, *The English Woman in History* (New York, 1977), 242, 243. For Thoresby see W. T. Lancaster (ed.), *Letters to Ralph Thoresby* (Leeds, 1912), p. 262.

[83] *George Whitefield's Journals* (London, 1960), 78; *The Parochial Libraries of the Church of England* (London, 1959), 24n. (but see SPCK Archives CS 2/ 20, p. 32).

[84] Leics. RO, 14D32/ 21, 3, receipt of Geo. Gell, 1729, and 14, 65, estimate of David Williams, 1732.

subscription, but after some confusion was discovered to be a donation.[85] She made a further donation in 1730, and continued to buy books and pamphlets from the society for distribution in the area around Donnington Park.[86] As late as 1745 she was concerned about the Society's Tranquebar mission in India and presented fifty prints of the native pastor there to the Society for distribution.[87] In 1737 Thomas Coram supplied her with information about his plan for a hospital for 'Helpless Infants daily exposed to Destruction', using his usual method of attracting female sympathies first.[88] She aided the unfortunate at Lady Betty's request.[89] Her sisters-in-law joined them in many of these good works, and many kind letters and presents passed between Ledston and Donnington Park.[90] It was therefore a serious blow to them all when it was discovered in 1738 that Lady Betty was seriously ill. On 13 May Lady Frances broke the sad news to her brother: 'It now appears that Dear Lady Bety about 18 years of Age as she has latly told us got a slight Bruise on her right Breast, but it neither gave her Pain eneugh then or ever since to take any Notice of it, tho' it wou'd spring up or be a little sore sometimes.' The pain had recently increased and her sisters had persuaded her to consult Dr Johnson about it. In his turn he also wrote: 'About 3 weeks ago Lady Betty Hasting's did me the Honour to consult me concerning a complaint in her breast. I was very sorry to find it was a Confirm'd Cancer, which would break and fix in a very short time.'[91] The operation, a few days later, was successful, and all looked well. It was particularly unfortunate that Lady Catherine Wheler was too ill to be told – she seems to have suffered from some mental disorder – and that Lady Huntingdon became pregnant soon after it became apparent that the cancer had not been defeated.[92]

[85] SPCK Archives, FT 9/ 1; CS 2/ 20, and minute book 13, p. 81; L. W. Cowie, *Henry Newman: An American in London* (London, 1956), 58.
[86] SPCK Archives, CS 27 (1733) and CN 2/5 (1739); Hunt. Lib., HA Misc., box 2, 1, SPCK circular, 29 June 1732; HA 9503, Newman to Lady H., 17 December 1730 (SPCK Archives, CS 22, p. 11).
[87] Leics. RO, 14D32/ 4, 7, copy of SPCK minute and 14D32/ 6, 28 Henry Hastings to Lady H., 13 September 1746. For an account of the Tranquebar mission see S. Neill, *A History of Christian Missions* (London, 1964), 228–31.
[88] The papers are in Leics. RO, 14D32/ 3, 2, 3 and 4, and Hunt. Lib., HA 1624. For Coram see 'Letters of Thomas Coram', *Proc. Mass. Hist. Soc.*, 56 (1923), 43. For Coram's Hospital see J. Brownlow, *Memoranda or Chronicles of the Foundling Hospital* (London, 1847).
[89] Hunt. Lib., HA 4730, Lady Betty to Lady H., 23 June [1729]; HA 4987, Lady Frances Hastings to Lady H., 19 December 1730.
[90] E.g. Hunt. Lib., HA 4746, Lady Betty to Lady H., 8 March [1735].
[91] Leics. RO, 14D32/ 8A, 35, Lady Frances to Lord H., 13 May [1738]; 14D32/ 7, 14, J. Johnson to Lord H., 20 May 1738.
[92] Leics. RO, 14D32/ 8A, 36, Lady Frances to Lord H., 20 May [1738].

The harrowing details of the operation and Lady Betty's subsequent decline are chronicled in the letters which passed between Ledston and Donnington Park during the next eighteen months. On 24 April 1739, during the course of the day, Lady Betty dictated her will and three codicils.[93] On Christmas Eve 1739 her nephew George sent the news of her death to his elder brother at school in London: 'All the Family here [at Ledston] as my Brother will easily believe are in the deepest sorrow for my Aunt Bettys Death which happen'd on Saturday last. It will be of the Greatest Service to all her Relations to Bear in Mind her Great and exemplary Virtues...'[94] Thomas Barnard, when describing the virtues of Lady Betty called upon the Countess to continue her pious works,[95] but the long and harrowing illness had the effect of turning Lady Huntingdon and her sisters-in-law towards Methodism.

---

[93] She also signed a deed for her educational charities and provided for her companion Sarah Hole. Borthwick Institute, LE/ A 1 (trust deed) and LE/ F 4 (will); Leics. RO, 14D32/ 10, 32, R. Wilson to G. Wheler, 26 October 1739; 14D32/ 8A, 30, Lady Betty to Lord and Lady H., 6 December 1739; 14D32/ 10, 35, G. Wheler to Lord H., 6 December 1739.
[94] Drew Univ., Hunt. A 116, Geo. Hastings to Frances Hastings, 24 December [1739].
[95] Barnard, *Lady Elizabeth Hastings*.

3

Conversion

An eighteenth-century Methodist if suddenly plunged into the present century would have difficulty in adjusting to changed circumstances. He would be surprised to see a building called a Methodist *Church*, something which he had never encountered. If he ventured inside he would find an emphasis on John Wesley to the almost total exclusion of all the other Methodist leaders he had known. The nineteenth century would have been even more confusing with its proliferation of Wesleyan, Primitive, Free and many other Methodist churches. It would only be in some small town where a Protestant church was holding an ecumenical revival meeting that he would find congenial surroundings. Eighteenth-century Methodism was not represented by a Church: it saw itself as a catalyst for the encouragement of conversions within all churches and as a means of stirring them to greater efforts. It was an evangelical movement which affected all the Protestant denominations. It was only in the nineteenth century that it inevitably became a separate denomination. Eighteenth-century Methodism was not even an homogeneous body, but was divided into many groups with no distinctive theology of its own. Even before John Wesley had been born the name of Methodist was employed as a term of abuse.[1] For much of the century it distinguished evangelicals or 'enthusiasts' of all kinds from the unconverted.[2] In England and Wales most of these evangelicals willingly took the name of Methodist, although it meant a different theology in Wales than in England. In New England and Scotland the title did not appear until much later. The revival was called the Great Awakening in New England (*Y Deffroad Mawr* in Wales): the Revival of Religion in Scotland. It was not until the end of the century

---

[1] For the early use of the term Methodist and its relation to the Pietists see K. H. Voigt, *Pietismus – Methodismus – Gemeinschaftsbewegung* (Bremen, 1979). Lady Betty Hastings owned a *Letter concerning Enthusiasm* of 1708 (Hunt. Lib., HA Inv., box 2, 28). It was in use in this sense as early as 1692.

[2] In different parts of England there can be found the monumental inscription describing a person as 'pious without enthusiasm' – an indication of one opposed to Methodism.

that the 'Methodist Church' was carried to these two countries by Wesleyan missionaries,[3] but the first Methodist movement in England and Wales is exactly the same as the early evangelism of Scotland and New England. There were many links between them, not the least of which were the evangelical periodicals published in England, Scotland and New England under such titles as *The Weekly History* or *The Christian's Amusement*.[4]

Many attempts have been made to establish a priority for the beginnings of Methodism, but all have failed.[5] In each of the four countries the evangelical movement began independently, but because of the ease and simplicity of printing by this period it was not long before experiences were being exchanged and their evangelical efforts were encouraged by the knowledge of similar developments elsewhere. In each country modern historians have placed the emphasis on one key figure for the revival – Jonathan Edwards in New England, William M'Culloch in Scotland, Howell Harris in Wales and John Wesley in England. But just as no one country can claim the sole credit for the evangelical revival, so no one man can receive all the credit. These are the men who have left a considerable quantity of literature or papers for our information. Others, equally important, have not done so and are therefore neglected. Lady Huntingdon can be included amongst the latter. She wrote nothing and insisted on no personal publicity, even after her death.

There were some precursors of the Methodists to whom they owe some inspiration and some of their organizational features. The earliest of these were the German Pietists, who became known in the English-speaking world through the activities of August Hermann Francke. In 1693 the new University of Halle established the *Franckesche Stiftung*, which eventually included schools, an orphanage, a dispensary and a printing works. Some of Francke's works were translated into English and had a great influence on all the early Methodists. William Law, Philip Doddridge, the Wesleys, George Whitefield and Lady Betty Hastings owned translations of his works. Lady Huntingdon had a copy of *Pietas Hallensis, or a publick Demonstration of the Foot-Steps of a Divine Being yet in the World: In an Historical*

---

[3] For the slow progress of 'Methodism' in North America and Scotland see F. A. Norwood, *The Story of American Methodism* (Nashville, 1974) and W. F. Swift, *Methodism in Scotland* (London, 1947).

[4] For these periodicals see S. Durden, 'A Study of the First Evangelical Magazines', *Journal of Eccles. Hist.*, 27 (1976), 255–75.

[5] See, for example, R. R. Williams, *Flames from the Altar* (Caernarvon, 1962) on the subject of priority. For an account of the revival in all these countries, see J. Gillies, *Historical Collections relating to the Remarkable Success of the Gospel* (Kelso, 1845).

Narration of the Orphan-House (London, 1705). Howell Harris planned an orphan house in Wales as early as 1736. Cotton Mather in New England corresponded with Francke.⁶ However Halle's greatest contribution to eighteenth-century evangelism was the education of a minor German noble, Nikolaus Ludwig, Count Zinzendorf. Zinzendorf later provided a home for the refugees from Moravia, descendants of the ancient Protestant Church there, encouraged their missionary activities, and eventually became their presiding bishop.⁷ The Moravians, the Church of the *Unitas Fratrum*, were to influence greatly the evangelical revival in both Britain and North America. So close were they in the first years that Moravians could be confused with Methodists.⁸ The Moravians also made some notable converts from the ranks of the early Methodists.

The last precursors needing to be mentioned here were the religious societies which proliferated in the early eighteenth century. Most of these were informal groups meeting to read a sermon or a homily, and have left very little written evidence of their existence. The majority would not have considered themselves as Methodist, but were probably evangelical. Records of these societes are sparse, but they can be found at Gloucester in 1735, Deptford in 1739, and Bury in Lancashire. David Brainerd met with similar societies in New England about 1740.⁹ In Scotland the societies usually met 'for prayer' and were more organized. In the Highlands there were fellowship meetings of the 'Men' and in the Lowlands the revival at Cambuslang and Kilsyth led to the establishment of similar societies.¹⁰ In England some of the societies were also organized with their

⁶ Hunt. Lib., HA Inv, box 2, 28. Lady Huntingdon's copy is now in Cheshunt College library; *George Whitefield's Journals* (London, 1960), 46; *A Catalogue of the Library at King's Cliffe* (1927); Cheshunt archives, F 1/ 1942, circular about a translation of Francke's *Footsteps of Divine Providence* (1787); M. H. Jones, 'Howell Harris, Citizen and Patriot', *Trans. Hon. Soc. of Cymmrodorion* (1908–9), 211; K. Francke, 'Cotton Mather and A. H. Francke', *Studies and Notes in Philology and Literature*, 5 (Boston, 1896), 57–67. See also G. F. Nuttall, 'Continental Pietism and the Evangelical Movement in Britain', in *Pietismus und Reveil* (Leiden, 1978), 207–36.
⁷ For the early history of the Moravian Church see J. E. Hutton, *A History of the Moravian Church* (London, 1909), and for its Revival, J. T. and K. G. Hamilton, *History of the Moravian Church* (Bethlehem, PA, 1967).
⁸ E. Welch, *The Bedford Moravian Church in the Eighteenth Century* (Bedford, 1989), 8.
⁹ *Whitefield's Journals*, op. cit., 61; W. Brockbank and F. Kenworthy, *The Diary of Richard Kay* (Manchester, 1968), 48; *The Christian's Amusement* (London, n.d.), no. 14; G. F. Nuttall, *New College and its Library* (London, 1977), 13, 14; *The Diary of David Brainerd*, 1, (London, 1902), 31.
¹⁰ J. MacInnes, 'The Origin and Early Development of "the Men"', *Scottish Church Hist. Soc.* (1942), 16–41, and *The Evangelical Movement in the Highlands of Scotland* (Aberdeen, 1951), 103, 105; G. D. Henderson, *The Burning Bush* (Edinburgh, 1957), 58; J. Robe, *A Continuation of a Faithful Narrative of the Extraordinary Work of the Spirit of God, at Kilsyth* (London, 1743), 63.

own rules, and two societies were even sufficiently wealthy to subscribe to Thomas Hartley's sermons in 1754.[11] For the Methodists and the Moravians the existence of these societies provided a useful model. By September 1740 Howell Harris had already organized bands of societies in the neighbourhood of Trefeca, and in 1742 he printed a set of rules for them.[12] In general they were considered to be part of a denomination, but for the Moravians it was the concept of the *ecclesiola*.[13] These societies also provided a base on which John Wesley could build.[14]

It is impossible to define eighteenth-century Methodism by either doctrine (some were Arminians and some Calvinists) or by church membership, so that the best indication of it is the emphasis on personal conversion. Both Moravians and Methodists agreed that there were three stages on this path:

1 Acceptance of the fact that one was a sinner and that good works alone could not redeem one. The argument about the value of good works was to perplex Methodists for many years.
2 Abandonment of 'reason' and complete submission to God. This was a reaction to the growth of rational religion in Protestant churches – a trend which led by way of Deism and Socinianism to Unitarianism.
3 The joy of a revelation of personal salvation. This might either be instantaneous or by slow stages. John Wesley believed in the former: Charles Wesley in the latter.[15]

Lady Huntingdon has left us no account of her conversion, but it can be dated to 1739. In her *Letter to a Student* of 1785 she refers to 'the long Experience of a poor unprofitable Servant, now near fifty Years facing

---

[11] J. S. Simon, *John Wesley and the Religious Societies* (London, 1921) prints some of these rules in chapter 1. For an account of religious societies later in the century, see J. H. Pratt (ed.), *The Thought of the Evangelical Leaders* (Edinburgh, 1978), 185–9. T. Hartley, *Sermons on Various Subjects* (London, 1754), list of subscribers – Markfield and Packington – both parishes are in north-west Leics. and were probably influenced by Lady Huntingdon.

[12] D. E. Jenkins, *Calvinistic Methodist Holy Orders* (Caernarvon, 1911), 17, 62.

[13] The Moravian Church, an episcopal church claiming the apostolic succession, did not wish to convert anyone from another Protestant Church. Its primary concern was its missions to natives and the heathen.

[14] See J. Wesley, *Rules of the Band Societies* (1738) and *A Plain Account of the People called Methodists* (Bristol, 1749).

[15] This was Jonathan Edwards's classic definition (C. C. Goen, *Revival and Separatism in New England* (Yale, 1962), 14); T. Jackson, *The Life of the Rev. Charles Wesley* (London, 1841), vol.1, p.125.

Hell and the world'.[16] In November 1740 the Moravian James Hutton visited Lord and Lady Huntingdon, and cross-examined her maid on the improvement of the Countess's temper, and was told that she had not been in a passion for more than twelve months.[17] But the best evidence is in the family letters for this period, both of her sisters-in-law and of Thomas Barnard, the Leeds schoolmaster. In July 1739 Thomas Barnard wrote two letters to the Countess giving her spiritual advice. In October of the same year he wrote that she had been 'four months employed in the blessed work'.[18] So the date of her conversion must be July 1739.

The links between the early Methodists and the Hastings family began with Lady Betty's interest in the work of the Society for the Propagation of the Gospel. Her friendship with Sir John Philipps introduced her to the SPG. The Society had supported John Wesley as a missionary in Georgia, and General Oglethorpe, the founder of the colony, took Charles Wesley as his secretary. When Charles returned to England in 1737 Lady Betty asked him about the spiritual needs of the new colony.[19] It was Lady Betty (and not the Countess) who at this time was interested in North America: she bequeathed money to the SPG as an endowment for an American episcopate.[20] When George Whitefield followed the example of the Wesleys and sailed for Georgia in January 1737/8 Lady Betty took an even greater interest because he was one of the students she had supported at Oxford. She received various reports about his progress, and collected information about his character and appearance: 'A great many of the clergy dislike him. I can't tell why unless it be that he labours more abundantly than they do ... I heard him once at our church. His sermon was moderate. Nothing fine ...'[21] Another early Methodist returned from Georgia who had closer links with the family at Lady Betty's home at Ledston was Benjamin Ingham. Ingham was born at Ossett in the West Riding, the son of a farmer and hatter, and went to Queen's College – the

---

[16] *A Copy of a Letter from the Countess of Huntingdon to One of Her Students* (Trefecka, 1785). Copy in Cheshunt archives, A 3/ 12, 1.

[17] D. Benham, *Memoirs of James Hutton* (London, 1856), 67.

[18] Leics. RO, DE 23/1/ 1428 (20 July 1739); 14D32/ 2, 12, 2 and 3 (30 July and 12 October 1739).

[19] T. Jackson, *The Journal of the Rev. Charles Wesley* (London, 1849), vol.1, p.71.

[20] By its original charter the SPG (which the Countess did not support) was confined to missionary activities in America. She preferred the eastern missions which the SPCK helped. No bishops were appointed for North America until the end of the century – a serious handicap to the Anglican Church there.

[21] *Hastings Wheler Letters*, 2, pp.140, 141, 153, 156.

college which Lady Betty chose for her scholarships. Whether she supported Ingham at Oxford is not known.[22] Like all those who had gone to Georgia with the Wesleys, Ingham was strongly influenced by the Moravians who went to the colony at the same time, and on his return to Yorkshire he began itinerant preaching. The Ledston sisters took a great interest in the Moravian missions. Lady Margaret sent Lady Huntingdon copies of hymns recommended by Ingham, and 'A Copy of part of a letter of Count Zinzendorf' describing the progress of the Moravian missions throughout the world.[23]

The Earl and Countess spent a short time at Ledston early in July 1739, when they learned more about the Moravians from Lady Margaret, and the Countess had discussions with Thomas Barnard and Benjamin Ingham.[24] It was then that Lady Margaret told her that 'since she had known ... Christ, she had been as happy as an angel.'[25] When they returned to Donnington Park, both the Countess and her husband were in either the first or second stage of the conversion process, having resolved 'to betake yourself to the Life of Religion'. Thomas Barnard hastened to send a long letter of advice to Lady Huntingdon on 20 July, but Lady Margaret sent Ingham in person 'from whose conversation and expounding of the Scriptures I doubt not but you will receive great Comfort'.[26] It was arranged for him to preach in Castle Donnington parish church, to the annoyance of the vicar.[27] However both Lord and Lady Huntingdon were already convinced by the time he arrived. On 26 July a letter to Ledston announced the glad tidings: 'I had not read near half of my Dear Lady Huntingdons last Letter before my Sisters Snatched it from me thinking it more than I cou'd bear. Indeed I was quite overpower'd with Joy and Thankfullness to Infinit Wisdom and Goodness for Mannifesting

---

[22] Many of Lady Margaret's letters to the Countess are undated. Although the earliest reference to Ingham in the Hastings correspondence is 17 January 1737/8 (*Hastings Wheler Letters*, 2, p.140), most of the letters are probably a year later. For Ingham see B. Scott, 'The Dewsbury Riots and the Revd Benjamin Ingham', *Thoresby Soc. Miscellany*, 17 (1981), 187–95); R. W. Thompson, *Benjamin Ingham and the Inghamites* (Kendal, 1958); R. P. Heitzenrater, *Diary of an Oxford Methodist* (Durham, NC, 1985).

[23] Leics. RO, 14D32/ 8, 8, fragment of an undated letter. Lady Betty owned 'Wesley's Hymns and Poems. London, 1739' (Hunt. Lib., HA Inv., box 2, 28). Leics. RO, 14D32/ 8a, 3, Lady Margaret to Lady H., Sat. night.

[24] *Hastings Wheler Letters*, 2, pp.168, 169.

[25] T. Haweis, *An Impartial and Succinct History* (London, 180, 241.

[26] Leics. RO, DE 23/1 / 1428, Barnard to Lady H., 20 July; 14D32/ 8a, 19, Lady Margaret to Lady H., 28 July [1739].

[27] Leics. RO, 14D32/ 8A, 37, Lady Anne or Lady Frances to Lady H., n.d.

himself in so extraordinary a Manner to my Dear Brother and Sister.'[28] She had sent the news on to Benjamin Ingham, as requested, and he wrote to the Countess 'by a Private Messenger' rejoicing in the news.[29] Lady Huntingdon left no account of her conversion – only two short pieces give a brief indication that it followed the usual Methodist pattern.[30] She continued to receive letters of good advice and pious information from Lady Margaret, who rejoiced at the appointment of an evangelical minister to the family living of Markfield. Ingham also wrote requesting a donation towards the new Moravian settlement at Herrnhaag, and recommending a text for her meditations.[31]

As it became more certain during the course of the year that Lady Betty would soon die, so her sisters and the Countess turned more and more to the Moravians for comfort. Just before she died Lady Margaret and Lady Frances wrote to Sister Anna Nitschman at Herrnhut, the principal Moravian settlement in Germany.[32] Both request the prayers of the Church for their salvation. Ingham brought them into contact with two other sympathizers with the Moravian church. One was James Hutton, the London bookseller. In November he wrote to thank the Countess for her gift to John Hagen, who went to Carolina on a mission to convert the Indians. This was probably the £8 which Hoare's bank paid to Hutton at this time on behalf of the Earl.[33] Until 1742 the Earl continued to make payments to Hutton, either for books purchased or for donations to the Moravians.[34] Another clergyman introduced to Donnington Park was the Revd Jacob Rogers who had been at school in Batley with Ingham. When he was expelled from his curacy in Bedford, he was sent to preach in the Midlands and Yorkshire by George Whitefield. For a time Rogers was very active, preaching in the area around Nottingham and Derby, and

---

[28] Leics. RO, 14D32/ 8, 1, [Lady Margaret] to Lady H., 29 July [1739]. This contradicts the often repeated anecdote of Lord Huntingdon's opposition to his wife's views (*Life and Times*, vol.1, p.18).

[29] Leics. RO, 14D32/ 8A, 18, Lady Margaret to Lord H., 28 July [1739].

[30] Leics. RO, 14D32/ 8, 9, undated fragment; *Hastings Wheler Letters* 2, p.170.

[31] Leics. RO, DE 23/ 1/ 1431, Ingham to Lady H., 23 October 1739; 14D32/ 8a, 11, Lady Margaret to Lady H., 7 November [1739].

[32] JRL, Meth. Archives, PLP 51.3.1 appears to be the original of this joint letter with a contemporary explanation in German of their social position added at the end. A modern transcript is in the Herrnhut archives (R13 A17/56a). Sister Nitschman's draft reply is at Herrnhut (R 13 A 17/57).

[33] Leics. RO, 14D32/ 4, 5, Hutton to [Lady H.], n.d.; Hoare's Bank archives, ledger O, fo. 427 (20 November 1739). For the date of Hagen's voyage see Benham's *Hutton*, op. cit., 44.

[34] Hoare's Bank archives, ledger p, fo. 434 and ledger Q, fo. 168; Drew Univ., Meth. Archives, A 26, Lady H: to Lord H., 7 May 1740.

probably visited Donnington Park. Lady Margaret reported his progress in an undated letter of this period.[35] However, by the end of 1740 he had become a Baptist, and contact with Ledston and Donnington Park was broken. Later he became a Moravian minister. In this way Donnington Park became a centre of the new 'sect' which aroused the disapproval of Lady Huntingdon's younger sister, Lady Kilmorey:

> my Complyments to Lady Margrit and am much oblidged to her for remembring me, but am sorry to find she Is turn'd Methodist as that sect Is so Generally exploded that It's become a Joke of all Compagnys, and Indeed I Can goe no whare but I hear of the uncommon piety of the Donnington familly ... I'm Conserned to think my Dear Sister who Is so reasonable In every thing Else should Encourage such a Cantting set of people...[36]

So far as we know, the Countess did not even follow Lady Betty's practice of prayers four times a day. The Earl and Countess had no resident chaplain, and the visits of Methodist preachers and exhorters were so short and rare that Donnington Park can hardly have been as Lady Kilmorey suspected. Despite the voluminous journals and diaries of the early Methodist leaders we have little information about when they first met Lady Huntingdon or visited one of the Earl's houses. Only Howell Harris records how Charles Wesley took him to meet 'a Lady of Quality – Lady Huntingdon' on 26 August 1743.[37] Only James Hutton has preserved a detailed account of one of his meetings:

> Last week I waited upon the Earl of Huntingdon and his lady, at no great distance from London. The Countess, who had sent for me, I found more eager to hear the Gospel than anyone I ever saw before. Of poor sinnership and of the Saviour she has not much to say; nevertheless, she receives the Gospel very simply, and believes it. I look daily for its striking deep roots in her heart; she has a great liking for the Brethren; she does not lack good sense, but has a very violent temper.[38]

This was the occasion on which Hutton advised her to be 'obedient, cheerful and loving' to her husband. Hutton can hardly have known how unnecessary the last two words of advice were. Neither the Wesleys nor Whitefield recorded their first meetings with the Countess. It is only by a letter which the Countess wrote on 19 February 1741/2 that we know she

---

[35] For Rogers, see Welch, *The Bedford Moravian Church*, 6–9 and J. Walsh, 'The Cambridge Methodists', in P. Brooks (ed.), *Christian Spirituality* (London, 1975). Leics. RO, 14D32/ 8a, 4, Lady Margaret to Lady H., n.d.
[36] Hunt. Lib., HA, Lady Kilmorey to Lady H., 9 June [1740?].
[37] T. Beynon, *Howell Harris, Reformer and Soldier* (Caernarvon, 1958), 50.
[38] Benham, *Hutton*, 67; letter of 18 November 1740.

had already met George Whitefield before that date.[39] His surviving journals show no evidence of a possible visit to Donnington Park at this early period. Neither John nor Charles Wesley mentions the Earl and Countess by name in their published journals for this period. They write of visiting Castle Donnington, the parish in which Donnington Park is situated, but do not say whom they saw. When Charles 'rode to Donnington, and asked, "Have ye received the Holy Ghost since ye believed?"' on 24 May 1743 (his first visit), Lady Huntingdon was at Enfield Chase.[40] Yet Lady Huntingdon was already corresponding with him as early as February 1741/2.[41] John Wesley paid four visits to Donnington Park to see the ailing Miss Cowper, and six visits to preach at Markfield, a few miles away, between June 1741 and November 1743, and Lady Anne Hastings hoped to meet him there, but he does not mention either the Earl or the Countess in his journals. His fragmentary diary, which he did not publish, records six visits to see Lady Huntingdon at Enfield Chase between April and August 1741.[42] Did he and Charles consider these meetings too unimportant, or did they find the Countess too ready to take the initiative in the new movement? The latter is more probable since George Whitefield was able to establish a long and close friendship with her later, whereas John Wesley, with a temperament similar to hers, was always uneasy and even unwilling to meet her.[43] For the Methodist leaders the Countess's role was to be a protector and a provider of patronage, to rescue their followers from riots, the press, and hostile incumbents and bishops.

After Lady Betty's death the Countess ceased to be so interested in the Moravians. With the benefit of hindsight, the growing affection of Lady Margaret for Benjamin Ingham is obvious to us. Lady Betty may have realized this before her death, and it may be the reason for a curious provision about Lady Margaret's possible marriage which she included in

[39] JRL, Meth. Archives, Hunt. 5, Lady H. to Mr Wesley, 19 February [1741/2].
[40] *Charles Wesley's Journal*, vol.1, p.308; Leics. RO, 14D32/ 24, 8, Lady H. to Lord H., 20 May 1743.
[41] JRL, Meth. Archives, Hunt. 4.
[42] Leics. RO, 14D32/ 11, 6, Lady Anne to Lady H., 21 May 1742; N. Curnock (ed.), *John Wesley's Journal* (London, n.d.), vol.2, pp.446–84. One meeting between John Wesley and the Countess has been frequently cited but did not occur: the story is that she accompanied him when he left from the Fetter Lane society on 20 July 1740 (e.g. J. S. Simon, *John Wesley and the Methodist Societies* (London, 1923), 14). She was probably in Ledston at that time and there is no evidence that John Wesley knew Lady Huntingdon then, that she belonged to the Fetter Lane society, or that she joined his new society.
[43] E.g. Simon, op. cit., 157, 158.

her will.⁴⁴ She had also bequeathed Ledston and much of her property in Yorkshire to Francis, the Countess's eldest son, and his parents decided to lease out the house until he came of age.⁴⁵ Therefore his aunts, the Ladies Anne, Frances and Margaret, were offered a home in Leicestershire. They decided on Ashby Place rather than Donnington Park. At first Lady Margaret was as enthusiastic as her sisters, looking forward to conversations with the Countess, but she found it difficult to leave Ingham. Lady Frances organized the move for herself and Lady Anne, but Lady Margaret did not join them. The Countess wrote to her husband from Ledston in April or May of 1740 'I have some uneasiness on my spirits about L – y M – te. I fear she will not return to Donington with me, but do not speak of this. I have sent this day for Mrs Hole hoping she will be of great use to me, but I am under great anxiety of mind, haveing acted with such Caution and to so little purpose.'⁴⁶ In July Lady Margaret was staying in Lightcliffe near Halifax with Mr and Mrs Holms, and in August Mrs Hole was reporting similar concerns to the Countess.⁴⁷ The rumours that she was to be married began as early as February 1740/1 when Lady Mary Wortley Montagu reported that she had 'disposed of herself to a poor wandering Methodist'.⁴⁸ It is difficult to see why the family was so upset about the marriage. The bride was older than the groom, but this was not often a problem in the eighteenth century, and both parties possessed a modest fortune which was sufficient for the life they intended. It is possible that their chief concern was the wandering life which Lady Margaret led for the next few months. James Hutton tried to dissuade Benjamin Ingham from the marriage, as his mother wrote to Lord and Lady Huntingdon.⁴⁹

In October the Earl received two letters from the vicar of Halifax about his meetings with Ingham and his future bride. He feared they intended to ask him to issue a licence, which would avoid any possibility of objections to banns. Lady Margaret 'was very desirous to see me at her new House', and 'would be disoblig'd' if she did not see him next week.⁵⁰ The new

⁴⁴ Borthwick Institute, LE/ F4, Lady Betty's will gave Lady Margaret an annuity of £150 a year unless she married before 1745.

⁴⁵ In 1745 it was leased to Mr Bowes (*HMC Portland 6*, (London, 1901), 182).

⁴⁶ Drew Univ., Meth. Archives A 125, Lady H. to Lord H., n.d. Sarah Hole had been Lady Betty's companion.

⁴⁷ Leics. RO, 14D32/ 8a, 5, Lady Margaret to Lady H., 30 July [1740]; 14D32/ 11, 2, S. Hole to Lady H., 9 August.

⁴⁸ R. Halsband (ed.), *The Complete Letters of Lady Mary Wortley Montagu*, 2 (Oxford, 1966), 225.

⁴⁹ Hunt. Lib., HA 7621, Elizabeth Hutton to Sarah Hole, n.d.

⁵⁰ Leics. RO, 14D32/ 14, 10, Geo. Legh to Lord H., 20 October 1741.

house was that at Aberford, just north of Ledston, where the newly married couple were to settle. The vicar of Halifax was spared the need to refuse them a licence. On 11 November Ingham persuaded the vicar of Aberford to issue a licence for his marriage with Lady Margaret, and to marry them on the next day.[51] Although he considered himself a Moravian, Ingham did not tell the Brethren of his forthcoming marriage, as they would have expected. However, on hearing the news a few days later, the congregation at Fetter Lane sang a hymn for them.[52] The Earl and Countess did not hear of the ceremony until December. On the 14th the Countess had heard the news from her husband: 'O how I lemant poor Sister Margrate and that Instance you give has so much of the world in it (as far as we Can see) that it quite shocks one. I have been asked hear much about it. It gives Lady Cox and all the religious people great trouble, as it may prove a stumbling block to the weak.'[53] On Christmas Eve Lady Margaret Ingham wrote to her sister-in-law from Aberford: 'I find an Inclination in my Heart to write to Your Dear Ladyship and I hope you will receive it as I write it, in Love. For as we have but one Common Lord and Master, all who are united to him will love one a Nother ...' The friendship between the two ladies was soon renewed. A few months later Lady Huntingdon was sending her sister-in-law accounts of her work with the local colliers and 'amongst the fine Ladys at Bath'.[54] Benjamin Ingham, on the other hand, resented the attempts made to prevent his marriage, and it was long before he visited Donnington Park again. Thomas Barnard broke his friendship with Ingham and used the preface to his account of Lady Betty's benevolence to denounce all 'Methodists'. The principal losers were the Moravians, and it was many years before the Countess resumed her contacts with them.[55]

Another cause of Lady Huntingdon's distaste for the Moravians may have been the influence which they had on her own evangelistic activities in north-west Leicestershire. As was fitting for a member of two mine-owning families, she began her efforts with the local coalminers. The early Methodists were particularly concerned with the plight of the miners at

[51] Borthwick Institute, ABE 2 (Aberford parish register) and marriage bond, 11 November 1741.

[52] Benham, op. cit., 75.

[53] Drew Univ. Meth. Archives A 100, Lady H. to Lord H., 14 December [1741].

[54] Leics. RO, DE 23/ 1 / 1436 and 1442, Lady Margaret to Lady H., 24 December 1741 and 27 February 1741/2.

[55] The differences between this account of the marriage and that given by Seymour in *Life and Times*, vol.1, p.248 should be noted. Barnard, op. cit., xxiii, xxvii, 57. The memoranda to which Barnard refers have not been found.

Kingswood near Bristol.[56] Later their interest spread to miners in the north of England and Cornwall. The Countess's interest was so considerable that John Wesley was to write in 1743: 'When I was first pressed by the Countess of Huntingdon to go and preach to the colliers in or near Newcastle ...'[57] The Hastings owned a mine near Oakthorpe which was being developed about this time.[58] There are various references to the Countess's efforts on behalf of the miners, but few details have been preserved.[59] There is, however, one letter from a mining contractor which casts considerable light on the problems of an evangelistic campaign:

> It will be a great pleasure to me if I can in any shape forward your good Intentions towards our truly Ignorant Colliers, and I do assure your Ladyship that you have my free Consent therein and I shou'd be glad If they wou'd adhere to any good Advice whatever, but they are a strong Sett of Obstinate People and under no kind of Government for whether they continue in this part of the World or go into any other they are their own Masters ... one thing I must observe to your Ladyship (which is) as I have a Considerable undertaking at that place, I must beg no notice may be taken of me, for fear of any Ill Consequence that may attend the present good Friendship and Interest I have in the Neighbourhood, besides if any uneasyness should happen on the occasion ... a Mobb might be of the utmost Ill Consequence in the World.[60]

The writer probably referred to the Oakthorpe mine. The riots in the Staffordshire coalfield around Wednesbury a year later show that his fear of a mob was not unjustified.[61]

Nothing more is known of this activity, but Wesleyan and Baptist chapels at Oakthorpe may have developed from it. Better results came from a parallel campaign of evangelism in a nearby area of Leicestershire centred on Markfield church. Lord Huntingdon was the patron, and the rector, the Revd Edward Ellis, who had been sent to Cambridge at the Earl's expense, adopted Methodist views. John Wesley preached in his church frequently between 1741 and 1743, as well as on later occasions.

---

[56] [O. Goldsmith], *The Life of Richard Nash* (London, 1762), 109 records a public subscription for the distressed colliers organized by Nash. *Charles Wesley's Journal*, vol.1, p.301.

[57] F. Baker (ed.), *Letters of John Wesley*, 2 (Oxford, 1982), 101.

[58] Warws. RO, CR 2131/ 16, L. Shirley to Conduitt, 31 March 1732/3; Leics. RO, 14D32/ 14, 39, B. Sparrow to Lady H., 14 April 1740). About this time Charles Wesley wrote a hymn for 'the colliers of Coldoverton', i.e. Coleorton (Cheshunt archives, B5/ 6, 9).

[59] Leics. RO, 14D32/ 29, 2, Wynter to Lady H., n.d.

[60] Leics. RO, 14D32/ 4, 2, H. Sparrow to Lady H., 3 June 1742.

[61] See J. L. Waddy, *The Bitter Sacred Cup* (London, 1976) for an account of the Wednesbury riots.

Charles Wesley preached there twice on 19 October 1743.[62] The link between Ellis and the Wesleys was Lady Huntingdon. Early in 1741 she provided suitable books for the society which Ellis had formed, before John Wesley's first visit, invited Ellis to preach at Donnington Park, and supplied him with medicines for the benefit of his parishioners.[63] This was not the only society which benefited from her benevolence. Amongst her papers is an address of the societies at Breaston and Draycott in Derbyshire 'To our Benefactors Unknown'. Both villages were on the opposite bank of the river Trent to Donnington Park. All of her charitable work at this time was confined to those parts of Leicestershire, Derbyshire and Staffordshire adjacent to her home,[64] and there is no evidence that she attended either the Wesleys' society at the Foundery in City Road or Whitefield's at the Moorfields Tabernacle at this time. One of her servants, David Taylor, now began to establish new societies in Leicestershire, and his enthusiasm caused problems. The Countess was obliged to apologize to the incumbent:

> Upon application of some of your parishioners to me I gave my servant David leave to go to some one of their houses to read to them ordering him at the same time to read one of Bishop Kenn [sic] sing a psalm and read a prayer – the same they use in all the religious Societys in Town – hoping by this means to promote the Glory of God ... [W]hat has inclined me to address you in this manner proceeds from being told that this night that David read out of doors which was both Contrary to my knowledge and approbation.[65]

David Taylor became a Methodist exhorter throughout the Midlands and Yorkshire,[66] but his activities soon became a source of distress to Lady Huntingdon and the Wesleys, because he refused to surrender control of the societies he had formed.[67] On 19 April 1742 the Countess wrote to John Wesley: 'your opinion of David Taylour will I fear be found true. I think it will be best to take no notice till I find a way open to do it

[62] Ellis had been presented to Markfield by the Earl in 1738) (Hunt. Lib., HA 2551). He was afterwards vicar of Ledsham (Hunt. Lib., HA 2553). *John Wesley's Journal*, 8, 12 and 14 June 1741, 22 July 1742, 27 July and 28 November 1743; *Charles Wesley's Journal*, op. cit., vol.1, p.337.

[63] Leics. RO, 14D32/ 4, 1 and 3, Ellis to Lady H., 14 February 1740/1 and 8 October 1742.

[64] Leics. RO, 14D32/ 4, 6 (22 June 1740).

[65] Leics. RO, 14D32/ 24, 1, Lady H. to [?Mr Rolston], n.d. For another account of the activities of a religious society, see Cheshunt archives, E 4/ 2, 6 (1773).

[66] V. S. Doe, *The Diary of James Clegg*, pt 2 (Derbys. Rec. Soc., 1979), 441, 446, 447.

[67] *John Wesley's Letters*, vol.2, p.74.

effectualy.'[68] Ten days later she forwarded to him a letter from David Taylor 'by which you will find he will have no one to rule over him and I think Mr I[ngham] has a hand in it ... I shall take no farther notice of David Taylours proceedings or give incourag[ement] to him ...'[69] In 1743 James Hutton was complaining that David Taylor was sometimes for and sometimes against the Brethren, and during the next year it was Charles Wesley's turn to complain about him.[70]

Despite being abandoned by David Taylor, the societies around Markfield continued to flourish. In 1742 John Taylor, another exhorter, took on the task.[71] Most of what is known about John Taylor's early life comes from a letter which he wrote to Howell Harris after hearing Harris preach at the Tabernacle in London.[72] Several months earlier Lady Huntingdon had told John Wesley that John Taylor proposed to settle at Ratby, the next parish to Markfield, where he would have 'a little shop to sell all your books and other things', together with a school.[73] She hoped that this would enable both John and Charles Wesley to preach there, whereby 'a litle Church might be rais'd there.' John Taylor soon began to follow his namesake's example and preach in the surrounding villages and hamlets, but his behaviour led to problems with persecutors and the courts.[74] Soon after this the society at Barton in the Beans decided to establish 'a kind of Moravian settlement', but this was soon abandoned.[75] Instead they began to evangelize the surrounding district. The writer of the earliest account of their activities predicted that although now obscure, these churches were 'likely to make a considerable Figure' in the future.[76] In this he was correct. In the nineteenth century the New Connexion of General Baptists founded at Barton became a large and flourishing denomination. Long before the church was formed at Barton in the Beans, the Countess had lost contact with its members. At this time she was a determined

[68] JRL, Meth. Archives, Hunt. 106, Lady H. to J. Wesley, 19 April [1742]. Printed in *Letters*, vol.2, p.75.

[69] Ibid., 105, Lady H. to J. Wesley, 29 April 1742. Partly printed in *Letters*, vol.2, p.76.

[70] Benham, *Hutton*, 120; *Charles Wesley's Journal*, vol.1, pp.309, 362.

[71] It should be noted that three Taylors (David, John and, later in the century, Daniel) were successively concerned with the Leics. revival. There is no evidence that they were related.

[72] NLW, Trev. letter 684, J. Taylor to H. Harris, 12 October 1742.

[73] JRL, Meth. Archives, Huntingdon 105.

[74] J. R. Godfrey, *Historic Memorials of Barton and Melbourne General Baptist Churches* (Leicester, 1891), 5. The 'Account of the late Persecution ... written by Br. Cennick appears in *The Weekly History*, 24, 19 September 1741; ibid., pp.6–9; Leics. RO, QS 3/ 119, 4, bail bond, 27 February 1743/4. No other record of the case has been found in the quarter sessions records.

[75] Godfrey, op. cit., 13.

[76] DWL, MS 38.6, fo. 44r, Josiah Thompson's list, 1772.

supporter of the Church of England, so the establishment of a dissenting meeting in the parish of Markfield was no doubt a blow to her hopes. There is no further reference in her correspondence to these evangelists.

However, the Methodist revival of the early eighteenth century affected almost all the Protestant churches. As we have seen, the Leicestershire Methodists progressed from Moravian to General Baptist principles. The Bedford Methodists, on the other hand, went from Particular Baptist to Moravian beliefs. In Plymouth the Methodist Tabernacle eventually became a Congregational church.[77] In all these examples the Methodists were originally Anglicans, but those already dissenters came under the same influence. The Batter Street Presbyterian church in Plymouth appointed a Welsh Methodist as its minister in 1760, expelled the Arian minority, and became a rival to the Tabernacle. About the same time another Methodist minister moved to the local Baptist church. In Southampton the Above Bar Independent chapel elected an evangelical minister, William Kingsbury, in 1764, and daughter churches sprang up in much of southern Hampshire. Charles Wesley's early journals have numerous references to Quakers who were sympathetic to Methodism and requested him to preach.[78] For much of the century the Society of Friends organized Circular Yearly Meetings which seem to have closely resembled the evangelical activities of the leading Methodists.[79] Thomas Story, a Quaker elder, held public meetings throughout the country, and particularly at those places where Methodism later flourished. In 1739 he discussed the Methodists with Lord Lonsdale at Lowther Hall, and expressed a favourable view of their activities.[80] There was a Quaker meeting house at Castle Donnington, and at least two of the Friends there were aided by Lady Huntingdon. One of them wrote an account of his beliefs to her.[81]

There would have been less difficulty in the early Methodist movement if there had not been division on doctrinal lines. John and Charles Wesley were Arminians and believed in the possibility of salvation for everyone. Since they held very firmly to this belief, they were never able to join with the majority of the dissenters, who were Calvinists. After quarrelling with the Moravians over Quietism, John Wesley was left with the Church of

[77] For Bedford see Welch, *Bedford Moravian Church*, 7–9. For Plymouth see E. Welch, 'Andrew Kinsman's Churches', *Trans. Devons. Assoc.*, vol.97, 1965 pp.233, 234.
[78] *Charles Wesley's Journal*, op. cit., vol.1, pp.158, 235.
[79] W. C. Braithwaite, *The Second Period of Quakerism* (Cambridge, 1971), 546, 547.
[80] *A Journal of the Life of Thomas Story* (Newcastle on Tyne, 1747), 675, 694, 718, 741.
[81] Leics. RO, 14D32/ 14, 79 and 29, 6, Thomas Cornwall to Lady H., 28 July 1746 and John Varnam to Lady H., n.d.

England as the only spiritual home for his kind of Methodism. Rarely, if ever, did either of the Wesleys preach inside a dissenters' meeting house, but George Whitefield, Howell Harris and many other Methodist leaders were Calvinists, and so were able to fraternize with the Calvinist dissenters without wishing to turn them into Anglicans. Whitefield preached in any congregation which was willing to invite him.

For her part Lady Huntingdon accepted the Wesleys' Arminianism for the next ten years. She refused to meet Spangenberg, Count Zinzendorf's companion, or other Moravians.[82] In February 1742/3 she happened to meet George Whitefield at Gloucester and debated the merits of Calvinism with him:

> he held forth above two hours [u]pon the Doctrine of election and reprobation [and] Collected all the Choicest flowers of all [t]hat was to be geather[ed] or said upon the [sev]eral heads to Charm me ... [I] told him upon what he had said the [u]pon the whole I found I should be such [a] looser by his way a thinking that no Consideration that I was yet able to see [fr]om any thing he had said Could have [a]ny waight – he seem'd surpriz'd and [s]aid how Could that be! I told him I [w]as so much happier than he was and [t]hat not from any thing in my self but on my Constant dependence upon Christ...[83]

They debated whether anyone could live without sin: Lady Huntingdon believing it possible (an antinomian doctrine) and Whitefield denying it. She was impressed that Whitefield could talk 'very sensibly, his manner agreeable, a Command of words and smothly put togeather', but complained of his behaviour towards the Wesley brothers. At this period she was closest to John Wesley – advising on the publication of his journal, and accepting the dedication of his *Collection of Moral and Sacred Poems*.[84] She was also allowed to read Charles Wesley's journals, though they were never published in his lifetime. Amongst the Hastings papers are copies of Charles Wesley's account of his visit to Devon and Cornwall from 15 June to 13 July 1746, which include the extra information which Charles had concealed in shorthand entries.[85] It was apparently the same copy which Elizabeth Cart lent to James Erskine in August.[86] Elizabeth Cart was a Quaker from Virginia who had married a prosperous London merchant,

[82] *John Wesley's Letters*, vol.2, p.67.
[83] JRL, Meth. Archives, Hunt. 5, Lady H. to [J.] Wesley, 19 February 1742/3. The original is in poor condition.
[84] *John Wesley's Letters*, vol.2, p.75.
[85] Leics. RO, 14D32/ 29, a journal letter from J. Merriton to John Wesley, 31 March 1746, copied by the same person, is included.
[86] G. M. Roberts (ed.), *Selected Trevecka Letters 1742–1747* (Caernarvon, 1956), 191.

and was now a widow.[87] She corresponded for a time with the Countess, not about her Quaker beliefs, but about millenarianism. In particular she was interested in a hermit who lived in a hut near Bexley, who had been visited by the Prince of Wales.[88] His praise of 'our Brethren Wesleys' interested Lady Huntingdon.[89]

The Countess's earliest acquaintance among the Methodists was probably John Wesley. In his surviving diary for the summer of 1741 he reports frequent visits to her at Enfield Chase, where he would eat a meal and expound on a text.[90] Most of the surviving early correspondence between them belongs to the years 1741 and 1742. However, from then onwards Charles Wesley becomes more important in her life. Despite her subsequent quarrels with John, she remained on good terms with Charles, and they corresponded frequently at this period and later. Most of the letters addressed to Charles are detailed accounts of her religious experiences and seldom dwell on doctrinal matters. But on occasion she was capable of sending him what was almost a personal journal:

> August the 5 We had this day much worldly Company of our politest neighbourhood to dine with us. I asked one if I should not help him to some fish. He Civily refused me and added that he should have made but a bad romanist for it was the only thing he thought of eatables he dislik'd. Another, who has been all his life bad in life and principles but has sense and at times has had meny Calls by fear, answer'd 'No I Could never have done for the Church of Roam for I Could neither eat fish or pray ten times a day' and it struck all at table that this was ment to me by his look.[91]

At that moment the second man's servant, who was waiting on him at table, fell down and was thought to be dead. However under the Countess's care he revived after an hour and 'said the stroke was instant'. She believed this 'to be a Call from God to his master and Lady'. The Countess employed Charles Wesley to dispense her charity, and offered him advice on how a clergyman should read prayers and the best way to

---

[87] Friends House Library, London and Middlesex registers. She married Joseph Cart 19 September 1717; he died in 1720 and she in 1773. I am indebted to Peter Daniels, the assistant librarian, for this information. See also F. Baker, *The Relations between the Society of Friends and Early Methodism* (London, 1948).

[88] Leics. RO, 14D32/ 4, 11, Cart to Lady H., 25 April 1746.

[89] Leics. RO, 14D32/ 14, 85, Cart to Lady H., 20 May 1746, enclosing 14D32/ 14, 86 (copy of letter from Piers to Cart, 3 May 1746); 14D32/ 14, 101, W. R. Pickering to Lady H., 31 May 1746; 14D32/ 4, 8, Cart to Lady H., September 1746. Elizabeth Cart was eventually baptized by Charles Wesley (*Charles Wesley's Journal*, op. cit., vol.2, p.13).

[90] *John Wesley's Journal*, vol.2, pp.446–84.

[91] JRL, Meth. Archives, Hunt. 87, Lady H. to C. Wesley, 16 August [1744 or 1745].

answer a letter.[92] She took an interest in the society at Bristol and the school at Kingswood, and reported on them when Charles Wesley was elsewhere.[93]

It was Charles Wesley who introduced Lady Huntingdon to one who was to be an even closer friend. On the evening of 25 August 1743 Howell Harris met Charles Wesley in London – 'On hearing I am to go to see a Lady, I was inflamed with praise to God' – and Lady Huntingdon at her house in Downing Street. It was to be the beginning of a long and somewhat tumultuous friendship. At first Harris was overawed by the nobility, not having previously encountered anyone more important than a squire in Wales. On 6 September Charles Wesley took him to breakfast with the entire family at Enfield Chase where they had 'Heavenly conversation' and the Countess gave him £5.[94] At first he appears to have been willing to accept information about Lady Huntingdon from other sources. In January 1743/4 he wrote in his diary of a son of Lady Huntingdon who continued in prayer for three days before he died.[95] Two months later he admitted being surprised to hear another rumour that the Prince of Wales had sent for Lady Huntingdon and made promises to the Methodists on behalf of the king.[96] It was certainly surprising since Frederick Prince of Wales had been at odds with his father for some years. His letters and reports of long conversations with her do not contain such rumours, but are mostly concerned with the spiritual benefits he gained from her conversation and in describing the work of the Welsh evangelists.[97] Early in 1744 Howell Harris introduced another of his important friends, James Erskine, to the Countess. James Erskine possessed an estate at Houghton Park in Bedfordshire, but was Member of Parliament for a Scottish seat. He in turn introduced the Countess to the work of M'Culloch and others in the Lowlands.[98]

---

[92] JRL, Meth. Archives, Hunt. 86 and 9, Lady H. to C. Wesley, n.d. and February 1743; Hoare's Bank Archives, ledger P, fo. 434; JRL, Meth. Archives, Hunt. 86 and 83, Lady H. to C. Wesley, n.d. and 25 October 1743.
[93] JRL, Meth. Archives, Hunt. 14, Lady H. to C. Wesley, 4 June 1743.
[94] Beynon, *Howell Harris Reformer and Soldier*, 50, 52.
[95] The Countess's sons, Ferdinando and George, were still alive when this was written.
[96] T. Beynon, *Howell Harris's Visits to London* (Aberystwyth, 1960), 41, 54.
[97] *Selected Trevecka Letters*, 135; NLW, Trev. letter 1276, Harris to Lady H., 11 January 1744/5. It should be noted that Trev. letter 790 is given too early a date by the editor – the meeting with Lady H. took place seven months later.
[98] NLW, Trev. letter 1186, Erskine to Harris, 25 May 1744. Erskine was the son of the Jacobite 'wicked Lord Grange' (T. Steel, *St. Kilda* (London, 1975), 31, 32). He was MP for Kinross and Clackmannan, 1734–41, and for Inverkeithing and other boroughs, 1741–7.

Howell Harris was frequently in London as George Whitefield's deputy at the Tabernacle. Erskine was there during the parliamentary sessions, and Lady Huntingdon now spent more time either in London or at Enfield Chase. The three were equally concerned to keep the Methodist movement united. Harris deplored 'the bitter and narrow spirit of many Eminent Christians'; Erskine the bigotry amongst 'our High flying Episcoparians, and to a Dismal Height among the greatest part of our seceding Presbiterians'; Lady Huntingdon 'the Babel of Oppinions and whence they spring'.[99] Harris soon ceased to be overawed by the Countess, and the three corresponded on equal terms.

James Erskine was resident at Houghton at least between 1743 and 1756 according to the Ampthill parish registers (information kindly provided by Miss Patricia Bell). NLW, Trev. letter 599, copy of letter from Mr Boyes to Erskine; *John Wesley's Letters*, vol.2, pp.124–9; G. F. Nuttall, *Correspondence of Philip Doddridge* (London, 1979), 208, 256, 257. James Erskine was also related to Lady Anne Agnes Erskine, Lady H's companion in later years.

[99] NLW, Trev. letter 999, Harris to Erskine, 8 October 1743; and Trev. letter 1016, Erskine to Harris, 24 October 1743; Leics. RO, 14D32/ 4, 10, Erskine to Lady H., 9 October 1744.

4

Widowhood

The death of Lady Betty also coincided with a change in the social life of the Earl and Countess. In the spring of 1740 the Earl went to London and his wife went to Ledston to make arrangements for their properties. The house at 2 Savile Row in London, which they had rented from William Kent, was given up, and it was generally assumed that Lady Betty's large donations to charities had disappointed them and obliged them to make savings. Kent wrote that it was 'with the utmost regrett that I loose so good a tenant and would rather I could have the satisfaction of calling you still so'. However it was not for reasons of economy, and they soon rented a house in Downing Street – 'a genteel street, within a few steps of the Parade, near the House of Commons, and very healthful'.[1]

The Countess's first letter to her husband from Ledston reported her melancholy feelings as she remembered Lady Betty: 'but I am perswaid'd ware you to see it you would think your exchange of Enfield and London for this would be a matter of approbation. I asure you it has of mine for I realy think a finer place, take it altogether, I never saw.'[2] With her usual energy she interviewed the servants, called in workmen to examine the state of the 'water house' and arranged for the plate and pictures to be secured. The Earl had a fever when he left Donnington, and her letters express concern that she had not received a letter from him. She told him that Thomas Barnard had brought George Hastings over from Leeds and recommended that he should spend four years at Westminster School.

---

[1] P. Willis, 'William Kent's Letters', *Architectural History*, 29 (1986), 166, 167; *HMC, Hastings 3*, p. 29; F. A. Pottle (ed.), *Boswell's London Journal* (New York, 1950), 50. It is believed to have been the present house of the Chancellor of the Exchequer (F. F. Bretherton, *The Countess of Huntingdon* (London, 1940), 11n.). Leics. RO, 14D32/14, 37, N. Harding to Lord H., 25 March 1740. An inventory of all the furniture for sale is in Hunt. Lib., HA Inv. 2, 26. Leics. RO, 143D32/14, 51, anon. to Lady H., 16 February 1739/40; Drew Univ., Hunt. A 125, Lady H. to Lord H. [Apr. 1740].

[2] Drew Univ., Hunt. A 115, Lady H. to Lord H., [Apr. 1740].

His mother thought that this would cure him of his thoughtlessness and indolence.³ The Earl was detained in London longer by the difficulty of trying to dispose of Enfield, and she wrote to assure him that she would be happy anywhere so long as he was with her.⁴ By 5 May she had taken to her bed and was let blood 'as an inflamation of my lungs seem'd to threaten me', but felt somewhat better. She had done little in the grounds, but had improved the house in many little ways: 'I have taken perticuler Care to have your rooms very warm by Door Curtains. I Can't say (tho' Certainly tender from my being so much out of order) that the house is so extreemly Cold. Carpets and a few such helps will do a great deal.'⁵ Two days later she rode out behind the steward to try a horse that was for sale. She left Ledston about the middle of the month, leaving behind instructions for various repairs.⁶ A fine day at Donnington tempted her to ride over to Ashby Place, from where she wrote to her husband to propose letting Enfield:

> I have thought if Gurney or some other that would live in the house and keep the Gardens Managing the lands for there own profit and paying a proportion of the rent, we by this means should be at a Certenty and have only the remaining part of the rent to pay, and allways have it in a Condition that you might see it for a short time without any expence.⁷

Enfield was not sold and Mr Gurney continued to manage it for them. In October he sent a detailed reply to various questions from Lady Huntingdon:

> I will take Care of Geese and turkeys according to your Ladyships order. I Cannot acquaint your Ladyship An Account of the price of swine, pork is sold here at a Groat a pound ... I will Go this afternoon to Mr Ward. He lately had some pretty Scotch or Welch Beasts, will come to about fifty shillings ... The Gardens I believe is fully stockt Except turnips.⁸

The Earl's return to Donnington was further delayed by his decision to transfer his eldest son from Westminster to Winchester College. The decision to send his brother George there led their parents to believe that he should be separated from his elder brother. The Countess approved

---

³ Drew Univ., Hunt. A 24, Lady H. to Lord H., 28 April 1740. He was sent to Westminster in June 1740 (information supplied by the Westminster School Archivist).
⁴ Drew Univ., Hunt. A 125.
⁵ Drew Univ., Hunt. A 25, Lady H. to Lord H., 5 May 1740.
⁶ Lady H.'s letters to Robert Dickinson about the Ledston renovations are in Hunt. Lib., HA2235–2238. Leics. RO, 14D32/11, 2, S. Hole to Lady H., 9 August [1741].
⁷ Drew Univ., Hunt. A 27 and A 29, Lady H. to Lord H., 12 and 19 May 1740.
⁸ Leics. RO, 14D32/14, 28, J. Gurney to Lady H., 4 October 1740.

'his resolution about Dear Frank'.[9] That the separation was needed is shown by two letters received from a Westminster schoolmaster about Master Hastings in 1741.[10] Francis got better reports from Winchester, and the headmaster reported that 'my Lord distinguisht himself very much in all their opinions.'[11] However Lord Hastings did not stay long at Winchester and had returned to Westminster by the summer of 1742, eventually to become Head Town Boy. His brother Ferdinando followed George to Westminster, where both died of smallpox in 1744.[12]

By the end of May 1740 the absence of the Earl from Donnington Park was almost unbearable to his wife: 'little Linny is standing by me and in a very whinning tone says Mamma fecht [sic] papa home for I love him dearly.'[13] The year 1740 had been difficult and busy for both the Earl and Countess. Writing to a Savile Street neighbour in September to apologize for the delay in answering his letter, Lady Huntingdon said:

> Lady Bettys affairs has brought us a good deal of Buissness as we find upon the whole the Intrest of our son is so nearly Concurned which engages us to take every step as much as possable to his advantage. This view has inclined my Lord to accept the proposals made by the Childs trustees to spend some time in yorkshire and to keep up that place for him which must run to utter ruin but by this means.[14]

In March 1740/1 Lady Frances Hastings wrote from Ashby Place to express the sympathy of Lady Anne and herself with 'the weight of worldly affairs' which Lady Huntingdon had 'upon her Mind' and to advise her not to 'Add to them the Management of the Yorkshire Estate':

> The Overpluse will rise slowly, and the Decendents of Sister Lewis's sisters to whom at present it belongs, as they are poor, will be very Clamorous. Mr Austin, as one of the Trustees said, is a very honest Man and a good Buttler, but doth he understand much of the Business of a Land Steward?[15]

They thought that the two local trustees for the estate could be trusted to supervise the steward since Leeds was 'not further from Ledstone than

---

[9] Drew Univ., Hunt. A 102 and A 31, Lady H. to Lord H., n.d. and 24 May 1740. He had left Winchester a year later (Hunt. Lib., HA 6121, Lord H. to Lord Hastings, 27 June 1741). The College Archivist tells me that there is no record of Lord Hastings' stay at Winchester. I am indebted to him for the information that Lord Hastings was probably a Gentleman Commoner. Leics. RO, 14D32/14, 41, P. Brooke to Lord H., 17 June 1740.

[10] Leics. RO, 14D32/22, 10, Bourne to Lady H., 30 May 1741.

[11] Leics. RO, 14D32/22, 6, J. Burton to Lord H., 6 May 1741.

[12] Drew Univ., Hunt. A 50, Lady H. to Frank, 5 July 1742; J. L. Chester (ed.), *The ... Registers of the Collegiate Church or Abbey of St Peter, Westminster (London, 1876)*, 363, 365.

[13] Drew Univ., Hunt. A 30, Lady H. to Lord H., 21 May 1740.

[14] JRL, Meth. Archives, Hunt. 108, Lady H. to Ferdinando Fairfax, 3 September [1740].

[15] Leics. RO, DE 23/1, 1434, Lady F. Hastings to Lady H., 13 March 1740/1.

Ashby is from Donnington'. However it was not long before it was decided to lease out the house and estate. By 1745 it was rented by a Mr Bowes.[16]

Another duty which the Countess assumed was to share in the care of Wheler nieces and nephews. Her other sister-in-law, Lady Catherine Hastings, had married Granville Wheler in 1724 as his second wife. She suffered more from ill health than Lady Huntingdon, and from time to time letters mention the necessity of not telling her any disturbing news. Although Granville Wheler had inherited the family estate of Otterden in Kent, his income was probably limited, and in 1737 he had taken orders to improve it. He was presented to the Hastings family living of Leake near Nottingham, and was immediately ordained by the archbishop of Canterbury.[17] This was hardly the procedure which would be approved by the Methodists and evangelicals, but Granville Wheler seems to have been a conscientious and good rector without being a Methodist. Six months later Lady Kitty appealed to 'My Dear Lady Huntingdon' for some financial assistance. They had overspent by several hundred pounds because of his ordination and institution.[18] Granville Wheler's wife died towards the end of 1740 leaving him with a number of young children, the eldest of whom, Theophilus, was only fifteen. His sons were sent to Westminster School, from where the Hastings boys sent frequent reports on their behaviour, and his daughters spent more and more of their time with the Countess, or at Ashby Place. Kitty Wheler became an especial favourite at Donnington Park.[19]

Disputes within the Shirley family had temporarily become less violent, probably because of the efforts of Lady Huntingdon's uncle, Laurence Shirley. The family register described 'his good nature' as 'engaging', an attribute rarely given to members of his family at this time, and his letters confirm this statement. He died on 27 April 1743, and his brother Henry two years later, when the title passed to Laurence's son and namesake. His father had been unable to settle all the lawsuits, most of which still continued. In 1740 the Countess received an unusual rebuke from her husband for interfering in a suit by sending instructions to the steward at

---

[16] *HMC, Portland 6*, p. 182.

[17] Leics. RO, 14D32/10, 9, G. Wheler to Lord H., 1 September 1737. Leake was then in the diocese of York, and Wheler was ordained both deacon and priest by letters dimissory from the archbishop of York.

[18] Leics. RO, 14D32/10, 13, C. Wheler to Lady H., 26 March 1738. The living was valued at £25. 4s. 7d. in the *Liber Valorum* (J. Ecton, *Thesaurus* (London, 1754), 551 which makes it one of the most valuable in the archdeaconry of Nottingham.

[19] Leics. RO, 14D32/6, 3, Henry Hastings to Lord H., 26 June 1740. Selina, Kitty (Catherine Maria) and Fanny Wheler do not appear in the family pedigree. Fanny probably died unmarried.

Staunton Harold, for which she apologized: 'I am extreem sorry My Dear Jewel should think we have suffered much by my haveing wrote to Coundit. I believe it was forgot that an examination was proposed for me and every article that I wrote to him I should have swore upon that examination.'[20] However, when matters concerning the executrices of her father were submitted to arbitration, her husband did nothing at all, and his brother-in-law, Lord Kilmorey, was obliged to send him a reminder that they needed a speedy decision.[21] We can also attribute to the Countess the attempts which were now made to collect debts due to her husband. These included £20 a year due from the sheriff of the counties of Cambridge and Huntingdon for 'creation money', and money due from courts held for the Rape of Hastings in Sussex.[22] Although he may have received the money from Sussex, £500 of creation money was unpaid in 1750 and was unlikely to be recovered, 'the Counties pleading poverty'. The twenty pounds for 1723 was not paid until 1763, and the remainder in succeeding years.[23] It was not until after her husband's death that the Countess was able to recover these and other debts due to his estate.

In addition to these problems the Countess's health did not improve and there was increasing concern over her husband's illnesses. The Earl was to have attended the opening of Parliament on 18 November 1741, when they both hoped to spend a few days at Enfield with their sons. The Countess would then go on to Bath with her elder daughter to take the waters once more. However the Earl must have returned to Donnington Park soon after the opening as he was sent all the parliamentary news.[24] At Bath Dr Cheyne gave the Countess medicine and told her not to drink the waters, but by Christmas Eve she was able to bathe and her health had improved.[25] She continued to send her husband all the Bath scandal, and

[20] Drew Univ., Hunt. A 28, Lady H. to Lord H., 14 May 1740. Conduit was the Shirleys' steward.
[21] Hunt. Lib., HA 9574, Lord Kilmorey to Lord H., 20 April 1741.
[22] Creation money is probably a commutation of the Earls' right in the Middle Ages to the 'third penny' of the county from which their title was taken. The 'rape' was a medieval division of the county peculiar to Sussex. The fees for the lathe or leet court were probably also commuted. Leics. RO, 14D32/26, 1, 2 and 4, W. Gardiner to Lord H., 25 April, 13 August and 19 September 1741.
[23] Cheshunt archives, E 1/2, 2, Mr I. Anson's accounts, 1777; Connexion archives, 2/1, abstract of the Earl's personal estate, 1750.
[24] Drew Univ., Hunt. A 36, Lady H. to Frank, 11 November 1741; Leics. RO, 14D32/27, 7, 8 and 9, J. Wright to Lord H., 15, 17 and 24 December 1741. John Wright was MP for Abingdon.
[25] Drew Univ., Hunt. A 100, A 105 and A 39, Lady H. to Lord H., 14 December [1741], 18 December [1741] and 24 [December] 1741.

described a meeting with her younger sister: 'Lord and Lady Killmorey have been to see me and she is just what she was forteen year ago. She is at all Corners of Bath in a moment and Lord Killmorey at all the great partys at whisk.'[26] It was not until February that Dr Cheyne finally allowed her to leave Bath.[27] Then in the summer of 1742 the Earl and Countess were in an accident when their coach overturned. She was bruised 'from head to foot', but was more concerned for her husband: 'I thought his Coller Bone was broke or indeed kill'd for upon the Coachs falling he gave so terrible a Groan that I think I would not hear him give it again for all the whole earth togiather.'[28] He suffered only a bruised shoulder. The following spring Lady Huntingdon was once more seriously ill, but on this occasion she went to Bristol with her youngest son to take the waters at the Hotwells.[29] While she was there her son Ferdinando was taken ill and died at Westminster School. The Earl took his other sons to Enfield to escape the infection as the Countess was still too unwell to leave Bristol.[30] Her two daughters had joined her at Bristol, and all three were taken ill – Henry, who was only four, with convulsions, and Elizabeth and Selina overcome with the heat.[31] They all recovered, but the sad events of the year were not over. On 20 December George Hastings died of smallpox and was buried in his brother's grave in Westminster Abbey.[32] Lord Hastings apparently caught the disease too, but recovered, and Lord and Lady Huntingdon decided to take the new and dangerous step of inoculating their other children against the disease.[33]

Letters now show that the Earl was not in the best of health; his bankers corresponded with Lady Huntingdon about her husband's accounts.[34] It was possibly for their health that they decided to have a house at Chelsea, as well as in London and Enfield Chase. It was leased from Sir Hans Sloane, and required extensive alterations which Lady Huntingdon

[26] Drew Univ., Hunt. A 37, Lady H. to Lord H., 7 December 1741. 'Whisk' was whist.
[27] Drew Univ., Hunt. A 41 and A 42, Lady H. to Lord H., 31 December [1741] and 2 February [1741/2].
[28] Drew Univ., Hunt. A 50, Lady H. to Frank, 5 July 1742.
[29] Drew Univ., Hunt. A 51 and 52, Lady H. to Lord H., 24 March 1742/3 and 8 May 1743; Leics. RO, 14D32/22, 2, John Hall to Lord H., 19 April 1743; 14D32/27, 12, John Wright to Lord H., 21 April 1743; Chester, op. cit., p. 363.
[30] Leics. RO, 14D32/24, 5, Lady H. to Lord H., 4 May 1743.
[31] Leics. RO, 14D32/24, 6, Lady H. to Lord H., 11 May 1743.
[32] Chester, op. cit., 365.
[33] One of the Wheler nephews also died. Hunt. Lib., HA 4995–4997, Lady F. Hastings to Lord H., 4, 11 and 18 January 1743/4.
[34] Cheshunt archives, E 4/8, 9, Geo. Campbell to Lady H., 21 January 1745/6.

supervised.³⁵ There was some delay in completing the work, and it was not until November 1745 that she was deciding on the garden fences and the best way to complete the drive. When the work was completed there were difficulties with Sir Hans Sloane.³⁶

All this was going on against the background of the Forty-five. The Young Pretender landed in Scotland on 25 July 1745 and marched south. From August onwards reports of his advance reached Donnington.³⁷ The rebels reached Derby on 4 December and were only ten miles from Donnington Park when they decided to return to Scotland. Neither the Earl nor the Countess was ever suspected of Jacobite sentiments, but it must have been a difficult time. In 1746 came the trials of the leading Jacobite lords, to which the Earl received a peremptory summons. Eardley Wilmot, a lawyer and an old family friend, supplied Lady Huntingdon with the text of an affidavit to be signed by a physician and a surgeon, or physician and apothecary, and sworn before a justice, that the Earl was too ill to travel to London. Lord Huntingdon himself wrote to the Duke of Newcastle to excuse his absence.³⁸ Writing from Lichfield on 13 June to thank the Countess for her entertainment at Donnington Park Magdalen Walmesley, a Methodist, added: 'whenever Mr Walmesley Speaks of his Dear old Friend my Lord Huntingdon, it is with pain and concern, and a great Distrust that he cannot hold out long. He wou'd come to Donnington Park on his hands and Knees, cou'd he prevale with My Lord to set in, in earnest for the Recovery of his Health – But That he almost dispairs of.'³⁹ These sentiments were echoed in a letter from Eardley Wilmot to Lady Huntingdon: 'It gives me a real concern that A person of Lord Huntingdons good sense, from pursuing a way of Living destructive of His Health together with want of faith in, or, rather,

---

³⁵ Leics. RO, 14D32/14, 74, Roger Morris to Lord H., 22 September 1744. The house was said to be near the Cremorne Arms tavern (*Wesley Hist. Soc. Proc.*, 13 (1922), 49).

³⁶ Drew Univ., Hunt. A 54, Lady H. to Lord H., 8 December 1744; Leics. RO, 14D32/25, 2 and 4, Philip Miller to Lady H., 21 November 1745 and 19 June 1746; 14D32/6, 18, H. Hastings to Lady H., 6 May 1746; 14D32/6, 19 and 25, H. Hastings to Lady H., 7 June and 26 July 1746; 14D32/25, 4, P. Miller to Lady H., 19 June 1746.

³⁷ Drew Univ., Hunt. A 55, Lady H. to Lord H., 19 August 1745; Leics. RO, 14D32/8, 2, Lady [Frances] to Lord and Lady H., [Nov. 1745]; 14D32/14, 93, Robert Gra[ ] to Mr Hastings, 28 November 1745.

³⁸ Leics. RO, 14D32/14, 80, Wilmot to Lady H., 17 July 1746. The certificate was delivered to the Lord Chancellor by Lord Chesterfield (Leics. RO, 14D32/14, 102, John Stamford to anon., 24 July 1746). *HMC, Hastings 3*, p. 57; BL, Add, MS 35588, fo. 266, Lord H. to Newcastle, 23 July 1746. For the summons of the peers see N. Sykes, *Church and State in England* (Cambridge, 1934), 49.

³⁹ Leics. RO, 14D32/14, 69, M. Walmesley to Lady H., 13 June 1746.

appetite to Remedies, shou'd still continue in the same Dropsical Disorder.'[40] In August Lady Huntingdon left him at Donnington Park to attend to urgent business in London. Tenants for the London houses had to be found and the final arrangements for landscaping at Chelsea made.[41] About the middle of the month she returned to Donnington, and almost immediately her husband went to London for medical advice.[42] All the business of the estates was now in her hands and she had accounts to check and tenants to meet. On 4 October she wrote her last love-letter to him:

> I shall long to have some account how my Dear Jewel is after his Journey, for I think should not your Legg be worse by it I am sure otherwise your health will be better for it. I hope you will my Dear Creature if you should find yourself the least ill will allow it not to be Conceal'd from me, for nothing Could in this world make me so throughly unhappy, the Consequence of keeping your good resolutions must have so Comfortable a prospect not only to you but to all who Love you so tenderly as I Can feel we all do, and I am asur'd Could my Dear Creature see the agonies of mind that at times I suffer on account both of your mortal and imortal part ... it would give you most sensible pain.[43]

He died on the morning of 13 October 'of a fit of apoplexy'.[44] Thirty years later the Countess told Augustus Toplady

> The late lord Huntingdon (who was remarkable for having hardly ever dreamt in his life) dreamed one night, that death, in the appearance of a skeleton, stood at the bed's foot; and, after standing a while, untucked the bed-cloaths, at the bottom, and crept up to the top of the bed (under the cloaths) and lay between him and his lady. His lordship told his dream, in the morning, to the countess; who affected to make light of it: but the earl died, in about a fortnight after.[45]

Since he made no will the Countess was obliged to take out letters of administration for his property.[46] On 23 October he was buried with his ancestors 'in the Vault under the Chancel' of the parish church of Ashby

---

[40] Leics. RO, 14D32/14, 80.
[41] Lord Granard's MSS, Lord H. to Lady H., 9 August, 1746; Leics. RO, 14D32/26, 3, W. Gardiner to Lady H., 26 July 1746; 14D32/25, 6, P. Miller to Lady H., 13 September 1746.
[42] Drew Univ., Hunt. A 57, Lady H. to Lord H., 12 August 174[6]; Leics. RO, 14D32/6, 27, H. Hastings to Lady H., 16 August 1746; Drew Univ., Hunt. A 59 and 60, Lady H. to Lord H., 6 and 8 September 1746.
[43] Drew Univ., Hunt. A 58, Lady H. to Lord H., 4 October 1746.
[44] *Stemmata Shirleiana* (1841), 151; *Gentleman's Magazine*, 16 (1746), 667.
[45] *The Works of Augustus Toplady*, 4, (London, 1794), 185. 'Told me, by the countess at Rumford, Essex, April 12, 1776.'
[46] The original letters of administration from the Prerogative Court of Canterbury (4 November 1746) are in the Connexion archives (11/1).

de la Zouch.[47] The vicar wrote in the burial register: 'This Nobleman had such Advantages of Person and fine Breeding as gave a peculiar Grace to all His Actions. In His Lordship were eminently united The good Christian, The Man of Honour, The Peer and the private Gentleman.' Over his grave the Countess erected a monument with a long inscription composed by Lord Bolingbroke, which echoed that in his obituary in the *Gentleman's Magazine*: 'Never was there a better father, or kinder brother, a more tender husband, or a more indulgent master.'[48] The Countess was left with four children, all minors, to care for, and a large estate to administer.

The death of her husband marks another turning-point in the life of the Countess. It cannot be doubted from the evidence of her letters to him that she was deeply in love. His death must have been a great emotional shock. There is no direct evidence because she never expressed her grief in writing. Indirectly we learn a little of what she must have felt from two sources. Howell Harris recording a private meeting with her in April 1747 says: 'She consulted me about which was best, to live retired and give up all, or fill her place, and I said the latter I thought was right...' A year later in a letter to the Countess of Hertford she spoke of her withdrawal from the world in 'a little retreat' close to her husband's tomb.[49] She did not become a recluse; but during her widowhood all her earthly reponsibilities were to disappear and she was able to devote all her time and abundant energy to religious matters. In 1748 she had two sons and two daughters to care for. Her eldest daughter, Elizabeth, married Lord Rawdon in 1752 and went to live in Ireland. Her youngest son, Henry, died in 1758 and her youngest daughter, Selina, in 1763. Her eldest son, the tenth Earl, went abroad on a prolonged Grand Tour after leaving Oxford. For some years after he reached his majority she continued to be responsible for his estates, but by 1763 she was free to do whatever she wished.

Her religious search did not begin in 1739 with her conversion to Methodism. Most Methodist conversions were not as sudden as is often supposed, and the Countess was no exception. Her interest in religious matters can be traced as far back as her visits to Bath and her friendship

---

[47] The accounts for his funeral can be found in Connexion archives 1. Leics. RO, Ashby par. reg., DE 1013/2.

[48] *Gentleman's Magazine*, 16 (1746), 667. *HMC, Hastings 3*, p. 65.

[49] T. Beynon, *Howell Harris's Visits to London* (Aberystwyth, 1960), 137; *HMC, Astley MSS* (London, 1900), 209, 210. It is most unfortunate that the originals of these two letters of the Countess to Lady Hertford have disappeared. This makes it impossible to check what is clearly a very poor transcript. Both letters are given the impossible date of 1718. The most probable on both biographical and palaeographical grounds is 1748. Connexion archives 1 – accounts for administration of Earl's estates.

1. Lord and Lady Huntingdon with their children, Selina and Henry. Painted by Soldi, c. 1744 (Cheshunt College Foundation).

2. Donnington House before it was rebuilt, from Nichols' *History and Antiquities of Leicestershire*, 1804 (Leicestershire Museums, Art Galleries and Records Service).

3. Monument to Theophilus, Earl of Huntingdon, in Ashby de la Zouch parish church, by Kent, Rysbrack and Pickford (photograph by Hugh Richmond).

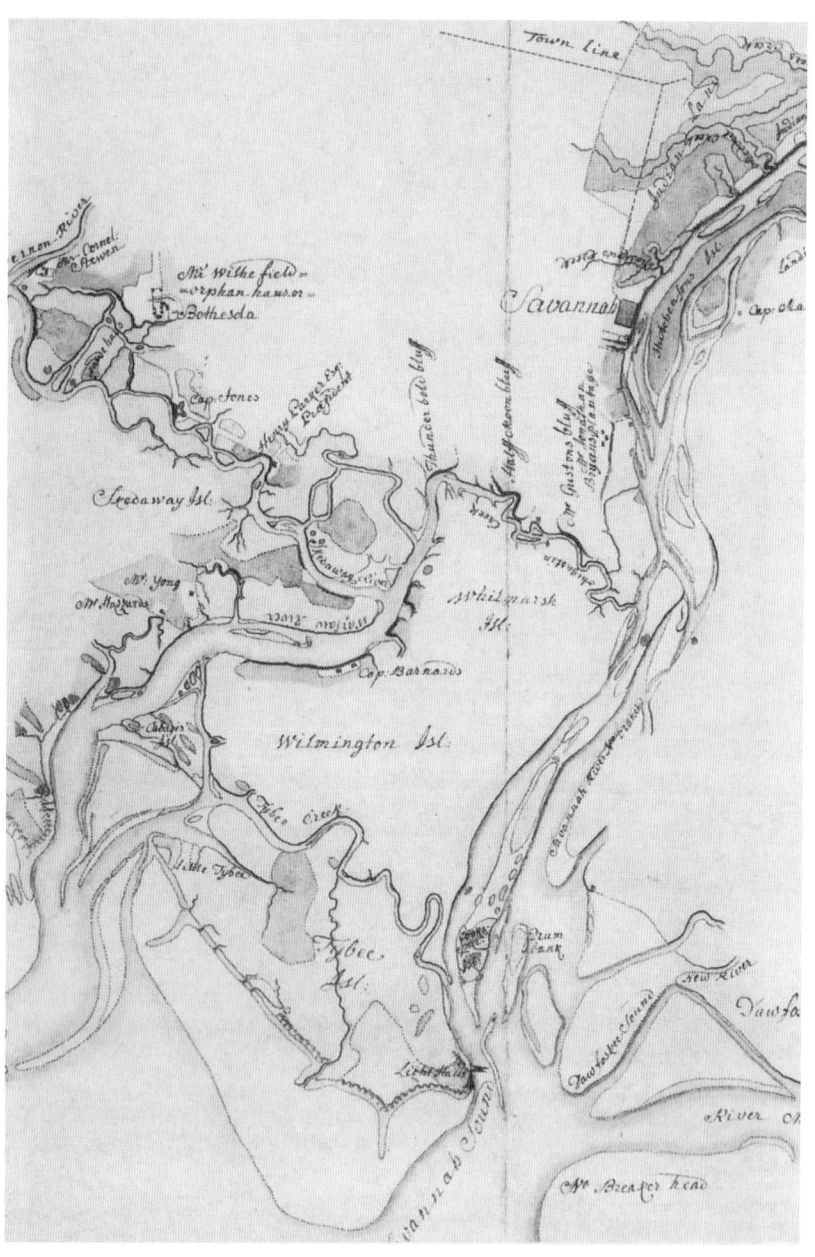

4. Map of Southern Georgia showing Bethesda, *c.* 1752 (Library of Congress, taken from De Brahm's map).

5. Portrait of Lady Huntingdon by J. Russell, which she sent to Bethesda (Georgia Historical Society, Savannah).

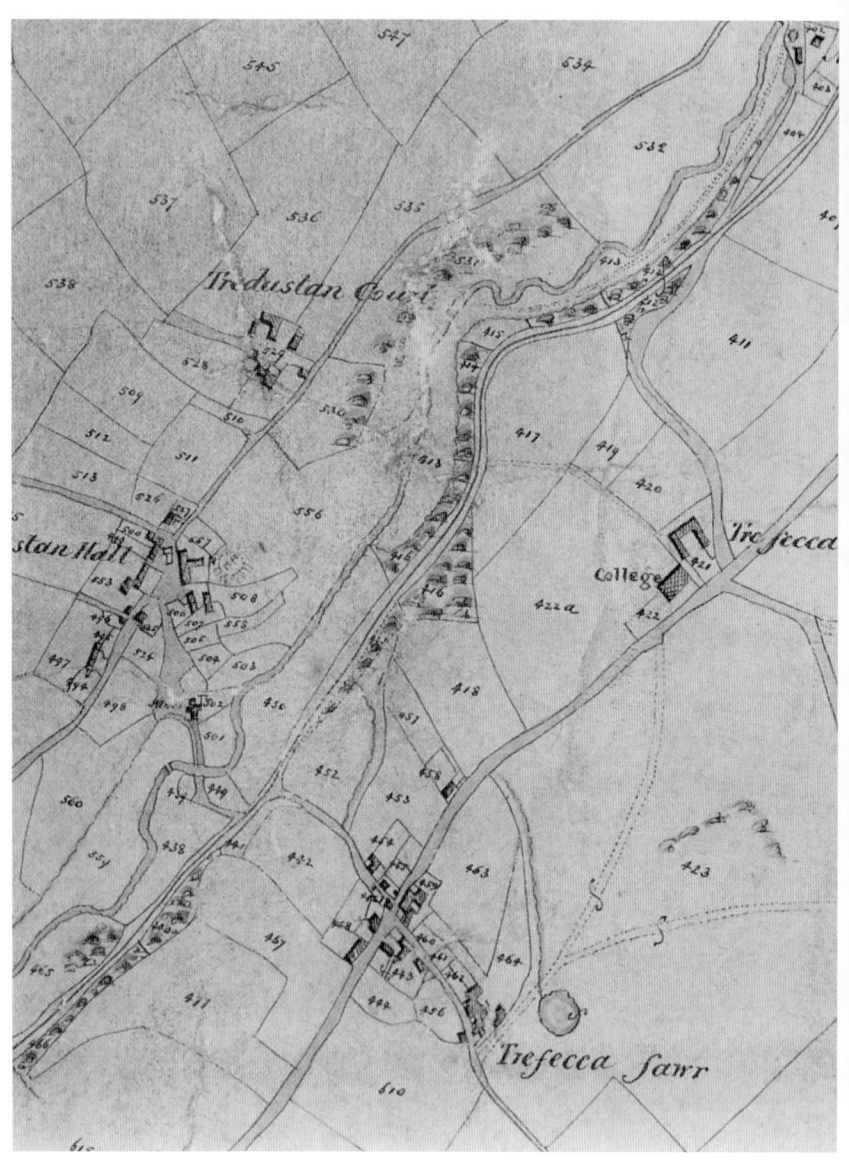

6. Map of Trefeca taken from the Talgarth tithe map, 1842 (National Library of Wales).

7. Trefeca College, 1768 (*Evangelical Register*, vol. 1).

8. Spa Fields Chapel and House (Guildhall Library, Corporation of London).

with Dr George Cheyne. He was not just a good physician. Religion was closely bound up with his medical advice, and their conversations at Bath must have touched on both topics. Cheyne was greatly influenced both by the German mystics and the French Quietists.[50] In the eighteenth century the French Quietists were best known by the works of Fénelon, archbishop of Cambrai (1651–1715), whose novel *Télémaque* was particularly popular. Lady Betty possessed a translation of his *Education of a Daughter*, which she bequeathed to her nephew George Hastings. Both she and her sister-in-law would have approved of his belief in the importance of female education. Lady Huntingdon owned a translation of the more popular *Dissertation on Pure Love* which included a life of another noted Quietist, Mme Guyon (1648–1717).[51] Mme Guyon's works were not so popular in England, and translations were not so readily available in the eighteenth century, but the Countess owned a volume containing manuscript translations of some of her works together with an extract from St John of the Cross.[52] She also owned a manuscript translation of the introduction to the Mons New Testament which was published in French by the Jansenists, but not translated into English until the year of her death.[53] The Jansenists and Quietists were popular with the English evangelicals not only because they suffered persecution by the Roman Catholic Church, but also because the sentiments which they expressed were similar to their own. The emphasis of the Quietists was on Justification and Sanctification: 'Justification inquires, How shall the sin, which is past, be forgiven? Sanctification inquires, How shall we be kept from sin at the present time and in time to come?'[54] Their answer was through faith, rather than by reason or good works.

Her knowledge of the German mystic Jacob Boehme was obtained through the works of William Law. Law had become one of the second generation of non-jurors who had been willing to serve the Stuart Queen

[50] For Cheyne's religious beliefs and writings see G. S. Rousseau, 'Mysticism and Millenarianism', in R. H. Popkin (ed.), *Millenarianism and Messianism in English Literature and Thought* (Leiden, 1988). In 1742 he received a gift of Boehme's works from Samuel Richardson, the author and publisher (C. F. Mullett (ed.), *The Letters of Dr George Cheyne to Samuel Richardson* (Columbia, MO, 1943), 107).

[51] Hunt. Lib., HA Inv., box 2, 27 and 28. Lady Huntingdon's copy is in the Cheshunt College collection.

[52] Cheshunt archives, B 5/4. William Cowper translated some of Mme Guyon's poems, but they were not published until the end of the century.

[53] Cheshunt archives, B 5/7. It should be noted that some of her books were sold when the College left Trefeca for Cheshunt in 1792. These probably included this work, which was restored to Cheshunt later, and Hunt. Lib., HM 30302, a manuscript commonplace book.

[54] T. C. Upham, *Life, Religious Opinions and Experience of Madame Guyon* (London, 1905), 128.

Anne, but were unable to accept the Hanoverian succession. In 1727 he published a denunciation of all 'Stage Entertainments', and in 1729 his best-known work, *A Serious Call to a Devout and Holy Life*. This work, together with an earlier one on *Christian Perfection*, had a great influence on the early Methodists. John Wesley included the *Serious Call* in the list of books to be read by the Kingswood scholars, and Charles Wesley said that he owed all he knew of the Christian religion to Law.[55] George Cheyne had introduced Law to the thought of Boehme, and later supplied him with his works.[56] The Methodists disapproved of Law's mysticism, but the Countess continued her friendship.[57] In 1739 he wrote to her from his home in King's Cliffe suggesting that she should 'draw up an Historical Account of [Lady Betty Hastings's] spirit, life and virtues'.[58] Only three of Law's later letters to the Countess have survived and none of her replies. All three letters were written in the last years of his life.[59] The first is a reply to a request for advice on behalf of a clergyman who had adopted Methodist views and thought he was obliged to resign his benefice. Law begins by comparing the adverse effects of taking too much advice on medical matters with that of taking too much advice on spiritual affairs, and concludes that 'The great Danger that new Converts are liable to, especially if they are young, arises from their conceiving something great of their Conversions, and that great Things are to follow from it.'[60] This sensible advice was probably in line with her own advice and was what she expected Law to say. His second letter gives his reasons for not replying to the attacks made on him by John Wesley.[61] His final letter also gives his reasons for not replying to an attack by 'a pious and very excellent Clergyman'.

Before the date of these letters Lady Huntingdon had included Law's works in her programme of tracts to be circulated. The earliest reference

[55] A. K. Walker, *William Law: His Life and Thought* (London, 1973), 69.
[56] Rousseau, op. cit., 99.
[57] J. B. Green, *John Wesley and William Law* (London, 1945), chapter 3; G. Whitefield, *Law Gospelized; or, An Address to all Christians* (London, 1748).
[58] J. H. Overton, *William Law, Nonjuror and Mystic* (London, 1881), 343.
[59] They were printed in W. Law, *A Collection of Letters on the most Interesting and Important Subjects, and on Several Occasions* (London, 1760), 122–32. Although it is only stated that they were written to 'a Person of Quality' it has been generally known since their publication that they were addressed to Lady Huntingdon. I have rejected the letter written by Hester Gibbon to the Countess on the grounds first stated by Canon Overton (*William Law*, 367, 368). Lord and Lady H. wrote to Law in July 1742 (*HMC, Hastings* 3, p. 35).
[60] Overton, *William Law*, 124.
[61] Ibid., 127–30. Although this letter is dated 16 February 1756, and Wesley's attack was published on 6 January 1756, the contents of Law's letter do not coincide with those of Wesley's book.

to these publications of which any evidence survives was in 1746, when Mrs Pickering of Warrington wrote to her about the cost of printing one: 'The Printer was with me ... and he said if I wou'd take a Thousand he must have 6d. a Dozen, but if 2000 he wou'd print them for 4d. a Dozen, stich them in Blew paper and print them on good writing paper.'[62] She added that it would be about 'the size of your other Books of Mr Westley' which implies that she was then reprinting John Wesley's works for free distribution. Mrs Pickering was willing to take 500 copies of Law's work and thought that a friend would take the same. In 1749 the Countess reprinted the first part of William Law's *The Spirit of Prayer*, soon after it first appeared.[63] It is probable that this is the anonymous and undated *The Spirit of Prayer* printed by R. Hawes of Spitalfields, since the title-page has a note that 'This Tract is not to be Sold, but given away.'[64] In 1754 a copy of *A Serious Call* was published with the same note on the title-page, which suggests it was another of the Countess's tracts. Later she printed a work of Miguel de Molinos, the Spanish Quietist.[65]

John Byrom was another follower of Boehme who knew Lady Huntingdon as early as 1735 and who introduced himself to Dr Cheyne with a reference to the good character which she had given him.[66] As early as October 1744 Byrom had been invited to stay at Donnington Park by the Countess, where he found two of her Methodist friends, Mrs Bartlet and Catherine Edwin: 'We are very freely and courteously entertained, and you may guess at our conversation; Mrs Edwin is a fine singer, has just been singing some hymns to us.'[67] Another friend of the Countess was the Revd Thomas Hartley, rector of Winwick in Northamptonshire from 1744. In his *Sermons on Various Subjects* (1754), which he dedicated to the Countess, he included 'A Prefatory Discourse on Mistakes concerning Religion, Enthusiasm, Experiences, etc.', in which he defended the mys-

[62] Leics. RO, 14D32/2, 12, 3, C. Pickering to Lady H., 7 July 1746; Drew Univ., Meth. Archives, Hunt. B 16 and B 84, Grinfield to Lady H., *c.* 1755. In 1789 Lady Huntingdon reprinted a puritan work, *Some Sermons by Rev. William Bridge* (London, 1789).
[63] For this work see *The Works of The Rev. William Law*, 7 (Canterbury, 1893), 3–48. John Byrom refers to this publication; see R. Parkinson (ed.), *The Private Journal and Literary Remains of John Byrom* (Chetham Soc., 1855–7), vol.2, p.492. In 1756 Lady H. reported a conversion brought about by reading Law's book (JRL, Meth. Archives, Hunt. 62, Lady H. to C. Wesley, 27 July 1756).
[64] There is a copy of this pamphlet in the library of the Garrett Evangelical Theological Seminary, Evanston, IL.
[65] A. W. Hopkinson, *About William Law* (London, 1948), 123 refers to this edition, but I have been unable to see a copy.
[66] Parkinson, op. cit., vol.1, pp.592, 610; vol.2, p.308.
[67] Parkinson, op. cit., vol.2, p.383.

tics.[68] He had already been a guest at Ashby Place, from where he wrote to George Whitefield in 1750.[69]

With these and other evangelical clergymen and lay people the Countess now carried on what must have been a voluminous correspondence. Only a small proportion of this has survived, perhaps the most complete being the letters which she wrote to Charles Wesley.[70] Much of this correspondence is devoted to what may be described as religious sentiments. At this period Lady Huntingdon had the ability on occasion to compose several pages of self-abasement and exhortations to others to persevere without giving any clear indication of her own beliefs on such questions as those which divided the Methodists.[71] Some of her earlier letters deal with local affairs – the progress of Edward Ellis, rector of the family living of Markfield, who she found had become a Methodist.[72] She refers to the difficulties of the Methodist society at Nottingham which had endured considerable persecution. Although sympathetic, she told a man 'who Came from Nottingham in the name of threescore' people to ask that the magistrates should be obliged to allow them to meet every night, that they should be content with the liberty which they had.[73] She also commented on the lukewarmness of the Methodists in Derby. When Charles Wesley spent part of the summer in Cornwall she expressed concern for 'the poor Tinners' and sent a gift to the society at St Ives.[74] Two of her letters written in the summer of 1742 are attempts to provide a journal similar to that of the other early Methodists, but she did not continue it for more than two or three months.[75] To both Charles and John Wesley she sent long accounts of the death of Miss Fanny Cowper at

---

[68] Published in London, 1754. Lady H.'s copy is in the Cheshunt College collection.

[69] *Christian Correspondence* (a catalogue of MSS sold by Clifton Books in 1984), 6. For Hartley's defence of Law see Overton, op. cit., 240. Hartley later became a Swedenborgian.

[70] These are now in the Methodist archives at JRL, but the folder includes letters to John Wesley as well as a number of Lady H.'s letters to others purchased or given to the archives more recently. The letters to other persons are at the back of the folder and most of the correspondents can be easily identified. The letters to John Wesley present a more difficult problem.

[71] For example JRL, Meth. Archives, Hunt. 90 (n.d.) is a long letter with only a few sentences of practical importance (about a curacy for Charles Greaves).

[72] JRL, Meth. Archives, Hunt. 92, Lady H. to [C. Wesley], n.d. For Ellis see also Hunt. 18 ([7 September] 1744) and Hunt. 96 (n.d.).

[73] JRL, Meth. Archives, Hunt. 18, Lady H. to C. Wesley. For early Nottingham Methodism see R. C. Swift, *Lively People* (Nottingham, 1982), chapter 1.

[74] JRL, Meth. Archives, Hunt. 16, Lady H. to C. Wesley, [July] 1743.

[75] JRL, Meth. Archives, Hunt. 88 (19 July 1742) and Hunt. 87 (16 August [1742]).

Donnington Park in 1742. Miss Cowper was one of the daughters of William Cowper of Enfield Chase. She joined Lady Huntingdon at Bath when they were both taking the waters in the winter of 1741/2. Against her father's wishes she was carried off to Donnington Park when the Countess left Bath, and died there on 27 May.[76] One of the Countess's letters to Charles Wesley concerns the return of a horse which she had lent him.[77] Good advice appears more often in her letters to his brother. She suggested that he should omit the celebrated passage in his journal for 5 June 1739 about his encounter at Bath with 'Beau' Nash and the following entry about the ladies who followed Wesley.[78] She also tried to persuade him not to print Charles's elegy on a Mr Jones because it emphasized his gentility rather than his Christianity.[79]

In 1747 or 1748 Lady Huntingdon finally decided that the Calvinistic doctrine of salvation was correct. Apart from the one letter on her encounter with George Whitefield in February 1742/3 there is little evidence that she had previously taken a strong line on the subject. Like Howell Harris, she always preferred to emphasize the agreements rather than the disagreements of Methodism. Her friendship with the Wesleys did not end at this time. Charles continued to be a dear friend, but John became more suspicious of her behaviour. In September 1748 he confided to his diary. 'Being not able with tolerable decency to excuse myself any longer, I went to Chelsea and spent two or three hours as in the times that are past. I hoped one journey would serve. But I was too hasty in reckoning. L[ady] H[untingdon] pressed me to come again on Friday, so that I could not handsomely decline it.'[80] On Friday he writes, 'I took up my cross once more and came to Chelsea a little after eleven.' She now began a lengthy correspondence with Whitefield and appointed him one of her chaplains – an honour which neither Charles nor John Wesley had been given. He was invited to stay at Ashby Place and to preach at her house in Chelsea. On 30 August 1748, after his return from North America, he preached twice, and both Lord Chesterfield and Lord Bath

---

[76] Her deathbed is described in JRL, Meth. Archives, 85 and 101 (to C. Wesley, c. 25 and 18 May 1742) and Hunt. 95 (to J. Wesley, c. 30 May 1742). Her father's letters to Lady H. are Leics. RO, 14D32/14, 110 and 113 (4 January 1741/2 and 15 July [1742]). She was buried at Ashby on 30 May 1742 (Leics. RO, DE 1013/2). Charles Wesley composed an 'epitaph' for her (Cheshunt archives, B 5/6, 44).

[77] JRL, Meth. Archives, Hunt. 9 and 83 (February 1743/4 and 25 October 1743).

[78] JRL, Meth. Archives, Hunt. 105, Lady H. to J. Wesley, 29 April 1742.

[79] JRL, Meth. Archives, Hunt. 111, Lady H. to [J.] Wesley, 4 August 1742.

[80] *John Wesley's Journal*, vol. 8, pp. 157, 158.

spoke kindly to him afterwards.[81] This circle included Chesterfield's sister-in-law, the Countess Delitz; his sister, Lady Gertrude Hotham; the Countess's aunt, Lady Fanny Shirley; Lady Archibald Hamilton; Bath's father-in-law, Col. John Gumley; and Lord Bolingbroke. Most of them were decidedly in need of Whitefield's admonitions. Chesterfield and Bolingbroke were thought to be infidels: Lady Fanny Shirley was Chesterfield's mistress, and Lady Archibald Hamilton the mistress of the Prince of Wales. Howell Harris was present on many of these occasions and excitedly recorded the information about the Prince's support and encouragement of the Methodists provided by Mrs Edwin.[82] From her conversations Howell Harris had a vision of Whitefield being made a bishop when the Prince succeeded to the throne, and of the Methodists being freed from persecution. It was not to be. Only Lady Fanny Shirley became a permanent convert to Methodism.[83] Lady Gertrude Hotham was already a Methodist, and so was her son, Sir Charles.

Because she shared their Calvinism, Lady Huntingdon was now able to add to her old friends an increasing number of evangelical dissenting ministers.[84] Isaac Watts she met only once, but Philip Doddridge visited her at Ashby Place and they often corresponded.[85] Doddridge had both preached at the Tabernacle and allowed Whitefield to occupy his own pulpit in Northampton, which had caused great concern among the more traditional dissenters.[86] In 1744 Doddridge sent Lady Huntingdon a copy of the sermon which he had preached to encourage the establishment of a county infirmary in Northampton. He hoped no doubt for a donation, but received instead an assurance that she could find nothing wrong in it and a

[81] J. Gillies (ed.), *A Select Collection of Whitefield's Letters*, 2 (London, 1772), 170, 350. The original appointment of Whitefield as her chaplain on 1 September 1748 is now JRL, Rylands charter 772. For a detailed account of some aspects of the Countess's life at this period, see G. F. Nuttall, 'Howel Harris and "the Grand Table": A Note on Religion and Politics 1744–50', *Journal of Eccles. Hist.*, 39 (1988), 531–44.

[82] The eighteenth-century usage of 'Mrs' for a more mature spinster has caused some confusion over the two 'Mrs Edwins'. The Methodist (and later Moravian) was Catherine Edwin who never married. Since the wife of John Edwin MP makes no appearance amongst the Methodists later, it is probable that only Catherine is referred to in Harris's diaries.

[83] The letters of the Revd James Hervey, the evangelical rector of Weston Favell, to her were printed in *Letters from the late Revd James Hervey ... to Lady Frances Shirley* (London, 1782). For his friendship with Lord and Lady H. see *HMC, Hastings 3*, p. 43.

[84] For the Methodists' attitude to dissenters, see J. M. Potts (ed.), *Letters of Francis Asbury* (London, 1958), vol. 3, p. 31.

[85] T. Milner (ed.), *The Life, Times and Correspondence of The Revd Isaac Watts* (London, 1834), 692. For their meeting see A. P. Davis, *Isaac Watts* (London, 1948), 31. For her letters to Doddridge, see G. F. Nuttall (ed.), *The Correspondence of Philip Doddridge 1702–1751* (London, 1979).

[86] M. Deacon, *Philip Doddridge of Northampton* (Northampton, 1980), 88.

request for a hundred copies which she would distribute.[87] In June 1746 he received a request not usually made to a dissenting minister. George Baddelley had succeeded Ellis as rector of Markfield and she wanted to find 'a gospel' curate for him. This would enable Baddelley to preach in other churches in Leicestershire as well as well as 'a little meeting' at Ashby Place.[88] By 1747 she was telling of the persecution endured by her little meeting, offering to support a student at Doddridge's Academy, and presenting Archbishop Leighton's *Select Works* to the Academy's library.[89] On 25 July 1748, while on a visit to London, Doddridge was invited to preach at Chelsea to the Countess, Mrs Edwin and Col. Gumley. He was not so optimistic as Howell Harris about the Prince of Wales's conversion, telling his wife that 'Mrs Edwin is building her self a House at Cookham where I hope she will preach her Neighbour the Prince of Wales into Religion' and adding that the two ladies would make good bishops.[90] In March 1750 he planned to visit Lady Huntingdon at Ashby Place, but this may have been postponed because the previous day the young Earl's coming-of-age was celebrated, and she warned him that 'all this part of the world will be quite in an uproar.'[91] She joined with Doddridge's friends in a subscription to send him to Lisbon in the hope of curing his consumption. He stayed with Lady Huntingdon at Bath in September 1751 on his way. A quarter of a century later the Countess remembered their last meeting:

> In the morning of the day that he set out for Falmouth (from which place he was to embark for Lisbon), lady Huntingdon came into his room and found him weeping over that passage in the prophet Daniel (chap. x. 11, 12), O Daniel, a man greatly beloved, etc. 'You are in tears sir,' said lady H. 'I am weeping, madam,' answered the good doctor, 'but they are tears of comfort and joy. I can give up my country, my relations, and friends, into the hand of God. And, as for myself, I can as well go to heaven from Lisbon, as from my own study at Northampton.'[92]

There were other correspondents and other visitors during this period of whom we know less. Thomas Gibbons of London, another dissenting

---

[87] J. D. Humphreys (ed.), *The Correspondence and Diary of Philip Doddridge*, 4 (London, 1830), 330, 331.

[88] Ibid., 501; Nuttall, *Doddridge*, 235.

[89] Humphreys, *Doddridge*, vol. 4, pp. 528, 535; Nuttall, *Doddridge*, 244, 249; G. F. Nuttall, *New College London and its Library* (London, 1977), 38.

[90] Nuttall, *Doddridge*, 281. John Byrom accompanied Doddridge to Chelsea a few weeks later (Parkinson, op. cit., vol. 2, p. 457).

[91] DWL, MS 28. 180, 9, Lady H. to Doddridge, 10 March 1749/50 (Nuttall, *Doddridge*, 324).

[92] Deacon, op. cit., 137; Toplady, op. cit., 149, 150. 'Told me, by lady Huntingdon, at Clifton, this day, August 19, 1775.'

minister and a friend of Doddridge, made a tour of the Midlands in the summer of 1750. He slept at Leicester and went on to Ashby to stay the night with Lady Huntingdon. His friendship with the Countess continued until 1778 or later.[93] Less well documented is her friendship with Col. James Gardiner and his wife, Lady Frances. Gardiner was killed at Prestonpans in 1745, and his life was commemorated by Doddridge in *The Christian Warrior Animated and Crowned* and in a biography. This was the period when Lady Huntingdon had the widest circle of acquaintances amongst the evangelicals.

---

[93] DWL, Cong. Lib., MS II a 3, p.10, Thomas Gibbons's diary.

5

Family and Friends

On Tuesday, 13 March 1749/50 there was a celebration at Donnington Park when the ninth Earl came of age.[1] No record of what occurred has survived, but on the evidence of the feasts given to his tenants during his minority, it was probably a very large assembly both of tenants and neighbouring landowners and friends. However the principal character in the celebration, the young Lord Huntingdon, was absent. He had left Westminster School and matriculated at Christ Church in 1747, but by June 1749 he was already in France beginning the Grand Tour, and he was still at Caen two weeks after the celebration.[2] In going to Westminster (and then to Christ Church) the young Earl had followed the common pattern for the nobility at this time.[3] He also found his Whig views at Westminster. In his first year at Oxford Dr Akenside dedicated an ode to him, in which he was advised

> To watch the State's uncertain Frame,
> And baffle Faction's partial Aim:
> But chiefly, with determined Zeal,
> To quell that servile Band, who kneel
> To Freedom's banish'd Foes.[4]

Lord Chesterfield had known and befriended him while he was still at Westminster School.[5] Now, when the young Earl began his travels, Chesterfield began a series of letters of advice about his behaviour, recommended him to learn French, Italian and dancing, and gave him

[1] DWL, MS 24. 180, Lady H. to Doddridge, 10 March 1749/50.
[2] Hunt. Lib., HA 13716 and 13718, Lord Chesterfield to Lord H., 26 June 1749 and 26 March 1750. These letters from Lord Chesterfield were printed in A. F. Stewart (ed.), *The Letters of Lord Chesterfield to Lord Huntingdon* (London, 1923).
[3] J. Cannon, *Aristocratic Century* (Cambridge, 1984), 40, 48.
[4] Mark Akenside, *An Ode to the Right Honourable The Earl of Huntingdon* (London, 1748), 18. Lord Chesterfield wrote of the Earl's Whig convictions later (Hunt. Lib., HA 13718).
[5] Drew Univ., Hunt. A 56, Lady H. to Lord H., 9 August 1746, quoted in *HMC, Hastings* 3, p. 61.

letters of introduction for each city he visited.[6] Chesterfield was anxious for his return because he had plans for the Earl to be one of the young Prince of Wales's Household when it was formed.[7] Lord Huntingdon lingered in Paris because of his liaison with Mlle Lang.[8]

Lord Huntingdon reached Madrid late in 1752, and Italy two years later.[9] Early in 1755 he finally decided to return home, and his mother was asked to prepare everything for his return. As her son-in-law wrote in April,

> I hear your Ladyship is Going soon to Leicestershire to put Donnington in order. I heartily hope you will have Good weather, as you will find a sensible difference between Clifton and Leicestershire air, tho' I believe the Park is the best air in that county. I shall long to see your Ladyships alterations as I am certain you will improve it Greatly.[10]

But by then work on the House and Park was proceeding well despite the heavy rains.[11] Lady Huntingdon was very concerned about the costs and tried to recover some of the 'hopeless arrears' from tenants. During his travels Lord Huntingdon had assembled a collection of paintings and sculpture and wished to have a new room added in which the latter could be displayed. In May he wrote to his mother from Florence,

> Hemington sends me word that the works out of doors at Donnington go on prosperously; but that many fears and difficulties arise about the house. I wrote to him about three weeks ago to beg he would send me a little drawing of the house, and park about it, that I might conferr with some people here, about placing my new room, as the proportions must be determined by the busts and statues.[12]

Although he said he preferred Donnington to Italy he went to Vienna, Dresden and Berlin at Lord Chesterfield's suggestion.[13] By July 1755 his

---

[6] Hunt. Lib., HA 13722 and 13723, Chesterfield to Lord H., 24 and 29 September 1750.

[7] Hunt. Lib., HA 13728 and 13729, Chesterfield to Lord H., 8 April and 18 May 1751.

[8] Hunt. Lib., HA 13731, Chesterfield to Lord H., 25 November 1751. Sir Charles Abney Hastings, who inherited some of the Hastings estates, was an illegitimate son from a different liaison.

[9] Hunt. Lib., HA 137736 and 13744, Chesterfield to Lord H., 21 November 1752, and 13745.

[10] Hunt. Lib., personal papers, box 34, 2, Lord Rawdon to Lady H., 26 April 1755.

[11] Drew Univ., Hunt. A 73, Lady H. to Lord H., [20] January [1755]. Part of this letter is printed in *HMC Hastings 3*, pp. 134–6 under the date 1758. The statement that Lord H. was abroad and the ages of Lady and Lord H. given at the end of the letter make it three years earlier.

[12] Drew Univ., Hunt. B 68, Lord H. to Lady H., 1 May 1755. An inventory of his Italian paintings is Hunt. Lib., HA Inv., box 3, 1.

[13] Hunt. Lib., HA 13747 and 13749, Lord Chesterfield to Lord H., 19 May and 2 July 1756.

mother hoped that the new building would be covered in the near future and proposed to attack the thistles and nettles in the Park, but was 'in the midst of more dust then ever one lived in'.[14]

Although everyone agreed that the house was old and in poor repair, neither the Earl nor his mother wished to rebuild the house. However, as the work proceeded new problems arose.[15] The original estimate of costs was soon exceeded.

> I Cannot say I am without my Cares how you will aprove what is done [she wrote] but I have the Comfort of thinking it is the best I Could do. I hope you will be as well satisfied as the Duke of Grafton in the like Circumstances. His House was so bad and so old and of the same kind as yours that they said he must build a new one. This he was not equal to, and so laid out two or three thousand pounds to make it Clean and Comfortable and when it was finish'd I find every body as well as himself likes it better then most modern new ones.[16]

Later she justified herself by saying that 'all must have been thrown away that had been done, had thare been less done.'[17] This information was passed on to Lord Chesterfield who advised the young Earl not to blame his mother.[18] However the results were universally criticized. Horace Walpole spoke of 'two tawdry rooms like assemblie rooms at Blackheath, added by the Countess Dowager'. John Byng thought that 'Dunnington House is of a capacity for a gentleman of 2000L a year, squatted in a hole, of most ugly building; and what was added by the present earl – is of the worst taste, a low dining room, with a tea room above it, like a mean addition to a villa near London.'[19] It was all eventually demolished and the present house built by the Earl's successor.

As Lord Chesterfield had planned, the Earl returned to England in 1756 to take up the appointment of Master of the Horse to the Prince of Wales, where he reorganized the Royal Mews.[20] At the Coronation of

---

[14] Drew Univ., Hunt. A 67, Lady H. to Lord H., 21 July 1755.
[15] 'Walpole's Visits to Country Seats', *Walpole Soc.*, 16 (1928), 64); W. Bray, *Sketch of a Tour into Derbyshire & Yorkshire* (London, 1783), 100.
[16] Drew Univ., Hunt. A 68; B. Falk, *The Royal Fitzroys* (London, 1950), 95. William Kent probably described the Duke's renovations to the Countess.
[17] Drew Univ., Hunt. A 69, Lady H. to Lord H., 14 September 1756.
[18] Hunt. Lib., HA 13750, Lord Chesterfield to Lord H., 9 October 1756.
[19] 'Walpole's Visits', op. cit.; C. B. Andrews (ed.), *The Torrington Diaries*, 2 (London, 1935), 76. The second room was intended for a library (Drew Univ., Hunt. A 95, Lady H. to Lord H., [May 1755]).
[20] M. M. Reese, *The Royal Office of Master of the Horse* (London, 1976), 228. For his appointment in 1760 see Lady Ilchester (ed.), *The Life & Letters of Lady Sarah Lennox*, 1, (London, 1901), 14 and W. R. Anson, *Autobiography & Political Correspondence of the Third Duke of Grafton* (London, 1898), p. 11.

George III he carried the sword of state.[21] He had inherited something of his mother's organizing ability, and also her quick temper. In 1767, after he had been promoted to Groom of the Stole, he quarrelled with Lord De La Warr, and a duel was only narrowly averted.[22] He was dismissed from his position at Court in 1770 for supporting John Wilkes in his attempt to sit as MP for Middlesex. As he wrote to his sister, Lady Rawdon,

> I have disliked the measures of government for some time and have been jealous of the imputation (which might have been thrown upon me) of being an accomodating man, that voted like a Swiss with every administration. The election of Mr Lutterel by the House of Commons, and not by the Freeholders of Middlesex, displeased me, and I did not conceal my sentiments upon it.[23]

He went abroad again the next year and spent several years in Italy. At Venice he visited the prison and complained of the injustice in that state. At Florence he quarrelled about servants with Lady Mary Coke 'beyond all accomodation'.[24]

The Earl's first long absence from England left the burden of administering his estates on his mother. Her eldest daughter Elizabeth was in her care until she escaped by marrying Lord Rawdon in 1752. She wrote to her brother: 'I lived a life of duty with my Mother. I own it grew wearisom at length, and was a strong inducement to my marrying – my Situation in Ireland is happy, extreemly so, in separating us so far asunder.'[25] She seldom left Ireland after her marriage and so was able to maintain a friendly relationship with her mother. The other two surviving children, Selina and Henry, were also the Countess's sole responsibility. When her youngest son Henry died in 1758 she had to act as his administratrix – a task which took until 1782 to complete. Even when her sister-in-law appointed their niece as executrix, the Countess found herself involved.[26] In September 1750 she had to take action against rioters who destroyed

---

[21] J. Beresford, *Letters of Thomas Gray* (Oxford, 1925), 237. He was obliged to borrow the Lord Mayor's sword to carry.

[22] *Letters and Journals of Lady Mary Coke*, 2 Edinburgh, 1896), 26, 27; J. Brooke, *King George III* (London, 1972), 298. For further evidence of his hot temper see Anson, op. cit., p. 33.

[23] *HMC, 13th Rep., App.* (1872), 430. Wilkes had been twice chosen by the Middlesex electors when the Commons voted to give his opponent Luttrell the seat. See also W. S. Lewis (ed.), *Horace Walpole's Correspondence with Sir Horace Mann*, 7 (Yale, 1967), 173.

[24] W. S. Lewis (ed.), *Walpole's Correspondence with Lady Mary Coke* (Yale, 1961), 153, 177; *Lady Mary Coke*, op. cit., vol. 4, pp. 262, 276.

[25] Hunt. Lib., HA 10413, Lady Rawdon to Lord H., 13 December 1752. Lord Rawdon became Earl of Moira in 1761.

[26] Connexion archives, 11/ 2, letters of administration, 4 October 1758 Cheshunt archives, E 1/ 2, 6, administration accounts, 1782; Drew Univ., Hunt. B 25, G. Ford to Lady H., 6 July 1755.

warrens on her son's estates in Leicestershire and Derbyshire. The local justices did not act to suppress the riots with the speed she expected, and she arranged for troops to be called in. However, when all was calm again, she was unwilling to prosecute 'these poor Creatures' under the Riot Act because they might be hanged.[27] Ten years later she was still involved in her son's affairs and she complained to Charles Wesley about 'Lord Huntingdons affairs wanting me so uncessantly'.[28]

Difficulties with the rest of the Shirley family, which had been largely smoothed over while her uncle Lawrence Shirley was alive, also began to occupy a larger portion of her time after 1743. Joseph Nightingale, Lord Kilmorey and Lady Huntingdon continued to have problems in collecting interest on the dowries from the new Earl, Lawrence's son and namesake.[29] The new Lord Ferrers was hardly more sane than his uncle Henry. In 1757 the friends of his wife were obliged to obtain an Act of Parliament to separate them on account of his cruelty.[30] The introduction of the Bill to provide her with an allowance from the estates obliged Lady Huntingdon and others to petition the Lords for their own interests to be protected.[31] The estates were placed in the hands of a receiver nominated by Lord Ferrers, John Johnson, his own steward and a family retainer. By 1760 Lord Ferrers had come to believe that Johnson was cheating him, and on 18 January 1760, having sent his mistress and all the servants away from the house, he had a meeting with Johnson at which he shot and fatally wounded him.[32] He was seized by one of the men from his own colliery, and carried to Ashby de la Zouch.

He was tried, according to his parliamentary privilege, by the entire House of Lords, and was persuaded by his family to plead insanity. If the M'Naghten rules had existed then he would have been found insane at the time that he committed the crime.[33] Evidence was given at his trial of frequent fits of insanity, and numerous assaults. No counsel being allowed

[27] Drew Univ., Hunt. A 64, 65, 108 and 109, Lady H. to E. Wilmot, 30 September and 12 October 1750, [1750] and n.d.
[28] BL, Add. MS 32910, fo. 25, Lady H. to Newcastle, 14 August 1760; JRL, Meth. Archives, Hunt. 60, Lady H. to C. Wesley, 29 June 1756.
[29] Hunt. Lib., HA 9576, Lord Kilmorey to Lady H., 5 January 1746/7; Drew Univ., Hunt. A 74, Lady H. to Lord H., 23 October 1768.
[30] *Lords' Journals*, vol.29, pp.36–280; Leics. RO, 26D53/ 147–9 and 1905.
[31] *Lords' Journals*, vol.29, pp.289–91.
[32] Leics. RO, 26D53/ 2123a, 7, coroner's inquest, 28 January 1760; *The Trial of Lawrence Earl Ferrers* ... (London, 1760). Lord Ferrers charged his estate with £2,000 for his mistress, Margaret Clifford (Warws. RO, CR 2131, 16, 5).
[33] The M'Naghten case was not tried until 1843. It remained a precedent in cases of lunacy for many years.

for the defence in criminal cases, Lord Ferrers found his arguments difficult to sustain. Despite the evidence of his relations and servants he was found guilty. The trial was a *cause célèbre* at the time, and the murder was obviously of great concern to all the family.[34] Lady Huntingdon visited 'their hardened Kinsman' with his sister, and accompanied the Earl's mother to the Queen in an attempt to get the sentence of death commuted. Seventeen years later she was to undertake a similar task on behalf of the Revd Dr William Dodd, who had been sentenced to death for forgery, but neither plea was successful. On 5 May Earl Ferrers was hanged at Tyburn.[35] Because he had been convicted of murder, such parts of his estate as remained in his own hands escheated to the Crown, and were not regranted to the family until December 1762.[36] This caused greater problems for the Earl's successor, and Lady Huntingdon was obliged to dispute the evidence of payments made to her from the estate. Earl Ferrers was

> in hopes that her Ladyship will reflect a little on the ill advice that has been given her and that she will not push things to extremities when I am so near paying off the Debt, for tho' this oppression may prevent my selling my Estate so well it will not forward the payment to her Ladyship a [single] hour.[37]

The debt continued to be a minor irritant to the Countess for the rest of her life, and the disputes, lawsuits, separations and quarrels continued until at least the end of the century.[38]

Despite all these troubles the Countess had already begun to plan for a future when family cares would cease and she could devote all of her time to her religious concerns. It would seem that the meetings of the nobility at her house in Chelsea came to an end about 1750. It is not known when she gave up the Chelsea house, but it may have been about 1751, when Count Zinzendorf bought the neighbouring Lindsey House and brought the Moravians into the parish.[39] Her reconciliation with them was not to come for another ten years. Howell Harris had retreated to his home at

---

[34] Beresford, op. cit., 205; H. Walpole, *Memoirs of King George II*, 3 (Yale, 1985), 106.

[35] PRONI, D. 2924/1, Lord Hillsborough to Lord Rawdon, 14 February 1760; Beresford, op. cit., 205; T. Jackson, *The Journal of Charles Wesley*, 2 (London, [1849] 171; T. B. Trowsdale, 'Laurence Ferrers, the Murderer-Earl', in W. Andrews (ed.), *Bygone Leicestershire* (Leicester, 1892), 187. Lady Huntingdon intervened on behalf of Dodd at the request of his hearers at the Magdalen Hospital (DWL, Cong. Lib., IIc 7/ 3, Lady H. to Mrs Wills, n.d. [1777]).

[36] Leics. RO, 26D53/ 2685, letters patent, 6 December 1762.

[37] Leics. RO, 26D53/ 2108, draft letter from Lord Ferrers, [1769].

[38] Most of this information can be found in Leics. RO 26D53/ 2119. Staffs RO, D 591/ A/ 1/ 1, Lord Ferrers to his son, 15 June 1779.

[39] *London County Council Survey of London*, 4, Chelsea pt 2 (London, n.d.), 35–41.

Trefeca, and no longer wrote to her. John Wesley was unhappy about the change in her opinions, but Charles Wesley continued his friendship with both Whitefield and the Countess, and they all attempted to moderate some of the actions of John Wesley.[40] However she now had more friends amongst the dissenters.

She had already abandoned her intention of living at Ashby de la Zouch when she decided to make her home at Clifton on the hills above Bristol. It was then nearly two miles from the city and overlooked the river Avon. About a mile below Clifton and on the river Avon were the Bristol Hotwells, the waters of which she had found particularly helpful.[41] Ashby may have been uncongenial. The town had the reputation of being very unfriendly to Methodists, while Bristol had the added attraction of Charles Wesley, who had taken a house in Charles Street when he married in 1749.[42] In order for Charles to marry, John Wesley had promised him £100 a year from the sale of his books. To reassure Mrs Wesley's father, the Countess had promised to make up any deficiency in that allowance.[43] She was able to attend meetings at the Methodists' New Room in the Horsefair from time to time and visited the newly married couple in their home.[44] Despite their disagreement about Calvinism, the Countess and Charles Wesley remained on very friendly terms, and now Sally Gwynne, the young Mrs Charles Wesley, was included in the friendship. Early on 29 November 1753 Lady Huntingdon brought them news that John Wesley was seriously ill in London.[45] Later in the day Charles received a letter that he should go at once if he wished to see his brother alive. He found John Wesley recovering, but was obliged to take services at the Foundery for him. On 4 December he returned there from visiting friends to find two letters from Lady Huntingdon telling him that his wife had smallpox, but assuring him to 'be under no Care I will do all that is possiable and all advice that Can be wanted . . .'[46] Sally had been

[40] J. Gillies (ed.), *A Select Collection of Whitefield's Letters*, 2 (London, 1772), 348–98; JRL, Meth. Archives, Hunt., 43, 54 and 55, Lady H. to C. Wesley, 29 May, 15 and 23 December 1755. There is little evidence that Lady Huntingdon was concerned about the ordination of Methodist preachers by the Greek Bishop Erasmus in 1764.

[41] For the relative positions of Bristol, Clifton and the Hotwells in the eighteenth century see J. Gill, *The Bristol Scene* (Bristol, 1973).

[42] J. B. Edwards, *Charles Wesley's House, Bristol* (Bristol, 1984).

[43] J. R. L., Meth. Archives, Hunt. 65, Lady H. to C. Wesley, 27 November 1756.

[44] Duke Univ.; an anonymous Methodist diary records her presence at the New Room on 26 October 1752. Univ. of California, Santa Barbara, Isaac Foot Coll., Lady H. to C. Wesley, [1752].

[45] [T. Jackson] *The Journal of Charles Wesley*, 2 London [1849]) 95. Mrs L. Galatin was a Scottish Methodist who corresponded with Lady Huntingdon.

[46] JRL, Meth. Archives, Hunt. 27, Lady H. to C. Wesley, 1 December 1753.

told that it was only the spotted fever, and Dr Middleton was optimistic about the mildness of the disease. Charles's return to Bristol was complicated by his travelling companion, John Hutchinson, who suffered from some mental disorder and attacked Lady Huntingdon as 'that vile wicked woman', a 'nasty baggage' and a 'hypocritical goat'.[47] Charles arrived home to find his Sally still very ill, but surrounded by friends. 'Good Lady Huntingdon attends her constantly twice a day, having deferred her journey to her son on this account.'[48]

It was about this time that Lady Huntingdon became closely acquainted with three remarkable women, probably by means of Catherine Edwin, who was their neighbour. The first of the three whose name appears in her correspondence was Ann Grinfield, who was 'Bed-Chamber Woman to their R.H. the Princesses Amelia and Caroline'.[49] In December 1753 Sarah Hodges wrote to the Countess from London to thank her for the 'Good Book' which Mrs Grinfield had delivered to her.[50] A few weeks later Lady Huntingdon asked Charles Wesley to call on Mrs Grinfield while he was in town: 'she is a sweet woman.'[51] In her efforts to adopt the Methodist way of life while remaining at Court she found many difficulties, and her persecution increased when she held religious meetings in her rooms. Ann Barlow, one of the other two friends, pitied 'her uncomfortable station', and wrote that 'Miss Grinfield is in waiting ... The place is enough to weary a person of the strongest constitution; their Highnesses rise early and go to bed late; are waited upon by the dressers at dinner. Princess Caroline has one to read to her continually.'[52]

During the next twelve months Mrs Grinfield sent about twenty letters to the Countess. Most are undated and all are concerned with her problems at Court. She obtained arguments from Lady Huntingdon

---

[47] JRL, Meth. Archives, Hunt. 32 and 28, Lady H. to C. Wesley, 3 and 6 December 1753; J. R. Tyson, 'Charles Wesley, Pastor', *Quarterly Review*, 4 (1984) 14.

[48] *The Journal of Charles Wesley; op. cit.*, vol. 2, p. 100; JRL, Meth. Archives, Hunt. 29, Lady H. to C. Wesley, [7?] December 1753.

[49] So described in the list of subscribers to Thomas Hartley's *Sermons on Various Subjects* (1754).

[50] Drew Univ., Hunt. B 54, S. Hodges to Lady H., 8 December 1753. Sarah Hodges may have been a relation of the Revd John Hodges, the vicar of Clifton and a friend of the Wesleys.

[51] JRL, Meth. Archives, Hunt. 31, Lady H. to C. Wesley, 31 December 1753. Mrs Grinfield's nephew, afterwards a Moravian minister, was at Westminster School with Lady Huntingdon's youngest son (Drew Univ., Hunt. B 56 and 61, Henry Hastings to Lady H., n.d.).

[52] Drew Univ., Hunt. B 36, Barlow to Lady H., 3 July 1755; E. J. Clemenson, *Elizabeth Montagu*, 1 (London, 1906), 256.

which she could use against one of her opponents at Court. 'Mr Scott who was here yesterday, when I read what your Ladyship Commanded me, said your arguments were very sensible, if they had any foundation, but absolutely denied that, talk'd a heap of Learned Nonsense that your Ladyship must have heard a thousand times over, and lamented over me as a lost friend.'[53] Scott borrowed her copies of William Law's works to read and raised objections to them, and said Elizabeth Elstob had told him that Ann Grinfield was not a sincere convert.[54] Mrs Grinfield felt that through his influence with the Princesses they might be led to Methodism, and in December 1754 suggested the Countess should rent a house in London in order to visit the Princesses.[55] In August 1755 she left her position at Court to go to live with Lady Huntingdon at Clifton. It was generally believed that she had been dismissed, but Ann Grinfield said she had been released because of her 'State of Health'.[56]

Lady Huntingdon's other two friends were related – widow and stepdaughter. Elizabeth Skrine was the daughter of the rector of Ockham and vicar of Cobham in Surrey. Her first husband died a month after they were married, and in 1719 she married Richard Skrine of Warley near Bath as his second wife. He died in 1737 and she went to live in Pembrokeshire with her stepdaughter, Ann Barlow, and her son-in-law. Two years later, when Ann Barlow also became a widow, they set up house together.[57] Her first introduction to Moravian and Methodist literature was from Catherine Edwin, and it was not until 1752 that she met with Methodist and Moravian ministers at Bath and attended their services. They divided their time between the house at Warley and another at Cobham. Mrs Skrine sent the Countess a detailed account of the latter together with a timetable of a typical day:

> We breakfast at half an hour after nine altogether, than Part till dinner, I with difficulty prevail upon Mrs Barlow to walk half an hour, by this time it is Eleven, then I sit in my own room and read and write till dinner ... We separate again at five and drink Tea between six and seven ... Then we read

[53] Drew Univ., Hunt. B 24 and Hunt. B 11, Grinfield to Lady H., n.d. [1755].
[54] Drew Univ., Hunt. B 14, Grinfield to Lady H., 2 January [1754].
[55] Drew Univ., Hunt. B 73, C 4 and B 23, Grinfield to Lady H., n.d. and December [1754].
[56] Clemenson, op. cit., vol.2, p.84; Drew Univ., Hunt. B 20, Grinfield to Lady H., 16 August [1755].
[57] This account is taken from her obituary notice (Bristol Univ. Lib., Moravian diary 2, 20 November 1763).

together till near Ten when we go to supper. A little before Eleven we read Prayers, then to Bed.[58]

Her stepdaughter is only represented by a few letters in the surviving correspondence. One contains her thanks to Lady Huntingdon for a book by William Law which Lord Huntingdon had delivered to her. Another describes a religious society at Bradford on Avon which they had discovered.[59] All three of these ladies were subscribers to a book dedicated to the Countess, Thomas Hartley's *Sermons on Various Subjects: With a Prefatory Discourse on Mistakes concerning Religion, Enthusiasm, Experiences, &c.* The list of subscribers is a guide to the number of the Countess's friends at this time. Amongst the subscribers who are friends of Mrs Grinfield is Mr Barham, a planter from the West Indies who had encouraged the Moravians to preach to his slaves there. Ann Grinfield feared that he would join the Moravians and recommended one of the recent attacks on them as an antidote, but without success. By 1756 he had joined the Moravian congregation at Bedford.[60] Another of her friends was Mrs Cresset, whose husband objected to her correspondence with Lady Huntingdon.[61] The Countess Delitz was another cause of embarrassment to Ann Grinfield. Lady Huntingdon warned her against confiding in the Countess, whose reputation was none of the best.[62] However, the chief mischief-makers amongst Lady Huntingdon's friends were Lady Charlotte Edwin and Catherine Edwin.

Lady Charlotte was the protagonist in an anecdote recorded by Thomas Haweis:

> The late Prince of Wales, one day at court, asked a lady of fashion, Lady Charlotte E. where my Lady Huntingdon was, that she so seldom visited the circle. Lady Charlotte, replied with a sneer, 'I suppose praying with her beggars.' The Prince shook his head, and said, 'Lady Charlotte, when I am

---

[58] Drew Univ., Hunt. B 87, Skrine to Lady H., 12 August [1755]. Verses describing the beauties of Cobham have been preserved in the Hastings papers (Leics. RO, 14D32/ 14, 64 (n.d.)).

[59] Drew Univ., Hunt. B 35 and 60, Barlow to Lady H., 24 May 1755 and 25 April [1756?]. For Samuel Walker's rule of 1754 see E. Sidney, *The Life and Ministry of The Rev. Samuel Walker* (London, 1838), 59–75.

[60] Drew Univ., Hunt. B 22, Grinfield to Lady H., n.d.; B36, Barlow to Lady H., 3 July 1755; Beds. RO, MO 4. Barham was a correspondent of two evangelicals, John Newton of Olney and William Bull of Newport Pagnell.

[61] Drew Univ., Hunt. B 24.

[62] Drew Univ., Hunt. B 14, Grinfield to Lady H., 2 January [1754]; R. Sedgwick (ed.), *Lord Hervey's Memoirs* (London, 1963), 125. The Countess was an illegitimate daughter of George I.

dying, I think I shall be happy to seize the skirt of Lady Huntingdon's mantle, to lift me up with her to Heaven.'[63]

When Ann Grinfield attended the Princess Dowager of Wales's court, Lady Charlotte refused to speak to her, saying to others that Ann Grinfield was too much of Lady Huntingdon's views to be acceptable at court.[64] A few years later Lady Huntingdon tried to use her presence at Court to assist the Methodist cause, but with very little success.[65] Catherine Edwin played a more important part in Methodist and Moravian circles – but it was usually disruptive. An anonymous letter of 1750 provides a good example of the backbiting in which she was frequently concerned: 'I find Mrs Edwin is angry on account of Your relating something to Mr Whitefield which Mr Whitefield related again to Mr Charles Wesley – and the Countess says you was strangely lifted up and you braged of having brought me away and Mrs Edwin from Mr Wesleys.'[66] She was pleased to tell Lady Huntingdon that when she returned to Court the Prince of Wales asked for 'a private conference' and proposed to sing hymns with her.[67] She joined the Moravians some years later and became a benefactor of the Bedford settlement.[68] She built a house at Cookham across the river from the Prince and Princess of Wales at Cliveden. There she was a neighbour of Nathaniel Hooke, a disciple of the French Quietists, and introduced him to Lady Huntingdon. Hooke and the Countess discussed Law's *Appeal to All that Doubt, or Disbelieve the Truths of the Gospel*.[69]

The two clergymen, apart from Charles Wesley, who were most closely associated with this circle of friends, were Walter Chapman and Thomas

[63] T. Haweis, *An Impartial and Succinct History* (London, 1800), vol.3, p.245. This anecdote was printed by Thomas Charles in *Trysorfa Ysprydd* (Chester, 1794–1802), 305. The incident must have occurred before 1751. The relationship between the two Edwins and a Mrs John Edwin needs further study. R. T. Jenkins, *Yng Nghysgod Trefeca* (Caernarfon, 1968), 76–8 gives some information. Mrs Edwin and Lady Huntingdon were friends as early as 1744 (Leics. RO, 14D32/ 6, 10, Henry Hastings to Lady H., 30 August, 1744).
[64] Drew Univ., Hunt. B 13, Grinfield to Lady H., 12 January [1754]. See also Leics. RO, 14D32/ 7, 6, Lady Kilmorey to Lady H., 11 July n.y.
[65] Cheshunt archives, F 1/ 751 and 1171, Lady Charlotte Edwin to Lady H., 7 December 1771 and n.d.
[66] G. M. Roberts, *Hanes Methodistiaeth Galfinaidd Cymru*, 1 (Caernarfon, 1973), 342, quoting Trevecka letter 1932. There is a similar incident in Drew Univ., Hunt. B 24.
[67] Leics. RO, 14D32/ 29, 21, C. Edwin to Lady H, 3 April [1752?].
[68] E. Welch, *Bedford Moravian Church* (Bedford, 1989), 163; D. Benham, *Memoirs of James Hutton* (London, 1856, 457; SMU, Hunt. 77, Lady H. to Mrs Wadsworth, 5 December 1768.
[69] A. W. Ward, *The Poems of John Byrom*, 3 (Chetham Soc., 1912), 124–6. I am indebted to Timothy Underhill of Pembroke College, Cambridge for this reference. *Howell Harris Visits to London*, op. cit., 164; Sedgwick, op. cit., 226. For Hooke's hermitage and Mrs Edwin's house, see Clemenson, op. cit., vol.2, p.41.

Hartley. Walter Chapman was a student at Pembroke College, Oxford. In 1737 he was appointed master of St John's Hospital in Bath, and in 1745 he became a prebendary of Bristol Cathedral.[70] He soon became acquainted with Lady Huntingdon, corresponding with her as early as 1742 about the ordination of Methodists. He was a warm supporter of the Moravians in Bristol and Bath. However, when his daughter wished to marry a Moravian, he opposed her – an affair in which Lady Huntingdon intervened.[71] Thomas Hartley, the rector of Winwick in Northamptonshire, helped her in her publishing ventures.[72]

In 1755 Lady Huntingdon, Mrs Skrine, Mrs Barlow and Ann Grinfield resolved to join together in a community at Clifton. She explained its purpose in a letter to Risdon Darracott:

> We had agreed upon this retreat, and taken a larger house among us for this purpose, and we all wish your prayers. To become the Lord's in body, soul, and spirit, is the one cry and desire of our hearts; and we know he will not reject us, nor cast us out; and though we can do nothing, yet we can receive of his fulness grace for grace; and in this world suffer reproach and persecution for his name's sake.[73]

Lady Huntingdon's daughter Selina and four of her Wheler nieces (whom she described as her chickens) were also to live there, but it was not until the summer that Ann Grinfield was able to complete the circle.[74] Meanwhile she wrote from Court that Lady Huntingdon had 'set the Moravians in a flame and Mrs Edwin beside Her Self at the News of the House being taken on Clifton Hill ... On being told how violent your Ladyship was against them all, I inserted I never saw you violent against any Creature ...'[75] A long and rather obscure letter which Lady Huntingdon

[70] L. Tyerman, *The Oxford Methodists* (London, 1873), 361, where he is wrongly described as William Chapman, which explains Tyerman's failure to find any information about Chapman, R. Young, *Mrs Chapman's Portrait* (Bath, 1926), 39–42.

[71] Leics. RO, DE 23/ 1, 1435, Chapman to Lady H., 12 June 1742; Welch, *Bedford Moravian Church*, 9; Benham, op. cit., 457; R. Young, *Father and Daughter* (London, 1952), 9; Cheshunt archives, F 1/ 1304, R. Chapman to Lady H., n.d.

[72] Lib. of Congress, Whitefield MSS, vol.2, fo. 12, Hartley to Whitefield, 15 March 1748; Drew Univ., Hunt. B 17, Grinfield to Lady H., n.d.

[73] J. Bennett, *The Star of the West* (London, 1813), 169, 170. Darracott was the dissenting minister of Wellington (Som.). After the date of this letter he visited Lady Huntingdon at Clifton (J. Gillies, *Historical Collections* (Kelso, 1845), 526). *Whitefield's Letters*, 3 (London, 1772) 150, 151 contain a reference to this community.

[74] Drew Univ. Hunt. B 35; JRL, Meth. Archives, Hunt. 48 and 49, Lady H. to C. Wesley, 20 and 27 August 1755.

[75] Drew Univ., Hunt. B 84, Grinfield to Lady H., [c. July 1755]. I am indebted to Miss Elizabeth Ralph, the former Bristol City Archivist, for the information that at this time Lady Huntingdon rented Clifton Wood House from the Quaker Thomas Goldney.

wrote to her son at this time is about her intention to form a community. In it she thanked him for his assistance and support in carrying out a project of which he disapproved., and concludes: 'I think I hear you say ... when will this old dull woman have done her Harangue – what has she to do to bring the Ideas of forty seven into those lively ones my present delightful sensations make for me at six and Twenty.'[76] The model for this 'Family' or 'Colony,' as the Countess described it, was almost certainly that of William Law, and perhaps also the family at Little Gidding, rather than a Moravian settlement in which everyone was expected to do manual labour.[77] Charles Wesley was asked to attend meetings of their 'little society'.[78] The community was soon disrupted by the greater attraction of the Moravians. In 1761 the three ladies joined the Moravian congregation at Bristol, and Lady Huntingdon was expected to join them. Mrs Skrine and Mrs Barlow together with Catherine Edwin had visited the Moravian minister at Bristol in 1759, and his diary is full of references to them.[79] In 1763 the Moravians described Elizabeth Skrine's part in the 'Family' as 'a Family-Connexion with Lady Huntingdon and our dear Sister Grinfield; but from many Incidents which happen'd in each of the Families so connected, they were separated, and our late Mother Skrine and Sister Barlow ... retired to Warley, from whence they attended the Brethrens Meetings at Bath.'[80] The Moravian chapel at Bath was not built until 1765, when Sisters Edwin, Barlow and Grinfield all contributed to the cost.[81]

At first the Countess's renewed interest in the Moravians appeared to

[76] Drew Univ., Hunt. A 73, Lady H. to Lord H. Part of this letter is printed in *HMC, Hastings 3*, pp. 134–6, with a date of 20 January 1758 taken from the endorsement. The unprinted part relates to the new building at Donnington Park, and the ages given in this quotation prove that it was written in 1756.

[77] Lady Huntingdon had a copy of Walton's description of Little Gidding (Hunt. Lib., HM 30302, Lady H.'s commonplace book).

[78] Drew Univ., B 18, Grinfield to Lady H., n.d.; B 26 and 27, G. Ford to Lady H., 3 and 24 July 1755; B 87, Skrine to Lady H., 12 August; JRL, Meth. Archives, Hunt. 39, Lady H. to C. Wesley, 19 November 1754. On 12 November 1756 Lord and Lady Chesterfield breakfasted with Lady H. at Clifton (Drew Univ., Hunt A 70, Lady H. to Lord H.). Lady Huntingdon still occupied a house on Clifton Hill in 1778 (SMU, Hunt. 99, Lady H. to T. Haweis, 8 August 1778).

[79] Bristol Univ. Lib., Moravian diary 1, pp.195, 261–74.

[80] Bristol Univ. Lib., Moravian diary 2, 20 November, 1763.

[81] Bristol Univ. Lib., Moravian diary 1, p.197 and diary 2, 9 April 1765. Earlier meetings had been held at Bath, but the Moravian records there were destroyed in World War II and Prof. R. T. Jenkins's notes taken from them (Bangor University College Library) contain no information on this subject. Bristol Univ. Lib., Moravian diary 2, 20 November 1763; Cheshunt archives, F 1/ 53, Benjamin La Trobe to Lady H., 13 March 1769. Mrs Skrine died at Bristol in 1763 and Mrs Barlow at Fulneck in 1769.

herald her conversion. In October 1760 the Moravian minister at Fulneck recorded one of several visits of gentry and nobility to their settlement:

> Brother La Trobe kept the Congregation Meeting during which Lady Huntingdon, Sir Charles Hotham, and 2 other maiden Ladies came hither to spend a Day amongst our People ... Br La Trobe gave a full account of the Work of our Saviour in the Dispersion in Lusatia and other Places ... which was all listened to attentively, as likewise the Account of the Heathen Congregations in Thomas and Crux.[82]

Lady Huntingdon then attended the Widows' meeting, her two companions the Single Sisters' meeting, and Sir Charles the Married Choir meeting.[83] This was an unusual favour, and early next morning they departed 'seemingly well pleased with their Visit'. Benjamin La Trobe corresponded with the Countess for some years after this visit.[84] In March 1761 the Countess began a similar, but longer, visit to the Bedford settlement. On this occasion she was accompanied by her son-in-law, Lord Rawdon, and a sister of Sir Charles Hotham, and their servants.[85] They attended the church meetings for four evenings, and for the second evening the minister, George Trancker, selected two discourses of Count Zinzendorf 'which they hearkened to with great attention, and afterwards expresst their admiration of the solidity and Depth of that dear Man's Sentiments'. On the same evening they attended a service in the chapel which so impressed Lord Rawdon 'that he wept as a Child'. On the last day Lady Huntingdon and Lord Rawdon spent two hours

> in a very agreeable and hearty Conversation with Brother and Sister Trancker, and we were glad to hear and feel, that their visit here has been a real Blessing to them ... Lady H[untingdon] said: I own before you, that I have been formerly much prejudiced against the Brethren, but I knew them not ... I love you most tenderly, and shall cultivate that Connection while I live.

---

[82] Fulneck archives, congregation diary, 1760–1. Lusatia is Lausitz in Saxony; Thomas and Crux are St Thomas and St Croix in the West Indies.

[83] Sir Charles Hotham was the son of Lady Gertrude. He was a friend of Lord Huntingdon as well as of the Countess and Henry Venn. When he died in 1767 he left the reversion of his Suffolk, Kent and Middlesex estates to the Countess. Hunt. Lib., HA 6889–6893, Hotham to Lord H., 1765 and 1766; Birmingham Univ. Lib., Venn MSS, C 11/3, Venn to Miss Wheler, November 1766; PRO, PROB 11/932.

[84] Cheshunt archives, F 1/1794, La Trobe to Lady H., 17 October 1777.

[85] Beds. RO, MO 342, Bedford diary, 9–14 Mar. 1761.

The following January Lady Huntingdon returned by herself and spent five days before returning to London, 'seemingly satisfied with her visit'.[86]

The Moravians had suffered from a series of attacks during the past few years. The language which they used and Count Zinzendorf's overextension of their missionary activities had aroused powerful enemies.[87] The principal and more vicious attacks against them came from Henry Rimius, a Prussian living in England.[88] All his complaints relate to Moravian excesses in Europe, few of which can be traced in the British settlements and congregations. The same objection applies to *A True and Authentic Account of Andrew Frey*, the book which Ann Grinfield wished to recommend to Mr Barham as an antidote against Moravianism.[89] Both John Wesley and George Whitefield published attacks, and even George Baddeley, Lady Huntingdon's vicar of Markfield, appealed to them not to empty the parish churches.[90] These were the allegations which had inspired Lady Huntingdon's dislike of the Moravians, and which she now decided were untrue. In October 1760 the Moravian minister at Bristol 'saw a pretty Letter, wrote by Lady H[untin]g[do]n to Mrs Grinfield, containing some very friendly Expressions towards the Brethren'.[91] Even as early as 1755 Lady Huntingdon had rejoiced 'at hearing from the Authority of an eminent Christian' that the Brethren had been slandered. The 'eminent Christian' may well have been Benjamin Ingham, who had now been completely reconciled to his wife's family. In the summer of 1755 he had visited the Countess at Ashby Place, and she in turn visited Aberford.[92] In April 1761 the Moravian minister at Bristol had 'a hearty effectual Conference' with the Countess. In May, 'Upon a pressing invitation Brother and Sister Nyberg waited on Lady Huntingdon at Milehill. She was uncommonly free and open; especially as long as the Discourse turned upon the Diaspora-Plan. Her visit at Gracehill and

---

[86] Beds. RO, MO 342, Bedford diary, 9–13 Jan. 1762.
[87] For an example of their verses on 'the blood' see Welch, *Bedford Moravian Church*, 13.
[88] H. Rimius, *A Candid Narrative of the Rise and Progress of the Herrnhuters* ... (London, 1753); H. Rimius, *A Second Solemn Call on Mr Zinzendorf* (London, 1757); J. Stanston, *A Pastoral Letter against Fanaticism, address'd to the Mennonists of Friesland ... Translated from the original Dutch by H. Rimius* (London, 1753). For further information about the controversy see J. E. Hutton, *A History of the Moravian Church* (London, 1909), 353–62.
[89] *A True and Authentic Account of Andrew Frey ... Faithfully translated from the German* (London, 1753); Drew Univ., Hunt. B 22, Grinfield to Lady H., [Jan. 1754].
[90] Hutton, op. cit., 349, 350, where Baddeley is described as curate of Melbourne.
[91] Bristol Univ. Lib., Moravian diary 1, p. 293.
[92] Drew Univ., Hunt. B 86, Skrine to Lady H., 15 July 1755; Fulneck archives, 82, B. Ingham to Br. Telschig, 12 November 1746; Drew Univ., Hunt. B 43, M. Ingham to Lady H., 12 July 1755; JRL, Meth. Archives, Hunt. 46, Lady H. to C. Wesley, 24 July 1755.

Bedford has been a Blessing to her ...'[93] In July the minister received 'a curious message from Lady Huntingdon that a Mrs Parrott had apologized for her slander of the Brethren'.[94] The minister was confused by this and concluded it was a 'comical affair'. It was a few days later that Sisters Skrine and Barlow were admitted as members of the congregation, but there is only one further reference to the Countess in the congregation diary for the next two years.[95] Whatever hopes Brother Nyberg may have had about a noble convert to the *Unitas Fratrum* were now at an end. However, she did succeed in reconciling the Wesleys with the Moravians, and Sally Wesley even asked permission to attend their meetings.[96]

Lady Huntingdon's interest in the Diaspora, the bringing together of the scattered 'saints', may have misled Nyberg. Howell Harris had left the settlement at Trefeca, which he had founded on Moravian lines, to pursue his passion for Methodist unity. In January 1760 he had answered his country's call and joined the Breconshire Militia as an officer. His regiment spent the first summer at Great Yarmouth and the second in the West Country, which gave him opportunities to renew his contacts with both the Moravians and the English Methodists. In September 1761 he was in Bristol, where he called on the minister to urge the importance of a union between Methodists and Moravians, and on Charles Wesley, probably with the same purpose. Harris felt that they were 'coming somewhat nearer'.[97] Although their paths never crossed until November 1763, Harris and the Countess had already begun to correspond. On 6 October 1760 Howell Harris read the account of the Revd James Hervey's death which Lady Huntingdon had obtained from his curate.[98] In March 1763, when Harris's travels brought him to Bristol again, he discussed the Countess with Charles Wesley, who 'mentioned of Lady Huntingdon's writing now to him against Perfection, but willing to do what she can on this occasion of persecution, and to suffer with them as she knows they mean well'.[99] In October the Countess wrote to Harris about the supply of ministers for the chapel which she had opened at

---

[93] Bristol Univ. Lib., Moravian diary 1, pp.332, 341. Milehill was at Bath. The Diaspora Plan was Zinzendorf's proposal to bring together the scattered saints (see Hutton, op. cit., 263). The reference to Gracehill is a mistake for Fulneck. There is no record of a visit to Gracehill in that congregation's diaries.

[94] Bristol Univ. Lib., Moravian diary 1, p.346.

[95] Ibid., pp.346, 370.

[96] Ibid., pp.431, 443.

[97] Ibid., p.356; T. Beynon, *Howell Harris, Reformer and Soldier* (Caernarvon, 1958), 120.

[98] Beynon, op. cit., 90. The account is now NLW, Trevecka letter 2244. A different version is printed in J. Brown, *Life of The Rev. James Hervey* (London, n.d.), 138–40.

[99] Beynon, op. cit., 162.

Brighton, and on 4 November they finally met there, but he did not preach for her.[100] In a long discussion she spoke of 'the young ministers', Martin Madan, John Berridge and Henry Venn, as impulsive, but 'must be borne with'. John Wesley she described 'as an Eel, no hold of him and not come to the truth'. In all these statements we can see Harris's usual exaggeration of her complaints, but when they discussed the question of union her sentiments and Harris's were completely in agreement. The meeting ended with Harris urging her to try to bring them all together.

The Countess played her part by calling 'most all the Religious Clergymen of the Church of England to meet at Bristol for a Conference' beginning on 8 August 1764.[101] It was attended by Martin Madan, preacher at the Lock Hospital in London, Joseph Townsend, the rector of Pewsey in Wiltshire, Howell Harris, the two Moravian ministers, and probably also John William Fletcher, vicar of Madeley. Although John Wesley had held his annual conference at Bristol which began two days earlier, and did not attend this one, he too emphasized union. 'The great point I now laboured for was, a good understanding with all our brethren of the Clergy, who are heartily engaged in propagating vital religion.'[102] Little came of their efforts except the muting of doctrinal disputes for a few years, but the friendship between Harris and Lady Huntingdon flourished. In 1763 Harris's niece spent some time with the Countess, and in 1765 his daughter also paid her a visit.[103] In 1768 Lady Huntingdon opened her College at Trefeca, and spent much of her time with her students and Howell Harris.

Another friend of Lady Huntingdon and Charles Wesley at this time did not attend her conference because he was not a Methodist. Theophilus Lindsey's mother had been a servant of Frances, Countess of Huntingdon, Lady Huntingdon's mother-in-law.[104] Her only son, Theophilus, born in 1723, was the godchild of Lady Huntingdon's husband. His education was provided by Lady Betty Hastings, who sent him to Thomas Barnard's school at Leeds, and after her death by Lady Anne, who sent him to St John's College, Cambridge. After Mr Lindsey's death

---

[100] Ibid., 205, 206; G. M. Roberts, *Selected Trevecka Letters 1747–94*, 2 (Caernarvon, 1962), 91–3.

[101] The best description of this conference appears to be that in the Bristol Moravian diary (Bristol Univ. Lib., vol. 2), and this account is based on it.

[102] *John Wesley's Journal*, 6 August 1764. See also J. Telford (ed.), *Letters of John Wesley*, 4 (London, 1931), 235.

[103] Beynon, op. cit., 206; *Selected Trevecka Letters* 2 (Caernavon, 1962), 98–101.

[104] This account of Lindsey's early life is based on T. Belsham, *Memoirs of the late Revd Theophilus Lindsey* (London, 1873), 1–5. For his friendship with Charles Wesley see JRL, Meth. Archives, Hunt. 67, Lady H. to C. W., 3 February 1758.

in 1742, his widow and her children moved to Ashby Place for some years.[105] Theophilus was given the charge of a chapel in Spital Square by Granville Wheler, and later recommended by Lord Huntingdon to the Duke of Somerset as his domestic chaplain.[106] He next accompanied the Duke of Northumberland on the Grand Tour for two years. During this time Lady Somerset kept him informed of the Countess's activities including a glimpse of her method of travelling: 'I was surprised to meet Lady Huntingdon upon the road last Saturday was fortnight; she was on her way to London, but her coach drove by so fast that I had only time to send Lomas after her with my compliments; she seemed to me to look as well as ever I saw her.'[107]

On 4 January 1755 Lindsey was presented to the Hastings family living of Piddletown in Dorset. As Lord Huntingdon was 'travelling in foreign parts' he had appointed his mother, Lady Anne Hastings, Granville Wheler and his agent or steward Robert Hemington to act on his behalf, and the two last named signed the deed of presentation.[108] In July he wrote to the Countess to thank her for sending the news of the death of Lady Anne Hastings – 'my kind and ever to be revered Benefactress' – and to ask if he could seek the Countess's advice at a more suitable time.[109] He presumably intended to consult her about his objections to the Thirty-nine Articles of the Church of England. However four days later he had a more pressing problem with which to trouble her. His sister, who lived with him, had decided to marry a man who Lindsey agreed was a good choice, but was the brother of one of his former servants. He had hoped that he and his sister would remain single and live together and her choice was a great blow to his pride.[110] His sister fled to Lady Huntingdon at Clifton and enlisted her aid as a peacemaker. Once again Lindsey suggested that he should write to her later about his religious doubts, and urged her not 'to cry out *heretic* upon a man who professes to believe the scriptures, who believed that his Savior Christ governs this world at

---

[105] Although Belsham says Mrs Lindsey was buried at Ashby de la Zouch in 1747, there is no entry in the parish register.

[106] The Wheler chapel, later St Mary's church, had been opened by Sir George Wheler, Granville's father, who died in 1723. Belsham mistakenly attributes the appointment to Sir George. At this time the church was a donative and exempt from the jurisdiction of the bishop of London (G. Hennessy, *Novum Repertorium Ecclesiasticum Parochiale Londinense* (London, 1898), 401).

[107] Belsham, op. cit., 323, 324.

[108] Bristol RO, EP/A/3/ 259, Piddletown Presentations, 1675–1763; EP/A/5/1/2, fo. 35, Institution Book. Belsham is in error in stating that the presentation took place in 1766.

[109] Drew Univ., Hunt. B 29, Lindsey to Lady H., 14 July 1755.

[110] Drew Univ., Hunt. B 31, Lindsey to Lady H., 18 July 1755.

present, *for all power is committed to him*, and that he will be his Judge at the great day'.

There is a long undated document which he sent to the Countess about this time in which he entered into great detail about his doubts, which he believed would oblige him to renounce his orders.[111] In August he acknowledged a helpful reply to his next letter, and explained that he thought himself a perjurer. 'When I took the oaths before the Bishop it was against my conscience. I thought I might afterwards qualify them and make them easy to me, which I have not been able.'[112] He hoped to visit Lady Huntingdon at Clifton during the winter, but for a time there is a gap in the correspondence. Lindsey's next letters to the Countess begin in 1762, and there is nothing more about his religious doubts. In 1763 he wrote to console Lady Huntingdon on the death of her daughter, and in 1767 he enlisted her aid for a fellow clergyman in difficulties.[113] He deplored the persecution of Methodists, and in particular the expulsion of the Methodist students from St Edmund Hall which showed

> the temper of the hierarchy of the present times, and how much further they would go, if the civil power did not restrain them. But whatever persecutions are set on foot, they will never be able to suppress the truth ... I only wish that some of the Methodists would cease from their hard speeches and intolerance towards some of their christian brethren.[114]

At this time Lady Huntingdon was providing Lindsey with books. He thanked her for the 'Quaker bible' and requested a copy of Matthew Henry's *Exposition of the Bible*.[115] Only one other letter to Lady Huntingdon survives, but he continued to correspond with her son until 1770 or later.[116] Lindsey sympathized with the Methodists even though he disagreed with their doctrines, and thought that they were the only clergy who could subscribe to the Articles with a clear conscience.[117] After leaving the Anglican Church for Unitarianism, Lindsey appears to have

[111] Drew Univ., Hunt. B 32, [Lindsey] to [Lady H.], n.d.
[112] Drew Univ., Hunt., B 30, Lindsey to Lady H. 11 August 1755.
[113] Cheshunt archives, F 1/ 10 and 16, Lindsey to Lady H., 15 June 1763 and 26 May 1767.
[114] Cheshunt archives, F 1/ 28, Lindsey to Lady H., 29 April 1768.
[115] The 'Quaker bible' is Anthony Purver, *A New and Literal Translation of all the Books of the Old and New Testaments* (London, 1764). Matthew Henry published his *Exposition of the Old and New Testaments* between 1708 and 1710. It was completed by others after his death. Lindsey probably required the complete (folio) edition of 1762.
[116] Hunt. Lib., HA 8306–8324 (1748–1770).
[117] *The Apology of Theophilus Lindsey, M. A., on resigning the Vicarage of Catterick* (London, 1774), 204.

ceased to write to many of his former friends, but in the summer of 1786 when visiting Wales he and his wife were received at Trefeca by Lady Huntingdon 'most graciously as usual'.[118]

---

[118] Belsham, op. cit., 2n.

6

Freedom

Lady Huntingdon's friendship and help for Theophilus Lindsey aptly illustrates the difficulty of assigning motives for her benevolence. While she probably helped him because he was her husband's godson, she was also sympathetic towards his early religious doubts, and not so opposed to his later Unitarianism as to refuse to welcome him to Trefeca. Throughout her life three different motives for her widespread charities can be traced. There was a general benevolence without any specific link to Methodism. In July 1749 she relieved thirty-four insolvent debtors who owed less than £10 each at Bristol. In 1757 she sent money to Mrs Charles Wesley 'for any of the *Poor Colliers*' who were sick or otherwise distressed. She made a shift for a poor woman. She got patients admitted to the Bath Hospital and children admitted to schools. She sought to provide them with places in the government and courts, and to get conscripted soldiers discharged.[1] In 1747 she successfully pleaded with the Prime Minister to reprieve a man condemned to death at Chelmsford Assizes because the family depended on an annuity on his life. She helped to find places for servants.[2] Orphans and poor children were brought up and educated at her expense. She clothed and educated five poor girls at Ashby, and protected children from a profligate mother. Henry Heron, who described her as 'a Father and a Mother' to him, was sent to a grammar school. Her efforts were appreciated. Towards the end of her life she heard from one of the early objects of her benevolence: 'During the time I

---

[1] J. Latimer, *Annals of Bristol in the Eighteenth Century* (Bristol, 1893), 279; J. R. L., Meth. Archives, Hunt. 66, Lady H. to Mrs C. Wesley, 30 June 1757; Hunt. 24, Lady H. to Mrs C. Wesley, 10 September 1753; Drew Univ., Hunt. B 89, M. Hotham to Lady H., 2 June 1755; Leics. RO, 14D32/14, 70, Lady Gertrude Hotham to Lady H., 25 May 1738; 14D32/8, 3, Anon. to Lady H., n.d.; Drew Univ., Hunt. A 66 and B 12, Lady H. to Eardly Wilmot, 1 January 1751/2 and anon. to Lady H., 14 July; BL, Add. MS 32712, fos. 442, 443, Lady H. to Duke of Newcastle, 27, 28 August 1747.

[2] Leics. RO, 14D32/14, 3 & 4, M. Fitzherbert to Lady H., n.d.

was with your Ladyship you told me several times that you bought me, and you was always pleased to call me Poll.'³

Favours for members of her family are less well documented. She intervened with the Duke of Argyle to allow Mr Needham to leave his regiment, and several of the pensioners of Lady Betty Hastings were taken over by the Earl and Countess after her death. Family members in trade received their custom, and some received an annual gift.⁴ After her son's death the Countess sent to school 'Mr Hastings who I am educating as preparity to his being Earl of Huntingdon from Just Claim'.⁵ All these, and many more charities, were common both before and after Lady Huntingdon's conversion. They were expected of the nobility and gentry of the period. Soon after her conversion in 1739 she began to help the Methodists and evangelicals in the same manner.

One important activity on behalf of Methodists was to obtain ordination for evangelical ministers. Walter Chapman had a friend, Mr Laseure or Lasere, and was improving his education in order that he might be ordained. Lady Huntingdon hoped to get him the title of a curacy so that the bishop of Bath and Wells could be persuaded to ordain him.⁶ John Jones of Radnorshire was refused ordination by the bishop of St David's because he had 'expounded' among the Methodists, and Catherine Edwin asked Lady Huntingdon to approach the archbishop of Canterbury about his case.⁷ In December 1752 Lady Huntingdon wrote to the bishop of Exeter about his refusal to ordain an evangelical deacon. Richard Elliott had annoyed the redoubtable Bishop Lavington by serving as curate to the Methodist vicar of St Gennys in Cornwall, George Thomson. Despite her pleas, Lavington refused to ordain him, saying that it was 'a dangerous thing to introduce an Enthusiast into the Church', and that this had led to madness, fornication, adultery, theft and murder in his

³ Drew Univ., Hunt. B 45, H. Heron to Lady H., 22 July 1755; Cheshunt archives, A 2/4, 12, 16 and 17; E 4/8, 20–2; F 1/688, Mary Davis to Lady H., 5 November 1787.
⁴ Leics. RO, DE 23/1/1425, anon. to [Lady H.], n.d.; Connexion archives, 1, administration accounts; Leics. RO, 14D32/6, 29, Henry Hastings to Lady H., 14 September 1746.
⁵ SMU, Hunt. 79, Lady H. to T. Haweis, n.d.; Yale, Osborn Coll., Lady H. to Eardley Wilmot, 16 December 1789.
⁶ Leics. RO, 14D32/14, 5 and 6, M. Cocks to Lady H., n.d. and Chapman to Lady H., 22 April 1742.
⁷ This was not the Mr Jones who later became curate at Markfield. Leics. RO, 14D32/4, 4, Mr Jones' Case; 14D32/29, 23, C. Edwin to Lady H., n.d.; JRL, Meth. Archives, Hunt. 48, Lady H. to C. Wesley, 20 August 1775; Drew Univ., B 33 and 34, T. Hartley to Lady H., 24 May and 10 July 1755. A letter of Jones to Whitefield in 1743 is in Lib. of Congress, Whitefield MSS, vol. 1, 13. See also A. B. Sackett, *John Jones: First after the Wesleys?* (Wesley Hist. Soc., 1972).

diocese.[8] She was more successful with Walter Sellon, a protégé of the Wesleys. He was ordained in 1752, and two years later was presented to the donative of Smisby in Derbyshire by Lord Huntingdon.[9] It was important for her to be personally acquainted with the bishops in order to persuade them to ordain Methodists; for this reason the Irish bishops who visited Bath for their health were more often willing to help.[10] In her early years she had a fairly extensive acquaintance with bishops. Bishop Benson was her husband's former tutor. Archbishop Potter was a close friend who sent her messages, received her with great attention at Lambeth and wrote to her in his last hours.[11] But Potter died in 1747 and Benson in 1752. Her acquaintance with Archbishop Secker was limited to an unsuccessful attempt to persuade him to employ a relation. By 1770 all the bishops who were alive when she had been converted were dead. She knew William Warburton some years before he became bishop of Gloucester, but his behaviour cannot have contributed to their continued friendship.[12] By 1781, during the crisis which led to the secession, she was known to them only by reputation.

There were other ways in which the Methodists needed her protection. In 1749 she wrote to Mr Stanhope on behalf of some 'poor distress'd people' in Cork who were being oppressed by the magistrates.[13] In 1744 she successfully interceded with Lord Stair for the release of John Nelson, the Yorkshire Methodist who had been taken up for a soldier in May 1744. She also offered to intercede for a Moravian minister who had been imprisoned by the Yorkshire magistrates 'as a Spy and an Unworthy Person without the least ground'.[14] Other examples of her intervention are known, and many probably passed unrecorded, but until she reached

---

[8] Lamb. Pal. Lib., Secker MSS, 8, fos. 122–30. Thomson was a friend of Philip Doddridge (G. F. Nuttall, *Correspondence of Philip Doddridge* (London, 1979), 253).

[9] JRL, Meth. Archives, Hunt. 23, Lady H. to C. Wesley, 13 June 1752; Hunt. Lib., HAM box 63, 37, presentation, 15 June 1754.

[10] JRL, Meth. Archives, Hunt. 64 and 56, Lady H. to C. Wesley, August & 13 January 1756.

[11] Leics. RO, 14D32/6, 30, Henry Hastings to Lady H., n.d.; 14D32/6, 21, Henry Hastings to Lady H., 17 June 1746; *The Works of Augustus Toplady*, 4 (London, 1794), 144.

[12] Toplady, op. cit., 150. Cheshunt archives, E 4/8, 12, Secker to Lady H., 30 March 1758.

[13] Yale Univ. Lib., Osborn Coll. 8, Lady H. to Mr Stanhope, 30 October 1749. This relates to the riots described by John Wesley, but the Countess's aid was enlisted by Whitefield (*John Wesley's Journal*, 19 July 1749; J. Gillies (ed.), *A Select Collection of Whitefield's Letters*, 2 (London, 1772), 291.

[14] R. Parkinson (ed.), *Byrom's Journal* (Chatham Soc., 1855–7), vol.2, p. 383; J. C. Hartley, *John Nelson* (London, 1988), 10; Fulneck Archives 82, petition to archbishop of York, [1745].

the age of sixty her efforts on behalf of Methodists were almost always the result of a request from another person.

For the greater part of the eighteenth century these were the semi-public activities permitted to ladies. A work popular during Lady Huntingdon's youth, *The Ladies Calling*, by the author of *The Whole Duty of Man*, allowed that compassion was a feminine virtue and that women should be permitted to help the poor.[15] However the author believed that women should submit to their superiors, control their affections and obey their husbands. After their husbands' death their work should be confined to the preservation of their husbands' memories, and he was convinced that 'Women of quality have few secular avocations.'[16] Bishop Sherlock expressed his dislike of female education in a letter of 1760: 'Nothing, I think, is more disagreeable than Learning in a Female, when the Mistress studies Newton, which perhaps she neither does nor ever will understand, to the absolute neglect of her Children and Servants.'[17] In practice, however, many women probably enjoyed as much freedom as Lady Betty Hastings and Lady Huntingdon did. A spinster, Elizabeth Baker, joined in a partnership for a company to search for minerals in north Wales in 1770. Edward Young the poet took no part in 'Family Affairs' and left all monetary transactions to his wife. Susanna Whatman, after her husband died, took over his estate and investments and ran them successfully.[18] Some women believed that they were only held back from competing with men by their lack of formal education. Mary Astell, a friend of Lady Betty, wrote that 'Ignorance is the Cause of most Feminine Vices' and proposed a 'monastery' for providing them with schooling.[19] Similar sentiments can be found in Lady Chudleigh's *Essays on Several Subjects* (London, 1710). Copies of these books were owned by Lady Betty Hastings, were bequeathed by her to her nephew George and passed to Lady Huntingdon on his death. But not even the most feminist authors of this period seem to have envisaged women taking part in public meetings and speaking. At the beginning of the century the author of *The Ladies Calling* reserved his strongest condemnation for women who spoke in public. This was im-

---

[15] Richard Allestree (1619–81) is usually considered to be the author of both these works. Lady Betty Hastings owned a copy of the sixth edn., but the quotations used here come from the complete *Works* (Oxford, 1726).

[16] *The Ladies Calling*, 15, 24, 52, 63. Lord Bute gave similar advice to George III (J. Brooke, *King George III* (London, 1972), 48, 262).

[17] E. J. Clemenson, *Elizabeth Montagu* (London, 1906), vol.2, p.198.

[18] *Journal of the National Library of Wales*, 3 (1944), 80–2; *Huntington Library Quarterly*, 2 (1938–9), 93; T. Balston (ed.), *The Housekeeping Book of Susanna Whatman 1776–1800* (London, 1956), 15.

[19] *A Serious Proposall to the Ladies*, pt 1 (London, 1697), 19, 36.

modest, led to lewdness and should be forbidden.[20] At the end of the century William Huntington, the coalheaver evangelist, was said to have taught that 'it was ever contrary to his principles that a woman should rule in the church. He had in the course of his ministry much opposed the Countess of Huntingdon on this ground.'[21] Mary Bosanquet, the future wife of John Fletcher, wrote a long letter to John Wesley about the prayer meetings which she and her friend had established in Leytonstone and later in Yorkshire.[22] She was convinced that women with an *extraordinary* call were permitted to exhort. John Wesley agreed with her but emphasized that there could only be 'a few exceptions' to the rule. Unfortunately the eighteenth-century examples of women preaching were generally amongst the least acceptable religious groups, and this cannot have helped Mary Bosanquet's case. The French Prophets, Mother Ann Lee and the Shakers, Joanna Southcott and her Box – all made it more difficult for Methodist women to take any active part in church activities of this kind.[23]

Lady Huntingdon's thoughts had led her along the same road as Mary Bosanquet. As early as 1736 she was enquiring about a woman who spoke at the Quaker meeting house at Winchmore Hill in Middlesex.[24] Her encouragement of religious societies had led her to make some attempts at exhortation. This could be seen as an extension of previous work, when attempts to convert individuals were overheard by others:

> Lady Huntingdon was once speaking to a workman who was repairing a garden wall, and pressing him to take some thought concerning eternity and the state of his soul. – Some years afterwards, she spoke to another, on the same subject: and said to him, 'Thomas, I fear you never pray, nor look to Christ for salvation.' – 'Your ladyship is mistaken,' answered the man: 'I heard what passed between you and James ... through an hole in the wall...'[25]

A few years after she had opened her chapel at Brighton her exhortations had established a society of sisters there who sent greetings to their 'dear

---

[20] *The Ladies Calling*, 3.
[21] E. Hooper, *Facts, Letters and Documents concerning William Huntington* (London, 1872), 94, quoting a letter of 1817.
[22] R. Davies (ed.), *A History of the Methodist Church in Great Britain*, 4 (London, 1988), 168–72.
[23] In 1743 Whitefield and Howell Harris discussed the question of women preaching. Whitefield approved, but Harris opposed it (Beynon, *Howell Harris, Reformer & Soldier* (Caernarvon, 1958, 49).
[24] Hunt. Lib., HA 1238, Thos Carte to Lady H., 8 January 1735/6.
[25] Toplady, op. cit., 165.

Wiltshire Sisters' at Pewsey.[26] Ten years later her views were very similar to those of Mary Bosanquet. When on a visit to the Revd Thomas Wills and his wife (her niece Selina Wheler) at St Agnes in Cornwall she was asked by him:

> Why had not I preached publickly – from the great knowledge and abillitys he supposed me to have – he urged the examples in scripture for it and did not a little of the fear of man occasion that restraint – I then spoke my whole heart on the subject ... that my own Conscience testified before the Lord and that I had re[*illeg.*] many many of my Dear Friends and even ministers who had reason'd with me on this subject, viz. that I did not see it scriptural that our Saviours General Commission was given only to men except in two Instances ... and that I Could [witness] before the Lord had I heard his voice ... and that the usage of the primitive Church (which might have reasons not now the same) Could be no president [precedent].[27]

It may be that Lady Huntingdon's interest in the Moravians and the Quakers led her to think that a greater role should be allowed to women in the Church. Both denominations were unusual in having meetings for women. The Society of Friends had a women's meeting outside the gates of Donnington Park while she lived there, and members of the Castle Donnington meeting corresponded with her.[28] Women Friends not only spoke at meetings, but also undertook missionary activities. In the sixties 'a simple, humble woman dressed in the severest garb of the Society of Friends' spoke to the company in the Pump Room at Bath on the vanities and follies of the world:

> as the speaker proceeded, and spoke more and more against the customs of the world, signs of disapprobation appeared. Amongst those present was one lady with a stern yet high-toned expression of countenance; her air was distinguished; she sat erect, and listened intently to the speaker ... Then the lady I have described arose with dignity ... she went up to the speaker, and thanked her, in her own name and in that of all present, for the faithfulness with which she had borne testimony to the truth. The lady added, 'I am not of your persuasion, nor has it been my belief that our sex are generally deputed to be

---

[26] SMU, Hunt. 53, Lady H. to Mrs Wadsworth, 7 March 1765. Lady Huntingdon always spelt her name Wadsworth (until the lady married Thomas Haweis), but Wordsworth is the more common spelling.

[27] SMU, Hunt. 86, Lady H. to Mrs Haweis (Mrs Wadsworth), 7 October 1775. For information about the few early Methodist women who were allowed to preach, see H. D. Rack, *Reasonable Enthusiast* (London, 1989), 244, and A. B. Lawson, *John Wesley and the Christian Ministry* (London, 1963), 176–81.

[28] The records of the Castle Donnington meeting are divided between the Notts. and the Leics. record offices. The eighteenth-century women's meeting minutes are at the former.

public preachers, but God who gives the rule can make the exception ...' This lady was the celebrated Countess of Huntingdon.[29]

About 1758 Lady Huntingdon took her son Henry to Brighton in the hope that his health would benefit from sea bathing. While there she encountered a gentlewoman

> who, seeing the countess, made a full stop, and said, 'O madam you are come!' – Lady H. was surprized at the oddity of such an address from an absolute stranger, and thought, at first, that the woman was not in her senses. What do you know of me? said the countess. – 'Madam,' returned the former, 'I saw you in a dream, three years ago, dresst just as you now are.'[30]

She had dreamed that Lady Huntingdon was to be 'an instrument of doing much good'. The Countess established one or more religious societies at Brighton and then built a house and chapel as a meeting-place for them. At that time the population of Brighton was beginning to grow and there was also a transient population of the more wealthy people who came for the sea bathing. It had only one parish church, an Independent meeting house and a very small Baptist meeting, so Lady Huntingdon's chapel provided extra space for churchgoers.[31] In order to build the chapel she borrowed £500 from Lady Gertrude Hotham, and later transferred to her as repayment the reversion of £2,000 which she had by Lady Betty Hastings's will.[32] The congregation grew so quickly that a new building was erected on the same site in North Street in 1767.[33] This building, which was not erected at the suggestion of any Methodist minister, was her first small step on the way to establishing her right to take independent action in the cause of evangelism. It was followed by a chapel at Ote Hall (or Oathall) in the parish of Wivelsfield (Sussex) where she had rented a house from a distant Shirley kinsman. On 27 March 1762 John Ollive registered this chapel in the bishop of Chichester's Lewes office as a

---

[29] C. C. Hankin, *Life of Mary Anne Schimmelpenninck* (London, 1860), 74. This anecdote was told to her by her mother who described what she had seen as a child, probably in 1764 or 1765 when Lady H. was in Bath.

[30] Toplady, op. cit., 183.

[31] West Sussex RO, Ep I/26/3, p. 37; Ep II/25/1, fo. 37.

[32] Cheshunt archives, F 1/6 & 7, deed and bond, 16 February 1762. The income from the money went to Lady Betty's servant, Sarah Hole, during her life. There is no contemporary evidence for the story that the Countess sold her jewels to build the chapel. The list in the Cheshunt archives cannot be older than 1792 (C 9/14, 3, the gift of Dr Henry Allon, 1818–92).

[33] JRL, Meth. Archives, Hunt. 79, Lady H. to C. Wesley, 4 February 1767; Hunt. 123, Lady H. to Mrs Harris, 15 February 1767. A photograph of the building erected in 1870 (and demolished in 1972) appears in D. R. Elleray, *The Victorian Churches of Sussex* (London, 1981), illus. 39. No picture of the original building has been found.

Presbyterian meeting house, but a year later 'May 6 1763. Mr Ollive desired me to take off the Licence for Oathall and says Lady Huntingdon desires it should be done.'[34] She was still a convinced member of the Church of England, and it is uncertain whether she allowed Howell Harris, a layman, to preach in her chapels at this period. In 1765 she built a chapel at Bath, and in 1769 another at Tunbridge Wells.[35] Little is known about the financial arrangements which she made for the erection of these buildings, but the only other chapel built entirely at her expense was at Swansea in 1789. All her other chapels were either existing buildings (which she usually leased) or chapels erected at the expense of others. Amongst the Hastings papers there is the plan of a meeting house which it was proposed to build at Markfield in 1761, but her involvement in this is uncertain and there is no evidence that it was ever built.[36]

These early chapels were planned as meeting-places for societies, the members of which would continue as loyal Anglicans and attend the parish services. However, from the beginning visiting evangelical ministers preached there outside regular church hours, and occasionally even administered the sacrament. The chapels also became centres for evangelism in the area. In 1768 ministers from Brighton preached in a private house at Rottingdean – the owner of which objected to Rowland Hill's 'many Theatrical Airs and ungarded Expressions'.[37] Cradock Glascott preached at Arundel in the same year: 'Last Sunday after a Volley of Eggs and huzzas, which obliged us to retreat some distance from the Tree, I preached to two or three hundred in the highway, who for the [most] part were very serious and attentive [and] intreated me to come again.'[38] Lady Huntingdon often experienced difficulty in finding Methodist ministers who were prepared to preach in her chapels.[39] She was also sometimes disappointed by their failure to arrive on the day they had promised. Because of these problems she considered the idea of transferring the

[34] West Sussex RO, Ep II/25/2, p. 31. This is the only known example of a meeting house licence being cancelled. Some Wesleyan chapels were already being licensed about this time.

[35] A 'model' of the proposed chapel was sent to her by Mr Harman (Cheshunt archives, F 1/1185). Bath chapel is now used as a community centre, but the one at Tunbridge Wells has been demolished.

[36] Hunt. Lib., HAM, box 53, 33.

[37] Cheshunt archives, F 1/34, Henry Peckham to Lady H., 14 June 1768. Other congregations were to make this complaint in later years.

[38] Cheshunt archives, F 1/1440, Glascott to Lady H., 28 July 1768.

[39] JRL, Meth. Archives, Hunt. 79, Lady H. to C. Wesley, 4 February 1767; Cheshunt archives, F 1/1391, Venn to Lady H., 29 August 1769; F 1/25, John Lloyd to Lady H., 21 March 1768.

chapels to John Wesley's care. This alarmed the Revd Thomas Maxfield because he had quarrelled with Wesley and joined Lady Huntingdon:

> to Day a Friend of mine told me that One of Mr Wesleys Stewards, told him a few days since, that Mr John Wesley was sent for to Town, by his Brother, to have the Chapel at Bath (if not that at Brighthelmstone also) to be made over to him ... and that he is to supply it for the Time to come, with such Preachers as he sees good. And he supposed that I should not be desired to go either to Bath, or to Brighthelmstone any more.[40]

In the event she did not turn her chapels over to Wesley, and a few years later she was even being asked whether John Wesley should be allowed to preach at Tunbridge Wells.[41] A new generation of Methodist preachers, of whom Maxfield was one, were itinerating for her and they proved more amenable to her wishes.

One of these preachers was her cousin, the Revd Walter Shirley. He was a son of Lawrence Shirley, and younger brother of the fourth Earl Ferrers. After graduating at New College, Oxford in 1746, he was given the family living of Loughrea in Ireland. According to tradition he kept a pack of hounds there until he became a Methodist. It was Walter Shirley whom she described to Thomas Priestley: 'There never was known to be but one person of the family, besides herself, who had the appearance of the fear of God.' His first acquaintance in the Hastings family was Lady Huntingdon's son, and the Countess first met him in 1755.[42] After Lady Huntingdon began to build chapels Shirley employed curates in Ireland and spent much of his time serving her societies in England. One of his curates was Richard De Courcy, a graduate of Trinity College, Dublin, who had his licence to preach at Loughrea taken away because of his Methodism, and who followed Walter Shirley to England. In 1769 he began preaching for the Countess at Brighton.[43] Two descriptions of De Courcy have been preserved, both unflattering, but he was one of her ministers who never quarrelled with her.[44] Another of the Countess's

---

[40] Cheshunt archives, F 1/1394, Maxfield to Lady H., 29 August 1766.
[41] Cheshunt archives, F 1/80, A. E. Godde to Lady H., 26 November 1769.
[42] Drew Univ. A 67, Lady H. to Lord H., 21 July 1755; C. H. Crookshank, *The History of Methodism in Ireland* (Belfast, 1885), 130; *Stemmata Shirleiana* (1841), 156. T. Priestley, *A Crown of Eternal Glory* (London, 1791), 25. The quotation is somewhat misleading. Lady Huntingdon was referring to the Shirley and not the Hastings family.
[43] Crookshank, op. cit., 201; Cheshunt archives, F 1/69, De Courcy to Lady H., 8 June 1769; G. D. Burtchell and T. U. Sadleir, *Alumni Dublinenses* (London, 1924), 220.
[44] Beds. RO, L 30/9/17/160, Lady Gray to Lord Breadalbane, 25 July 1771; B. Andrews (ed.), *The Torrington Diaries*, 3 (1938), 234. De Courcy is one of the few preachers for whom descriptions of this kind have survived.

relations who preached for her for many years was Thomas Wills. He was one of the group of Cornish Methodists inspired by the example of Samuel Walker, and became curate at St Agnes in Cornwall. In 1772 he met Selina Wheler, Lady Huntingdon's niece, while on a visit to Bath. Two years later he returned to Bath and married her. In 1778 he left his curacy to preach for Lady Huntingdon.[45]

Laurence Coughlan and Thomas Maxfield were two of John Wesley's preachers who preached for the Countess after he denounced them for disagreeing with him on the subject of Perfection. Coughlan later went as a missionary to Newfoundland, and Maxfield ministered to a chapel in London.[46] Other ministers who served the Countess at this time were Henry Peckwell, Thomas Pentycross and Cradock Glascott. Henry Peckwell, the son of a Chichester gentleman, studied at that Methodist stronghold, St Edmund Hall. He built a chapel at Chichester which became part of the Connexion, but was reluctant to give up to the Countess his chapel at Westminster.[47] Thomas Pentycross, the son of a London merchant, preached for the Countess both before and after he became rector of Wallingford in Berkshire.[48] Cradock Glascott, a Welshman, left the Connexion during the secession crisis to become vicar of Hatherleigh in Devon, but he remained a Methodist, continued to preach for the Countess and later welcomed the Bible Christians to his parish.[49] All these young ministers were as much the objects of the Countess's affection as the students at her College were to be later. All (except Walter Shirley, who died in 1786) eventually left her Connexion; not all remained her friends.

Another friendship which endured until the Countess's death was with the Revd Thomas Haweis, but in its early years it was neither very close nor happy. Haweis was the principal character on the Methodist side in the dispute about the presentation to Aldwinkle All Saints, which provided the enemies of Methodism with much ammunition. The Aldwinkle affair also marks the first time that Lady Huntingdon took action contrary

---

[45] *Memoirs of the Life of Rev. Thomas Wills ... by a Friend* (London, 1804), 12–18; W. Wilson, *The History and Antiquities of Dissenting Churches and Meeting Houses in London*, 3 (London, 1808), 118, 119.

[46] I am indebted to Dr Hans Rollman of Memorial University, St John's, Newfoundland for allowing me to read an advance copy of his paper on 'Laurence Coughlan and the Origins of Methodism in Newfoundland' (1990). Crookshank, op. cit., 190; Rack, *Reasonable Enthusiast*, 210, 334.

[47] J. S. Reynolds, *The Evangelicals at Oxford* (Oxford, 1953), 44. In 1776 Peckwell became rector of Bloxham (Lincs.).

[48] JRL, Meth. Archives, PLP 83, 20, 1.

[49] *Methodist Historical Soc. of the Plymouth and Exeter District*, 7 (1988), 8.

to the wishes of some Methodist leaders. At the age of sixty-one, she at last felt able to come to a decision on a public matter. In doing so she settled a controversy which might have dragged on for many years to the detriment of the Methodist cause, but she annoyed Thomas Haweis.

The Aldwinkle affair turned on a complicated, and not entirely resolved, legal problem, and the causes of the dispute have been completely obscured by the incorrect account printed by Seymour.[50] Aldwinkle is still a small, quiet village in Northamptonshire, having two parish churches – one at each end of the village street. The advowson of All Saints belonged at the end of the seventeenth century to Miles Fleetwood, a nephew of Oliver Cromwell's general. One of his sons, Charles William Fleetwood, was the vicar of All Saints, but the advowson itself had passed to another son. He had three daughters, one of whom married John Kimpton, a fellmonger of London and a dissenter.[51] His other two daughters were unmarried. In 1748 the three daughters inherited the advowson. According to his widow, Kimpton had been 'cordially intimate' with his father-in-law, but all this changed on William's death. Kimpton produced a new will disinheriting the widow. He drove her from the family home, did not attend his father-in-law's funeral and behaved insolently and morosely.[52] It is clear from this and other information that the Fleetwood family was not very prosperous, and the advowson of All Saints was probably the only remaining piece of property of value.

In 1763 Kimpton concocted a plan to buy the shares of his two sisters-in-law in the advowson for £700. He would then sell it for £1,100 thus providing himself with a comfortable profit. Since the incumbent, his wife's uncle, was elderly, the value was considerably higher than if the vicar had been a young man. However Kimpton was obliged to borrow the £700 which he needed to pay his sisters-in-law. His plan, simple in essence, was dogged by legal complications. The widow discovered that if the advowson was sold, she could claim part of the purchase price as dower.[53] Kimpton stated that he did not obtain a clear title to the advowson until early in 1764, but the Revd C. W. Fleetwood died at

[50] See Seymour, *Life and Times*, vol. 1, p. 413, where Kimpton is described as the vicar of Aldwinkle.
[51] For the Fleetwood family see A. J. Shirren, *The Chronicles of Fleetwood House* (London, 1951), 176–82; *Northants. Notes & Queries* (1905–6). In the composition with his creditors Kimpton is described as a fellmonger of Stratford in the parish of West Ham, but such descriptions of bankrupts are not always reliable.
[52] Cheshunt archives E 2/1, 10, printed legal opinion of R. Wilbraham, 16 November 1767.
[53] *A Letter to The Rev. Mr Madan. occasioned by reading two Pamphlets relative to the Presentation to the Rectory of Aldwinkle. By the Widow of the late Mr Fleetwood* (London, 1767).

Finchley on 30 August 1763. There had been 'no great harmony between the two families' and the owners of the advowson first heard of their uncle's death through the newspapers.[54] According to ecclesiastical law the advowson was unsaleable until the benefice had been filled. Kimpton now faced a dilemma. If he presented a younger man to the benefice it would reduce the amount he would receive when he sold the advowson, but if he did not present within six months, then the bishop of Peterborough could fill the vacancy.[55] However there was a legal solution to the problem. Kimpton could take a bond from anyone he presented to the bishop that he would resign whenever the patron requested, or alternatively pay a large sum in damages. In 1618 the court of King's Bench had declared such bonds illegal, but by the end of the century they were apparently in frequent use by patrons.[56] Although it was more usual for the benefice to be held until a member of the family was old enough to obtain orders, there was little to prevent Kimpton from using the same device. Even in Methodist eyes it could be justified if it enabled an evangelical clergyman to occupy the church for a time.

Kimpton's nonconformity meant that he was not well acquainted with ecclesiastical law and not particularly acceptable to the bishop. He did not seek a lawyer's advice, possibly from lack of funds, and the bishop of Peterborough was prepared to put every difficulty in his way. When Kimpton approached a Mr Elliott to hold the benefice until he could sell it, the bishop disapproved and Elliott withdrew; and when Kimpton finally presented Thomas Haweis, the bishop insisted on a searching examination of a kind unusual for those times.[57] The bishop was principally concerned with the possibility of simony, although this was an issue rarely raised in the eighteenth century.[58] Early in 1764, with only a few days remaining before the benefice lapsed to the bishop, Kimpton took the problem to his minister, the Revd Samuel Brewer of Mile End.

[54] *A Faithful Narrative of Facts, relative to the late Presentation of Mr H – s to the Rectory of Al – w – le* (London, 1767), 2.
[55] For a cynical view of the sale of advowsons in the next century see 'The Revd Simon Magus', in W. S. Gilbert's *The Bab Ballads*.
[56] W. Gibson, 'Dangerous Snares', *Journal of Soc. of Archivists*, 10 (1989) 26, 27 Richard Burns, *Ecclesiastical Law* (London, 1763), vol. 2, p. 346. Even a Methodist would hold a benefice on these terms (E. Sidney, *The Life and Ministry of Rev. Samuel Walker* (London, 1838), 4).
[57] *An Answer to a Pamphlet, Intitled A Faithful Narrative* ... (London, 1767), xi, 8.
[58] In the diocese of Norwich the oath against simony was only administered once in the eighteenth century (E. H. Carter, *The Norwich Subscription Books* (London, 1937), 17, 32). Burns, op. cit., vol. 2, pp. 334–45. See also Thomas Ken, *Ichabod or the Five Groans of the Church* (1663).

Brewer was completely out of his depth and sent Kimpton to an evangelical Anglican friend, the Revd Martin Madan, at the Lock Hospital. Madan was then its chaplain, and also one of Lady Huntingdon's chaplains.[59] Although Madan had trained as a lawyer and subsequently been ordained, he had no experience of parish work or the legal complexities of holding a benefice. In addition he had an uncompromising and determined character of a kind which later caused him to write a book in favour of polygamy because he felt it was an acceptable alternative to prostitution.[60] On 17 February 1764 Kimpton met Madan at the Lock after the evening service and explained his dilemma. Madan's first reaction was to send for the 'great book of common prayer' out of the chapel and read a denunciation of simony from it, probably canon 40 of 1603.[61] He then took Kimpton into the vestry, where his assistant, the Revd Thomas Haweis was sitting after preaching the evening sermon. As Haweis recalled the incident many years later,

> Mr Madan brought into me with him a Man whom I had never before seen, and informed me he was the Patron of a Living, and by Mr Brewer's recommendation of him as a very serious Man, who had the living of Aldwinckle All saints to dispose of, and it was near a Lapse; he had come to consult him (Mr M) on that subject and he had told him, as he must present, he knew of no person he could more cordially recommend than myself. The Man, a Dissenter told us a long story of a treaty he had been in with a person who had failed him, and that he wished to prevent the living from a Lapse if I would hold it for him. Mr Madan said all such traffic as he had been engaged in was illegal. He professed his ignorance, and that he would on no account do a wrong thing. My friend thought me rather uncivil in my reply, which was to this purpose, without thought and on the impulse of the moment, Sir if I could stand in the Gap for you I would, but if the Matter is as my friend says, you must if I take it give it me out and out, or seek some body else.[62]

According to Kimpton, on the other hand, Haweis said, 'I am very willing to stand in the gap', and Madan added that if bonds of resignation were legal, he would have acted as Haweis's bondsman.[63] If we accept both accounts, written after the event, as correct then there was a serious misunderstanding of intentions. Madan thought he had made it clear that Kimpton's proposal was completely unacceptable; whereas Kimpton

---

[59] Lamb. Pal. Lib., Faculties, register of chaplains, 5 October 1761.
[60] *Thelyphthora* (1780).
[61] *An Answer*, op. cit., 1, 4. As the Book of Common Prayer does not usually contain the institution service, it is unlikely that Madan read the oath against simony.
[62] Mitchell Lib., Haweis MS, autobiography, chapter 9. This was written much later and contains several errors of fact.
[63] *A Faithful Narrative*, op. cit., 4.

believed that Madan was willing to evade the law by a gentleman's agreement. Alternatively, Kimpton, being later faced with heavy debts, revised what had been said to suit his own ends; Haweis undoubtedly made his account as much as possible on the other side.

Thomas Haweis was the son of a Cornish lawyer who had lost the remnants of the family fortune 'by a series of improvidences'.[64] He was educated at Truro where he came under the influence of two evangelical clergymen – his headmaster, George Conon, and the curate of St Mary's, Samuel Walker. He went to Oxford in 1755 to train for the ministry. Like Madan he was a man of strong views, and in his first curacy in Oxford he succeeded in irritating both undergraduates and his bishop.[65] Driven out of the diocese, he took refuge with Madan at the Lock. Haweis was no more fitted to advise Kimpton than was Madan. They had decided that what Kimpton wished to do was both immoral and illegal, but they made no effort to help him to find a way out of his difficulties. As was suggested later, Madan might have suggested a more suitable candidate than Haweis, who was very young to receive such preferment and was to live another fifty-six years as vicar of Aldwinkle All Saints.[66] Neither did Madan help Haweis, who, as the result of the subsequent scandal, received no further preferment in the Church.

For the events of the next few days there are two conflicting accounts, both written after the event and intended to justify either Madan and Haweis or Brewer and Kimpton. Haweis alleged that he had a dispute about dilapidations to the vicarage with the last incumbent's widow and eventually spent £300 himself on repairs. He also claimed that Kimpton had tried to make a match between his niece (said to have a fortune of £4,000) and Haweis, which the latter declined.[67] Kimpton alleged a gentleman's agreement that Haweis had made to resign whenever requested by Kimpton. Both Kimpton and Brewer (though he was not present at the interview) seem to have believed that this was Haweis's intention. After this meeting Kimpton is reported as saying:

> Mr B[rewer] I see nothing Can be Done. I shall be a Ruined man, as these Gentlemen Mr M. and Mr H. seem to be worthy men, Christians, and men of honour I will put myself into their hands and present Mr H – and Doubt not but their Humanity and goodness will be such that some how or other they will

[64] A. S. Woods, *Thomas Haweis* (London, 1957), 24.
[65] W. N. Hargreaves-Mawdsley (ed.), *Wooodforde at Oxford 1759–1776* (Oxford, 1968), 62, 63.
[66] *Aldwinkle: A Candid Examination of the Revd Mr M – n's Conduct* (London, 1767) 28; *Remarks on the Answer of the Revd Mr M – n to the Faithful Narrative* (London, 1967), 7.
[67] *An Answer*, op. cit., 9.

Either (knowing my unhappy Circumstances) make me a Compensation or Resignation some time hence.

On 20 February Madan wrote out a presentation which Kimpton signed. The bishop insisted on a bond of indemnity from Haweis before instituting him to the living on 25 February.[68] At the end of the year Kimpton became desperate for his money and several meetings between Haweis, Brewer, Madan and Kimpton led to an offer from Haweis to pay £600 for the advowson. This was rejected by Kimpton who was desperate to raise £1,100.[69] Soon rumours began to circulate in London that Haweis had a moral obligation to resign but had not done so. John Newton, the evangelical curate of Olney and a friend of Haweis, wrote that 'As to Aldwinkle, I can say no more: time will shew. I hope the Lord will direct for the best; but I can hardly either think or wish that Mr H[awei]s should have the place. I expected him and Mr M[ada]n last week; but the latter had some slight illness which prevented.'[70] At Christmas Newton was visited at Olney by Revd Samuel Brewer and Alexander Clunie, who was soon to play an important part in solving the problem of Aldwinkle. They must have discussed it then without reaching any conclusion.[71] Allegations were circulated in manuscript which must have reached Madan and Haweis, making them less likely to agree to a compromise. After two years had passed, the principal parties became involved in an open quarrel.[72] The Kimpton party now printed *A Faithful Narrative of Facts Relative to the late Presentation of Mr H – s to the Rectory* [sic] *of Al – w – le in Northamptonshire*. This was the beginning of a pamphlet war which included Mrs Fleetwood's denunciation of Kimpton. Haweis complained that Kimpton was making his life at Aldwinkle difficult.[73] Both Newton and William Cowper the poet, who was Madan's cousin, were caught up in the controversy.

As early as April 1766 Lady Huntingdon was attempting to solve the problem.

---

[68] *A Faithful Narrative*, op. cit., 7, 8; Northants. RO, Episc. A5/8/5.
[69] Cheshunt archives, E2/1, 2, letter of Clunie to Brewer, 15 January 1768, quoting from *A Faithful Narrative*.
[70] *The Christian Correspondent* (Hull, 1790), 87.
[71] J. Bull, *John Newton* (London, 1868), 142, 146.
[72] *An Exact Copy of an Epistolary Correspondence between the Rev. Mr M – and S – B –* (London, 1768), 5; Gillies, *Whitefield's Letters*, vol. 2, p. 342; *An Exact Copy*, 7–23; *A Correspondence* (London, 1768), 14, 47.
[73] Cheshunt archives, E 2/1, 1, letter of Clunie to Brewer, 10 December 1767; *Christian Correspondent*, op. cit., 31; Birmingham Univ. Lib., Venn papers, C 11/2, Venn to Miss Wheler, 8 April 1766.

L[ord] D[artmouth] was with me for two hours the other morning but Mr W – being hear it ended in nothing but a desire from him that I would speak my sentiments to our friend fully on the All[dwin]kle affair which does make a dreadfull noise and has so very [*illeg.*] appearances against H[aweis] and our friend that all dread the publication of it.[74]

She proposed that Haweis should resign Aldwinkle and go to Pennsylvania to take charge of 'the great Church' there. Brewer, also a peacemaker, was anxious to find a compromise which would release Kimpton from his burden of debt without involving Madan and Haweis in further scandal. To this end he persuaded two London Methodists, Daniel West, a member of the Tabernacle congregation, and Captain Alexander Clunie, a friend and correspondent of John Newton, and a member of Brewer's congregation, to negotiate a settlement.[75] Both George Whitefield and John Thornton also became involved. Little would be known of the negotiations but for five letters of Clunie to Brewer of which copies were given to Lady Huntingdon. On 10 December 1767 Clunie reported on a meeting with Madan at the Lock at which the latter refused to make any payment to Kimpton even though they might 'Cut and mangle him to Death'.[76] It must have been about this time that Kimpton, unable to repay the £700, was imprisoned for debt, which added to the scandal and made efforts to reach a settlement even more urgent. The scandal affected both the Methodists and the Dissenters. In London they felt its effects very severely. The leaders both of the London Dissenters and the Tabernacle tried for an accommodation, but Madan escalated the controversy because one of his relations was standing for Parliament. To avoid its becoming an issue at the election, Madan proposed to sue one of his detractors for libel and justify his actions in open court.[77]

It was shortly after this, at the end of February, that Lady Huntingdon intervened. Although she had given Madan her opinion the previous April, as she was entitled to do to one who was her chaplain, she had not made it public at that time. At an interview she had said that 'she could not see how Mr Haweis as an honest man could continue to keep that living.' She had also proposed that Kimpton should go to the bishop of Peterborough and state that simony was not involved in the presentation. This

[74] SMU, Hunt. 68, Lady H. to Mrs Wadsworth, 15 April 1766.
[75] Daniel West and Robert Keen were Whitefield's (and later the Countess's) London agents for Bethesda. Both were members of the Tabernacle congregation. Clunie had first met Newton in the West Indies. For Capt. Clunie see B. Martin, *An Ancient Mariner* (London, 1950), chapter 16.
[76] Cheshunt archives, E 2/1, 1–4.
[77] Cheshunt archives, E 2/1, 2; E2/1, 5, letter of Clunie to Brewer, 21 January 1768.

would leave the way open for Haweis to submit his resignation to the bishop, who might either accept or refuse it. It was very close to the compromise later suggested by Clunie, but was not acceptable to either side. She said no more, but 'became satisfied to share in the certain shame or reproach so many of God's people' would endure as a result of the scandal.[78] Now by February 1768 she had decided that drastic action was needed to help 'a miserable family and to stop all further grief to Gods people'. Without any consultation with Madan or anyone else involved she decided to buy the advowson herself. On 1 March she sent a bank draft for £1,000 to John Thornton by the hand of George Whitefield, and instructed Thornton to use the money to pay off Kimpton's creditors. At the same time she notified Lord Dartmouth, who had apparently been drawn into the negotiations, of her intentions.[79] On the following day, after arrangements had begun, she informed Madan by letter, and exhorted him and Haweis 'to make every proper and publick concession to the world for any *Conscious* Infirmity, weakness, Temptation or mistaken Step through this Transaction'.[80] Madan's reply was not friendly:

> Your Ladyship acquaints me that you have sent £1000, for the purchase of the Advowson of Aldwinkle. This step your Ladyship may have taken with the best intentions – but, under all the circumstances of the case, it is very evident to me, that the necessary consequence of it will be an increase of reproach and injury to my Friend Mr Haweis's Character, and my own: and therefore I hope your Ladyship will do us the Justice, upon all Occasions to declare, that this Step has been taken without our knowledge, privity, consent, or Approbation...
>
> As to the *concessions* which your Ladyship is pleased to mention, as we do not conceive we have any to make, so we must assure you that none can ever be made, by *us* I mean, for I by no means despair, that some may appear on the other side of the Question, when conscience shall do its Office in respect to the Wrongs we have sustain'd, and our just dealing shall be as the Noonday Sun.[81]

Kimpton's friends were delighted that 'poor Kimpton has found so Noble and generous a Friend as Lady Huntingdon'.[82] In a remarkably quick operation Kimpton's creditors signed a composition for 11*s.* in the pound by 21 April, and all were paid by the end of the year. A meeting was called at the White Hart Tavern in Bishopsgate Street, counsel were employed

[78] Cheshunt archives, E 2/1, 6, letter of Lady H. to Madan, 2 March 1768.
[79] Cheshunt archives, E 2/1, 8, letter of Lady H. to Thornton; E2/1, 9, Thornton's reply, n.d.; E2/1, 11, Lady H's draft to Lord Dartmouth, 1 March 1768. The original letter to Lord D. is in Staffs. RO, D(W) 1778/111/246.
[80] Cheshunt archives, E 2/1, 6.
[81] Cheshunt archives, E 2/1, 7, Madan to Lady H., 3 March 1768.
[82] Cheshunt archives, E 2/2, 1, Yorke to West, 10 March 1768.

to investigate Kimpton's title to the advowson, and enquiries were made both in Northamptonshire and Leicestershire before a deed conveying the patronage of Aldwinkle to the Countess was drawn up. On 7 December all was settled, and attempts were made to stop the flow of pamphlets and libels.[83] In May John Thornton wrote to the Countess about Kimpton 'I am afraid he is of an unsubdued Spirit and not much to be trusted further than Intrest may bind him and therefore Mr Whitefield and I were afraid he would make an improper use of your Ladyships Letter which upon that account he with held from him.'[84]

Of the characters involved in this affair, John Kimpton disappears from the scene. Thomas Haweis reappeared at a later date as a friend of the Countess, and was eventually a trustee of the Connexion. The advowson of Aldwinkle was transferred by the Countess to her relation and supporter, the Revd Walter Shirley with the intention that he would present himself to the living after Haweis's death or resignation.[85] This would have enabled him to give up his Irish living and to spend more time in serving her chapels in England. However Haweis lived on as vicar of Aldwinkle until 1820, long after Shirley had died. His son, another Revd Walter Shirley, finally sold the patronage in 1810 for £3,850 to pay off his mother's debts.[86] The scandal, though no longer fuelled by pamphlets, lingered on for many years. Ten years later Samuel Foote when recommending a new career for Invoice in his *Devil upon two Sticks* suggested that of Methodist preacher, for whom there was only one sin to be avoided – simony: 'Simony, Sir, is a new kind of canon, devised by those upstart fanatics, that makes it sinful not to abuse the confidence, and piously plunder the little property of an indigent man and his family.'[87]

---

[83] Cheshunt archives, E 2/2, 2, original composition with creditors, 21 April 1768; Leics. RO, 26D53/2123a, lawyer's bill; Cheshunt archives, E 2/2, 3, accounts with creditors, n.d.
[84] Cheshunt archives, E 2/2, 6, Thornton to Lady H., 20 May 1768.
[85] Leics. RO, 26D53/2119, 2, Lady Moira to Walter Shirley, 22 January 1801.
[86] Leics. RO, 26D53/2123a, Walter Shirley's accounts of his debts.
[87] S. Foote, *The Devil upon two Sticks* (London, 1778), 67 (quoted in A. M. Lyles, *Methodism Mocked* (London, 1960), 69).

7

The College at Trefeca

Almost the last letter written about the Aldwinkle affair, that from John Thornton to the Countess, relates to her next independent action:

> My Friend Dr Dixon is somewhat discouraged on now finding his young Men leave him, the heads of the Houses having taken off the restriction they had laid themselves under of receiving none of the Students from St Edmunds Hall, but he seems to wish to act his part faithfully and to commit the Issue to the Lord, I assured him if your Ladyship sent the two Young Men you once mentioned to the University I was persuaded you would on no consideration send them to any other College.[1]

Dr George Dixon was the Principal of St Edmund Hall in Oxford, which had become a sanctuary for evangelical students. The Hall was noted for its commitment to religion, and had previously been a home for the non-jurors. Dixon himself was described as devout, kindly and sympathetic.[2] As Thornton's letter shows, the heads of the other colleges had been opposed to his support of the Methodists, but were now beginning to soften their hostility. However the entire controversy was in the process of being revived by the actions of Dixon's vice-principal, the Revd John Higson of Wadham College. He was opposed to Methodism, but also seems to have had a personal grudge against some of the students. Getting no satisfaction from Dixon in his attempt to root out Methodism, on 29 February 1768 Higson made a formal complaint against seven of the students to the Vice-Chancellor.

He alleged that John Matthews, Thomas Jones and Joseph Shipman had been bred to trades, that these three and Erasmus Middleton and

---

[1] Cheshunt archives, E 2/2, 6, Thornton to Lady H., 20 May 1768.
[2] S. L. Ollard, *The Six Students of St Edmund Hall expelled from the University of Oxford* (London, 1911), 4. This gives a full account of the incident. Dixon's predecessor at St Edmund Hall, Dr Fothergill, subscribed to Thomas Hartley's *Sermons on Various Subjects* (1754) together with many other Methodists and their sympathizers.

Benjamin Blatch had no knowledge of Latin and Greek, and that all except Blatch had preached illicitly and were enemies of the Church of England. Two other students, Benjamin Kay and Thomas Grove, were also accused of preaching although unordained.[3] The charges against Blatch were abandoned since he chose to leave the University, but the other six were cited to appear before the Vice-Chancellor and his assessors on 11 March. Although the charges were not particularly serious by the standards of the period, all six were found guilty and expelled from the university. The proceedings excited a great deal of interest, and a pamphlet war began. It was soon alleged that Lady Huntingdon was financing their education at Oxford, but this was untrue.[4] Matthews and Shipman were protégés of the Revd Edward Davies, a friend of the Countess and vicar of Bengeworth near Evesham.[5] Thomas Jones had been at Olney under the tuition of John Newton, and returned there after his expulsion. Little is known of the origins of the other three. None of the six is known to have corresponded with the Countess before the expulsion,[6] and only two of the six students, Shipman and Matthews, went to the Countess's college when it opened in the summer of 1768. The Countess did not enter into the controversy, but continued her efforts to provide an alternative to Oxford and Cambridge for training Methodist evangelists. Her interest in this can be traced back to Howell Harris – the man who had been so horrified by what he saw that he remained at Oxford only a few weeks. Harris's diaries abound with evidence of his enthusiasm for Francke's *paedagogium* and his wish to establish one at Trefeca, but it is not always clear if he meant a grammar school, a theological college or a combination of both. Twenty years earlier, for example, he confided to his diary: 'To Glanyrafon-Ddu-Ganol where I had especial freedom to cry for a school at Trevecka to train young men to the Lord.'[7] By 1761 this had become 'an Academy for preachers' which was to be attached to his

---

[3] [Richard Hill], *Pietas Oxoniensis: or a Full and Impartial Account of the Expulsion of Six Students* ... (London, 1768), 8, 9.

[4] *The Annals of a Yorkshire House* (London, 1911), vol.1, pp. 227, 228.

[5] J. P. Shawcross and E. A. B. Barnard, *Bengeworth* (Evesham, 1927). Shipman wrote to Lady H. from Davies's house in 1767 (Cheshunt archives, E 4/5, 1) and Matthews sent a message from Davies to Lady H. in 1768 (Cheshunt archives, F 1/26). Davies afterwards became rector of Coychurch in Glamorgan (G. Redford, *The Autobiography of William Jay* (London, 1974), 91).

[6] Cheshunt archives, E 4/5, 1, Shipman to Lady H., 26 March 1767 [sic]. Since this letter speaks of his 're-admission into the University and Church of England' it was probably written in 1768.

[7] T. Beynon (ed.), *Howell Harris's Visits to Pembrokeshire* (Aberystwyth, 1966), 158.

settlement at Trefeca, and after renewing his friendship with the Countess in 1763 he began to impress her with the need for such an academy.[8]

Towards the end of 1764 Lady Huntingdon was already seeking a man who could take charge of such an institution. She approached Francis Okely of Bedford, probably at Harris's suggestion.[9] Okely had joined the Moravians, but left them in 1757 to preach for John Wesley for a brief period. He then returned to Bedford, where the Moravians allowed him to open a school.[10] As a Cambridge graduate with teaching experience and an evangelical, Okely met the Countess's requirements. His interest in the German Pietists may also have appealed to her. But Okely was concerned about the arrangements for the college, as he explained to Howell Harris:

> In a Letter from L. Huntingdon of December 27, she acquaints me, that she has transmitted to you my Answer to her upon a Proposal made to Me; to which it seems you are no Stranger. As I am desir'd by her Ladyship to request further Information upon that Head and settle all Preliminaries with you, and then let her know the Result: I beg the Favour of you to give me all necessary Knowledge of the Affair, in a still and private Manner; that (if of God) it may arrive at due Maturity to lay before the Brethren... Pray will the Tutors House be furnished?...[11]

Three months later he wrote to Harris declining the honour.[12]

Nothing more happened until 1767 when Lady Huntingdon approached the Revd John William Fletcher, the vicar of Madeley.[13] He had corresponded with the Countess for 'several years, and she had offered him employment as tutor to her nephew in 1760.[14] At the beginning of June 1767, when on her way to visit Edward Davies at Bengeworth and her sister Lady Kilmorey in Shropshire, she stopped at

---

[8] T. Beynon, *Howell Harris, Reformer and Soldier* (Caernarvon, 1958), 114, 197.

[9] Harris had met Okely at the Swan Inn in Bedford, probably in October 1763 (M. H. Jones, *The Itinerary of Howell Harris*, pt 3, Connexional Press, Caernarvon, 1927, p.25); JRL, Meth. Archives, Hunt. 70, Lady H. to C. Wesley, [7] December 1758.

[10] For Okely see E. Welch, *The Bedford Moravian Church* (Bedford, 1989) 6–9, 153.

[11] G. M. Roberts (ed.) *Selected Trevecka Letters*, 2 (Caernarvon, 1956), 99, 100, quoting Trevecka letter 2593 (5 January 1765).

[12] Ibid., 102, quoting Trevecka letter 2599 (10 April 1765).

[13] For Fletcher see P. P. Streiff, *Jean Guillaume de la Fléchère. John William Fletcher* (Frankfurt am Main, 1984) and J. Benson, *The Life of the Rev. John W. de la Fléchère* (London, many editions).

[14] Copies of Fletcher's letters to the Countess can be found in JRL, Meth. Archives and Connexion archives 3. The latter does not contain as many letters, but is a more accurate transcript than the former, which was prepared for publication by A. C. H. Seymour. JRL, Meth. Archives, 392/89, Fletcher to C. Wesley, 14 September 1760.

Madeley.[15] While staying with Fletcher, Abiah Darby, wife of the Quaker ironfounder of Madeley, offered her the use of a carriage,[16] but there is no report of her discussions with Fletcher. However, while at Madeley, the Countess wrote to Mrs Harris at Trefeca about the project, and spoke of Hannah Bowen, the Family's housekeeper, as a suitable housekeeper for the college.[17] Five months later her plans were well under way. Fletcher agreed to help the project and proposed James Glazebrook, a collier from Madeley, as a student.[18] In December 1767, before the expulsions from St Edmund Hall, work had begun on the college buildings.

It was inevitable that the College would be at Trefeca, where Howell Harris could provide both advice and supervision. On 17 December Lady Huntingdon assured Howell Harris that all was going well:

> Seven young men I have heard of that I believe really are precious souls. Mr Fletcher sends [one]. Dr Conyers another two from Bristol ... I have ordered my bit of furniture linning etc. that can be wanted and I hope all can be ready by the first or second week of May ... Mr Fletcher has agreed to give us all assistance ... I trust it will be the mind of you all by the children of the Lord to give dear Hanah Bowen as housekeeper.[19]

The building chosen was Trefeca Isaf (now known as College Farm) about 500 yards nearer to Talgarth than Harris's settlement on the road from Talgarth to Llangorse. It is a sixteenth-century building.[20] The original farmhouse had a central hall, with rooms at either end. The hall became a chapel and 'gothick' windows were added there and at the south end of the building. An extension at the back of the chapel provided rooms for the students. The north end was probably reserved for the Countess, Fletcher and visiting preachers.[21] Howell Harris had leased the house, then called Lower Trefeca, and extensive lands in 1765 for twenty-one years from his elder brother Thomas, and in October 1768 he sublet the house, orchard and a part of the land to the Countess for the remainder of

---

[15] NLW, Trev. letter 2627; Lady H. to H. Harris, 1 June 1767; part printed in *Sel. Trev. Letters*, 2, op. cit., 111.
[16] Friends House Library, MS vol.310, 1 June 1767, printed in R. Labouchere, *Abiah Darby* (York, 1988), 152.
[17] NLW, Trev. letter 2627, Lady H. to H. Harris, 1 June 1767 (includes a message to Mrs Harris).
[18] Connexion archives 3, copy of letter of Fletcher to Lady H., 24 November 1767.
[19] NLW, Trev. letter 2635, Lady H. to H. Harris, 17 December 1767, printed in *Sel. Trev. Letters*, 2, op. cit., 115–16. As Mr Roberts there remarks, the letter is very difficult to decipher.
[20] For a description of the house see J. T. Smith, 'The Houses of Breconshire' (*Brycheiniog*, 10 (1964), 90–4). The date of 1576, now illegible, was originally read as 1176.
[21] In 1986 the building was in need of urgent repairs. The original fittings of the chapel were still *in situ*, but the Countess's additions were too dangerous for access.

his lease at ten guineas a year. This sublease expired in September 1786, but the Countess continued as a yearly tenant of the new owner, a Mr Hughes, who was probably the husband of Howell Harris's niece.[22]

Howell Harris supervised the building work for the Countess. He later prepared 'Lady Huntingdon's accounts ballanc'd to March 24/1769', but the document has been damaged and is now partly illegible. Work began on the alterations on 1 December 1767 and continued until 26 November 1768 at a cost of £550, and another £100 was spent on furniture The chapel was not completed until the day before the college opened. Howell Harris also spent £114 on housekeeping from the opening of the College on 24 August 1768 to 24 March 1769.[23] The Countess kept a careful eye on all the details relating to her college. On 4 June she wrote a long letter to Howell Harris about the domestic arrangements:

> Mrs Leighton will mention the servants that she thought might be wanting, but I have thought by another scheme it might be better managed, on further thoughts about Dear Hannah Bowen I have considered some difficultys attending her situation and that upon the which it might not do so well, she is too young a woman and being rather more amiable than the generality of her orders it might be a great temptation to her and more so to Trusty young men that she must of necessity be much with.[24]

Instead she had selected a Mrs Bowlling, who had spent all her life 'in great familys'. With her, Lady Huntingdon would not have to concern herself with domestic arrangements even when at Trefeca. Mrs Bowlling would find a cook 'of the same stamp' and 'a boy to go of errands and bring Coles, water, etc., and the young man is to help, that more than those three I will not hear of and but these 2 women, unless on a washing day or a brewing, and then the present help and no more'. The final section of her letter is concerned with the teaching:

---

[22] Connexion archives, College lease, 1768; Cheshunt archives F 1/47, Lloyd to Lady H., 21 January 1769; A 2/4 and 5, vouchers, 1770; F 1/2043, A. Powell to Lady H., 2 October 1788. Gareth Davies, in 'Trevecka', *Brycheiniog*, 15 (1971), 45 states that the owner was Thomas Harris, and John Bulmer in *Memoirs of the Life and Religious Labours of Howell Harris Esq.* (Haverfordwest, 1824), 62, says it was rented from Howell Harris. Both are therefore correct. The Apostolic Society minute book (Cheshunt archives C 1/1, p. 51), which records the negotiations for terminating the tenancy in 1792, gives the owner as Mr Hughes. He was probably Samuel Hughes, who married Joseph Harris's daughter (M. H. Jones, *The Trevecka Letters* (Caernarvon, 1932), 47).

[23] NLW, Trev. letter 3227 is a summary account. It would appear that Harris wrote this for his own information, because most of the sums are round figures. See also NLW, Trev. diary 250.

[24] NLW, Trev. letter 2642, Lady H. to H. Harris, 4 June 1768, printed in *Sel. Trev. Letters* 2, op. cit., 119–20.

I have found that less than 2 masters will not do as [torn] will want the first principles of knowledge. I have got an honest Soul, a Welsh man, who has served with great Credit in a large boarding school and has a heart to desire nothing but a Crust and Jesus Christ. He teachs writing arithmetick, Latin and the Greek testament and he is Comfortably happy by his situation. I have agreed on a supposition Mr Fletcher shall approve.[25]

The opening of the College was fixed for the Countess's birthday, 24 August, and she invited all the Methodist clergy to attend. John Wesley accepted:

> On this day se'nnight, the sixteenth instant, our Conference is to begin. What Business it may be needful for me to do immediately after, I do not know. But if nothing pressing calls me another way, I shall be glad to wait upon your Ladyship at Trefeca. And I nothing doubt, so will my Brother too.[26]

But he went to Cornwall instead. He complained to his brother about the organization of the college, and asked 'who penned it, man or woman?'[27] George Whitefield, who performed the opening ceremony, gave an exhortation to the students on the next day, and on 'Sunday, August 28 Preached in the court before the College (the congregation consisting of some thousands) from 1 Cor. iii. 11.'[28] The Countess had arrived at Howell Harris's house as early as 29 July together with four ladies, the schoolmaster, the housekeeper and two maids. The numbers were augmented by the arrival of twelve students during the next few weeks, so that the 'Family' provided four tables 'every day till August 24th when the Chappel was open'd and a great Congregation and publick Diner'.[29] It must have been a busy time for the settlement, and there is a note of relief when all were safely settled in Trefeca Isaf. The Countess left Trefeca for Tunbridge Wells, where she was to open her chapel, on 27 September. She had finally decided to take Hannah Bowen as the College housekeeper, and E. Roberts as the steward. She took

> B: Roberts (E. Roberts Son) with her as her footman and one of our women as her maid at Trefeca El[izabeth] Hughes and a boy (Richard Davies's Son), and to have 2 Women to wash every fortnight, and toke 3 fields to the House and drew a Plan of a Garden, and has increased the number of students to 15.[30]

---

[25] This was probably the Mr Williams whom in September 1769 Lady H. gave over to Satan (NLW, Trev. diary 254).

[26] Cheshunt archives, G 2/1, 23, J. Wesley to Lady H., 9 August 1768.

[27] *John Wesley's Letters*, vol.5, p.88.

[28] J. Gillies (ed.), *A Select Collection of Whitefield's Letters*, vol. 3, p.373; J. Gillies, *Memoirs of the Life of the Rev. George Whitefield* (London, 1772), 254, quoting from Whitefield's memorandum book.

[29] NLW, Trev. diary 250. Unfortunately Harris did not keep a full diary for this period, only memoranda under the heading 'July 1768'.

[30] NLW, Trev. diary 250.

The garden and fields were intended to provide food for the students, and later for the Countess and her household in London.

Information on the College during the Countess's lifetime is limited by the absence of a diary or minutes, and its history must be reconstructed from letters, Howell Harris's diaries (until his death in 1773), and the occasional descriptions of visitors. Even the names of the masters and the period in which they served are uncertain. Neither can we be certain that the name of every student has survived.[31] The 'huge Plan for the Establishment of the College, printed at Bath, on a sheet of paper' which could be seen at the College has not survived.[32] Perhaps the most informative description is one written by an enemy of Methodism:

> The House, modern gothic, stands in a pleasant spot, about 3½ miles out off the Road, on the Right, exactly half way between Brecknock and Hay. At present it contains 7 students, whom I happened to find at their Studies, which were in the New Testament, both in Greek, Latin, and English. They were about 20 years of age, dressed chiefly in black, very grave and attentive to their Business. Their Master was a decent man, about 30 years of age. The Schoolroom is a very pleasant Apartment with a Collection of Books in it. Over the Chimney is a painting of Frank, a German Divine ... and there were 20 Desks in the Room. The Chapel is a neat pretty room. A handsome Eating Room, used when her Ladyship is among them, for thither she sometimes comes, and makes a short Residence. The Common Eating Room is small. The Walls of the whole House are adorned with Scripture Passages, and that selected over the Chimney in the Eating Room is, 'Feed my Sheep.' Her Ladyship's Apartment is very small, but the whole is extremely neat, and all the Rooms cheerful, calculated to improve much more lively and pleasant sentiments than seemed to reign there.[33]

For the remainder of 1768 there was a procession of evangelical clergy to the new College. Charles Wesley spent a week there in September preaching and administering the sacrament to the students. He was followed in October by Cradock Glascott.[34] John Fletcher stayed at the College until November, after which he returned to his parish, but before leaving he was able to report that an evangelical atmosphere reigned in the College. On 2 November he and Howell Harris spent the evening 'seeing students'. Harris 'had much freedom to speak on an Important

[31] For a comprehensive list of students see G. F. Nuttall, 'The Students of Trevecca College 1768–1791', *Trans. Hon. Soc. Cymmrodorion* (1967), 249–77.

[32] *Brycheiniog*, 15 (1971), 47, quoting Sir Thomas Gery Cullum in 1775. The original has not been identified, but NLW has a modern transcript. I am indebted to Mrs Beryl H. Griffiths for this information.

[33] Ibid., 46, 47. The portrait of Francke is probably the one now at Cheshunt College.

[34] NLW, Trev. diary 253.

Subject, vizt. how we need to know the Will of God'. On the following evening they heard a sermon from Fletcher 'most home indeed' on Philippians 3.3.[35] Two nights later the students had an exhortation from Howell Harris when he found his 'mouth vastly open'd indeed'. On the following day, which was Sunday, 6 November, Fletcher despaired of success in their efforts, and complained in a letter to the Countess of the 'spirit of levity, irony and trifling' in the College.[36] That evening Fletcher reproved the students one by one and suggested that Lady Huntingdon would send all but six away if they continued at 'this poor trifling formal rate'. Under this pressure two of the students proposed a day of humiliation and fasting, which Fletcher fixed for the following Wednesday. However, on Monday noon the revival began.[37] Fletcher assembled them all in his room to sing hymns and pray for five hours. After leaving they went to pray with Betty the maid, who had joined them unseen in the darkness of the study. On the next evening Howell Harris visited the college, and the students invited 'His oeconomy' (the 'Family' at his settlement) to join them in the revival. Joseph Shipman, the student from Oxford, was particularly affected by the revival which surprised Fletcher because he thought him dry and bigoted. The revival continued until at least 15 November, but Harris went on a preaching tour of south Wales, and there is no further information about its progress. The Countess spread the news of this development. In December John Berridge wrote to congratulate the Countess on 'the plentiful effusion from above on Talgarth'.[38]

However the evangelical fervour did not last long, as Berridge predicted in his letter. After Harris returned he had to reprimand Williams, Glazebrook and Aldridge for their views on Justification. In February he had difficulties with a proposal for the hand of his daughter from Mr Williams the master at the College.

> I was very home last night to Williams the Master how he had sined against the students by opening a way for them to turn to Courtship against Lady Huntingdon by bringing this to the College in its Infancy against H[annah] –

---

[35] Ibid. The text is 'For we are the circumcision, which worship God in the spirit, and rejoice in Jesus Christ, and have no confidence in the flesh.'

[36] Cheshunt archives, F1/1449, Fletcher to Lady H., 10 and 15 November 1768. There is some discrepancy between the days of the week in this letter and those given by Howell Harris in his diary.

[37] Ibid.

[38] Connexion archives 3, Berridge 17, Berridge to Lady H., 30 December 1768, printed in *Life and Times*, vol.2, p.94. This was probably the only revival at Trefeca College.

by exposing her to Bet[ty] against me in my only Child going over my head to speak to her against the child ... I said I had done with him.[39]

In July Fletcher also complained about Williams whom he thought too young and 'deficient in point of Christian experience. Nor is he a proper Master of the Classics, so that he can hardly maintain his superiority over those who read Cicero and Horace.'[40] Peace returned when Howell Harris departed on a preaching tour, but in September the same problems arose. On 13 September he reported that Williams and Hannah Bowen had been 'turned away before the College'. Harris now felt that Lady Huntingdon was unfair to Williams.

> I had combats with Lady Huntingdon, she giving W[illiams] to Satan, and I told her she had no power, that being an ecclesiastical concern, that she had no power but as head of her family, and if any would assume any power over me that they had not, I would only turn away when any gave themselves such airs ... Then she said I was prejudiced for Williams: I then charged her with sinning against my spirit, and going to God's Throne, and that she had done the same last year and never owned it ... I shewed the danger of making our Impulses a rule to act by, and that in judging we should consider ourselves, and not think ourselves infallible...[41]

But when Hannah 'in a bad spirit' demanded her wages, Harris reprimanded her. To the great annoyance of John Wesley, Williams was soon replaced by Joseph Benson, a master at the Wesleys' Kingswood School. His salary was £25 a year, and he began his work there in January 1769.[42]

John Wesley did attend the first anniversary of the College on 24 August 1769 and preached on the evening before the ceremonies 'to as many as her chapel could well contain, which is extremely neat, or rather elegant, as is the dining-room, the school, and all the house. About nine, Howell Harris desired me to give a short exhortation to his family. I did so,

---

[39] NLW, Trev. diary 254, 4 February and 26 March 1769. Harris's anger made him somewhat incoherent, but the outline of his complaint can be deduced. See J. T. Lloyd, 'Nathaniel Rowland', *Cylchgrawn Cymdeithas Hanes y Methodistiaid Calfinaidd*, vol.45, pp. 60–66).

[40] Connexion archives, 3, 16, copy of letter from Fletcher to Lady H., 1 July 1769. Mr Jones was then being considered as William's replacement.

[41] NLW, Trev. diary 254, 13 and 14 September 1769.

[42] A. G. Ives, *Kingswood School in Wesley's Day and Since* (London, 1970), 68; Cheshunt archives, A 2/5, 3, receipt 1 September 1770; Conlan records (courtesy of Peter Conlan, Esq.), letter of Lady H. to Benson, 14 December 1769.

and then went back to my Lady's, and laid me down in peace.'[43] On the following day he administered the Lord's Supper, and this was followed by sermons given in the courtyard ('the chapel being far too small') by Fletcher, Williams (Pantycelyn), Wesley, and Fletcher for a second time. There was a break in this marathon at two o'clock for dinner, when 'a large number of people had baskets of bread and meat carried to them in the court.'[44] It was the only time John Wesley visited the College though he preached to Harris's 'Family' on 'the strait gate' in August 1772, and reported Harris as saying that

> I have borne with those pert ignorant young men, vulgarly caled students, till I cannot in conscience bear any longer. They preach bare-faced Reprobation, and so broad Antinomianism, that I have been constrained to oppose them to the face, even in the public congregation. It is no wonder they should preach thus. What better can be expected from lads of little understanding, little learning, and no experience?[45]

Harris was clearly suffering from one of his moods of depression at the time, and his comments have not lost anything through being reported by Wesley, who was jealous of her Ladyship's College.[46]

The final breach between John Wesley and the Countess came in 1771, and it began, as so many times before, in a dispute between the Calvinist and the Arminian Methodists. The Arminians feared that Calvinism would lead to Quietism – the belief that the sinner should await his salvation without taking any steps himself to seek it – and to Antinomianism – the belief that a person saved was freed from the law.[47] At his annual conference held in London in August 1770, John Wesley had made a stand against Calvinism:

> Take heed to your Doctrine.
> We said in 1744, 'we have leaned too much towards Calvinism.' Wherein?
> 1. With regard to *Man's Faithfulness*...
> 2. With regard to *working for Life*...

---

[43] *J. Wesley's Journal*, 23 August 1769.

[44] Ibid., 24 August 1769. The chapel is indeed very small, and the congregation must have gathered behind the house in 'the court' as there is insufficient room in front.

[45] Ibid., 14 August 1772.

[46] From 1768 onwards Harris's diary has entries concerning his denunciations of the students and staff for their doctrinal misdeeds. They become more frequent towards the end of his life. By March 1773 members of his 'Family' were actively opposing the College (Cheshunt archives, A 3/15, 1).

[47] For the popular view of Antinomianism see J. Hogg, *The Private Memoirs and Confessions of a Justified Sinner* (1824).

3. We have received it as a Maxim, That 'a Man is to do nothing, *in order to Justification*': Nothing can be more false...[48]

This was thought by the Calvinists to lead to Universalism and Unitarianism. Although the Wesleys were not about to propagate these doctrines, there was a real fear that their followers might do so, and this accounts for the failure of the Arminians to make much progress in Calvinist Scotland or Wales in the eighteenth century. The Calvinists now felt obliged to defend their doctrines, and Lady Huntingdon asked her students to state their own views on the subject. So far as is known, all the students passed Lady Huntingdon's test, but Joseph Benson was an adherent of John Wesley, expressed his views and left his post at the end of 1770.[49] In March 1771, after remonstrating with the Countess, John Fletcher resigned his post as President. Howell Harris exercised his talents as a mediator without success.[50]

Fletcher submitted his resignation on 7 March 1771, when he sent to Lady Huntingdon the students' declarations on the subject. From this letter it would appear that the controversy was not his only reason for resigning. He told her that he had given his reasons for resignation to the students under three heads. The first was Lady Huntingdon's declaration to him on the previous day 'with the highest degree of positiveness, that whosoever did not fully and *absolutely* disavow and renounce the Doctrines contain'd in Mr Wesley's minutes, should not, upon any terms, stay in her college'.[51] His second reason was his 'want of freedom in the College,' and '3. (And he should have begun by this, which alone is more than sufficient to make him take that step) his own *compleat insufficiency*. To this he added his fears least party spirit, and rash censures of things not properly examin'd and understood, or persons not sufficiently known, began to take place in the college.' This is confirmed by a letter which Fletcher sent to Charles Wesley a few months later, which adds that 'we parted in love', and expressing his continued admiration for the College's 'extraordinary Foundress'.[52] After leaving the College, Fletcher began to

[48] *Minutes of some late Conversations, between The Revd Mr Wesley, and Others* (Bristol, 1770), 11. Lady Huntingdon's copy with a mark against this minute is in Cheshunt archives, F 1/ 2486. According to Wesley's *Journal* the conference ran from 7 to 10 August, but he gives no further details.
[49] J. Benson, *Life of Fletcher* (London, n.d.), chapter 5.
[50] NLW, Trev. diary 263.
[51] The letter of resignation is Cheshunt archives, E 4/7, 2. It refers Lady H. to the declaration of Fletcher, which is Cheshunt archives E 4/7, 1, and was sent to her at the same time. The first quotation is from the latter; the other from the former source.
[52] R. Davies (ed.), *A History of the Methodist Church in Great Britain*, 4 (London, 1988), 172-3, quoting from a MS at Duke Univ.

write an even longer apologia for John Wesley and the minutes of 1771, which he intended for publication. This he submitted to Wesley for approval.

In the meantime the Calvinistic Methodists resolved to make a further attempt to promote peace. As early as March 1771 they had established 'the plan of our summer campaign'.[53] The next Wesleyan conference was to be held at Bristol from 6 August. Walter Shirley sent a circular letter asking all those who disapproved of the minutes to meet at Bristol at the same time. An advance copy was given to Charles Wesley by the Countess, and immediately the objection was raised that the Calvinists had no right to attend the Wesleys' conference to 'insist upon a formal Recantation of the said Minutes'.[54] On 2 August Lady Huntingdon therefore wrote to John Wesley a conciliatory letter regretting the lack of 'christian Tenderness due upon such an Occasion' and withdrawing their demand. Walter Shirley sent a similar letter saying that they were suggesting a private discussion as a better alternative to a public protest at the minutes.[55] In his reply John Wesley invited a delegation to attend the conference on the third day. Three of Lady Huntingdon's ministers, two students, and three other Calvinistic Methodists therefore made their appearance, and Walter Shirley was allowed to read all the correspondence to Wesley's people for the first time. John Wesley defended the minutes on Justification, and 'complain'd of ill Treatment from many Persons, that he apprehended had been under Obligations to him, and said that the present Opposition was not to the Minutes, but to himself personally'.[56] Shirley assured him that it was not a personal vendetta, and quoted many letters which he had received, especially from Scotland, objecting to the tendency of the minutes. John Wesley and fifty-three of his preachers then agreed to sign a 'Declaration' disavowing the doctrines objected to, and Walter Shirley stated that he had misunderstood the intention of the minutes and was satisfied with the declaration.[57] Wesley contented himself with a very brief description of the events of the day in his journal: 'We conversed freely for about two hours; and I believe they were satisfied that we were not so "dreadful heretics" as they imagined, but were tolerably sound in the faith.'[58]

[53] NLW, Trev. letter 2693, Lady H. to H. Harris, 26 March 1771.
[54] W. Shirley, *A Narrative of the Principal Circumstances relative to The Rev. Mr Wesley's Late Conference at Bristol* ... (Bath, 1771), 7, 8.
[55] Ibid., 8–12.
[56] Ibid., 13.
[57] Ibid., 14.
[58] *John Wesley's Journal*, 6 August 1771.

As Walter Shirley said, 'thus far all was well', but John Wesley now proceeded to muddy the waters by publishing Fletcher's pamphlet without first obtaining the author's permission. This distressed Fletcher, who promised to pay the costs of printing if it could be suppressed.[59] Nevertheless the *Vindication of the Revd Mr John Wesley's Minutes* duly appeared, and led to another pamphlet war.[60] Lady Huntingdon took no part in the controversy, except to distribute copies of Shirley's *Narrative*. One hundred copies went to Jonathan Parsons, Whitefield's friend at Newburyport, for distribution in New England.[61] Despite all this controversy, John Fletcher continued his friendship with the Countess.[62] However the uneasy peace between the Arminians and the Calvinists which she, Howell Harris and others had helped to sustain over thirty years was shattered. Never again were the leaders to be more than distantly friendly. Never again were there to be discussions of the points at issue. The followers of both parties were now encouraged to oppose each other's views in a way which their leaders had previously discouraged. In particular John Wesley took exception to the activities of the growing number of students leaving Trefeca College.[63] 'I am afraid Lady Huntingdon's preachers will do little good wherever they go. They are wholly swallowed up in that detestable doctrine of Predestination, and can talk of nothing else.'[64]

Although the dispute was principally about doctrine there was probably also a personal element. Even before the minutes of 1770, John Wesley had complained of Lady Huntingdon and her college. In November 1769 he complained to one of his followers: 'It is exceedingly strange. I should really wonder (if I could wonder at any weakness of human nature) that so good a woman as Lady Huntingdon, and one who particularly piques herself on her catholic spirit, should be guilty of such narrowness of spirit!'[65] In the following month, in reply to Joseph Benson's criticisms of the Kingswood School which he had just left for Trefeca, Wesley wrote,

[59] Shirley, op. cit, 18–20.
[60] *Five Letters to the Reverend Mr F – r relative to his Vindication of the Minutes* ... (London, 1771); *A Review of all the Doctrines Taught by The Rev. Mr Wesley* ... (London, 1772); *Logica Wesliensis: or, The Farrago Double Distilled* ... (London, 1773); *The Finishing Stroke: contains some Strictures on The Rev. Mr Fletcher's Pamphlet, entitled Logica Genevensis* ... (London, 1773). Fletcher replied in several pamphlets, including *A Third Check to Antinomianism; in a Letter to the Author of Pietas Oxoniensis: By the Vindicator of The Rev. Mr Wesley's Minutes* (London, 1775).
[61] Cheshunt archives, A 3/5, 21, Parsons to Lady H., 29 December 1772.
[62] Cheshunt archives, A 1/13, 11, Fletcher to Lady H., 28 May 1777.
[63] E.g. John Wesley's *Journal*, 7 December 1772.
[64] J. Telford (ed.), *Letters of John Wesley* (London, 1931), vol.6, p.51.
[65] Ibid., vol.5, p.162.

'Trefeca is much more to Lady Huntingdon than Kingswood is to *me*.'[66] This was undoubtedly true. The Countess lavished her care and affection on her students in a way which John Wesley never had time or inclination to do, but he did not make the remark in a complimentary way. A year later he found it necessary to send a letter of reproof to her. As he explained to Joseph Benson,

> For several years I had been deeply convinced, That I had not done my Duty with regard to that valuable Woman: That I had not told her what I was thoroughly assured, no one else would dare to do, and what I know she would bear from no other person, but *possibly* might bear from me. But being unwilling to give her pain, I put it off from time to time. At length I did not dare to delay any longer, lest Death should call one of us hence. So I at once deliver'd my own soul, by telling her all that was in my heart...[67]

There is a great deal more self-justification in the letter, as well as his dismissal of her because 'she rewards me evil for good.' He then takes up the further grievance of George Whitefield's will which left his Orphan House at Bethesda to Lady Huntingdon. John Wesley had received nothing except the request to preach Whitefield's funeral sermon. It is difficult to avoid the conclusion that he resented the appearance of a rival at this time, and this is supported by his repeated references to the reproof he gave her: 'This morning I have calmly and coolly read over my letter to Lady Huntingdon. I still believe every line of it is true. And I am assured I spoke the truth in love ...'[68] Little about the dispute appears in Lady Huntingdon's own letters, and this may well be an indication that she was very distressed by the breach with John Wesley. However she was so concerned about John Wesley's illness in 1775 as to make enquiries of his brother. It is certain that she regretted the split between Calvinists and Arminians, and the antagonism which spread amongst their supporters. It is equally clear that if Charles Wesley had undertaken the task of 'reproving' her, the problem might never have arisen.

Meanwhile the College continued to flourish despite John Wesley's continued complaints about the students.[69] To replace Fletcher as president Lady Huntingdon tried to persuade the Revd Henry Peckwell and

---

[66] Ibid., vol.5, pp. 164–6.
[67] Duke Univ. Lib., Wesley Family Papers, J. Wesley to Benson, 30 November 1770, printed in *Letters*, op. cit., vol.5, pp.211, 212.
[68] *Letters*, op. cit., vol.5, pp.214, 215, 258, 274.
[69] Cheshunt archives, E 4/3, 3 and G 2/1, 24, J. Wesley to Lady H., 15 September 1776 and 13 August 1779; NLW, MS. 7005C, Lady H. to C. Wesley, 4 July 1775.

probably other ministers to undertake the task, but all declined.[70] The Countess then decided that a formal president was no longer needed and her frequent visits would provide sufficient supervision. She sought another master, but arranged for the senior student to provide the elementary teaching required.[71] Despite the considerable number of letters and journals available, little is known of the masters at Trefeca until John Williams took over after 1782. Edmund Jones of Pontypool, who frequently preached at the College, refers only to 'the tutor'.[72] Howell Harris mentions a Mr Wilson in November 1771 who may have been the tutor then.[73] After Howell Harris's death Thomas Roberts's diary makes frequent references to the Revd Peter Williams, which may imply that he was tutor between 1774 and 1775.[74] Each year on 24 August Lady Huntingdon held the Anniversary at the College, and all the clergymen who attended were expected to preach. Howell Harris made a special effort to be at the second Anniversary.

> This morning I was awaked at 5 sleeping about 3 hours after riding about 15 hours yesterday and was refresh'd in Soul and Body... I saw Lady Huntingdon and congratulated her on her birthday and was full of life to all the company... and amazing that there being Company here last night sleeping 17 beds and 3 kept empty expecting more and yet here is no hurry.[75]

The preaching continued for two more days, and a lovefeast was held on the second evening. In 1771, at the Anniversary, Howell Harris went to the lovefeast 'being among the poor and by the Door' and refused to speak when Lady Huntingdon begged him to do so.[76] The relationship between Harris and the Countess had always been a stormy one. In September 1769 he expressed his thankfulness to her for setting 'the College down here near me'. Two days later he was denouncing her for her autocratic ways.[77] In September 1771 he confided to his diary: 'I feel it a great Tryal to my faith and Truth on any to be faithful now on this occasion with L[ady] H[untingdon] and to keep the Balance true and not to be [*illegible*] by her seeing all her friends bow to her and she can't bear contradiction – I

[70] Cheshunt archives, F 1/1618, Peckwell to Lady H., 31 October 1772; F 1/203, Lloyd to Lady H., 13 November 1772; F 1/1630, Peckwell to Lady H., 29 December 1772.
[71] NLW, Trev. letter 2693, asking Harris to send 'full particulars' of a clergyman recommended to her. The senior student continued to teach in the years after Lady H.'s death (Cheshunt archives, C 1/2, fo. 93).
[72] NLW, MS 7026A, Jones' diary for 1770.
[73] NLW, Trev. diary 264, 18 November 1771.
[74] NLW, Trev. MS 3154, Thomas Roberts's diary, 1774–5.
[75] NLW, Trev. diary 262, 24 August 1770.
[76] NLW, Trev. diary 264, 24 August 1772.
[77] NLW, Trev. diary 254, 11, 12 and 14 September 1769.

shew'd last night much of the Blessing of Reproof...'[78] A letter written by James Hawksworth to the Countess in March 1772 suggests that Harris had hoped to become the next president, but was rejected. Shortly before Howell Harris died in July 1773 there was a violent quarrel between the 'Family' and the College: 'they now maintain Hall to oppose the College and he Comes to the Chapel and as soon as it is over preaches over against it in the Lane publicly abusing all in it... all the students and Mr Glascott in a manner that is quite Infamous.'[79] Nevertheless, despite all their differences, they remained close friends, and she grieved for his death in July 1773.

Future Anniversaries were not always recorded. The Countess did not attend the Anniversary in 1773, but Cradock Glascott sent her an account.[80] Thomas Roberts attended in 1774 and 1775 and gives a brief account of the sermons preached.[81] In 1776 Richard Hill's sister was at the Anniversary and provides a longer account. Proceedings began in the evening with a sermon in Welsh from Mr Davies and an English exhortation by one of the students. Sermons in English and Welsh began again at six o'clock the next morning and continued throughout the day. Augustus Toplady was the third preacher, and had just announced his text when the scaffolding erected for the ministers and students collapsed. Miss Hill was impressed both with the Welsh appetite for sermons and with the calm which followed the accident.[82] There were other similar occasions at the College, including two when students were sent out as missionaries. The first of these was as early as 1769, when Howell Harris received a letter from Lady Huntingdon asking for two students to go to the East Indies.

> This morning 2 out of 7 were Chosen by lot in the Colledge to go to the East Indies to preach the Gospel, vizt. Mr Peache and Mr Euer both from London. 7 offered... The form was thus, the 7 names were set in one Hat and 5 blanks in another Hat and 2 pieces of paper with the Words, thou art the man, written on them. There were several Texts very pertinent opened to each of those two that went...[83]

---

[78] NLW, Trev. diary 264, 22 September 1771.

[79] Cheshunt archives, F 1/176, Hawksworth to Lady H., 28 March 1772; A 3/15, 1, Lady H. to Cosson, 10 March 1773.

[80] Cheshunt archives, F 1/1656, Glascott to Lady H., 27 August 1773.

[81] NLW, Trev. MSS 3154, 3157.

[82] E. Sidney, *The Life of the Rev. Rowland Hill* (London, 1844), 135–7. Another account of this accident appears in Toplady's *Works*, 4, (London, 1794), 283.

[83] NLW, Trev. diary 254, 26 and 27 December 1769. The correct names of the students were Hewer and Pecore.

Little is known of their progress. William Hewer wrote from the Cape of Good Hope describing the gales they had encountered. The only other information comes from Howell Harris's diary – that Hewer 'did nothing' while at Bencoolen.[84] The second occasion, the departure of the students for Georgia in 1772, will be described in the next chapter.

As we have already seen, the students were received by Lady Huntingdon on a recommendation from an evangelical clergyman or layman; many were cross-examined on their religious experience. They were first admitted as probationers, and confirmed as students later.[85] Fletcher himself nominated James Glazebrook 'Collier and getter of ironstone, in Madeley Wood. He is now 23, by look 19 – he hath been awakened seven year ... Notwithstanding his strong desire to exhort, he never attempted it yet ...'[86] John Cosson, who afterwards went to Georgia, was recommended by the Revd Thomas Maxfield, who sent him to the Countess hoping that he 'will answer your Ladyship's expectations'. Maxfield seems to have proposed three of the original students, since he wrote: 'I shall *not* send the Other two Young Men till I hear from your Ladyship, and till Mr Whitefield or some one beside myself has talked with them.'[87] A friend of the Countess, John Lloyd, sent a prospective candidate's statement to her, wishing 'he had comprised what he had to say in a more reasonable Compass'.[88] As the College became better known, Lady Huntingdon received applications from those who did not wish to become ministers.[89] William Williams, Pantycelyn, writing to Lady Huntingdon that he could not give a *testimonium* to the son of one of his friends, spoke of the problem of the many parents who

> would be glad to put 'em in your Colledge, some only for pious education, others on a further view of training 'em up for the Ministry without weighing whether they are call'd or not thereto; and others from that base end of riseing up their children in the world to be men, without empt[y]ing their own pockets by so doing.[90]

[84] Cheshunt archives, F 1/95, Hewer to Lady H., 25 May 1770; NLW, Trevecka diary 264, 22 October 1771, printed in Beynon, *Howell Harris's Visits to London*, 287.
[85] Cheshunt archives, F 1/1636. Many of the practices of the College at Trefeca, including this one, were continued after it moved to Cheshunt (see Cheshunt archives, C 1/1, p. 132).
[86] Connexion archives 3, Fletcher 13, Copy of letter from Fletcher to Lady H., 24 November 1767.
[87] Cheshunt archives, F 1/1444, Maxfield to Lady H., 17 August 1768; F 1/. 1419, Maxfield to Lady H., 16 April 1768.
[88] Cheshunt archives, F 1/1430, Lloyd to Lady H., 18 May 1768.
[89] Cheshunt archives, F 1/96, M. Ling to Lady H., 7 June 1770; F 1/265, Gough to Lady H., 10 January 1774.
[90] Cheshunt archives, F 1/1475, Williams to Lady H., 9 August 1769.

He suggested that the solution might be a grammar school attached to the College under Howell Harris's supervision. The parents would be obliged to pay for their sons' education.

A practice with no parallel in the older dissenting academies, or the universities, was that the entire cost of the students' education and maintenance was met by the Countess. The black cloth for their gowns was bought by her and made up locally.[91] She always took a great interest in their health, as might be expected from her earlier interest in medicine. Joseph Benson was asked for the particulars of Henry Mead's illness, after he had written to her about his 'costive habit of Body' which required a diet of water gruel with currants and butter, instead of the beer and cheese with which the students were served.[92] John Meldrum was put under the care of Elizabeth Thomas of Tredomen to be cured of what was believed to be the 'Itch', but proved to be 'the effect of much cold'. Joseph Benson's letter to the Countess when leaving the College for Oxford was almost entirely devoted to the illness of Brother Hull.[93] Joseph Shipman requested permission to leave College soon after arriving because he was 'oftimes oblig'd to eat that which does not well agree with my constitution', and John Holmes left because the 'Country' did not agree with his constitution.[94] Some students died at College. William Gibbons was so sick in May 1769 that Howell Harris advised the students to get the Countess's instructions for his burial, which duly took place.[95] Students were sometimes expelled. We learn accidentally of one Smith in 1771 only because he did not deliver a letter to Thomas Maxfield.[96]

For their instruction the students had a library at Trefeca. No catalogue survives, and some of the books were disposed after the College moved to Cheshunt.[97] What now remains of the original library is almost entirely limited to the Countess's own books. However we have Fletcher's proposed collection of books for their edification:

[91] Cheshunt archives, E 4/3, 4, Harris to Lady H., 5 February 1772. Specimens of cloth are included with the letter.
[92] JRL, Meth. Archives, Hunt. 113, Lady H. to Benson, March 1770; Cheshunt archives, F 1/76, Mead to Lady H., 18 August 1769; F 1/1222, Mead to Lady H., n.d. Mead also had financial problems for which he needed help.
[93] Cheshunt archives, F 1/120, Eliz. Thomas to Lady H., 14 February 1771; F 1/1493, Benson to Lady H., 9 May 1770. Brother Hull was probably Christopher Hull, who was expelled later.
[94] Cheshunt archives, E 4/5, 6, Shipman to Lady H., 6 October 1768; F 1/262 and 264, J. Holmes to Lady H., 18 December 1773, 8 Jan. 1774.
[95] Cheshunt archives, F 1/63, G. Pecore to Lady H., 14 May 1769.
[96] Cheshunt archives, F 1/1528, Maxfield to Lady H., 21 February 1771.
[97] Cheshunt archives, C 5/1 (1793).

Grammar, Logic, Rhetoric, and Ecclesiastical History, and a little Natural Philosophy and Geography, with a great deal of practical Divinity, will be sufficient for those who do not care to dive into languages ... Watt's Logic and his History of the Bible by questions and answers ... Mr Wesley's Natural Philosophy contains as much as is wanted. Mason's Essays on Pronunciation will be worth their attention. Henry and Gill on the Bible, with the four volumes of Baxter's practical works, Keach's Metaphors, Taylor on the Types (printed at Trevecca), Gurnel's Christian Armour, Edwards on Preaching, Johnson's English Dictionary and Mr Wesley's Christian Library.[98]

A series of exercises set by Fletcher have also survived in one of his letters:

I desire you to turn the 39 Articles in as good classical Latin as you possibly can. 2 Write an English letter to a Deist to convince him of the truth of the Scriptures. 3 Draw a parallel between John's baptism and Christ's, and prove the superiority of the latter over the former. 4 Make an English Theme upon the mischief of unsanctify'd learning...[99]

Although Fletcher had departed, the curriculum did not change. Surprisingly most students managed to acquire Latin, Greek and some theology, despite frequent calls to go out preaching. Above all, the students listened to sermons – by their tutor, by Howell Harris, by visiting clergy, and by one another. Edmund Jones of Pontypool spent five days at Trefeca in October 1770 and preached twice a day to the students and Lady Huntingdon. During the six days he was there in July 1773 he preached to the students every day, and often at Howell Harris's settlement too.[100] In their regular letters to the Countess when she was absent the students recorded their pleasure: 'Last Lords day was an extraordinary day with some of us that will not soon be forgotten. John E[yre] preached in the morning at the Chapel to a large congregation of people and David Jones in the Evening, both with great light and power.'[101] The College was the Countess's own. She kept a check on everything that happened in her absence. The president or master submitted detailed reports, and the students wrote of their personal matters and experiences.[102] As Dr Nuttall has shown, Trefeca was a new departure in theological colleges, and

---

[98] JRL, Meth. Archives, Seymour vol., no. 21, copy of letter from Fletcher to Lady H., 3 January 1768. Few of these books can now be found in the Cheshunt library.
[99] Cheshunt archives, A 3/3, 25, Fletcher to Lady H., n.d.
[100] NLW, MSS 7026A, 7027A, diaries of E. Jones, 1770 and 1773.
[101] Cheshunt archives, F 1/241, Thos. Molland to Lady H., 13 August 1773.
[102] Cheshunt archives, F 1/1464, Fletcher to Lady H., 12 April 1769.

became a model for those established by other evangelicals, but above all the College was the Countess's own 'Family'.[103]

---

[103] G. F. Nuttall, *The Significance of Trevecca College 1768–91* (London, 1969); Cheshunt archives, F 1/55, Cosson to Lady H., 30 March 1769. 'Your Ladyship was pleased to declare it gave your Ladyship joy every time you heard from your Family at the College.'

8

The Bethesda Orphan House

In 1770 Lady Huntingdon took on a fresh responsibility. George Whitefield died at Newburyport in Massachusetts on 30 September, bequeathing the Orphan House at Bethesda in Georgia to her care. A letter from Boston written the same day arrived in London on 5 November, and Thomas Maxfield hastened to send the news of Whitefield's death to Lady Huntingdon at Trefeca. However the newspapers reached Trefeca first, and Howell Harris described its arrival in his diary:

> Yesterday (after I had seen it in the paper) Lady Huntingdon came to my room all in tears at the news of the death of a dear and faithful servant of the Lord, and the first that brought me to London and to the Brethren ... Being asked by Lady Huntingdon to discourse last night on his death, I thought it was against me as I had many objections to, as I saw him the head of a great spirit. However, to shew my faith and conquering self, I yielded.[1]

The newspaper report was soon followed by more letters from North America. Phyllis Wheatley, 'the black poetess', sent a poem she had composed on the subject, and this was followed by the offer of a lifesize wax image of Whitefield.[2] As soon as Whitefield's will had been proved, James Habersham, his friend and supporter in Georgia for many years, sent several copies of the exemplification and other legal documents relating to Bethesda to Lady Huntingdon. The steward at Bethesda expressed his willingness to continue at Whitefield's 'Beloved Bethesda'.[3]

Bethesda was one of the results of the early Methodist interest in

---

[1] Cheshunt archives, F 1/1519, Maxfield to Lady H., 6 November 1770; T. Beynon (ed.), *Howell Harris's Visits to London*, (Abeystwyth, 1966), 19.

[2] Cheshnut archives, A 1/13, 30 (Cary to Lady H., 1 October 1770) & A 3/1, 28 (Wheatley to Lady H., 25 October 1770). This letter is printed in *The Journal of Negro History*, 57 (1972), 212. For the poem see D. Porter (ed.), *Early Negro Writing 1760–1837* (Boston, 1971), 532–4. Cheshunt archives, A 3/1, 14, Mrs Patience Wright and Mrs Rachel Wells to Lady H., 7 March 1771.

[3] Georgia Hist. Soc., coll. 337, pp. 33–40, copy of letter from Habersham to Lady H., 10 December 1770. Cheshunt archives, A 3/1, 6, M. Jollie to Lady H., 29 May 1771 & A 3/1, 1, John Crane to Lady H., November 1770.

Professor Francke (1663–1727) and his *Stiftung* at Halle. Prominent in this work was the concept of a refuge for orphans. In 1737 the Georgia trustees asked Charles Wesley to draw up a scheme for an Orphan House there, but it was George Whitefield who established it.[4] Even before Whitefield's first voyage to Georgia he had taken up the trustees' proposal and they had given him a licence to collect money for it in Britain.[5] In 1739 Whitefield had written from Philadelphia to Howell Harris on the subject. Three years later he was to send Francke's son an account of its progress.[6] On Whitefield's arrival in Savannah he had discovered that the Salzburgers already had their own orphan house, but it was intended for their fellow-countrymen. On his return to England the Georgia trustees gave him 500 acres on which to build.[7] When he reached Savannah early in 1740, James Habersham, his schoolmaster, had chosen a suitable site about ten miles out of Savannah at the junction of the Vernon and Skidaway rivers.[8] Even today, when all of Whitefield's and the Countess's buildings have disappeared, Bethesda is still remote from Savannah's urban sprawl, on a hill overlooking the rivers.

Here, on 30 January, Whitefield laid out the plan of his buildings:

> It is to be sixty feet long and forty wide. The foundation is to be brick, and is to be sunk four feet within, and raised three feet above the ground. The house is to be two stories high ... there will be twenty commodious rooms. Behind are to be two small houses, the one for an infirmary, the other for a workhouse.[9]

He already had some twenty-four orphans in temporary quarters in Savannah and had another sixteen before it was opened.[10] They were to be taught to spin and card cotton so that the Orphan House would be self-financing. James Habersham was placed in charge of administration and a Mr Jonathan Barber of Rhode Island was the spiritual advisor. Although Habersham left Bethesda to set up in business in 1744, he remained a friend and supporter of Bethesda for the remainder of his life.

---

[4] *Charles Wesley's Journal*, op. cit., vol. 1, p. 79. Georgia had been founded by General Oglethorpe as a philanthropic venture, and was governed by a board of trustees in London. R. J. Charleton, *History of Newcastle upon Tyne* (Newcastle, 1950), 390.

[5] *HMC, Egmont Diary 1*, pp. 457, 516.

[6] J. Gillies (ed.), *A Select Collection of Whitefield's Letters* 1 (London, 1772), 84, 469.

[7] *George Whitefield's Journals* (London, 1960), 158, 159; A. L. Fries, *The Moravians in Georgia* (Raleigh, NC, 1905), 18, 152; *HMC, Egmont Diary 2*, pp. 2, 37, 56.

[8] *Whitefield's Journals*, 395.

[9] Ibid., 396. A few months later Whitefield planned a similar institution in Pennsylvania, but surrendered it to the Moravians (*Two Centuries of Nazareth 1740–1940*, (Nazareth, PA, 1940), 5–7.

[10] J. Gillies, *Memoirs of the Life of the Rev. George Whitefield* (London, 1772), 50, 51.

This helped the Countess when he became a leading politician in the colony.[11]

Whitefield was the victim of many calumnies about Bethesda.[12] To these we owe the existence not only of Whitefield's own account of Bethesda, but also an independent description, defending him from 'false Unreasonable aspersions':

> The Orphan House Stands On a Riseing Ground, having A Descent on All Sides, – On the North and South, are Yards about 120 feet Long, planted with Orange Trees. On the East, is a Water Passage to Carry You to any part of Georgia, Carolina, etc. it lyes Open for several Miles, and is Accounted Twelve Miles from the Sea – On the West (which is the front of the House) are four small Houses Standing a proper Distance from the Great House and from Each other. Above these there is a beautiful Garden and a fine Orchard Containing allmost all sorts of fruits, Trees and Herbs which the Country will afford – A little further Up, There are two Inclosures for Cattle...[13]

The writer described the daily routine:

> Att five oClock (in Summer) and Six in Winter, the Bell rings to Call all the family out of their Beds, half an Hour is allowed to wash and perform secret Duties. Then the Bell Rings Again, to Call everyone to Publick Prayers in the Chappel ... Afterwards all Go to their proper Work, The Children some of them Spin, others pick Cotton etc. at eight oClock the Bell Rings Again, to Call all to Breakfast ... After Breakfast a Hymn is sung, then they are Discharged. In a Hour or Less the Bell Rings to Call to school. At twelve oClock it Rings to Dinner ... Att two oClock it Rings for School again which Continues to 5 oClock. Att Sunsett the Bell Rings for Supper – After Supper the family is Called to Prayers...

The children were taught Latin, arithmetic, writing and reading.

At this time Bethesda was considered the best educational institution in Georgia, but it was not successful financially.[14] Whitefield, along with other colonists in Georgia, thought it essential that the ban on slavery should be lifted if the province was to prosper. He suggested this to the

---

[11] Habersham was born at Beverley (Yorks.) in 1712 and accompanied Whitefield to Georgia in 1738. He later became Provincial Secretary and President of the Upper House. *Whitefield's Letters*, op. cit., vol. 3, p. 460. E. M. Coulter and A. B. Saye, *A list of the Early Settlers of Georgia* (Athens, GA, 1967), 21. *Georgia Hist. Soc. Collections*, 6 (1904), 5, 6. By this period Georgia was governed in the same way as the other North American colonies, with a governor, an elected assembly and civil servants.

[12] Cheshunt archives, A 3/1, 31, benefactions and collections.

[13] Georgia Hist. Soc., coll. 249. This has been printed in the Society's *Collections*, 45 (Savannah, 1961), 364–6.

[14] R. B. Strickland, *Religion and the State in Georgia* (New York, 1939), 95.

trustees in 1748 without success. Whitefield was very concerned about 'the miseries of the poor negroes', who were without food, clothes or houses, but as an evangelical he emphasized the opportunity to convert them to Christianity while providing for their physical needs.[15] When slavery was legalized in Georgia they were employed to grow rice on the land around Bethesda.[16] Nevertheless Bethesda continued to decline,[17] and Whitefield proposed turning Bethesda into a college or academy, using as his model the College in New Jersey. A petition to London for a royal charter for his college was unsuccessful because the archbishop of Canterbury insisted that the draft charter should be amended to limit the position of head of the college to an Anglican.[18] This was unacceptable in a colony in which the Anglicans were probably in a minority. However it did not prevent Whitefield from attempting to establish a public academy at Bethesda, and the Houses of Assembly were asked to pass a Bill to this effect, with a clause stating that it should not take effect until approved in London. The Bill reached Lady Huntingdon after Whitefield's death.[19] The decision to abandon this Bill was probably taken by her in consultation with Lord Dartmouth, then President of the Privy Council, who must have pointed out the difficulty of obtaining confirmation of any Act which did not safeguard the Church of England.

The Bill, Whitefield's will and other papers for Lady Huntingdon were brought back to England by Cornelius Winter, a young man placed in charge of Bethesda by Whitefield.[20] With the papers was a letter from James Habersham, lamenting the loss of 'The oldest and Dearest Friend I had upon Earth. My first acquaintance with him was 34 years ago soon after he left Oxford and on his first Visit to London, before he was known as a popular preacher, and from the first Hour we saw each other, to the

---

[15] Gillies, *Memoirs*, 179. 'A Letter to the Inhabitants of Maryland' in *Works*, (London, 1771) vol. 4, p. 35. 'A Prayer for a poor Negroe (ibid., p. 473).

[16] See D. Doar, *Rice and Rice Planting in the South Carolina Low Country* (Charleston, 1970) and M. Granger, *Savannah River Plantations* (Savannah, 1947) for an account of the cultivation of rice in this area.

[17] Lib. of Congress, Whitefield letters, vol. 1, 26, John Portrees to Whitefield, 2 July 1757; and 61, Thomas Dixon to same, 3 July 1762.

[18] Gillies, *Memoirs*, op. cit., 179, 281; Strickland, op. cit., 134, 135. W. M. Manross, *The Fulham Papers* (Oxford, 1965), 114. *Whitefield's Letters*, vol. 3, pp. 471–83.

[19] *A Letter to His Excellency Governor Wright* (London, 1768), copy in Cheshunt archives, A 3/1, 9. See also *Whitefield's Letters*, vol. 3, p. 485. Cheshunt archives, A 3/1, 2, Habersham to Lady H., 31 December 1770. Copy from Habersham's letterbook is in Georgia Hist. Soc., coll. 337, pp. 43–5. Cheshunt archives, A 3/1, 10.

[20] W. Jay, *Memoirs of the Rev. Cornelius Winter* (Bath, 1808), 76, 78.

Hour of Death, our Affectionate and real Friendship never abated...'[21] Habersham was unhappy with the wording of the bequest to the Countess as he felt it did not express Whitefield's intentions clearly and might enable his relations to contest the will. Almost as soon as the news of the will reached England a caveat against its probate was filed in the Prerogative Court of Canterbury. However, two years later one of Whitefield's nephews conveyed any interest he might have in the Bethesda estate to Lady Huntingdon.[22]

It might have been expected that Whitefield would bequeath his two London chapels to Lady Huntingdon since she was already in possession of similar chapels in the provinces, but instead he left them to Daniel West and Robert Keen, two London merchants.[23] Lady Huntingdon had very few links with Georgia and Bethesda. She had followed Whitefield's progress there and had contributed towards the costs of Bethesda, but nothing more. Whitefield's obvious choice would have been James Habersham himself, but he was only to take control if Lady Huntingdon had died before Whitefield. It shows Whitefield's great trust in the Countess and her abilities to leave her the problems of Bethesda and its future when she lived several thousand miles away. The eventual difficulties were far greater than he could have anticipated, but she struggled with them, even planned to visit Georgia, and tried to carry out his wishes. Bethesda was to be her biggest problem and her worst failure.

Lady Huntingdon proposed to promote 'the Knowledge of the Lord not only in the various Provinces', but also to provide missionaries for 'the back settlements and among the Heathen Nations'.[24] Her first requirement was for a clergyman, a schoolmaster, and students to put all in order and continue the work. She decided to replace the steward and superintendent at the College, and the temporary replacement in the post of

---

[21] Georgia Hist. Soc., coll. 337, copy of James Habersham's letter book, pp. 4–13. This is printed in the Society's *Collections*, 6 (Savannah, 1904), 103. The original letter has not survived, but a copy of it was amongst the records taken to America by Mr Laurens (Cheshunt archives, A 4/6, 37). Gillies' *Memoirs*, op. cit., lxii.

[22] Georgia Hist. Soc., coll. 337, pp. 50 and 51, copy of Habersham's letter to Lord Dartmouth, 9 January 1771; Cheshunt archives, A 3/1, 23. The conveyance was dated 9 July 1772 (see Cheshunt archives A 4/6, 37). Cheshunt archives, A 3/1, 34 is a list of queries about the rights of Whitefield's two nephews and the future of Bethesda after the Countess's death.

[23] For the earlier history of the Tabernacle see *Two Calv. Meth. Chapels*. For Keen's behaviour later see I. M. Fletcher, 'John Reynolds, 1740–1803' (*Trans. Cong. Hist. Soc.*, 18 (1958), 65. The diary from which these quotations are taken is not (as stated in the article) in the London Misionary Society archives.

[24] Cheshunt archives, G 2/1, 4. An inaccurate version appears in *Life and Times*, vol. 2, p. 257n.

schoolmaster had already decided to leave.[25] All this took time, because of the need to communicate with James Habersham, and to persuade the right persons to venture to one of the remoter colonies on the other side of the Atlantic. Finally she called a meeting of ministers and students at the College. The first ministers arrived on 3 October and immediately plunged into a round of hymn singing, prayers and sermons. There were meetings with Lady Huntingdon in the study. A few days later more ministers arrived. The final choice of a clergyman to lead the party to Georgia was the Revd William Piercy, a preacher at the Lock Hospital under Martin Madan. Lady Huntingdon had asked him to preach at Tunbridge Wells in 1771, when he was about to leave the Lock, but he replied that he was fully occupied in building 'a large place at Woolwich, for preaching'.[26] Chosen at the same time were the schoolmaster, the Revd C. S. Eccles, the superintendent, John Cosson (a student), and the housekeeper from Trefeca College, Elizabeth Hughes. The students who offered themselves for America were seven in number – John Cosson, William White, Joseph Cook, Daniel Roberts, Thomas Jones, Thomas Hill and Lewis Richards. All were provided with clothes and money to buy books and other items.[27] On 12 October the Countess, William Piercy and the students set off for London where the latter stayed at the Tabernacle house. A further service of dedication was held at Tottenham Court chapel, and a lovefeast at the Tabernacle. A hymn was composed for the occasion. Lady Huntingdon wrote to one of her students in Dublin: 'Nothing ever was so blessed as the Spirit in which they all went and such a remarkable an out pouring of the spirit that we trust is a pledge of their promised blessing to the heathen.'[28]

The atmosphere of enthusiasm and determination did not sustain the mood of the group for long. The first complaint came from the housekeeper, Betty Hughes, while still in London. As she wrote to the Countess

[25] Cheshunt archives, A 3/1, 2. The Revd Edward Ellington, the master, had been offered a parish in South Carolina.

[26] Piercy was at St Edmund Hall, but did not graduate. Cheshunt archives, F 1/133 Piercy to Lady H., 7 September 1771; F 1/1546, H. Godde to Lady H., 25 August 1771.

[27] The proceedings are very fully reported in *Some Account of the Proceedings at the College ... Relative to those Students called to go to Georgia ... In Three Letters. By One who was present* (London, 1772). Henry Mead listed the contents of his chest after failing to go to Georgia (Cheshunt archives, F 1, 256, Mead to Lady H., 1 November 1773).

[28] A lovefeast or *agape* was a Moravian service adopted by the Methodists. It was not discontinued by the Arminian Methodists until the beginning of the twentieth century, but was less popular amongst the Calvinists. *Some Account*, op. cit., 56, 57. Cheshunt archives, G 2/1, 5 – Lady H. to Hawksworth, 4 November 1772. The *Gentleman's Magazine* reported their departure (F. F. Bretherton, *The Countess of Huntingdon* (London, 1940), 42.

from Bethesda she almost turned back at that point: 'I am greatly obliged to your Ladyship for your sweet letter that I received in the Downs, it comforted my heart ... I was so cast down in London hearing so many prayers given up for the Students and not one grone for me.' Worse was to follow. Lady Huntingdon had planned to send her students on a boat sailing directly to Georgia and with a captain who would give them 'many Advantages'.[29] Since more boats sailed from London to Charleston in South Carolina, than to Savannah, it was convenient not to expose the students to a second sea voyage from Charleston, and (as will be seen) there were additional advantages in carefully choosing a reliable captain. The boat was the *Georgia Packet* under the command of Captain Anderson. At the end of October six students and Betty Hughes sailed from London as steerage passengers. While the captain waited in the Downs for a favourable wind to take him down the English Channel, William White was taken ill and put ashore. When they anchored off Deal Joseph Cook, Daniel Roberts and Thomas Hill went on shore, but Lewis Richards, John Cosson and Betty Hughes remained on board.[30] The wind improved and they all returned on board, but on the next day, being unable to sail, the captain, the cabin passengers, the students and Betty all spent the day ashore. A few days later all the students except Cosson and Betty went ashore again, 'which was some small trial to us as it exposed us to the censures and Jests of the Gentlemen on board'. Next came a message on board from William White at Dover asking Cosson to preach his funeral sermon. Taking Betty and Cook with him, he took a coach for Dover, arranging that if the ship sailed before dawn it would signal as it passed Dover. White did not die, and the three were rowed out to the *Georgia Packet*. But they then found that the other four students were not on board. In his letter to the Countess, Cosson advanced the alternative explanations that the four had never intended to go to Georgia, or that God had prevented them. He claimed that Hill's sole purpose in going was to qualify for ordination as quickly as possible, while Roberts only went to please the Countess. Both they and Cook had been extravagant while at Deal studying 'nothing but how to appear grand, powdering their hair, buying of Goold rings (Hill bought and wore two at Deal). Hill and Cook also bought Pieces to make them selves morning gounds, one of which cost six and thirty shillings, till they had spent almost all their money.' As the Countess had already paid to equip the entire party with clothes and other

[29] Cheshunt archives, A 3/4, 1, E. Hughes to Lady H., 26 December 1772; G 2/1, 4.
[30] The whole of this account is based on John Cosson's letter to Lady H., 9 January 1773 (Cheshunt archives, A 3/4, 2).

necessaries, this was an extravagance, but they had justified the expense, saying that there would be plenty of money in Georgia for them.[31]

The Countess now booked places on the *Montague* bound for Charleston for Hill, Roberts and Richards, another student, Henry Mead, William Piercy and his brother Richard, a servant and a horse, for £97. Piercy travelled as a cabin passenger, the students went steerage. This time Robert Keen, acting for the Countess, carefully stipulated that there would be no charge for any student who failed to go and Keen collected seven guineas for Mead's absence.[32] Piercy seems to have had a tolerable voyage despite being ill on the way, but the wayward students suffered by the change of ship. Daniel Roberts told the Countess: 'we had a very disagreeable passage: bad Weather, a cursing cruel Captain, and a sett of ungodly companions. We never eat one meal with the Cabban passengers; we lived day and night in the Steerage; where we had thirteen Steerage passengers in company with us; all which were of the lowest rank, or the bassest sort of people.'[33] He felt that his fellow passengers did not treat them with proper respect, and even Piercy who preached several times on the voyage was unable to hold his congregation. Lewis Richards also complained, but, unlike Roberts, did not see the voyage as a punishment for their negligence in missing the ship chosen for them by the Countess.[34] Thomas Hill added that the captain had also accused them of being responsible for the bad weather they encountered – a common superstition about the clergy – and threatened to throw them overboard like Jonas [*sic*].[35]

The *Georgia Packet* with Cosson, Betty and Cook arrived at the mouth of the Savannah river on Boxing Day 1772, having had the best weather Captain Anderson could remember in twenty-eight years.[36] They had to wait for a pilot and a fair wind before reaching Savannah on Monday, 28 December. They were kindly received by James Habersham, and in his parlour the same day John Cosson and Betty Hughes were married. Habersham found this surprising since the Countess had not written to him about it.[37] The happy couple and Joseph Cook then went to Bethesda to inspect their new home. Their first impression was one of desolation, and they went 'to the bottom of the burying ground' to hold a prayer

[31] Many of the bills for the clergy and students can be found in Cheshunt archives, A 2/6.
[32] Cheshunt archives, A 2/6, 9, agreement with Capt. Pickles, 19 November 1772.
[33] Cheshunt archives, A 3/4, 11, Roberts to Lady H., 16 February 1773.
[34] Cheshunt archives, A 3/5, 19, Richards to Lady H., February [1773].
[35] Cheshunt archives, A 3/5, 15, Hill to Lady H., 20 February 1773.
[36] Cheshunt archives, A 3/4, 2, J. Cosson to Lady H., 9 January 1773.
[37] Cheshunt archives, A 3/4, 2.

meeting.[38] John Cosson reported that all was in a state of neglect, the house contained no furniture or sheets, and there was no livestock. Both the steward and the superintendent were preparing to leave having set themselves up with a plantation, and were using the Orphan House slaves to their own advantage. He was told that the House was seriously in debt, and suggested that the remaining students and Mr and Mrs Eccles should wait in England as there would not be enough to support them at Bethesda.[39] A second letter complained that Cook employed the tailor to make up the cloth he had brought into morning gowns, when new clothes were needed for the slaves.[40] He suggested that more lay persons from Trefeca were required – the gardener and a herdsman would be particularly useful. A letter from Cook confirmed the picture of neglect:

> The provision we have to eat is rice Cornbeef and India Bred – There is neither Mutton, veal, Eggs, Cheese or Fouls in the Hous or Money to buy any... The Students Rooms are not near done, and it will amount [to] two hundred pounds to make them compleat. The dwelling-House likewise is very much out of repair.[41]

Their attitude to the slaves was ambivalent. They all deeply regretted their unconverted state, but they also said that the slaves were dishonest and stole beef from the cellar. They immediately began to preach to the Bethesda slaves. Elizabeth Hughes spoke to some with considerable success, but her husband could neither understand nor be understood by them. Cook went with Mr Wright to the plantation where they sang a hymn, gave a prayer and made an exhortation to 'the poor Negroes'.

All these reports about Bethesda contradict what was said by James Habersham and other inhabitants of Savannah, who undoubtedly felt that the Orphan House was in reasonably good condition, even though Whitefield had been dead for more than a year and supervision had been minimal. Habersham had undoubtedly done his best to supervise what was being done, even though his business kept him in Savannah for much of the time. The differing accounts probably arose from the different approach of the new arrivals. All were very young – even William Piercy – and most had little experience outside England and Wales. Arriving in a strange country and living on a frontier which from time to time was threatened by Spaniards and Indians required considerable adjustment. In addition they were probably given inaccurate information by the

[38] Cheshunt archives, A 3/4, 4, Eliz. Cosson to Lady H., 10 January 1773.
[39] Cheshunt archives, A 3/4, 2.
[40] Cheshunt archives, A 3/4, 5, J. Cosson to Lady H., 2 February 1773.
[41] Cheshunt archives, A 3/4, 8, Cook to Lady H., 8 January 1773.

steward and others, who had no further interest in the success of Bethesda.⁴² In reply to Cosson the Countess sent an optimistic letter with best wishes for his marriage, and the offer of sending anything which was wanted as soon as William Piercy had arrived and checked over the inventory which he was bringing with him.⁴³

The ship with Piercy and his party arrived off Charleston on 31 January, but no one went ashore until 2 February, when the two Piercys and James the servant did so, leaving the students to their own devices. The students went ashore on the following evening and were fortunate to find 'a gentleman that had come to Charlestown in a little boat, four Negroes rowing it, to sell Indigo and was returning, and he was kind enough to take us to Savanah for nothing.'⁴⁴ The new arrivals added to the story of neglect at Bethesda. The garden was derelict, there was only a cow and calf, a lame horse and four oxen at the Orphan House. Most of the goods in the inventory had disappeared and the negroes said that they had been taken by Wright and Crane for their own use. Wright and Crane had taken one of the slaves who was a good carpenter and used the wood from the Countess's land to make furniture and other goods. They also bought goods for themselves with rice from the plantation.⁴⁵ William Piercy and his brother remained at Charleston, William having been told that a further two days of sailing would kill him.⁴⁶ He did not reach Bethesda until 13 March a few days after Mr Eccles, who had sailed directly from London to Savannah in the *London Packet* at the end of December.⁴⁷ Both Piercy and Eccles made light of the difficulties listed by the students. They had been warmly welcomed by both Habersham and the Governor, and Piercy had been invited to preach at the Charleston meeting house, where he had great success.⁴⁸ Piercy saw himself as George Whitefield's successor and began to devote much of his time to travelling the American seaboard and preaching.

Soon William Piercy too began to complain to the Countess. He found that the two wings planned for the students had not been completed.

⁴² Cheshunt archives, A 3/4, 14, Edw. Langworthy to Lady H., 2 January 1773.
⁴³ Cheshunt archives, A 3/15, 1, draft letter from Lady H. to J. Cosson, 10 March 1773.
⁴⁴ Cheshunt archives, A 3/4, 11.
⁴⁵ Cheshunt archives, A 3/4, 12, Daniel Roberts to Lady H. 16 February 1773.
⁴⁶ Cheshunt archives, A 4/1, 1, W. Piercy to Lady H., 22 February 1773.
⁴⁷ Cheshunt archives, A 4/1, 2, W. Piercy to Lady H., 17 March 1773; A 2/6, 10, receipt for £21 for Eccles's passage, 24 December 1772.
⁴⁸ Cheshunt archives, A 3/5, 10, Eccles to Lady H., [February 1773]. The minister was William Tennant, probably the son of the Revd William Tennent jun. (1705–77) and grandson of the founder of the Log College (A. Alexander, *The Log College* (London, 1968), 124n, 146.

There was little furniture or linen, but he believed that it had been worn out by students at the school which Habersham had established rather than stolen. He also said that many of the slaves on the plantation were too old to work, so that they were unable to produce enough rice even to feed themselves.[49] Piercy also provided reports on his brethren for the Countess, but only one has survived: 'My dear Cosson could he be kept from reasoning and worldly Schemes would be one of the most excellent of the Earth in his Place; but to my Grief frequently something seems to come in his Head and he talks about that he shall not stay. Marrying I fear has much hurt his Soul ...'[50] Cosson had asked him for an apartment on the first floor of the house rather than in the place allotted, so as to be prepared for 'the Care of a little Family'. Piercy had refused the request, as he explained to Lady Huntingdon, for a great variety of reasons, but clearly did not realize that Elizabeth Cosson was about to give birth. The first news of the scandal reached the Countess from James Habersham: 'On Tuesday Evening [6th April], when Mr Piercy returned to Bethesda after preaching here, he found the House in Confusion, occasioned by Mrs Cosson being in Labour, and on Wednesday Morning I think she was delivered of a Child.'[51] Habersham was particularly unhappy since he had performed the marriage ceremony, and had ignored rumours from the other passengers on the *Georgia Packet* that Mrs Cosson was already pregnant. He consulted the Governor who agreed that the Cossons should be discharged immediately and sent back to England as soon as possible. This was followed a few days later by a letter from Mr Eccles who imported an air of melodrama: 'two days after the opening of the College publicly Mrs Cosson was delivered of a Boy, and so privately that none of us had the least suspicion; untill after the poor Babe proclaim'd his mother's shame by loud cryes.'[52] Piercy informed the Countess of Cosson's excuse. He said that they had been previously married at Trefeca on Brecon fair day, but this was only by a layman reading the service in one of the college parlours.[53] The two culprits wrote to the Countess expressing their sorrow for the offence. Betty Cosson complained that she was about to be turned out of Bethesda 'altho' I have not where to lay my head nor the poor infant ex[c]ept the ground', and her husband had been told that if he tried to stay in Georgia William Piercy

[49] Cheshunt archives, A 4/2, 1, W. Piercy to Lady H., 19 March 1773.
[50] Cheshunt archives, A 4/1, 3, W. Piercy to Lady H., 22 March 1773.
[51] Cheshunt archives, A 3/5, 14, Habersham to Lady H., 9 April 1773.
[52] Cheshunt archives, A 3/5, 11, Eccles to Lady H., 11 April 1773.
[53] Cheshunt archives, A 4/1, 5, W. Piercy to Lady H., 15 April 1773. This would have been a valid marriage before the passage of Hardwicke's Marriage Act in 1753.

would write and preach against him.[54] John Cosson left for London almost immediately, but it was considered too soon for Betty to risk the voyage. At the end of the year she was living with friends in Charleston and wrote to Mr Keen that 'If I do not greatly mistake myself I would rather sell my Gown of my back than to put my Lady into any expence. Blessed be God He supplyes all my returning wants.'[55]

The Countess was more kindly disposed towards the Cossons than were William Piercy and others in Georgia. She paid the cost of John Cosson's return voyage and probably contributed to his expenses when he began to preach in various London chapels.[56] He continued to write to her and sent her a copy of a hymn which he had composed. In March 1774, when Betty had still not returned to England, John Cosson wrote to ask about his future, whether to seek employment with the government or to continue preaching. In May he wished to be restored to the number of Lady Huntingdon's preachers, and to return to North America as an ordained minister. This was also the Countess's advice, and she eventually organized and paid for the entire cost of his return to Georgia.[57] At some point she had met a negro student, David Margrate or Margate, who probably spent a short time at the Trefeca College, and he was sent with Cosson to preach to the slaves. She paid numerous bills for the pair, and at the end of October they went aboard the *Mermaid* bound for Charleston.[58] Cossons and Margrate spent some time at Bethesda, but David caused problems with his preaching and Cosson still chafed at the restrictions which William Piercy imposed on him.[59]

They returned to a Bethesda which had lost almost all the buildings in a fire. On Whitsunday, 30 May, between seven and eight in the evening, when only Mr Eccles and a few slaves were there, the roof caught fire. One of the slaves got on the roof 'and well nigh put out the Flames, but in brushing off the Smoke and Flames from his face, he missed his hold, and fell to the ground, which was a Terrible Fall as the House is the highest in this Province, by which he was much hurt'.[60] While Eccles was attending

[54] Cheshunt archives, F 1/218, E. Cosson to Lady H., 20 April 1773.
[55] Cheshunt archives, A 1/9, 2, E. Cosson to Keen, 15 December 1773; A 3/5, 24, J. Cosson to Lady H., 14 April 1773.
[56] Cheshunt archives, A 3/6, 1, J. Cosson to Lady H., 7 December [1773].
[57] Cheshunt archives, A 3/6, 3 and 4; F 1/232 and 316, J. Cosson to Lady H., 19 March, 25 May, 16 June, 26 July 1774.
[58] Cheshunt archives, A 2/8, 20–35, various invoices, 1774.
[59] Cheshunt archives, A 3/6, 9, John Edwards to W. Piercy, 11 January 1775; Georgia Hist. Soc., coll. 337, copy of letter of Habersham to Keen, 11 May 1775; Cheshunt archives, A 1/13, 19, R. Piercy to Lady H., 16 June 1775. David Margrate was sent back to England.
[60] Georgia Hist. Soc., coll. 337, copy of letter of Habersham to Lady H., 3 June 1773.

to his injuries, others arrived, attracted by the flames. One gentlemen brought his slaves to help, but others only came to steal. Almost all the books in the library were lost and a portrait, bust and a wax image of George Whitefield were all burned. The heat had been so intense that the communion plate and the branch for candles in the chapel had melted. James Habersham recommended that the new buildings should be made of brick rather than wood and proposed improvements to make them less liable to fire. William Piercy, who had been preaching in Savannah, set out almost immediately for Charleston. From there he wrote to the Countess that although all the money and many of their clothes had been lost, the two new wings and other buildings had been saved.[61] The 'Gentlemen of the Province' had started a subscription to rebuild in brick and £500 had already been promised. Daniel Roberts was not so optimistic and he believed that Bethesda had been taken away from William Piercy as a punishment for his autocratic ways.[62] Both he and Lewis Richards wished to leave Bethesda and preach in the backwoods, but were forbidden to do so by William Piercy, who preferred to use them to read the service when he went preaching.[63] Soon after the fire Mr Eccles returned to England where he created more problems for the Countess.[64] The extent of her concern about Bethesda is seen by some notes which she jotted down on an old draft letter at this time

> Plantation
> Settlement of Land – doubtfull...
> Mr Eccles...
> No Plan of Building to be thought on till that sent by the arrears
> Hill and other Students Consider'd
> No accomptant yet found – reasons why one [abroad] might now be found better
> On the Cross.[65]

Only Richard Piercy seems to have caused no difficulties at this time. Having no clerical ambitions he settled into Cosson's place as superintendent and ran the Orphan House and plantation very creditably.

[61] Cheshunt archives, A 4/1, 8, W. Piercy to Lady H., 8 June 1773.
[62] Cheshunt archives, A 3/6, 20, Roberts to Lady H., 26 August 1773.
[63] Cheshunt archives, A 3/6, 11, Richards to Lady H., 30 July 1773; A 3/6, 6, Roberts to Lady H., 1 January 1774. For Berridge's views on the fire see R. Whittingham, *The Works of the Rev. John Berridge* (London, 1838), 382.
[64] Cheshunt archives, A 4/1, 7, W. Piercy to Lady H., 27 May 1773; E 4/9, Eccles's letters. Eccles also claimed to have written Henry Mackenzie's *The Man of Feeling* which was published anonymously in 1771 (B. Lenman, *Integration, Enlightenment, and Industrialization in Scotland* (Toronto, 1981), 98).
[65] Cheshunt archives, E 4/8, 17, Lord H. to Lord Moira, n.d.

The Countess's position as George Whitefield's successor in North America also led to an increased correspondence for her from the other side of the Atlantic. The Revd Nathaniel Whitaker of Salem asked to be sent tracts for distribution. David Vanhorne of New York consulted her about his religious beliefs.[66] She also became involved in the perennial dispute about the boundary between the provinces of New York and Pennsylvania. The Revd Mr Page, an Anglican clergyman of Methodist views, appealed to Lady Huntingdon to approach Lord Dartmouth, who was then Secretary of State for the American Colonies, on their behalf, but the dispute was not settled.[67] One of Page's letters on the subject was taken to England by Phyllis Wheatley, 'the Christian Poetess'.[68] She had already sent the Countess a copy of her poem on the death of George Whitefield. Now she was being brought to England for the benefit of her health. Her mistress put her in the care of the Countess: 'I did not think it worth while nor did the time permit to fit her out with cloaths: but I have given her money to Buy what you think most proper for her, I like she should be dress'd plain. Must beg your Ladiship to advise my son to some Christian Home for Phillis to board at.' Unfortunately Lady Huntingdon was at Trefeca during Phyllis's very short stay in London and they did not meet. She had already agreed to have the book of her poems dedicated to her. The printer of the poems reported that she 'was greatly pleas'd with them, and pray'd him to Read them; and would often break in upon him and Say, "is not this, or that, very fine? do read another," ... [she] Question'd him much, whether she was Real without a deception?'[69]

The final problem to trouble the Countess was her inheritance of slaves. Slave-owning had only been introduced into Georgia a few years before she inherited Bethesda, at a time when public opinion was beginning to move against it in Britain. The Society of Friends urged all Quakers, both in England and in Pennsylvania, to free their slaves and oppose all trade in them.[70] Anthony Benezet, the principal Quaker campaigner against

[66] Cheshunt archives, A 3/1, 20, Whitaker to Lady H., 7 December 1770; A 3/3, 10, Vanhorne to Lady H., 20 October 1772.

[67] Cheshunt archives, A 3/5, 18, B. Page to R. Cary, 26 April 1773; F 1/2488, petition, n.d. See also *HMC, Dartmouth 2*, p. 100; *Minutes of the Supreme Executive Council of Pennsylvania*, 14 (Harrisburg, 1853), 220.

[68] Cheshunt archives, A 3/5, 8, R. Cary to Lady H., 3 May 1773.

[69] Cheshunt archives, A 3/5, 3, Susanna Wheatley to Lady H., 30 April 1773, printed in *The Journal of Negro History* 57 (1972), 214; J. D. Mason (ed.), *The Poems of Phyllis Wheatley* (Chapel Hill, NC, 1989), 7. Lady Huntingdon's own copy of the *Poems* is in Cheshunt College library.

[70] R. M. Jones, *The Later Period of Quakerism* (London, 1921), 318; R. M. Jones (ed.), *The Quakers in the American Colonies* (London, 1911), 515.

slavery and spirituous liquors in Philadelphia, took it upon himself to convince Lady Huntingdon that slavery was immoral. He recognized her dilemma and the difficulty of disposing of her slaves in a humane manner:

> I understand that since the decease of my dear Friend George Whitefield, the direction of his Settlement in Georgia is under thy direction. I am persuaded if thou art rightly inform'd of the situation of the Slaves in that as well as the other South Colonies, thou wilt be engaged to give such direction with respect to the Managers there, making any further purchase of Slaves, as well as their treatment of them already under their Care, as will be agreeable to best Wisdom.[71]

Her reply, which has not survived, was sufficiently favourable for him to send a second long letter, together with copies of John Wesley's *Thoughts on Slavery* and Woolman's *Journal*, but it seems improbable that she promised that the employment of slaves 'should never have her countenance'.[72] Her attitude towards slavery was similar to that of other evangelicals – since the future life was more important than the present one, it was better to keep slaves in a comfortable and Christian setting than to release them into a harsh and pagan world.[73] Unfortunately this did not take account of the managers at Bethesda, who were accused of selling them or depriving them of clothes and food.

The cost of Bethesda to Lady Huntingdon was high, despite her efforts to economize. She had equipped everyone who went there with clothes and paid their passages. After they had reached Georgia she continued to send them clothes.[74] The fire caused her even greater expense. All this, together with the disputes which constantly arose there and were referred back to her, and her inability to visit Georgia as she had intended, were responsible for her decision to surrender the trust. In 1773 she planned to recall William Piercy and 'to put an end for the present to the Orphan House Plan and either for a Season to let every thing lie dormant or give up the whole Grants of the Orphan House Lands to the Province in Case the Governor Council and Assembly will reimburse you as to the Moneys ... already expended.'[75] A long letter from Georgia urged her not to give

[71] Cheshunt archives, A 3/1, 33, Benezet to Lady H., 20 May 1774.
[72] Cheshunt archives, A 4/7, 9, Benezet to Lady H., 10 March 1775; R. Vaux, *Memoirs of the Life of Anthony Benezet* (Philadelphia, 1817), 41.
[73] See for example W. Piercy's letter to Lady H., 11 June 1774 (Cheshunt archives, A 4/2, 10). James Hervey bought a slave for Bethesda (J. Cole, *Herveiana, Part the Second* (Scarborough, 1823), 99. For the earlier Christian approach to slavery see S. Neill, *A History of Christian Missions* (London, 1964), 4.
[74] Cheshunt archives, A 2/7, 10.
[75] Cheshunt archives, A 3/6, 21, anon. to Lady H., 29 October 1773; F 1/1656, Glascott to Lady H., 27 August 1773; *HMC Dartmouth 2*, p. 166.

up the work, and by February 1774 she had become more optimistic. An American visitor to London obtained from Mr Telfair, a merchant in Savannah, answers to a number of questions about the profit which might be made by raising rice to sell in London, which reassured her that Bethesda might be self-supporting.[76] Robert Keen and Daniel West, having read Mr Piercy's 'pleasing account of the Orphan House and promising prospect of the produce of your Ladyships Estate' approved her decision to continue, but urged her

> to postpone Erecting any New Building or being at any further Expence till you see what this Crop actually produces – and send Mr Piercy word as soon as the Rice is Barrelled to send them over to your Ladyship and if there is the Quantity of 600 Barrels as He thinks there will, and it proves to be a good sort and suitable – your Ladyship will have the most rational grounds to go upon to enlarge your designs.[77]

Although the accounts kept by Richard Piercy do not show the large profits intended and the rice was sold in Savannah, nevertheless the estates began to show a small profit over the next few years.[78]

These problems were soon dwarfed by the troubles which beset the American colonies. Even before George Whitefield's death the Stamp Act and other efforts to tax the colonies had caused trouble.[79] In September 1774 the first Continental Congress met at Philadelphia. Georgia was not represented there, but it was already becoming clear that civil war was threatened. The Countess's grandson was present at Bunker's Hill and wrote to Lord Huntingdon describing the British victory. William Piercy's account sent to the Countess, on the other hand, describes the condition of the 'poor oppress'd and distressed Provincials'.[80] His brother was equally pessimistic: 'The political State of Affairs is such that altho' I write so frequently I am fearful very few come to hand. The awful and gloomy Appearance strikes me with Horror and I shudder at the Approach of a Civil War, a War always replete with Terror in which the Innocent and Guilty are promiscuously involved.'[81] His was almost the last letter Lady Huntingdon was to receive from Bethesda for many years. The break in

---

[76] Cheshunt archives, A 3/3, 19, Telfair's replies, March 1774; F 1/1680, Green to Lady H., 12 March 1774.

[77] Cheshunt archives, A 1/9, 8, Keen and West to Lady H., 5 February 1774.

[78] Cheshunt archives, A 2/3, 2.

[79] Georgia Hist. Soc., coll. 337, p. 61, copy of letter from Habersham to Whitefield, 7 February 1766. This letter is also addressed to 'the Countess of Sussex', which is probably a mistranscription of the address to 'the Countess of [Huntingdon at Brighton in] Sussex'.

[80] J. Thorpe (ed.), *Letters in Manuscript* (Huntington Lib., 1971), 11–14. Cheshunt archives, A 4/2, 17, W. Piercy to Lady H., 26 June 1775.

[81] Cheshunt archives, A 3/3, 22, R. Piercy to Lady H., 11 September 1775.

communications frustrated a further attempt by her to transfer the Bethesda trust to the Americans.[82] Although they regretted the outbreak of violence, Lady Huntingdon and most of the people at Bethesda supported the Americans in their attempts to break free. In July 1775 the Marchioness Gray wrote from Clifton about the Countess's attempts at peacemaking:

> We had here an Oleo of Lady Huntingdon, Mrs Macaula[y], and Dr Wilson famous in the Bill of Rights Club, lodging in the same house, and their three heads often seen together very earnest in a window. The first is gone to her flock at Bath, Mrs Macaula[y] is writing something; 'tis said to be a Plan of Government for the Americans.[83]

Many of her friends in England also supported the cause of the colonists. They believed it was their 'bounden Duty not to suffer myself [or my] countrymen to be made slaves ... I conclude ... that whenever Gods Word prevailed in forming the Constitution, as in the Kingdom of Israel, there was always equal Liberty. Let Subjects know their place; let Kings and Ministers also know theirs.' Lady Huntingdon herself wrote to her daughter in 1775 regretting 'the measures taken to Correct the poor people in America'. Her son was also a Whig and a member of the Leicestershire Revolution Club.[84] James Habersham died in 1775, but his three sons all supported the colonists. When the British army left Savannah, William Piercy stayed behind and took services in the churches there until the British returned.[85] One of the Countess's preachers, Cradock Glascott, preached a fast day sermon at Tottenham Court chapel on 'The Best Method of putting an End to the American War' which was very different from John Wesley's denunciation of the American colonists.[86] Their support for the American cause was eventually to save Bethesda from confiscation, though not from spoliation.

[82] Cheshunt archives, A 1/14, 5, Keen to Lady H., 13 November 1775.
[83] Beds. RO, L 30/9/17/88, Lady Gray to Lord Breadalbane, 6 July [1775]. An olio is a mixture of heterogeneous things, a farrago or mixture. For Macaulay and Wilson see C. L. S. Linnell (ed.), *The Diaries of Thomas Wilson* (London, 1964), 17–20. Macaulay wrote many political works, e.g. *Observations on the Reflections of the Right Hon. Edmund Burke* (London, 1790). Wilson was the son of the celebrated bishop of Sodor and Man.
[84] Lord Granard's MSS Lady H. to Lady Moira, 19 May 1775; Birmingham Univ. Lib., Venn papers, C 14/5, Venn to J. Stillingfleet, 15 November 1775. A. T. Patterson, *Radical Leicester* (Leicester, 1954), 64.
[85] R. B. Strickland, *Religion and the State in Georgia* (New York, 1939), 149. *Georgia Hist. Soc. Coll.*, 6 (Savannah, 1904), 7.
[86] C. Glascott, *The Best Method of putting an End to the American War ... with an Address from Henry Peckwell* (London, 1776). It was sold at the Tabernacle, Tottenham Court and the Countess's chapels. For John Wesley's opposing views see his *Calm Address to our American Colonies* (1775).

9

Secession

Lady Huntingdon, like all the other eighteenth-century Methodist leaders, had a problem to reconcile membership of the Anglican Church with itinerant evangelism. Eventually almost all the Methodists found it impossible, but the Connexion was to be one of the first to leave the Established Church. This was the result of her particular approach to the problem, which at the time seemed to offer more chance of success in reconciliation. Her continuing desire to remain an Anglican is shown by many events after her formal secession. Most of her chapels continued to use the Book of Common Prayer. Her college remained open to future Anglican ordinands. All its early presidents were Anglican clergymen, and the trustees whom she appointed were all Anglicans.

The Church of England, to which most of the early Methodists belonged, was organized on a parochial basis. Its ministers were appointed to a well-defined geographical area with one or more churches, and provided the services traditionally expected there. On the whole it carried out its objectives with reasonable efficiency. In some areas the ministers were underpaid and tried to serve too many churches on every Sunday: this was the result of poor endowments and a failure to redistribute income. Some parishes had no congregation, while others lacked seating for all the parishioners: this was caused by the movement of population. Throughout the eighteenth century the Church slowly dealt with this problem. Queen Anne's Bounty encouraged the endowment of new parishes, and Parliament authorized the building of fifty new churches in London. However progress was slow, and often a plurality was the only means of providing a clergyman with an adequate income. Evangelists, on the other hand, had no wish to observe parish boundaries, and paid little attention to the requests or orders of archdeacons and bishops. Their real objection to the great majority of clergymen was not that they neglected their duties, but that they were not evangelical. Most parishes had one or more services and sermons every Sunday. Communion was administered several times a year. Baptisms, marriages and burials were performed, and parishioners were visited, but Methodist practices were not followed. Most Methodists set out to provide evangelical sermons without respect for parish boundaries. They provided communion where it was thought that the minister was not sufficiently religious. Both parties were certain that they were right. Both were so inflexible that a clash was inevitable.

Lay Methodists were fortunate because in practice they were no longer subject to the discipline of the Church. In the seventeenth century a puritan attending an illicit service, or even reading sermons aloud, would find himself punished in the ecclesiastical courts. After the passing of the Toleration Act the only possible compulsion was to attend a place of worship, whether Anglican or dissenting, and even this soon ceased to be enforced.[1] It now became possible for persons to 'sermon-taste', attending different services on Sunday, either for variety or to find a spiritual home.[2] Richard Kay could attend a Quaker meeting in the morning and the Manchester collegiate church in the evening. While in London, he tried almost every denomination.[3] Methodists could safely attend both their own services and those of the parish church, and their meetings were arranged at different times from those of the Anglican services in order to permit this. The Anglican clergy, however, were still subject to the bishop and archdeacon, and discipline could be enforced – particularly when they held a benefice. It was possible for a clergyman to be prosecuted for preaching in another parish without the incumbent's permission. The procedure had become cumbersome and costly with the decline of the church courts, and bishops were reluctant to authorize it since most of the costs fell on them. They had other and more efficient ways of enforcing their orders. A clergyman might be inhibited from taking any services in the diocese. For example the bishop of London inhibited the third president of the Countess's college for accepting that position.[4] If a list of banned clergy was circulated in the diocese, this could be very effective.[5] More often it was an administrative decision. An incumbent could be persuaded to dismiss his evangelical curate, as Thomas Haweis was

[1] In the diocese of Chester in the early eighteenth century persons were cited for failure to attend any place of worship on Sundays.
[2] E.g. C. B. Andrews (ed.), *The Torrington Diaries* (London, 1934–8), vol.1, p.69; vol.3, p.234; J. Holloway, *The Journals of Two Poor Dissenters* (London, 1970), 46.
[3] W. Brockbank and F. Kenworthy, *The Diary of Richard Kay 1716–51* (Manchester, 1968), 67–82, 123.
[4] R. Hodgson, *Life of the Rt Rev. Beilby Porteous* (London, 1811), 267–8.
[5] Leics. R., 1D41/ 19/5, list of persons not permitted to serve cures, n.d.

expelled from his Oxford church. An evangelical incumbent could be harassed in various ways, even if he could not be removed. But the principal method of reducing the number of evangelical clergy was to prevent known Methodists from being ordinand. Each ordinand was required to have a title – a position which would provide him with an income – and a *testimonium* signed by three neighbouring clergymen of their own knowledge of him. The acquisition of these two pieces of paper was a frequent subject of the Countess's correspondence. Having surmounted these hurdles, the candidate for ordination then had to face an examination by the bishop or someone appointed by him. John Fletcher records how he escaped the rigours of examination by an enemy to Methodism. Isaac Nicholson persuaded his diocesan of his good faith.[6] If Methodism was to flourish, this question of ordination had to be solved, either in the Anglican Church or outside it.

A second problem which faced both clerical and lay Methodists was how to obtain protection from ill-treatment and rioting. Although persecution was spasmodic and confined to certain areas, it was an ever-present fear for evangelicals. The local incumbent might get the parish constable to threaten a visiting preacher with arrest, or might even raise a mob to end his sermon. The frequency with which visiting preachers were asked to promise not to return to the parish demonstrates the motive for many of the disturbances. However some of the disputes may have been caused by rivalries among the Methodists themselves. At Plymouth Dock (Devonport) a dispute between Arminians and Calvinists led to physical violence without any intervention from others.[7] In these situations the Methodists might either appeal to the local magistrates to restore order – just as they would in food or press-gang riots – or seek the protection of the Toleration Act. Local magistrates were frequently unsympathetic to any form of evangelism or dissent.[8] If they refused to suppress the riot, or even to prosecute the Methodists for starting it, then an application had to be made to the courts at Westminster for a *mandamus* to compel the magistrates to do their duty. Costs might be recovered and damages paid, but the procedure was slow and the expenses high.[9] Where there was a sympathetic local landowner an appeal for him to exert pressure behind the scenes might be more successful. However there was considerable

[6] Connexion archives 3, John Fletcher to Lady H., 28 October 1760; T. Bennett, *Funeral Sermon* for Isaac Nicholson (London, 1807), 26.

[7] E. Welch, 'Andrew Kinsman's Churches at Plymouth', *Trans. Devons. Assoc.*, 97 (1965), 221.

[8] B. L. Manning, *The Protestant Dissenting Deputies* (Cambridge, 1952), 98.

[9] E.g. J. L. Waddy, *The Bitter Sacred Cup* (London, 1976), 38, 39.

encouragement for Methodists to declare themselves dissenters and seek the protection of the Toleration Act in times of trouble. For example, on 27 March 1762 the house of Mr Ashdowne in Wivelsfield was licensed in the bishop of Chichester's court by John Ollive for the use of 'Presbyterians'. This was Lady Huntingdon's congregation at Oathall. A year later, on 6 May 1763, 'Mr Ollive desired me to take off the Licence for Oathall and says Lady Huntingdon desires it should be done.'[10] Eventually all the Methodists found themselves obliged to take the road of dissent. For the Countess it came in 1782, but for others not until the early nineteenth century.

The Countess's unique solution to the dilemma was to use her legal right as a widowed peeress to appoint Anglican chaplains. The practice began in the Middle Ages, but at the Reformation it was authorized by Act of Parliament, and the use of the privilege was changed.[11] Benefices worth more than £8 a year were not to be held in plurality unless the incumbent was the chaplain of a peer, bishop or senior state official. The Act also regulated the number of chaplains whom each could appoint, ranging from six for a duke or archbishop to two for the widow of a peer, and no one could license more than that number. While the Act states no more than that the deeds of appointment must be exhibited on request, it became usual to register them in the Court of Faculties. By the earlier eighteenth century this became an accepted method of authorizing pluralities.[12] For example, in 1752 attempts were made by Lady Fanny Shirley and others to get for James Hervey an appointment as chaplain so that he might accept a second benefice.[13] Younger, unbeneficed clergy seeking preferment now acted as domestic chaplains without formal appointment. Although earls were entitled to five chaplains, the Hastings family in the first half of the eighteenth century seems to have been as slow at making appointments as the Shirleys were keen. The Countess's husband made only three appointments before their marriage.[14] In the year after her husband's death, Lady Huntingdon appointed John Warcopp of Teddington as her chaplain. Although no further appointments

[10] West Sussex Record Office, Ep. II/ 25/ 2, p. 31. For a similar example see T. Jackson, *Life of Rev. Charles Wesley* (London, 1841), 187.

[11] 21 Henry, VIII, c. 13. See E. Gibson, *Codex Juris Ecclesiastici*, 2 (London, 1713), 945–9, and R. Burns, *Ecclesiastical Law*, 2 (London, 1763), 159.

[12] Gibson, op. cit., 949n.

[13] *Letters from the late Rev. James Hervey* (London, 1782), nos. 31, 33; Cheshunt archives, E 4/ 13, 31, appointment, 3 January 1780; F 1/ 617, Pentycross to Lady H., 13 August 1781.

[14] Lamb. Pal. Lib., FV/ 1/ VIII. For the appointment of George Gell by Lord Huntingdon, see Leics. RO, 14D32/ 10, 51, G. Wheler to Lord H., 14 September 1743. The Earl also offered an appointment to James Hervey in 1744 (*HMC, Hastings 3*, p. 43).

were registered until 1761, we know from other sources that George Whitefield had received her scarf.[15] At this time she considered it as no more than a mark of favour for evangelical clergymen, since few of these Methodists held even one benefice. The Countess also encouraged her friends to appoint evangelical (usually Calvinist) clergy as their chaplains.[16] However, about 1770 the Court of Faculties had begun to enforce the Act more closely, and earlier appointments had to be revoked or certificates of death provided when the number of appointments exceeded the allowance.[17]

It was probably about 1778 that the Countess began to use the privilege of appointing chaplains to protect the ministers serving her chapels. The idea may not have originated with her, because in the previous year the two clergymen who opened Northampton chapel in Clerkenwell had made an unsuccessful attempt to obtain the protection of a peer.[18] Shortly afterwards Lady Huntingdon took Henry Peckwell and his Westminster chapel 'under her patronage' for his protection.[19] Because the chapels which she had built herself had houses attached in which she lived they could be described as her private chapels, and therefore exempt from the local incumbent. The disadvantages of this procedure were that she could appoint only two chaplains legally, though this might escape attention if the appointments were not registered.

Her expedient was challenged by the Revd William Sellon, son of that Walter Sellon who was a Methodist and a protégé of the Hastings family. In 1770 the Earl gave Walter the benefice of Ledsham and received a very fulsome letter of thanks, but a year later Walter Sellon sided with John

---

[15] Lamb. Pal. Lib., FV/1/XI, 26 June 1747 (repeated in 1761), and FV/1/XIII, 3 January, 5 October and December 1761. John Warcopp was not the incumbent of Teddington and probably had an independent income. He was a friend of two evangelicals, Col. Gardiner and Mrs Edwin (Leics. RO, 14D32/ 14, 92, Warcopp to Lady H., 20 November 1745). A. Dallimore, *George Whitefield*, 2 (Edinburgh, 1980), 264. James Robe congratulated the Countess on this appointment on 18 October 1748 (Drew Univ., Hunt. B 46). Similarly John Wesley was appointed as chaplain to the Countess Dowager of Buchan (R. Green, *Works of John and Charles Wesley* (London, 1906), 266). This was probably at the Countess's request (NLW, MS 7005C, Lady H. to Lord Buchan, 5 July 1779).

[16] Lamb. Pal Lib., FV/1/XIV; Connexion archives 3, copy of letter of Henry Venn to Lady H., 18 December 1767.

[17] On 14 November 1772 the Countess had to revoke Madan's appointment before making another, and on 7 September 1773 the Countess Dowager of Chesterfield had to certify Howell Davies's death (Lamb. Pal. Lib., FV/1/XIV).

[18] Cheshunt archives, A 3/ 2, 16, undated statement by Lady Huntingdon.

[19] Cheshunt archives, F 1/ 1823, T. Wills to Lady H., 10 March 1778.

Wesley in the Calvinist controversy.[20] His son William was a notable pluralist. In 1758 the parishioners of St James Clerkenwell elected him vicar, and in 1779 he became minister of the newly erected Portman Chapel in Marylebone. In addition he was evening preacher at the Magdalene Hospital, and lecturer at St Andrew's Holborn and St Giles in the Fields. His total annual income was estimated at £1,300.[21] His stipend from Clerkenwell was only £4. 18s. 9d. a year, to which was added £6 for preaching regularly. The greater part of his income there came from voluntary subscriptions by his parishioners, which made him particularly liable to a reduction of income from Methodist competition.[22]

At this time Clerkenwell was a flourishing suburb of the City, and in 1769 William Craven leased land on the south side of Exmouth Street to provide a resort for drinking 'Tea and spiritous Liquors'. It was called the Pantheon, and it was later described by Lady Huntingdon as 'an Elegant Building erected at a great expense for public diversions'. She added that it became so notorious 'that the Civil Magistrate was obliged by his authority to put it down'. This probably occurred after the unhappy Mr Craven had been unable to pay the rent of £110 a year and been made bankrupt.[23] When the Pantheon closed in 1776 it was offered to the Countess, but she found that alterations would be too great when she had other commitments.[24] Instead it was rented by a group of Calvinistic Methodists, who licensed it as a dissenters' meeting house under the Toleration Act, and it was opened on 5 July 1777 by the Revd John Ryland, the Baptist minister of Northampton.[25] The immediate result seems to have been the transference of part of Sellon's congregation to the new chapel and a reduction in the subscriptions which he had received. In February 1778 Sellon proceeded against the Revd Herbert Jones and

[20] T.J. Williams, *Priscilla Lydia Sellon* (London, 1950), xi; Hunt. Lib., HA 10729, Sellon to Earl, 21 May 1770.
[21] W. J. Pinks, *The History of Clerkenwell* (London, 1880), 69; G. Hennessy, *Novum Repertorium Ecclesiasticum Parochiale Londinense* (London, 1898), 244, 329; M. H. Port (ed.), *Commission for Building Fifty New Churches* (London, 1986), xix; Lamb. Pal. Lib., FV/1/XIII.
[22] GLRO, DL/C/281, evidence of Benjamin Long.
[23] Cheshunt archives, E3/ 2, 16, note on Northampton chapel, n.d.; Pinks, op. cit., 141–3; [F.W. Willcocks], *Spa Fields Chapel and its Associations* (London, c. 1884), 8; GLRO, DL/C/281, evidence of Wm Brown.
[24] Pinks, op. cit., 144; Cheshunt archives, A2/ 10 and F1/ 1823.
[25] This was probably John Ryland (1753–1825), who later became president of the Bristol Baptist College (N. Moon, *Education for Ministry* (Bristol, 1979), 27, 28), but may have been his father, John Collett Ryland (1723–92), who was also minister of the Northampton Baptist church at this time.

the Revd William Taylor for preaching at the chapel.[26] Sellon 'promoted the office of judge for the correction of their manners' – a criminal prosecution.[27] In May the two appointed a proctor to appear in court on their behalf, and at the beginning of June a meeting was held at Northampton Chapel to raise a subscription to pay for their defence. A committee of thirteen City merchants and tradesmen was appointed to manage the defence.[28] The trial proceeded rapidly for an ecclesiastical court, and in February 1779 Jones and Taylor were admonished by the judge not to preach or hold any services at Northampton Chapel without Sellon's permission.[29]

The Countess had already decided to intervene in October, when she had a meeting with Thomas Wills, Cradock Glascott and William Taylor at Northampton Chapel.[30] When the news of Sellon's victory reached her at Bath she wrote: 'I set out to morrow for London in order to finish all things for the possession of N[orthampton] Chapel – and to have it opened ... Mr Taylour and Jones must not appear there Just at first and one may go to Bath and the other to Brighthelmstone for a time.'[31] To John Hawksworth in Dublin she wrote: 'I *think* I see my way Clear. I leave this place to morrow to take possession of Northampton Chapel a Congregation of near five thousand souls in London. It is a great undertaking for such a poor worm but the things that are despised God Chuses.'[32] She also wrote to the bishop of London, on her arrival in town, deploring the registration of the building as a dissenting chapel and seeking an interview to explain her plans.[33] Included with this letter was a copy of one she sent simultaneously to Sellon to tell him that she had taken the chapel 'under her protection'.[34]

When the bishop replied to her on the following day, he ignored her request for an interview and gave a veiled warning of his intentions to

---

[26] The practice of some Anglican clergy preaching in dissenters' meeting houses was not entirely unknown at this time (N. Sykes, *Edmund Gibson, Bishop of London* (Oxford, 1926), 237). In 1777 the new bishop of London, Robert Lowth, had declared his intention of stamping out the practice of clergy preaching in dissenters' meeting houses in his diocese (SMU, Hunt. 96, Lady H. to T. Haweis, 17 October 1777).

[27] GLRO, Acts of court, 28 February 1778.

[28] GLRO, Acts, 8 and 27 May 1778; Cheshunt archives, D1/ 2, printed in *Two Calv. Meth. Chapels*, 46. Several members were later enthusiastic supporters of the Countess.

[29] GLRO, Acts, 4 June 1778 9 February 1779.

[30] JRL, Eng. MS. 338, 10, Lady H. to Mr and Mrs Wills, 26 September 1778.

[31] JRL, Eng. MS 338, 6, letter, 16 February 1779.

[32] JRL, Eng. MS 338, 7, letter, 16 February 1779.

[33] Cheshunt archives, E 3 / 2, 3, copy of letter, 25 February 1779.

[34] Cheshunt archives, E 3 / 2, 4, copy of letter, [25 February 1779].

challenge her right to appoint chaplains.[35] Sellon's reply echoed the bishop's sentiments, asserting the justice of his prosecution of those who had attacked 'his character and fortune', and asking her to seek legal advice before proceeding further.[36] These replies depressed the Countess and led her to discuss alternatives, including secession.[37] All this time services at the chapel had been taken by dissenting ministers whom Sellon could not touch. Now notice was given that it would be closed for two Sundays in March, and reopened as Spa Fields chapel by Thomas Haweis, Thomas Wills and Cradock Glascott, 'her Ladyship's Chaplains'. The registration as a dissenters' meeting house was cancelled, and all persons attending the chapel were asked to exchange their tickets of admission for new ones issued in the Countess's name.[38] Every effort was made to provide a defence against another lawsuit by William Sellon. A door was opened between the chapel and the house, and Lady Huntingdon moved into the house as soon as it was habitable. On the day before the chapel reopened she formally appointed Thomas Haweis as her chaplain.[39] Both the bishop and Sellon took these moves as a good reason to decline the proffered visit of Lady Huntingdon. Both the bishop and Sellon seem to have feared the Countess's persuasive tongue, and so carefully avoided personal contact. Her final letter to the bishop was apparently ignored.[40] In it she raised the question that if Spa Fields chapel was now attacked, it would be an invasion of her rights as a peeress — and therefore the bishop might find himself sued in court under the common law. The two parties had incompatible objectives and neither would compromise. So far as we can judge, the congregation at Spa Fields was indifferent to the entire controversy. No defections were reported either when it became Anglican or when it reverted to the dissenters.[41]

Spa Fields chapel was opened on Palm Sunday, 28 March 1779: 'thousands attended and a sensible Blessing attended, the ordinances (Good Friday) was also Gloriously attended and spirit and life appear'd and that in a sacrament of hundreds — all have fear'd for me but my path has such light upon it to me that all enemys or as many fearing friends

[35] Cheshunt archives, E 3 / 2, 5, letter, 26 February 1779.
[36] Cheshunt archives, E 3 / 2, 13, letter, 27 February 1779.
[37] Nashville archives B, Lady H. to Beale, 9 March 1779. For Thomas Beale see J. P. Shawcross and E. A. B. Barnard, *Bengeworth* (Evesham, 1927), 61–7.
[38] Cheshunt archives, E 3/ 2, 12, copy of notice, n.d.
[39] GLRO, DL/C/281, Wm Brown's evidence; Lamb. Pal. Lib., FV/1/XV, fo. 40.
[40] Cheshunt archives, E 3/ 2, 7, bishop to Lady H., 11 March 1779); E 3 / 2, 15, copy of letter of Lady H. to Sellon, 25 March [1779]); E 3/ 2, 14, reply by Sellon, 25 March 1779; E3/ 2, 8, copy of letter of Lady H., 19 March 1779.
[41] See *Two Calv. Meth. Chapels*, 46–8.

have not been able to shake my Confidence.'⁴² But Sellon lost no time in promoting the office of judge against Thomas Haweis.⁴³ The Countess was optimistic and wrote to her niece in May: 'the appearances the more they are examin'd into assure the learned of its not being in their power to affect my privileges and it is supposed it will soon be dismist the spiritual Court and thus we shall tread upon the serpent ... and all the powers of darkness.'⁴⁴ Her optimism may have been encouraged by efforts behind the scenes to influence the bishop and his court. Her son had consulted with a 'noble friend who has been so kind to consider my present circumstances'. In a letter to an unknown correspondent she spoke of getting a legal opinion on her privileges as a widowed countess, which privileges she thought should be defended by the House of Lords.⁴⁵ The charges brought against Haweis were 'for publicly preaching and administering the Holy Sacraments and performing other Ecclesiastical Duties and Divine Offices in a certain Building lately ... called the Pantheon and since become known by the name of Northampton Chapel ... not Consecrated or in any manner Dedicated to Divine Worship ... without sufficient Licence or Authority first had and obtained ...' Proceedings pursued a leisurely course in the consistory court, and it was thought at first that 'Sellon would satisfy himself with the Cause against Haweis.'⁴⁶ However in November Sellon began proceedings against Cradock Glascott for the same offences. Witnesses in both causes were examined between December 1779 and February 1780, and the depositions give much information about the nature of the services which they had attended.⁴⁷ William Brown, an enameller of Cold Bath Fields, said that the Revd William Taylor told him that tickets of admission were not sold, but issued to subscribers. He paid half a crown for admission to the lower gallery for three months. Richard Walford, a brewer of St James Walk, asked Taylor for a ticket for the lower gallery, but Taylor urged him to pay a guinea for the 'Pulpit Desk ... where he said all the genteel People sat'.

⁴² Nashville archives C, Lady H. to Beale, 6 April 1779.
⁴³ GLRO, DL/ C, Acts, 30 April and 4 June 1779.
⁴⁴ JRL, Eng. MS. 338, 8, Lady H. to Mrs Wills, 11 May 1779.
⁴⁵ Cheshunt archives, E 3/ 3, 3, copy of letter of Lady H. to the Earl, 11 August 1779; E 3/ 3, 1, copy of letter of Lady H., written 16 October and sent 26 October 1776.
⁴⁶ Cheshunt archives, F 1/ 1830, Wills to Lady H., 16 July 1779. It is interesting to note the reference to the lack of episcopal consecration in a century when it was sometimes neglected. GLRO, Acts, 30 April 1779, and Acts, 12 June 1779. Most of the proceedings in ecclesiastical courts were in writing. Cheshunt archives, F 1/ 1830; GLRO, Acts, 2 July 1779. Haweis was seriously ill from overwork and the poor living conditions at Spa Fields (Mitchell Lib., B 1226, pp. 127, 128).
⁴⁷ All the information in this paragraph is taken from GLRO, DL/ C/ 281.

When he renewed his subscription in August, he was told that Haweis no longer preached there 'on account of a Spirit of Persecution which had prevailed for some time'. Instead he heard a young man preach who he thought was Glascott. Not all those attending were subscribers. Some 200 seats were reserved for people without tickets.[48] The chapel was said to have 2,000 or 2,500 seats and it was usually full. Richard Walford had difficulty in getting a seat even though he held a ticket. Little was said about the services, which were conducted in accordance with the Anglican Book of Common Prayer. All the witnesses admitted that they attended with Lady Huntingdon's permission.

In April 1780 the judge prepared to hear the arguments on both sides, and in May he admonished Haweis (but not Glascott) against reading prayers or administering the sacrament at Spa Fields in future.[49] While Sellon waited for Lady Huntingdon's next move, she considered the possibility of seceding from the Church. She was probably still weak from 'putrid fever', and her recovery cannot have been helped by the pessimistic letters which she received.[50] Most advised her against secession. A third sect 'between the Establishment and Dissenters' would not be permitted, and her congregations elsewhere might suffer 'for the sake of a place which many have never seen, and others never heard of'. The Countess anticipated abandoning the Church and lamented its decline:

> The few scattered professing clergy who will not venture out of a Curacy to save a soul, will not, cannot be supposed to be more venturesome when their greater interests or even their own lives might be at stake – Thus every hope of the fundamental doctrines of the Church, as it now stands, being maintained must be by a body of those that will defend them by every loss ... To pursue legally this matter further is only to be rejected ... Let the peers take up their own rights...[51]

By the end of June a declaration had been drafted by which Wills, Glascott and Taylor were to announce their intention of withdrawing from the Established Church: 'And this we desire to do; not from a factious or schismatical Spirit, not from a Design to propagate Heresies in the Church of God, not from any sinister or lucrative Motives whatsoever; but from a simple view of glorifying God, of preaching the Gospel, and of

---

[48] GLRO, DL/ C/ 281, evidence of Richard Walford.
[49] GLRO, Acts, 13 March, 21 April, 26 May 1780. Judgment was reached by the lawyers on both sides drawing up a sentence. The judge would then accept that of the successful party.
[50] Cheshunt archives, E 3/ 3, 1, copy of letter of Lady H. to anon., 26 October 1779; F 1/ 448, Shirley to Lady H., 14 September 1779; F 1/ 469, Peckwell to Lady H., 31 July 1780.
[51] Cheshunt archives, E 3/ 3, 2, copy of letter of Lady H. to Mr Way, 25 July 1780.

being useful to our fellow-creatures ...' Lady Huntingdon had even written a draft of the note to be sent to the Archbishop asking for an interview, when she decided not to be too precipitate.[52] In August when she wrote to her son she was prepared to secede:

> The alternative for me plainly appears this at present (viz.) either to shut up all my Chapels in England or Wales, which are numerous, with the still greater number of places not yet under that Character, or to submit to a dismission from the Church by a Law now existing against me ... fear nor care not about me my dear Son, I have a faithful friend who has said 'I will never leave nor forsake you' ... I extremely love you.[53]

But before doing so she decided to appeal to the archbishop's Court of Arches, and from there to the court of Delegates if necessary.[54] It was also possible to take action in the common law courts, and early in 1780 her lawyer applied for a rule in the court of King's Bench. She still hoped that the House of Lords would take up the question of their privileges, but was not successful in either attempt.[55] These efforts were probably the result of objections to her secession from some of the evangelicals.[56] It did not assist Lady Huntingdon's cause when she discovered that 'there is now arose a secret new dissenting ordination which none in Connection with me had any information of – it is for Itinerants only, by which means great publick Confusion must follow.'[57]

In November Haweis's appeal was produced in the Arches and Sellon was admonished to put in his reply, but before this could be done Haweis abandoned the appeal. The cause was returned to the bishop of London's court for a final decree to be issued.[58] No further entries appear in the court records and nothing further was attempted against Glascott. During all this time the services at Spa Fields chapel had not been interrupted. Lady Huntingdon had appointed a committee and it had negotiated with

---

[52] Cheshunt archives, E 3/ 3, 10 is the first draft of this document; E 3/ 3, 11 is the final version, which was printed almost verbatim in *An Authentic Narrative of the Primary Ordination* (London, 1784), iv; E 3/ 3, 9, draft note, n.d.

[53] Cheshunt archives, E 3/ 3, 3, copy of letter of Lady H. to Lord H., 11 August 1780.

[54] GLRO, Acts, 31 May 1780; Lamb. Pal. Lib, Arches Aa 75, fo. 8.

[55] Cheshunt archives, E 4/ 10, 8, copy of letter from Lady H. to anon., 29 May 1780; SMU, Hunt. 103, Lady H. to [T. Haweis], 20 November.

[56] Cheshunt archives, E 3/ 3, 12, Romaine to Lady H., n.d.; F 1/ 472, Lloyd to Lady H., 15 August 1780. For John Wesley's opinion on her secession, see *Letters*, vol.8, p.92.

[57] SMU, Hunt. 113, Lady H. to T. Haweis, 12 February 1780. Nine years later Rowland Hill caused similar problems when a new chapel was opened at Haverfordwest in Pembs. (*Two Calv. Meth. Chapels*, 79). For Hill, see E. Sidney, *The Life of The Rev. Rowland Hill* (London, 1844).

[58] Lamb. Pal. Lib., Arches E 45/ 10; Aa 76, fo. 9; G 151/ 5. GLRO, Acts, 1 March 1780.

the leaseholders to buy out all their interest. In February 1780 they had sent a petition to the bishop of London signed by 'as many inhabitants of the parish as chose to sign it'. When it was delivered to the bishop, 'his lordship was pleased to say he would consider [it] with particular attention', but nothing more was heard from him.[59]

After the court proceedings ended, the Spa Fields committee began to take a more active part. At the beginning of April they decided to make a direct approach to Sellon, but found him 'inflexible in his demands', insisting that the chapel should be put in his hands. The committee then wrote to the Countess suggesting an immediate secession. In May another delegation visited Sellon, who replied that 'it is not in his power to make any concessions or agree to any terms but those of an absolute right to and authority over the chapel as a chapel of ease to the parish of Clerkenwell.'[60] The committee again suggested an immediate secession, fortifying their advice with a legal opinion which they had obtained, but once again the Countess temporized. In December 1781 the committee wrote to her again: 'It is with real concern we hear Mr Sellon perseveres in prosecuting our dear ministers and has so far succeeded as to silence that faithful and upright man of God, Mr Glascott, whose ministry was so much blest to this congregation, and whose loss will be greatly regretted.'[61] Finally on 7 January 1782 the Countess replied agreeing to their request. Thomas Wills agreed to secede, saying that he was 'a dissenter from principle'. A few days later Spa Fields was once again registered as a dissenters' meeting house. This was an extreme measure, and one which which the Methodists had hitherto avoided.

Apart from the information in the Spa Fields minute book, there is little evidence about the act of secession. Of the three ministers who had agreed to sign the draft, only Wills and Taylor did so. There is no evidence that it was ever handed to the archbishop of Canterbury, and it was not published until 1783.[62] Of the other ministers, Thomas Haweis protested to the Countess and refused to secede. As an incumbent he had more to lose than either Wills or Taylor. Cradock Glascott also found himself unable to secede because he had been appointed vicar of Hatherleigh in Devon the

---

[59] *Two Calv. Meth. Chapels*, 48–51.
[60] Ibid., 54, 55.
[61] Ibid., 62. Cheshunt archives, E 4/ 10, 11, copy of letter from Lady H. to Glascott, 8 June 1781.
[62] *An Authentic Narrative*, op. cit., iv.

previous December.⁶³ William Piercy, who had also preached at Spa Fields, soon left the Connexion in a dispute with the Countess. Some ministers continued to preach for her as if the secession had never occurred.⁶⁴ The Countess signed the Fifteen Articles of the Connexion with a flourish as 'S: Huntingdon Seceder', but this was her only public action.⁶⁵ The entire process of lawsuits and secession seems to have attracted little attention outside the Connexion. Surprisingly no pamphlets were published by either side in the dispute, and there was no public comment, although it appears that some publication was planned by the Countess. Amongst her papers are several draft statements, one of which describes the Methodists as divided into three groups – the Anglicans, 'Mr Wesley's people' and the dissenters. It suggests that nothing could be done with the Wesleyans 'as they will make a sect of themselves tolerated as not belonging to the principles of the Church'. The dissenters, on the other hand, 'exclude themselves uprightly' from the Church. If the bishops do not allow the Angican Methodists to make provision for 'the thousands that must be neglected Collieries Manufactories Towns in different Places which only one Minister has the charge of, and his labors day and night during his life from the succession of Strangers, and Miles distant from any place of Worship', then many would turn to the dissenters for spiritual comfort.⁶⁶ Another of these drafts is a defence of Taylor and Jones by the Countess, which denies a rumour that they had profited by fees from the Spa Fields burial ground – a commercial operation which had no links with the chapel.⁶⁷ Her failure to publish these papers may be linked to the arguments advanced earlier – publicity about the secession might well damage the Connexion in other places and provide arguments to be used against her. Sellon now ceased his attacks, since a nonconformist chapel could not be claimed as an Anglican chapel of ease. Until another incumbent took similar action against one of her chapels it would be as well for her to remain quiet. A letter which the Countess wrote to Mr and Mrs Wills in 1781 implies that this was her intention.⁶⁸ Two years later in a letter to her Thomas Wills wrote: 'Poor Sellon is just now struck with the Palsy; and his mouth so

⁶³ Mitchell Lib., A 3023 (131), draft letter of Haweis to Lady H., n.d.; M. Cook (ed.), *The Diocese of Exeter in 1821*, 2 (Torquay, 1960), 92.
⁶⁴ Connexion archives, 3, Jones no. 10, copy of letter of David Jones to Lady H., 21 May 1783.
⁶⁵ Cheshunt archives, C 18/ 1.
⁶⁶ Cheshunt archives, E 3/ 2, 17.
⁶⁷ Cheshunt archives, E 3/ 2, 16. For the burial ground see Pinks, op. cit., 150.
⁶⁸ JRL, Eng. MS. 338, 11, Lady H. to Wills, 14 April 1781.

distorted as to be unable to speak for two days. I believe few persecutors go even out of this world without some signal afflictive dispensation in a Day of Judgment.'[69]

The seccession solved one of Lady Huntingdon's problems: she was no longer dependent on reluctant bishops to ordain her students. Instead a presbyterian form of ordination was adopted, by which two or three of her ministers could ordain others. Her 'primary ordination' was held at Spa Fields chapel on 9 March 1783, and it was made a special occasion. Thomas Wills and William Taylor ordained six of the Trefeca students.[70] The proceedings were prolonged because it was felt necessary to make a public explanation of the secession and to read the Fifteen Articles. There was a second ordination in London in July, but after that they were held at any location which suited the convenience of the ministers and students.

---

[69] Cheshunt archives, F 1/ 1909, Wills to Lady H., 8 October 1783. Sellon did not die until 18 July 1790, when Lady Huntingdon described him as 'my poor and sure Enemy and Persecutor' (SMU, Hunt. 126, Lady H. to T. Haweis, 19 July 1790).

[70] *An Authentic Narrative.*

10

Bethesda Again

The early stages of the War of Independence saw very little violence in Georgia. It was the southernmost of the English colonies, with a small population, and a governor who was personally popular. A provincial congress was called in 1775, but Governor Wright (now honoured with a baronetcy for his support of the Crown) was able to prevent any disturbance until January 1776, when he was arrested but succeeded in escaping to England. However it proved impossible to raise an adequate force to defend the colony.[1] George Whitefield's relations in Georgia all supported the colonists, and so did William Piercy, who preached before the Provincial Congress.[2] Piercy's last letter to reach the Countess described the Battle of Bunker Hill in very different terms from those used by her great-nephew writing to Lord Huntingdon. The 'rebels' are described by Piercy as 'the poor oppress'd and distressed Provincials' and Charlestown (by Boston) 'all laid in Ashes and the poor People driven into the Fields'.[3] For more than two years Lady Huntingdon heard nothing more of Bethesda, her chaplain and her students. In March 1777 she heard rumours of Piercy's progress:

> I suppose it is true that he is married, as a relation of Mr Hawkins's in Cheapside declared he was in company with him and his wife at Philadelphia, but I did not see this gentleman, as I was then in the country. I never heard that he was settled in any place, nor do I suppose that half the prevailing reports are true.[4]

[1] For an account of the War as it affected Georgia see K. Coleman, *The American Revolution in Georgia* (Athens, 1958), and the appropriate chapters of H. Lee, *The American Revolution in the South* (New York, 1869).

[2] *Minutes of the Georgia Council of Safety* (Georgia Hist. Soc. Coll., 5, pt 1, 1901), 35, 85, 87. A. D. Candler (ed.), *The Revolutionary Records of the State of Georgia*, 2 (Atlanta, 1908), 127.

[3] Cheshunt archives, A 4/ 2, 17, W. Piercy to Lady H., 26 June 1775; F 1/ 1326, G. Green to Lady H., 4 May 1776. The Countess's grandson Lord Rawdon was taken prisoner by French troops (Cheshunt archives, E 4/ 10, 7).

[4] Cheshunt archives, F 1/383, J. Grove to Lady H., 4 March 1777

It was not until October that she heard directly from William Piercy.[5] He reported that Bethesda had been spared the 'surrounding Troubles and Horrors of War' and was even flourishing since the rice crops had been good. Three slaves had been carried off by the loyalists and he could not recover them. Because of the troubles he had been obliged to restrict his preaching to Georgia and South Carolina, but he was now married and had 'the Prospect of a Family'. Piercy was also able to tell her that Betty Cosson had died when her husband took her off to the backwoods in 1776.

That the Bethesda plantation was comparatively prosperous can be demonstrated from the accounts kept by Richard Piercy from 1776 to 1779 and later copied for the Countess.[6] This came to an end in December 1778, when Georgia was recaptured by the British. Many of the inhabitants fled and were 'drove about as the operations of the War progressed'.[7] Very heavy inflation now played havoc with the economy, and the Piercys were reduced to selling slaves. William Piercy felt it necessary to withdraw his family from 'the merciless insults of savage Indians and more than savage Hessian Soldiers who often plundered and destroyed without pity' and finally took them to safety in South Carolina, from where he sailed to England.[8] The first news of these events reached Lady Huntingdon in a letter from a stranger, George Baillie, who had been placed in charge of Bethesda by Sir James Wright:

> The person with whom your Ladyship was pleas'd to entrust the management of the affairs of the Orphan House in this Province having (I may venture to say) improperly taken part in the American contest in opposition to his Majesties Government ... he has fled from hence, carried off a considerable number of the Negroes, and left the Orphan House in a very confused State.[9]

Nevertheless Bethesda once again benefited from having friends in both parties. In July Baillie wrote again to say that he had sent an inventory of all that remained at Bethesda.[10] He had heard that General Prevost, Campbell's superior officer, had ordered much of the property to be carried away, but had later returned it to Bethesda.

The Countess now found William Telfair, who was on his way to Georgia, to report on Bethesda. In 1780 he was able to tell her that Piercy

---

[5] Cheshunt archives, A 4/2, 20, W. Piercy to Lady H., 3 October 1777.
[6] Cheshunt archives, A 2/ 3, 2.
[7] Georgia Hist. Soc., coll. 152, letter book copy, J. Clay to Lady H., 16 February 1784.
[8] Cheshunt archives, A 4/2, 21, W. Piercy to Lady H., 15 January 1781; A 4/ 5, 3, copy of permission to leave, 13 September 1780).
[9] Cheshunt archives, A 3/ 7, 1, Baillie to Lady H., 13 April 1779; A 2/ 3, 2, records of transactions as late as November 1779 and the payment of outstanding debts.
[10] Cheshunt archives, A 3/ 7, 2, Baillie to Lady H., 29 July 1779.

had left two attorneys, Josiah Tatnall and Nathaniel Hall, in charge of Bethesda.[11] They had recovered the estate from Baillie with some difficulty, and the Countess sent them a new letter of attorney to regularize the situation.[12] They continued to act for the Countess until July 1782 when the British troops were withdrawn from Georgia. Nathaniel Hall went to Jamaica from where he wrote to Lady Huntingdon:

> The middle of June last Orders arrived for His Majestys Troops to Evacuate Georgia in Consequence of which Mr Tatnall and myself (Our Estates being Confiscated by the Americans) were obliged to abandon our property – he is gone to East Florida and I arrived here Yesterday with my Negroes and the property of Sir James Wright etc. under my Care – The Orphan House property and your Ladyships, being exempt from Confiscation We left it intire.[13]

The Countess now turned to two inhabitants of Charleston, John Glen jun. and Roger Smith, who had been appointed attorneys along with Hall and Tatnall in 1781. They were able to do little to help her, and by 1783 Glen left Roger Smith in sole charge.[14]

Meanwhile William Piercy had landed at Cork in Ireland and hastened to assure the Countess that he had always remained loyal to her.[15] Between her failure to reply to his letters (which she had not received) and the censure of Sir James Wright for supporting the colonists, he told her that he felt he had been 'separated from your friendship and love'. He denied that he had entered into politics, and said he only remained in Georgia to save Bethesda from plunder. During the period before the British occupation he had not only preserved the estates, but

> particular Parts [were] greatly improved – A new Rice Plantation was settled – a new Indigo one from the wild wood of Nazareth – and the two whole wings which were falling down by being built at first with bad Timber were actually taken down and the whole rebuilt with Bricks made on the Place without a single Shilling being spent.

[11] In Cheshunt archives, A 3/ 3, 23 Lady H. says he was 'on the board of Police in Georgia'. Cheshunt archives, A 3/ 7, 4–6, Telfair to Lady H., 15 June–23 September 1779; A 3/ 7, 7, Telfair to Lady H., 28 August 1780.

[12] Cheshunt archives, A 3/ 7, 8, Tatnall to W. Piercy, 24 December 1781; A 3/ 7, 10 and 11, Tatnall and Hall to Lady H., 11 July 1781, and 27 January 1782; A 4/ 4, 10, Lord George Germain to Lady H., 25 May 1781, enclosing A 4/ 4, 11 from Wright, 25 February 1781); A 4/ 4, 17, draft letter of Lady H. to Glen and Smith, n.d.

[13] Cheshunt archives, A 3/ 9, 1, Hall to Lady H., 15 August 1782; A 3/ 9, 2 and 3, Hall to Lady H., 26 October 1782, 10 July 1783.

[14] Cheshunt archives, A 3/ 7, 22, Glen to Lady H., 20 March 1782; A 3/ 9, 4, Smith to Lady H., 10 December 1783.

[15] Cheshunt archives, A 4/ 2, 21, W. Piercy to Lady H., 15 January 1781.

With the arrival of the British troops all was changed, according to Piercy. General Prevost had seized linen and other goods for his personal use and then permitted 'a very bad Woman' to take charge and destroy the rest. 'Nor could he plead Ignorance as I wrote him and Governor Wright very fully upon the Subject at the very Time I gave my Reason for leaving Home and requested all things in your Ladyships name might be preserved by a safe Guard from Ravage and Plunder.' He also offered his account books and other records for the scrutiny of 'some Person of Business'.[16] Since Piercy had arrived back at a most critical stage in the Spa Fields crisis Lady Huntingdon welcomed the arrival of a friendly minister who would support her there and might well secede with her if this became necessary. Piercy was very much on the defensive about his conduct of the affairs of Bethesda, and complained of her coldness towards him.[17] He eventually met the Countess at Bath and persuaded her of his innocence. He alleged that he had left behind in the hands of various merchants at least £500 sterling from the profits of Bethesda, and she gave him a promissory note for that amount to be paid after it had been remitted from Georgia.[18] She also appointed him to preach at Spa Fields chapel, and he moved his family into the chapel house. He soon complained of the exertion of both conducting the service and preaching at Spa Fields, and asked the committee there to appoint a student as reader. After several moves to other chapels he decided to settle at Woolwich in the Plumstead Road chapel where he had preached before his departure for Georgia.[19] He arrived at Woolwich in October 1782, but encountered some difficulties. Before Piercy went abroad he had obtained £500 from Lady Huntingdon towards the erection of a chapel, and she continued to support the congregation until a Mr Groves came to her aid.[20] The subsequent dispute between Piercy and Lady Huntingdon

---

[16] Cheshunt archives, A 4/ 2, 22, W. Piercy to Lady H., 20 January 1781.

[17] Cheshunt archives, A 4/ 2, 24, W. Piercy to Lady H., 2 March 1781; A 4/ 2, 25, W. Piercy to Lady H., 9 March 1781.

[18] Cheshunt archives, A 4/ 6, 7 9, 23 6 March 1781; *Two Calv. Meth. Chapels*, 54, 55. His text was Exodus 14 13.

[19] Ibid., 56 8; Cheshunt archives, A 4/ 7, 6, Spa Fields accounts, 2 July 1783; Hunt. Lib., HM 43197, Lady H. to W. Piercy, 14 October 1781, Cheshunt archives, A 4/ 4, 1 lists letters from Piercy written at Woolwich on 10 October and 5 December 1782; A 4/ 7, 4, W. Piercy to Lady H., 14 September 1782).

[20] Cheshunt archives, A 4/ 7, 5, W. Piercy to Lady H., 7 November 1782; A 4/ 4, 6, queries for Mr Piercy, n.d. (another copy of this is Essex RO, Acc. 4497, B 6, a collection of Thomas Day's papers). O. F. G. Hogg, *The Royal Arsenal* (Oxford, 1963), vol.2, p.1319. For this and other references to the chapel I am indebted to Ms Veronica Moore of Eltham.

about Bethesda caused problems with Groves, and the chapel ceased to be part of the Connexion.

Not only had a merchant to whom Lady Huntingdon had sent Piercy's Bethesda accounts been 'much dissatisfied with them', but further information received from Georgia painted a very different picture of Piercy's activities there.[21] Although she had paid his travelling expenses in North America for the first few years, she had never been able to obtain an account of what he had spent. Now she was told that 'he Travelled with a Pheaton and four fine Horses – Caused himself to be drove by one of Lady Huntingdons Students – Hired a Servant at Philadelphia to whom he gave 25 Guineas a Year Wages, besides having two stout Negroe Boys to attend him...'

Some of this information came from his brother, Richard Piercy who had defended his brother at first, but now alleged that he 'had sometimes carried [William] a hundred Guineas in a morning for the Sale of Cattle etc. and that on such occasions his Brother used to throw him a couple of Guineas for the use of the Family, and carry away the rest'.[22]

The students continually complained that he would not let them preach, and all the students whom Lady Huntingdon had sent over in 1772 left Bethesda within two years. Piercy now demanded that she should pay him for the years which he had spent in North America, as well as £250 that Mr Groves demanded for the Woolwich chapel.[23] In June 1783 he proposed that each side should appoint two arbitrators to settle the matters in dispute. A month later he threatened a suit in Chancery unless she immediately agreed to arbitration about her 'most unjust cruel and dishonourable Conduct'.[24] She replied: 'Revd Sir, Every part of that very extraordinary letter except the above passage [suggesting arbitration], appears unnecessary to be answered at present, yet always wishing that Equity that met the heart of Zacheus may ever be retained in mine "If I have wronged any man I am willing to restore him fourfold."' On 26 July Piercy nominated Robert Keen and Mr Durrant as his arbitrators, although it was clearly undesirable that Keen should arbitrate on matters in which he had been closely involved. This action provoked a quarrel between Keen and Lady Huntingdon and led to her withdrawal

---

[21] Most of the information in this paragraph is taken from the 'queries' cited in the previous footnote.

[22] Cheshunt archives, A 4/ 6, 3, R. Piercy to Lady H., 20 September 1779.

[23] Cheshunt archives, A 4/ 2, 26, W. Piercy to Lady H., 10 October 1782.

[24] Cheshunt archives, A 4/ 2, 29, W. Piercy to Lady H., 2 June 1783; A 4/ 2, 30, W. Piercy to Lady H., 3 July 1783; A 4/ 2, 33, copy of letter of Lady H. to W. Piercy, 2 July 1783.

from the Tabernacle and Tottenham Court chapels.[25] Piercy's father now complained that she had ill-treated Richard Piercy, having promised to 'send him to your College in Wales as a Tutor for a time, and then to Oxford or Edinburgh to Study Physic or Divinity, either of which Providence might point out as the most eligible of the two'. The Countess promised to help him as soon as she received funds from Georgia, but meanwhile Richard sailed as surgeon aboard a Liverpool ship.[26]

To arrange for the arbitration Lady Huntingdon employed a different attorney, Oliver Cromwell. They met at Bath and chose Thomas Day of Chertsey in Surrey as one arbitrator. Later they chose Mr Bridgen of Paternoster Row as the other. Cromwell pointed out the difficulties which might arise from the number of arbitrators: 'by the nomination of four (two by each party) there is a chance and perhaps a probability of there being no decision, by an equal division of the references, which seems to render the choice, by the four referees of a fifth necessary.'[27] Piercy had chosen two Methodists who might be expected to sympathize with him; Lady Huntingdon chose two professional men who probably had some knowledge of Georgia. Her choice was made on the advice of an American politician, Henry Laurens, who had been imprisoned in the Tower on a charge of high treason. Released on bail at the end of 1781, he and his daughter went to Bath for his health, where he met the Countess.[28] As early as August 1782 he had suggested that she should consult Thomas Day about the dispute, and he also introduced her to other American politicians who visited England after the war was ended by the Treaty of Paris in October 1782. They were able to give some help with the problem of Bethesda after they returned home.[29]

[25] Cheshunt archives, A 4/ 2, 32, W. Piercy to Lady H., 26 July 1783; 34, copy of letter from Lady H. to W. Piercy, 14 July 1783; A 3/ 12, 11, copy of letter from Lady H. to Henry Laurens, 18 January 1787).

[26] Cheshunt archives, A 4/ 7, 1, W. Piercy sen. to Lady H., 21 February 1783; A 4/ 7, 2, copy of letter from Lady H. to W. Piercy sen., 4 April 1783; A 4/ 7, 3, reply, 16 May 1783.

[27] Oliver Cromwell was the last male descendant of the Protector – for his life see D. Slatter, 'Oliver Cromwell, Clerk of St. Thomas' Hospital', *Archives*, 8 (1968), 81–5. Cheshunt archives, A 4/ 9, 1 and 2, Cromwell to Lady H., 17 and 24 July 1783; Essex RO, Acc 4497, 1, Cromwell to Day, 21 July 1783; Cheshunt archives, A 4/ 9, 4, Cromwell to Lady H., 11 August 1783; A 4/ 10, 3, Day to Lady H., 26 July 1783.

[28] Cheshunt archives, A 4/ 9, 4, Cromwell to Lady H., 11 August 1783. For Laurens's life see P. M. Hamer, *The Papers of Henry Laurens*, 1 (Columbia, SC, 1968), xiv–xxii. His Tower diary is printed in *Collections of the South Carolina Hist. Soc.*, i (1857) from a MS in New York Public Library.

[29] Cheshunt archives, A 3/ 10, Laurens to Lady H., 23 August 1782. For the lives of the Peace Commissioners see H. A. Johnson, *John Jay 1745–1829* (Albany, 1976); J. Shepherd, *The Adams Chronicles* (Boston, 1975), chapters 1–4; B. Franklin, *Autobiography* (Oxford, 1970), 99–102. Lady H. did not meet Adams or Franklin. Essex RO, Acc. 4497, 1.

Lady Huntingdon, having declined any further direct communication with William Piercy, asked Cromwell to inform him that any 'needfull information' should be sent to Cromwell 'as from her business and infirm state of Health it is neither in her power or choice' to do otherwise.[30] Meanwhile, with the aid of an amanuensis she had assembled copies of all the letters and other papers which were relevant to the arbitration, and had begun to compare the various inventories of her properties which she had received from Georgia. She also drafted a set of questions to be put to Piercy which were probably the basis for those finally used in his examination.[31] By the end of August Cromwell had drafted a bond to accept the decision of the arbitrators, but Piercy insisted that no award could be made unless one of the four arbitrators changed sides.[32] In September Piercy and Keen called on Cromwell,

> alledging that [Piercy] went to America as President of the College and as employed by your Ladyship in the mission only, that he was retained by your Ladyship as one of your Chaplains, in support of which assertion he produced an Instrument of Appointment executed by your Ladyship, for all which he claims a Salary, and the only question before the Arbitrators he understood was meant to be not whether he was, or was not entitled to a Salary or Allowance but the Amount of such Salary or Allowance.[33]

By denying that he had ever been Lady Huntingdon's agent for the Orphan House and Plantation he evaded the principal accusation against him – of wasting its assets and not accounting for his receipts. By limiting the arbitrators to deciding how much he was owed by Lady Huntingdon he prejudged the issue. Cromwell rejected Piercy's demands and left him to continue with a suit in Chancery if he wished. The Countess considered suing Piercy in Georgia for an account of the Bethesda estate.[34] Two years later Piercy expressed his willingness to have a fifth arbitrator appointed and to enlarge the scope of their award, but Cromwell thought that Piercy and his lawyer were deliberately procrastinating.[35] As no further correspondence about the arbitration can be found he was probably correct.

These endless difficulties over Bethesda do not appear to have discouraged Lady Huntingdon, but rather persuaded her to take a greater

[30] Cheshunt archives, A 4/ 9, 3, copy of note from Lady H. to Cromwell, 28 July 1783.
[31] Cheshunt archives, A 4/ 9, 5, copy of letter from Lady H. to Cromwell, 14 August 1783.
[32] Cheshunt archives, A 4/ 9, 7, Cromwell to Lady H., 28 August 1783.
[33] Cheshunt archives, A 4/ 9, 10, Cromwell to Lady H., 16 September 1783.
[34] Cheshunt archives, A 4/ 9, 12, copy of letter from Lady H. to Cromwell, 20 September 1783; A 4/ 9, 16.
[35] Cheshunt archives, A 4/ 9, 18, Cromwell to Lady H., 18 November 1785.

interest in North America. This may perhaps be attributed to her increasing acquaintance with the American politicians, and she proposed a mission to the Indians.[36] She began her campaign with letters to George Washington. The first, written in 1782, failed to reach Washington because (as he later explained to her) 'letters are so often intercepted by negligence, curiosity or motives still more unworthy.' The second, written on 8 April 1782, did not reach him until 17 January 1783.[37] The contents of both letters have not survived either in Washington's papers or in Lady Huntingdon's,[38] but those of the second letter can be deduced from his reply, and a draft of a third letter sent a little later is in the Cheshunt archives: 'Sir, Ill qualified as I am to pay you the various honours due to your uncommon priviledges, you must nevertheless allow me to express the high esteem that so much belongs to that of your private Character, and which I am but Justly ambitious to acknowledge by every mark of my confidence.'[39] In this letter Lady Huntingdon claimed relationship with him through her grandmother, Elizabeth Washington, and conveyed her intention of appointing him one of her executors 'for the establishing a foundation in America principally intended as a College for a Mission to the Indian nations'. This plan was not, as might be expected, a change in the purpose of the institution at Bethesda, but a completely new project. From Washington's reply to these letters it can be deduced that she proposed to establish colonies of immigrants in North Carolina, Virginia, Pennsylvania and New York, which would become centres for the civilization and conversion of the Indians. Washington particularly approved her plan because 'all attempts to reclaim, and introduce any system of religeon or morallity among them, would prove fruitless until they could first be brought into a state of greater civilization.'[40] He thought that when the treaty between Congress and the western Indians had been signed, it might well be possible to obtain grants of some of the lands ceded by the Indians. Lady Huntingdon's intentions to carry out her plan were sufficiently strong for her to propose to visit North America herself – one of

[36] For eighteenth-century missions to the Indians see J. Gillies, *Historical Collections* (Kelso, 1845), 464–70.

[37] Lib. of Congress, Washington letter book 12, pp. 22–6; 22, copy of letter from Washington to Lady H., 27 February 1783.

[38] Cheshunt archives, A 4/ 4, 24 contains proposals for a letter to Washington which may have been drawn up by Sir James Jay for this purpose. It is amended by the Countess, but undated.

[39] Cheshunt archives, A 4/ 5, 16, draft letter from Lady H. to Washington, 20 February 1783.

[40] Lib. of Congress, Washington letter book 12, pp. 22–6.

several such proposals which she made at different times. In December 1783 Thomas Wills sent her his thoughts on this project:

> I will allow every thing you say and wish about America, provided your Province there is to be held *in Commendam* with poor old England. But I think, whilst we have so many ignorant *Pagans* here, and whilst the Lord is so eminently blessing the Work in general ... I cannot consent to your *entirely* giving up this poor Country, and taking your flight to America, for an *Abode* there during your earthly Pilgrimage.[41]

In August 1783 Washington replied to her letter of 20 February declining the position of executor, but promising to assist the plan in any way he could. He referred to her claim of being a relation. 'My Ancestry being derived from Yorkshire in England, it is more than probable that I am entitled to that Honourable [Connexion], which you are pleased to mention – Independent however of this priviledge, the veneration in which your Ladyships character, heretofore known, has impressed me, justly entitles you to rank high in my esteem.'[42]

The Countess wrote to Washington again on 20 March 1784, repeating her request for land grants, and probably enclosing the copies of her letters to the four States and her 'plan'.[43] The plan, addressed to 'the Friends of Religion and Humanity in America', describes the difficulties of converting wandering tribes by means of missionaries. She therefore proposed to send groups of tradesmen and mechanics from Britain under the guidance of evangelical clergymen, who would establish settlements intended to attract the Indians to a less roaming way of life. One of those proposed for this enterprise was John Evans of Bala, a Methodist exhorter, who was introduced to her by David Jones of Llangan.[44] The migrants, who would not be 'loose idle Vagabonds', and the schools for their children would provide good examples for the Indians, and especially their women and children. The plan was carefully devised by Lady Huntingdon to prevent land speculators and others from taking

---

[41] Cheshunt archives, F 1/ 1918 – Wills to Lady H., 7 December 1783.

[42] Cheshunt archives, A 3/ 12, 30, Washington to Lady H., 10 August 1783. The word 'Connexion' accidentally omitted from this original letter can be recovered from Washington's own copies (Lib. of Congress, Washington letter book H 3, 166 and Washington letters, series 4, p. 271). Lib. of Congress, Washington letter book, 21, p.252.

[43] There are slight difficulties with the dates of these letters, which are not eased by the ambiguity in her letter to Washington (Lib. of Congress, Washington letters, series 4, 20 March 1784). The draft letters and plan sent to Washington are dated 8 April (Ibid.). A further copy of her letter to the States is in Lib. of Congress, Acc. 2547.

[44] Cheshunt archives, F 1/ 599, J. Evans to Lady H., 24 February 1784; Connexion archives, 3, Jones 13, copy of letter from D. Jones to Lady H., 28 February 1784.

advantage of the project for their own ends.[45] When one of her correspondents sent her the printed proclamation of the United States Congress about the lands ceded or purchased from the Indians it must have seemed to the Countess that her plan was on the brink of success. However Sir James Jay was unsuccessful in interesting the politicians of his home State of New York in the proposal.[46] Sadly only one of the four States, Virginia, ever made any attempt to consider her proposal. On 5 February 1785 the Governor of Virginia, 'having laid before the board the plan of the Countess of Huntingdon ... together with some observations of Sir James Jay', was advised to consult Congress for their opinion. Sir James's letter and the covering letter of Governor Patrick Henry are amongst the papers of the Continental Congress, and its journals note that they were read on 17 February, but nothing further was done.[47] The failure of either Congress or the States to pursue the matter further may be attributed in part to the need to restore commerce after a long war, the struggle to draft an acceptable constitution for the United States, and disputes over the territories. Lady Huntingdon's plan cannot have been helped by the accompanying letter of Sir James Jay, which principally referred to the need to encourage domestic manufacturers by protecting them from foreign imports. On 30 May Washington wrote his last letter to the Countess. Governor Henry had informed him: 'his private opinion of the matter was, that under the pressure of debt to which this Fund [from the ceded lands] was to be appropriated; and the diversity of sentiment respecting the mode of raising it, that no discrimination would, or indeed could be made, in favor of Emigrants of any description whatever.'[48] So her plan for converting the Indians ceased to interest the Americans. The Countess continued to hope for its success until she died, but the problem of the future of Bethesda was more urgent.

In 1784 Henry Laurens returned to South Carolina. He set off with a

[45] A similar plan had been proposed for Massachusetts in 1730 (W. Kellaway, *The New England Company* (London, 1961), 269). Some of Lady H's notes can be found on the back of a note sent by Mrs Taylor, 4 May 1785 (Cheshunt archives A 3/ 12, 7).

[46] Cheshunt archives, A 3/ 12, 32, proclamations of 23 April and 20 May 1785; A 3/ 12, 2 and 3, Sir James Jay to Lady H., 4 November 1784 and 2 February 1785. Lady Huntingdon also corresponded with his brother, John Jay (Columbia Univ. Lib., letters of 7, 9 and 13 December 1783). Cheshunt archives, A 3/ 12, 4–6, Sir James Jay to Lady H., 9 and 19 February and 13 March 1785. I am indebted to the State Archivist of New York for the information that it was never considered by that Legislature.

[47] *Journals of the Council of State of Virginia* (Richmond, VA, 1952), 416; National Archives, RG 360; J. C. Fitzpatrick (ed.), *Journals of the Continental Congress 1774–1789*, 28 (Washington, DC, 1933), 77n.

[48] Cheshunt archives, A 3/ 12, 31, Washington to Lady H., 30 June 1785; copy in Lib. of Congress, Washington's letter book 12, p.130.

tin box containing a large number of original documents relating to Bethesda, together with a new power of attorney.[49] Laurens, however, had to re-establish his own business in Charleston before he could make the journey to Savannah. Letters seem to have miscarried very frequently and seriously hindered attempts to communicate with Georgia. Early in 1787 Lady Huntingdon complained that she had heard from Laurens only once since he went to America, and it was not until March 1788 that she finally received his report on Bethesda.[50] In it he described the damage caused to his property, which had detained him so long in South Carolina. He had not yet visited Bethesda, but had begun proceedings for the collection of her debts in South Carolina. He had not even been able to obtain replies to letters to Joseph Clay in Savannah after more than three years.

Meanwhile another solution to the problem of Bethesda had been proposed. John Habersham, one of James's sons, wrote to the Countess on 25 June 1786, to suggest that it should become a university. The General Assembly of Georgia had decided to establish the University of Georgia, and John Habersham, as the Secretary of the Board of Trustees, asked for her support. Lady Huntingdon approved the proposal, but had one objection to the College charter: '"that all professions of Christianity are alike to be established" a Latitude which may infer in the end that even Popish Bishops and Tutors may become the Guardians of the Youth and their instructors – this as it appears to Lady Huntingdon must sooner or later end in the most wretched slavery both in Church and State.'[51] However if Henry Laurens approved the clause, she would transfer the Bethesda property to the trustees. She thought that after all the problems and expense she had endured the 'present Event has opened a door yet to secure if possible the intended end of my Trust'.[52] Oliver Cromwell, after reading all the relevant documents, was not so happy with the proposal, believing that it would be a breach of the trust established by George

---

[49] Cheshunt archives, A 4/ 6, 37, schedule of contents of box, n.d. [1784]); F 1/ 1901, Wills to Lady H., 9 September 1783.

[50] Cheshunt archives, A 4/ 9, 19, Copy of letter from Lady H. to Cromwell, 11 January 1787; A 3/ 10, 28, Laurens to Lady H., 26 March 1788.

[51] Cheshunt archives, A 3/ 12, 8, John Habersham to Lady H., 25 June 1786; F 1/ 626, John Case to Lady' H., 6 May 1787; A 3/ 12, 10, copy of letter from Lady H. to Trustees, 15 January 1787. The copy of the charter is A 3/ 12, 12.

[52] Cheshunt archives, A 4/ 9, 19 and 20, copies of letters from Lady H. to Cromwell, 11 and 18 January 1787; A 3/ 12, 11, copies of letters from Lady H. to Cromwell and Laurens, 19 and 18 January 1787.

Whitefield to transfer Bethesda to what would be a secular university.[53] However, nothing further was heard from Georgia, and the University was not established for another fourteen years.

It is very doubtful whether any of the money owed to the Orphan House was ever recovered. Some of the debtors had died or left Georgia; other debts had been lost by the inflation which had swept the country during the later stages of the war. Poor communications and Piercy's optimistic account of what was owed to Bethesda led the Countess to expect some income and to make several attempts to recover it. This created difficulties with those merchants who had forgiven money owed by Bethesda and therefore were less inclined to continue their support of the institution.[54] It was not until the Countess, finally despairing of any action by Henry Laurens, sent out a student, David Phillips, in 1788 to take charge of Bethesda that the full extent of Bethesda's indebtedness became clear.[55] The only information about his disastrous trip to Georgia is contained in a letter from Joseph Clay, a merchant who had voluntarily taken over the management of Bethesda.[56] Phillips had annoyed Clay soon after his arrival by dismissing the overseer of Bethesda and telling him to get his wages from Clay. He next implied that Clay had been taking money from the estates, instead of supporting it, though 'he knew (or might have known) 'twas in my possession contrary to my desire and that only in daily expectation that your Ladyship wou'd send some person to take charge of it was I induced to pay any attention to it, and what I did was without fee or reward, or expectation or desire of any.'

Phillips had requested Clay's accounts thinking that Bethesda was in credit with Clay, but instead received a demand for £277. 1s. 11½ d. together with interest. Phillips was succeeded at Bethesda by a second student, John Johnson. Lady Huntingdon wrote: 'He is quite the man for me. He is not Eight and Twenty and two noble chapels erected by his means, one at Wigan in the very heart of Popery, and another at New Manchester. He now goes to America for me, to labour to fulfill, my long desired Plan for the Indian Natives.'[57]

---

[53] Cheshunt archives, A 4/ 9, 22, Cromwell to Lady H., – February 1787; A 4/ 9, 24, copy of letter from Lady H. to Cromwell, 27 February 1787.
[54] Cheshunt archives, A 2/ 3, 1, E. Bridgen to Lady H., 4 May 1784.
[55] NLW, CM MS 13354, Lady H. to T. Charles, 8 July 1790; Cheshunt archives, F 1/ 614, S. Phillips to Lady H., 23 April 1784; *Georgia Gazette*, 5 June 1788, p. 2.
[56] Georgia Hist. Soc., coll. 152, copy of letter from Clay to Lady H., 10 May 1790.
[57] SMU, Hunt. 127, Lady H. to T. Hawies, 7 August 1790; Cheshunt archives, F 1/ 2139, Johnson to Lady H., 12 July 1790.

He arrived at Savannah at the beginning of 1791 bringing another letter of attorney – this time addressed to Thomas Gibbons, a lawyer.[58] The Countess's wish that he would attend a meeting of the 'Chiefs of the [Indian] Nations' was overtaken by events, because on 11 September he was told that Lady Huntingdon's death was reported in the Charleston newspapers. Soon afterwards he received a copy of Thomas Haweis's printed account of her last moments, and early in November the details of her will.[59] Even before he received this, rumours were circulating in Savannah that a local lawyer and politician, James Jackson, and Joseph Clay were conspiring to take over the property by means of an Act in the State legislature.[60] The news that Lady Huntingdon had left it in trust to Lord Dartmouth, Sir Richard Hill, Oliver Cromwell and other Englishmen cannot have pleased the Americans. Lord Dartmouth had been a member of the Government which had recently carried on the war against them, while the others had done nothing to rescue Bethesda from its abandoned state.

Joseph Clay may well have felt that the time had come for Americans to take over the trust, but Johnson was very active to defend the property. He talked to the local politicians, and tried to get Thomas Gibbons to take up the case of its legal owners. An Act 'to explain an act, entitled an act to establish an academy in the county of Chatham, and for vesting certain property in Selina, countess dowager of Huntingdon' was passed on 20 December.[61] It appointed thirteen trustees to establish Bethesda College – a number which enabled Johnson to compare them all to Judas. The trustees included some familiar names – Joseph Habersham, Joseph Clay jun. Josiah Tatnall jun. and James Whitefield jun. On 9 January 1792 Johnson received an official letter taking possession of all the property and warning him against removing any property without their authority.[62] Johnson now commenced a battle on three fronts – by letters which the local newspaper refused to print, by legal action which local lawyers

---

[58] Georgia Hist. Soc., coll. 430, Johnson's letters, p. 1, copy of letter of Gibbons to Smith, – January 1791.

[59] The *Georgia Gazette* reported her death on 15 September. SMU, Hunt. 129, Lady H. to T. Haweis, 2 November 1790. Most of the details given here come from Johnson's 'Official Journal' (Georgia Hist. Soc., coll. 430), a copy of that which he sent back to England.

[60] James Jackson (1757–1806) had fought in the Georgia Militia, but was only a lieutenant-colonel, and not a general as Johnson thought. He was governor of Georgia from 1798 to 1801.

[61] *Digest of the Laws of the State of Georgia* (Savannah, 1802), 565, 566. The second quotation mark is missing in the original title.

[62] Georgia Hist. Soc., coll. 430, Johnson's letters, p. 3.

would not pursue, and by preparations for a siege of Bethesda. Although he reported considerable local feeling on his behalf, and said that he had difficulty in restraining the Bethesda slaves from taking violent action in his defence, the trustees managed to gain possession by 10 January. On the following day, since he continued to give orders to the slaves, Johnson and his wife were arrested and detained in Savannah. No charges were laid, and eventually they were released. Johnson then sailed for Charleston, where he not only tried to recover the debts due to the Countess, but also published a poem, *The Rape of Bethesda or the Georgia Orphan House Destroyed* in which he compares the seizure to the destruction of Troy.[63] He then returned to Savannah to continue his lawsuit against the trustees, but soon returned to England.[64]

But this was not the end of the disputes arising from the Countess's death. The Revd William Piercy left the chapel at Woolwich in the hands of his brother in 1796 and went to America. There, on 5 August 1797 the trustees received a writ issued on behalf of 'Revd Mr Percy' claiming his lost salary or damages.[65] In this, as in all previous claims, he appears to have been unsuccessful. Although Bethesda College continued as a school until 1808, various difficulties led to its abandonment in the following year.[66]

---

[63] Printed by Markland & McIver, Charleston, 1792, copy in Georgia Hist. Soc. collection.

[64] Georgia archives, typescript copy of the trustees' minutes, 1792–1809. Johnson returned to Tyldesley, where he was imprisoned for the chapel debt. Later he moved to Manchester, where he became minister of St George's church. He died in 1804 (W. E. A. Axon, *The Annals of Manchester* (Manchester, 1886), 133).

[65] W. T. Vincent, *Records of the Woolwich District*, 2 (London, 1890), 181. Georgia archives, trustees' minutes, 5 and 14 August 1797; Chatham County minute book C, p. 222.

[66] For the later history of Bethesda see T. Gamble jun., *Bethesda: An Historical Sketch* (Savannah, 1902). The present Bethesda was only opened in 1855.

11

The College and the Apostolic Society

Until her eightieth year, when she grew too old to leave London, the Countess spent much of her time at Trefeca with the students. When she was not there the senior student sent her regular letters reporting progress and asking for advice or money. From 1787 these letters are supplemented by those of the master and the housekeeper sent to her at Spa Fields. It is only during these last four years of her life that sufficient information has been preserved to give a complete picture of life at Trefeca. For most of the time after 1771 there was a master or tutor at the College, but much of the teaching was done by the senior student, and it is sometimes difficult to distinguish between the two positions. Samuel Phillips, who wrote a number of letters from the College in 1784, was first a student and then a tutor. This may have been while the Countess was seeking another tutor, or might have been a more permanent position which ended when she sent him out preaching.[1] When the College had moved to Cheshunt after the Countess's death, the practice of employing the senior student to teach the others was continued, but placed on a more formal basis.[2] After both Fletcher and Benson left the College in 1771 the senior student must have been in charge for a year, though he was undoubtedly closely supervised by Howell Harris. In March 1771 the Countess hoped to appoint a clergyman recommended to her, but the post had not been filled by October 1772, when she offered 'the superintendency' to the Revd Henry Peckwell. He was diffident and eventually proposed 'the only person in the world fit to be a Master' in December.[3] Since all three letters appear to relate to the same position, it will be seen

---

[1] Cheshunt archives, F 1/ 609 and 614, S. Phillips to Lady H., 19 March and 23 April 1784 are examples of his letters. For additional details about Trefeca students see Dr Nuttall's list in *Trans. Hon. Soc. of Cymmrodorion* (1967), 269–77.
[2] Cheshunt archives, C 1/ 1, fo. 11.
[3] Cheshunt archives, F 1/ 1618 and 1630, Peckwell to Lady H., 31 October and 29 December 1772; F 1/ 203, John Lloyd to Lady H., 13 November 1772; NLW, Trevecka letter 2693, Lady H. to Howell Harris, 26 March 1771.

how difficult it is to construct a list of presidents, tutors and masters. Both at Trefeca and later at Cheshunt, the College attracted Anglican clergymen who had been disappointed in hopes of a benefice.[4]

Lady Huntingdon wrote to Howell Harris just after Fletcher and Benson had left that 'the College [is] nearer and nearer to me before the Lord than any thing in this whole world.'[5] Despite all the problems and difficulties caused by individual students, she continued to find the College closer to her heart than her chapels. James Nicoll, seeking admission to the College in 1773, repeated what he had been told by a student:

> hir Ladyship (meining your Ladyship) is such a woman that no Body Can refuse any thing that she asks them, she is a mother to us all and indeed she Calls us hir Children ... she teaks so maney of us into hir [room] every night and makes us to read a Chapter to hir and she explens it to us and there is few ministers Could do'it beter and she prayes with us...[6]

In 1785 one of her students asked her 'Opinion and Advice with respect to the Ministry' and she wrote a long letter, which was afterwards printed at Trefeca.[7] The advice is that which she gave to all her students: 'The more Scriptural and Simple your address (in the Ministry) to the heart the better; applying to Facts – [stating] there the positive Evils, there Scripture.' It is echoed in the letter which she wrote in the following year which again expresses the need for simplicity in ministering to 'the miserable poor and ignorant'.[8]

Dr Nuttall has calculated from his list that the number of students at Trefeca was about ten a year, but the figures varied widely. Lady Huntingdon thought that there were twenty-four or twenty-five students at College in October 1773, but ten years later there were only six. In 1787 ten students signed a testimonial for a college servant, and in 1788 there were ten present (and at least two itinerating).[9] In the absence of a complete list of students and of details about their origin and social

[4] Cheshunt archives, F 1/ 478, Neale to Lady H., 17 September 1781.

[5] NLW, Trevecka letter 2693.

[6] See her letters to John Clayton in T. Aveling, *Memorials of the Clayton Family* (London, 1867), and to James Hawksworth in Cheshunt archives G 2/ 1. Cheshunt archives, F 1/ 221, Nicoll to Lady H., 3 May 1773.

[7] A copy was used to wrap a bundle of letters in the Cheshunt archives (A 3/ 12). The letter was also printed in D. Jones, *A Funeral Sermon preached at Spa Fields chapel* ... (London, 1791), 21–24.

[8] Quoted in Nuttall, op. cit., 260.

[9] Cheshunt archives, G 2/ 1, 9, Lady H. to Hawksworth, 13 October 1773. This in the letter printed by Seymour (*Life and Times*, vol. 2, p. 168) is '*Twenty-four*'. Cheshunt archives, F 1/ 562, Phillips to Lady H., 31 October 1783); E 4/ 15, 11, testimonial, 20 July 1787; F 1/ 769, J. Williams to Lady H., 29 September 1788.

background, it is difficult to draw many conclusions about the students trained at Trefeca. Of the thirty-four students for whom a birthplace can be found, eleven were Welsh, two came from Scotland and one from Ireland. Eighteen other students have distinctively Welsh surnames, so that about 20 per cent of the students were drawn from Wales. That this was not caused by the College being in Wales is proved by Welsh students continuing to apply to the College after it moved to Hertfordshire. Most of the English students were born in southern England:

Bristol
Cornwall
Devon (2)
Gloucester
Lancashire
London
Middlesex
Norwich
Oxfordshire (2)
Somerset (2 from Bath)
Staffordshire (2)
Sussex
Warwickshire (2)
Wiltshire
Yorkshire

From the list of students admitted at Cheshunt between 1792 and 1800 it can be established that most of them were of a lower social status than the governors of the college,[10] and it would seem that many of the Trefeca students were of the same standing as James Glazebrook, the miner from Madeley. The criteria used by Lady Huntingdon to select her students were the same as those used later by the governors at Cheshunt. They were to be young (in their early twenties) and unmarried. Each was to give a satisfactory account of his call to the ministry and hold paedobaptist views.[11]

Illnesses were frequent at Trefeca according to the surviving letters:

> Lloyd and Hayes who came home ill have continued so ever since, Hayes is the same as when he came, very Nervous and low, and is also troubled with Rheumatic Pains all over him ... Lloyd who has been exceeding ill with a Cough and Tightness in his Breast, is now somewhat better, but seems to be going into a decline ... Here is only Jenkins, Porter and Samuel Lloyd who are

[10] Cheshunt archives, C 9/ 9, 1 and 2, lists of applicants and admissions, 1791–1801, printed in E. Welch (ed.), *Cheshunt College: The Early Years* (Herts. Rec. Soc., 1991).
[11] DWL, Cong. Lib., II c 7/ 13, Lady H. to S. Wills, 1 April 1782.

capable of supplying the Places: and Jenkins complains of a Pain in his Breast after Preaching and Porter is sometimes bad with the Rheumatism.[12]

In 1788 William Davies who had 'that nasty Complaint the Itch' asked the Countess's permission to go 'to the Salt Sea for a Month'.[13] Neither the health nor the education of the students was improved by their being sent on preaching tours by the Countess whenever there was a demand. When John Clayton was taken ill while preaching in London, Lady Huntingdon immediately consulted a doctor about the relative merits of drinking goat's milk at Trefeca or the waters at the Bristol Hotwells. Another letter went to Clayton himself, and a third to a fellow student to persuade Clayton to accept the doctor's advice.[14] Some students disliked the interruption to their studies caused by their itinerating, and pleaded to be allowed to return to College: 'Theophilus Jones has been dispatched for Minehead some Time back. We sent him off with all his Murmurs, Grumblings and Discontentedness along with him. I have been repeatedly afraid that his Motives, in undertaking the Ministry were never genuine.'[15] Other problems arose among the students at Trefeca. In the summer of 1774 there was an outbreak of 'shaking' or 'leaping'. This had begun amongst the Welsh Methodists about 1760, and consisted of 'groaning and loud talking, as well as of loud singing, repeating the same line or stanza over and over thirty or forty times ... [jumping] until they were quite exhausted, so, as often to be obliged to fall down on the floor'.[16] Some of the ministers approved: others attempted to suppress the practice. At College on 6 July 1774, as Thomas Roberts wrote in his diary, 'The Revd Peter Williams Preach'd. Gwen Vaughan Leaped and Evan Moses quarrelled about it sadly – Evan Moses wanted to quiet Her – the students took her part but he bore his Testimony against it with a becoming Zeal [and] told Mr Williams that He must and shall give an Account for Encouraging such Unruly Passions.'[17] The Revd William Llewelyn, the Independent minister at Leominster, reported to the Countess 'I never saw jumping till this time at the College, and I suspended my

---

[12] Cheshunt archives, F 1/ 609, S. Phillips to Lady H., 19 March 1784.
[13] Gloucs. RO, D 2538, 4, J. Williams to Lady H., 21 April 1788.
[14] Aveling, op. cit., 26–8.
[15] Cheshunt archives, F 1/ 2027, J. Williams to Lady H., n.d.
[16] J. Evans, *A Sketch of the Denominations of the Christian World* (London, 1811), 182.
[17] NLW, Trev. MS 3154. All those mentioned were members of the Trefeca 'Family'. The Revd Peter Williams (1723–96) was an itinerant Methodist preacher. This year (1774) was the year that Mother Ann Lee and the Shakers left England for North America.

Judgment about it, till I had made some observations upon the Jumpers and those that put them on.'[18] Other disputes at the College led students to ask to be dismissed or allowed to leave.[19]

For a time it would appear that 'rounds' or circuits were established for the students at College. William Moody went on the 'Staffordshire-round' for ten weeks and John Meldrum took a round in Glamorganshire in 1774.[20] In 1777 the Countess required nine students 'to labour with all their strength' on the East Coast.[21] Other students were sent out to be temporary assistants to both Anglican and Dissenting ministers. Even before the secession the Countess drew no distinction between them. In 1777 a student assisted the Independent minister at Portsmouth for a time.[22] Such appointments might lead to a more permanent position. In 1771 'a Society of Dissenters Call'd Independents', who had left the Presbyterian congregation at Warwick because of its Arianism, petitioned Lady Huntingdon for a minister.[23] John Clayton left the Connexion in 1777 to join Sir Harry Trelawny, who had established a chapel at Looe in Cornwall, after he and other students had been sent to help Sir Harry. The Countess had come to disapprove of Trelawny's activities, but accepted Clayton's decision. Sir Harry was able to convince the students of 'his profound Learning, rare Abilities, and great Graces', but Lady Huntingdon's fears of his constancy eventually proved correct.[24] Sending some students to preach before their education was complete sometimes caused difficulty in that their native language was not English. The 'poor welch people' of Talgarth were pleased to have Daniel Rowland, 'the Welch Student', to preach to them, but the people of Wolverhampton had difficulty with James Pritchard's accent: 'The peopol at Wolverhampton are Dissatisfied with Mr Prickets Preaching as The[y] Cannot Understand him, if you can Cause a Change to take place we Think it would be

---

[18] Cheshunt archives, A 3/ 6, 24, Llewelyn to Lady H., 28 August 1774.
[19] Cheshunt archives, F 1/ 572, A. Dixon to Lady H., November 1783.
[20] Cheshunt archives, E 4/ 8, 2, Moody to Lady H., 11 February 1774; E 4/ 8, 6, Meldrum to Lady H., 12 February 1774.
[21] SMU., Hunt. 93, Lady H. to T. Haweis, 20 February 1777.
[22] Cheshunt archives, E 4/ 4, 11, Tuppen to Lady H., 20 June 1777.
[23] Cheshunt archives, F 1/ 148, J. Harmer to Lady H., 26 November 1771. Rowley accepted the offer.
[24] Aveling, op. cit., 36; Cheshunt archives F 1/ 376, J. Eyre to Lady H., 14 January 1777. Sir Harry Trelawny (1756 1834) was ordained an Independent minister in 1777, adopted Unitarian views, was ordained by the bishop of Exeter in 1781, joined the Roman Catholic Church in 1810, and was ordained a priest in that Church in 1830.

well.'²⁵ This was a difficulty of which the masters frequently reminded her.²⁶

Other students caused scandal wherever they went. John Williams wrote to the Countess's secretary, George Best, about the behaviour of Weston: 'He has a wife in Hereford, almost they say, stark naked; and by what I was inform'd must apply soon to the Parish, and at the same Time she has not received a single Line from her Husband since he left this Place. His Child is actually on the Parish already at the Hay.'²⁷ Travelling created difficulties for students and members of the congregation. Some students were able to move by sea, but others were obliged to use one of the 'college horses' or to borrow from a member of their congregation. Thomas Jones borrowed a mare in order to return to College, and arranged for Green to return it when he went to Tunbridge Wells.²⁸ By some oversight the mare was not collected by the owner and Green found himself faced with a demand to pay eight guineas for its care. Robert Satchell took 'a borrowed horse' with him to Cornwall and did not return it.²⁹ All these problems involved the Countess in more correspondence and expense.

About 1787 John Williams, the second son of William Williams (Pantycelyn, the Methodist hymn-writer), was appointed master at Trefeca with Averina Powell as the housekeeper.³⁰ Both wrote frequently to the Countess at Spa Fields. John Williams often consulted her about the admission of students. Thomas Davies, a Carmarthen schoolmaster, was required to get a recommendation, but told he could not be admitted immediately as there were already twelve students in residence. The Revd Peter Williams sent a young man called Lewis from Carmarthen without first asking permission from the Countess.³¹ Williams also submitted reports on the progress of each student. 'Holland . . . is a very bright young Man, and will do for some Capital places exceedingly well, such as Bristol or Brighthelmstone. Cureton is come and seems to have a tolerable

---

²⁵ Cheshunt archives, F 1/ 672, Talgarth people to Lady H., 24 November 1787; A 1/ 13, 33, Isaac Creswell to Lady H., 24 March 1782.

²⁶ Cheshunt archives, F 1/ 1964 and 1991, J. Williams to Lady H., 13 October 1787 and 31 January 1788.

²⁷ Cheshunt archives, F 1/ 1981, J. Williams to G. Best, 12 January 1788.

²⁸ Cheshunt archives, A 1/ 13, 18, copies of Lady H.'s letters, April 1782. It is not certain whether this was Samuel or William Green.

²⁹ Hunt, Lib., HM 39808, Lady H. to Mr Tanner, 21 September 1779.

³⁰ For William Williams (a correspondent of Lady H.) see G. T. Hughes, *Wiliams Pantycelyn* (Cardiff, 1983). Averina Powell may have been the housekeeper before 1787.

³¹ Cheshunt archives, F1/680, J. Williams to Lady H., 9 August 1787 and F1/706 Tels 21/1788. Both students were admitted.

Talent for Learning.' He was not always so optimistic and agreed with the Hereford people who preferred to close their chapel rather than endure another student.[32] 'Indeed the Senior Students that are here now are by far more stupid upon the whole than any I ever had. I know not when they will be able with Propriety to read a chapter of English.' John Williams had to leave the College when his father died at the beginning of 1791, and Lady Huntingdon enlisted the aid of Thomas Charles of Bala in the search for 'a proper Person' to succeed him.[33] However the unidentified Mr Jones who held the position at the Countess's death was generally considered unsuitable.

Averina Powell wrote about the farm attached to the College which provided food for the Countess as well as the College. In 1775 a goat was sent from Trefeca to Lady Huntingdon at Clifton to provide a supply of milk for the 'ladies' there; the accompanying letter accidentally describes one of the leisure activities of the students: 'She is very tame for she would be almost always in the great dining room, and often came into the studdy, she is very fond of A crust of Bread and will follow any one she is aquainted with for it till they give it... She will eat Bran, Oats, Barly, Cabbage-leavs, carrats, Teatos etc.'[34] In 1791 Mrs Charles Wesley was supplied with a turkey from Trefeca.[35] Averina Powell raised large numbers of turkeys; so many that the Trefeca 'Family' found their barns and ricks attacked by 'above 100 Turkeys Ducks Fowls etc. and 4 pigs'.[36] A considerable amount of food reached Spa Fields by the coach or Mr Golding's wagon: '1 small Ham, 2 turkeys, a goose, with the pigs Cheeks – I did [k]now your Lady ship did use to be fond of them.'[37] The supply of meat from the farm must have helped to provide a better diet for the students, but it did not prevent the College from getting into debt with the butcher. Henry Howell, 'the poor old Butcher that used to supply the College', pleaded with the Countess to pay his bill, and Averina Powell had to send to

---

[32] Cheshunt archives, F 1/ 738, J. Williams to Lady H., 26 June 1788; Gloucs. RO, D 2538/8/ 1, 3, J. Willams to Lady H., 3 April 1788.

[33] Cheshunt archives, F 1/ 956 and 963, T. Charles to Lady H., 21 January and 23 March 1791.

[34] Cheshunt archives, F 1/ 1716, William Aldington to Lady H., 31 May 1775. 'Teatos' were potatoes (*tatws* in colloquial Welsh).

[35] JRL, Meth. Archives, PLP 38. 23. 2, Lady Anne Erskine to Mrs Wesley, 20 January 1791.

[36] Cheshunt archives, F 1/ 653, Evan Roberts to Lady H., 10 September 1787; F 1/ 1965, J. Williams to Lady H., 16 October 1787.

[37] Cheshunt archives, F 1/ 1984, A. Powell to Lady H., 19 January 1788.

Brecon when he refused to supply her with any more meat.[38] The Trefeca 'Family' provided the College with various goods, services and loans for which the Countess eventually paid with a bank draft.[39]

In 1788 a rough account of her indebtness was drawn up:

Mr Roberts' Bill from the 10th April 1787 (when your Ladyship left College) to the 17th of July 1788 is	101	10	8
Mrs Jones' frm Ditto to the 4th July 1788 is	75	18	9
The Butcher about	50	0	0
Malt and hops about	40	0	0
Mrs Powell about	70	0	0
...			
The amount of the Expense of the College (within at most 30L) Between the 10 April 1787 and 10 July 1788, 1 year and a quarter	337	9	5

The master's salary and servants' wages not included.[40]

The cost of maintaining the College and providing for an increasing number of students was obviously too great a burden on Lady Huntingdon's income. Joan Jones of Tredustan Court complained that she had not been paid for 'the materials' which she had supplied, and the owner of the College lands applied to Averina Powell for his rent: 'I took the Liberty of Riting to Let your Ladyship know that Mr Huse [Hughes] of Tregunter did send to me Ister [yester] day for two years Rent and did desier of me to let your Ladyship know of it.'[41] Even the students had to wait for payment. John Lloyd, a student serving the chapel at St Agnes in Cornwall, had spent £32 10s. 5d. on clothes and travelling expenses which had not been paid three months after writing to the Countess for payment, neither had he received his year's salary of £52.[42] At the time of the Countess's death her debts amounted to about £3,000, but most had been incurred in the

[38] Cheshunt archives, F 1/ 1996, H. Howell to Lady H., 19 March 1788; F 1/ 2064, A. Powell to Lady H., n.d.

[39] John Williams probably kept an account book while at College. His commonplace book (NLW, Add. MS, 269A) begins, 'An Account Book belonging to me John Williams De Collegio Selinee [sic] comitissae Huntingdoniensis Anno Domini 1791', but contains only religious notes, medical receipts and notes about books.

[40] Cheshunt archives, E 4/ 15, 12, accounts; F 1/ 2054, E. Roberts to Lady H., 4 December 1788.

[41] Cheshunt archives, F 1/ 736, J. Williams to Lady H., 18 June 1788; F 1/ 762, Joan Jones to Lady H., 4 August 1788; F 1/ 2043, A. Powell to Lady H., 2 October 1788.

[42] Cheshunt archives, F 1/ 1916, J. Lloyd to Lady H., 21 November 1783. John Lloyd the student was not related to John Lloyd the friend of Lady Huntingdon and (later) one of her trustees.

purchase and repair of Sion chapel, and almost all the College bills had been paid.[43]

However, the debts of the College caused great concern among the Countess's friends in London, and on her eightieth birthday some of the members of Spa Fields Chapel decided to find alternative sources of income for the College after she died. As she sustained the entire cost of the College and its students and rarely accepted donations it was agreed that their activities should be confined to collecting subscriptions until after her death. The formation of a society 'for the supporting and perpetuating' of the College was discussed in October 1787. After the proposal was accepted by Lady Huntingdon, several meetings 'chiefly [of] hearers at Spa Fields Chapel' were held at the Castle and Falcon in Aldersgate Street.[44] Lady Huntingdon next invited a number of hearers from Spa Fields and some ministers to a dinner at the Castle and Falcon, where a 'plan' drafted by her was laid before them. Five days later a public meeting was held, but no clergy were invited.[45] The committee of Spa Fields, together with members drawn from her other two London chapels, were firmly in control. At a second public meeting her 'Plan' was approved and the 'Apostolic Society' formed.

Her plan, with a few minor amendments proposed at the second meeting, was comprehensive. When the College had been moved to Swansea, she would convey the buildings to seven persons (who were to be laymen and not ministers) as governors. Until her death the nomination and dismissal of the governors was to be in her hands; afterwards new appointments were to be made by co-option. On appointment all the governors were to subscribe to the Fifteen Articles of the Connexion, as were the students on admission to the College. There was to be a Master or Tutor, receiving no more than £50 a year together with board and lodgings; an Assistant at £30 a year, a housekeeper at £12 a year, and no more than three servants with £6 a year each. Twenty students were to be admitted after examination by either a minister of the Connexion or the Master. For three months the students were probationers, and then they were to be examined again, but on this second occasion five questions devised by Lady Huntingdon were to be put to them. As soon as practicable, the students were to be sent to preach on weekdays at towns and

[43] *Two Calv, Meth, Chapels*, 81.

[44] Cheshunt archives, C 5/2, p. 1, records of the Apostolic Society. Matthias Dupont, the owner of the Castle and Falcon, was a member of Spa Fields (see G. H. Hodson and E. Ford, *A History of Enfield* (Enfield, 1873), 332).

[45] Much of the information in this section is based on records printed in Welch, *Cheshunt College: The Early Years*.

villages within ten miles of the College, and on Sundays at places up to thirty miles away. After completing their education, the Connexion was to have priority in employing them, but 'the Trustees shall be at liberty to permit any Student or Students to go into and serve in the established Church, or other Churches in case there should be openings in Providence for their admission therein.' The College was the only theological institution which was prepared to train students for any evangelical ministry, and which made no charge for tuition or accommodation.

The students' day was fully occupied:

1. The Students are to rise at the sound of the Bell; which is to be rung at 5 O'Clock – to appear in the Study at a quarter after 5, before the Master, to sing a Hymn.
2. From this time 'till 6 they are to retire from private prayer and meditation; and to make their Beds, and clean themselves.
3. At 6 O'Clock, the Morning exercise begins.
4. Breakfast at 7. NB To be over in a quarter of an hour.
5. At eight, the Academical Studies begin and continue 'till 12.
6. Dinner at half past 12. NB Dinner to be over in half an hour.
7. At 2, the Academical studies to begin again and continue 'till 5.
8. At six, the evening exercise begins.
9. Supper at 7. NB To be over in a quarter of an hour.
10. At nine Family Prayer.
11. At half past 9 all retire to their Chambers – to be in bed by 10.

Any spare time which they might have was to be spent in 'wholesome bodily exercise and profitable conversation'. The 'academical studies' included English, Latin and Greek, Logic and 'the Sciences', together with divinity lectures every day. The teaching of English was more important here than at other theological colleges because many of the students were Welsh.[46] The Plan reflects the way in which the College had been carried on before 1787. The solitary exception to this was the provision that students should spend at least two years at their studies. As we have seen, Lady Huntingdon frequently sent them out to preach after only a few months at College, and after her death the governors had a battle with Lady Anne Erskine to prevent this practice from continuing.

The Society's attempt to solicit donations, legacies and subscriptions produced only £163. 1s. in the first year of the Society. As the writer of the Society's 'Record' said it was a 'day of small things' and he attributed this 'to two causes, first, that the Society was to have no operation till the demise of Lady Huntingdon; and secondly, that her Ladyship having

[46] A few years later the governors of Cheshunt College sat uncomprehending while Thomas Charles examined a student in Welsh.

chosen Laymen only as Trustees of her College, and given no share in managing the outward concerns thereof to Ministers.' Subscriptions fell to £43. 14s. 6d. in 1789, and the quarterly meetings of the subscribers were very poorly attended.

The minister who felt himself most affected by this Plan was Thomas Wills. He had left his curacy at St Agnes in Cornwall in order to itinerate for the Countess, and since the secession he had been stationed at Spa Fields as its resident minister each winter. His position as husband of the Countess's favourite niece, and the many affectionate letters which they received from Lady Huntingdon, led him to believe that he would be her adviser and her successor. As his obituary in the *Evangelical Magazine* stated, 'he probably felt himself of importance, and thought he might advise, and act with a freedom that Lady Huntingdon chose not to admit.'[47] In December 1783 he had sent her a long letter of advice about the future of both Trefeca and Bethesda.[48] He thought that Trefeca College was 'a vast burden and expense', and that the students acquired only 'a little smattering knowledge', which was 'so superficial as to be of little use to themselves or others; whilst they are so fond of throwing out hard words which they do not understand, as to subject them to ridicule from the wise of this world.' He proposed that the College should be given up and the students boarded with some evangelical minister 'in a cheap part of Wales' for training. His later letter to Lady Huntingdon about the Plan has not survived, but he 'did not accede to, or recommend' it, which 'occasioned a Shyness' between them. However, even before the Plan had been proposed, dissension had arisen between Wills, his fellow seceder William Taylor, and another minister in the Connexion, John Bradford. Bradford was accused of preaching antinomianism at Spa Fields in the summer of 1787, and when Wills returned there in March 1788 he thought that the congregation had been disturbed by Bradford's preaching.[49] Wills' statement that the Countess was now senile and had taken to antinomianism had greatly distressed her, and she received him with 'a kind of silent contempt'. He preached his last sermon at Spa Fields on 6 July; two days later he received his letter of dismissal.[50] Because he was not

[47] *Memoirs of the Life of The Rev. Thomas Wills ... By a Friend* (London, 1804), 210, quoting the obituary.

[48] Cheshunt archives, F 1/ 1918, Wills to Lady H., 7 December 1783.

[49] *Memoirs*, op. cit., 214; Gloucs. RO, D 2538/8/ 1, 2, Edmund Jones to Lady H., 9 January 1788.

[50] NLW, minor deposit 350A, Lady H. to N. Rowland, 25 July 1788; *Cong. Hist. Soc. Trans.*, 10 (1927–9), 44; *Memoirs*, op. cit., 219.

permitted to say farewell to the Spa Fields congregation he published a *Letter* to them and the other congregations in the Connexion.[51] Various attempts were made by friends to reconcile Wills and the Countess without success.[52] The attempted reconciliation caused a serious split in the Spa Fields committee. William Astle threatened to resign if Wills was reinstated; and Dr Benjamin Ford, the treasurer of the Apostolic Society, resigned because he was not reinstated.[53]

The Apostolic Society maintained a tenuous existence for another three years until the Countess's death. Then, on 6 July 1791, a meeting of subscribers was called at the Castle and Falcon. Twenty-five persons attended, only one of whom was a minister.[54] It was decided to continue the College at a more convenient place somewhere between ten and fifty miles outside London. An appeal was made for funds, but few of the Countess's aristocratic friends subscribed. The congregations at Spa Fields and Mulberry Gardens were more enthusiastic and £360 was raised in the first year. Although the College did not reach its total of twenty students for many years, enough money was raised to fill the building which was acquired at Cheshunt in Hertfordshire. Negotiations to rent it were carried on by James Oldham, a wealthy ironmonger of Holborn, but eventually the freehold was purchased with the help of a further appeal.[55] Lady Huntingdon had never executed a trust deed for any of her properties, and they would all have passed to her daughter if Lady Moira had chosen to exercise her rights. Now the governors had a trust deed prepared and registered in Chancery.[56] The College became the responsibility of a group of laymen who exercised as tight a control over the tutor and students as Lady Huntingdon had done.

A complete and detailed list of all those who subscribed to the Apostolic Society from its foundation in 1787 until 1816 has survived.[57] From the details of the 382 who began to subscribe before 1800 it is possible to

---

[51] T. Wills, *A Farewell Address from the Rev. Mr Wills to the Various Congregations and Societies in the Countess of Huntingdon's Connection* ... (London, 1788).

[52] Gloucs. RO, D 2538/8/ 1, 2.

[53] Cheshunt archives D 1/ 1, fo. 33; C 5/ 2, p. 4; *Memoirs*, op. cit., 220–229; W. Wilson, *Dissenting Churches and Meeting Houses in London*, (London, 1808) 116–22. Wills preached at Silver Street Chapel until two years before his death in 1802.

[54] See Welch, *Cheshunt College: The Early Years*.

[55] For James O. Oldham see E. Kaye, *A History of Missenden Abbey* (London, [1973]).

[56] The original deed of purchase and the trust deed are now in the Cheshunt archives (C 21/ 3 and 4). The Mortmain Act (9 Geo. II, c. 36) permitted charitable gifts of property to be made if the deeds were registered in Chancery.

[57] Cheshunt archives, C 5/ 3, summarized in Welch, *Cheshunt College: The Early Years*, 197–207.

discover from where the Countess drew her support and the social class of the wealthier members of the Connexion. Nine subscribers chose to be anonymous, and gave no address. Of the remaining 373 only forty-one lived outside the London area. Fifteen were clergymen. Thomas Charles, Cradock Glascott and Thomas Haweis were Lady Huntingdon's ministers, and most of the others had been students at Trefeca or Cheshunt. Five (who only subscribed after 1791) lived at Cheshunt, and the homes of most of the remainder were scattered across southern England. The greater part of the 332 London subscribers lived near to at least one of the three Connexion chapels there – Spa Fields, Clerkenwell; Mulberry Gardens, Wapping; and Sion chapel, Whitechapel. Of these, 115 lived within a mile of Spa Fields (most within half a mile) and sixty-five within a mile of Sion.[58] In the absence of lists of members of these three congregations it is only possible to say that twenty-five are known to have worshipped at Spa Fields. Few trades are noted in the list, but from Lowndes's *London Directory* for 1791 and the College trust deed it is possible to discover the trades or professions of 81 subscribers.

Attorney	Mercers (3)
Bacon factor	Merchants (8)
Brass founder	Oil men (2)
Cabinetmaker	Orange merchant
Cheesemongers (2)	Packer
Chemist	Printer
Coal merchants (2)	Seedsman
Corn chandler	Shoe warehouseman
Curriers (2)	Silk manufacturer
Doctors (2)	Skinner
Druggist	Slopseller
Engine and pump maker	Starchmaker
Factor	Stationers (5)
Glazier	Stockbroker
Glover	Sugar cooper
Grocers (3)	Sugar refiners (2)
Haberdashers (4)	Tallow merchant
Hat maker	Timber merchant
Ironmongers (2)	Tinplate manufacturer
Jeweller	Watch and clock maker
Leather seller	Weaver
Linen draper	Wholesale haberdasher
Manchester warehousemen (2)	Wholesale mercer
Mathematical instrument maker	Wine merchants (3)

[58] It should be noted that some lived within a mile of both chapels, and are therefore included in both totals.

Almost all of these men subscribed at least one guinea a year to the College and some gave more.

The later history of the College was not marked by any serious disputes – as was the Connexion. The buildings at Cheshunt were enlarged and eventually rebuilt. The number of teachers was increased, because most of the early presidents succumbed to overwork. The majority of the students became ministers in Independent (Congregational) churches, although the college retained its ecumenical character. As institutions of higher learning increased and the two ancient universities ceased to be the preserve of the Church of England, it became unnecessary to provide a general education, and it was agreed to move the college to a university town, where students could attend academic lectures. After some hesitations the choice fell on Cambridge, where the College occupied Cintra House until its new building in Bateman Street was opened. Two centuries after it was founded, Cheshunt College was amalgamated with Westminster, the Presbyterian Church of England college in Cambridge.[59]

---

[59] For a brief history of the college to 1968 see S. C. Orchard, *Cheshunt College* (Cambridge, [1968]). The Presbyterian Church of England and the Congregational Church now form part of the United Reformed Church.

12

The Connexion

In 1788 Lady Huntingdon supplied the Apostolic Society with a 'List of the Chapels and preaching places in the Connexion being 116 in number'.[1] Her intention was that these chapels and preaching places should be approached for donations to the Society. Unfortunately the list, which would be extremely useful, has since disappeared. The only extant complete list compiled during the Countess's lifetime is dated 1790 and names only sixty-three chapels.[2] The explanation of this large discrepancy between the two figures can probably be found by the earlier list's inclusion of 'preaching places'. In 1790 the West Country was represented by 'St Columbe District' with two chapels and 'a horse ride'. However, an undated 'Travelling Plan for the Ministers and Students' names nine towns between Exeter and St Agnes, only one of which (St Columbe) is in the 1790 list.[3] The next comprehensive list appears to be that compiled for the Connexion's conference of 1884.[4] Thirty-five chapels are listed, but the number is incomplete because none of the congregations outside the Connexion trust were allowed to attend. It is improbable that a complete list of all the chapels can now be compiled.[5]

It has been a tradition for many years that Lady Huntingdon's chapels were established in the spa or watering places which she visited in

---

[1] Cheshunt archives, C 1/1, p. 17.
[2] Cheshunt archives, D 3/2, Plan of Association, March 1790 (printed in *Two Calv. Meth. Chapels*, 93).
[3] Cheshunt archives, E 4/10, 16, printed in *Cirplan*, 5 (1973), 96, 97). The list was probably compiled about the time of the secession.
[4] *Report of Proceedings at a Conference of the Ministers and Managers of the Countess of Huntingdon's Connexion, together with the Trustees* (London, 1885). In 1831 twenty-seven chapels contributed to the Connexion's Society for the spread of the Gospel (Cheshunt archives, G 3/15), but this is probably not a complete list.
[5] For example, Brettle Lane near Dudley, where students preached (DWL, Thompson's List of Dissenters, 1772), was never in the Connexion. The Revd Ian Mallard produced a very useful typescript history of the Connexion chapels in 1957 (indexed copy in Cheshunt archives, G 3/14), but it is probably incomplete.

southern England. However only three of the chapels listed in 1790 – Bath, Brighton and Tunbridge Wells – fit this description.[6] Almost half the chapels in that list were situated in the Midlands or North of England. The principal factors in their geographical distribution were the activities of her preachers and the prior existence of a Whitefield Connexion chapel. For example, all the Sussex chapels, except Brighton and Ote Hall, were established as a result of Henry Peckwell's itinerancy in that county. On the other hand in such towns as Plymouth and Dursley in Gloucestershire, which already had flourishing Whitefieldite Tabernacles, a separate chapel was not established. The only indication of a consistent policy is the large number of cathedral cities in which a chapel was established. Ten such cities are included in the 1790 list, and several others were frequently visited by the Countess's students.[7] She appears to have been more willing than John Wesley to challenge the Church of England in its strongholds.

The chapels founded during the Countess's lifetime fall into three or four different groups. First there are those chapels which she owned and bequeathed to her trustees by her will: Bath, Brighton, Hereford, London and Tunbridge Wells. The London chapels were probably Spa Fields, Sion and Mulberry Gardens. The first two are in the Connexion trust deed of 1807 and the third was leased by her, but it is uncertain why she omitted Birmingham, Gloucester and Swansea, which are also in the trust deed and were opened in her lifetime.[8] Of all these chapels only Bath, Brighton, Tunbridge Wells, and possibly Mulberry Gardens chapel, were built by her – the others were buildings which already existed – and a distinction should perhaps be drawn between them. The next group comprises the chapels built by other Methodists and transferred to her Connexion with or without a trust deed being executed. Hereford was the result of a local initiative, and the trust was transferred to the Countess later. Chichester and Worcester had a similar origin, but their trusts were separately vested and never in the Countess's hands.[9] The last, and by far the largest group at her death, consisted of those meeting-places provided by societies or congregations formed by her students, which were described for varying periods of time as part of the Connexion. It is not

---

[6] Bristol is not included, because the chapel was built in the city, while the Hotwells which she visited were several miles away.

[7] London, although a cathedral city, is omitted because her chapels there cannot be described as a challenge to the cathedral clergy. After her death chapels were established at Canterbury and Chester.

[8] See Cheshunt archives, C 16/3 for copies of the will and trust deed.

[9] Worcester remained a separate trust until it closed recently.

surprising that, when the Connexion finally decided to grasp the nettle and define membership in 1884, there was so much dispute about the qualification.

Only the Bath chapel has survived from those built by Lady Huntingdon, and only Worcester from those built by others. Neither is now used by the Connexion. Swansea is the only chapel for which there is sufficient information to enable us to see how the Countess proceeded.[10] The society at Swansea was established about 1774 when one of the students wrote to the Countess: 'We have got a good Room intirely to ourselves at Swansea for preaching in. Mr Wesley's preachers have turned their backs upon it, because Mr Jones the Anchorsmith (whose property it is) is free and open hearted to the students, and by constantly attending to it, I think there would be a good work there.'[11] The society must have flourished, because in 1786 she visited Swansea and hired a local architect, William Jernegan, to find a house for her. The search was rendered more difficult by her insistence that the house should command a view of the sea. In October insuperable difficulties about buying a suitable house led to Jernegan recommending a house at Llanelli, but Swansea corporation was persuaded to lease land for ninety-nine years, and building began almost immediately despite the 'almost incessant rain'.[12] By 2 August 1788 the chapel was ready for use, but Jernegan was still seeking a house for the Countess's use.[13] By this time disputes had arisen about the cost of the work, and the Countess employed Oliver Cromwell to settle them. Jernegan had agreed to supervise the work for £570 and had already been paid £560. It is not clear whether the architect ever received any more money.[14]

Similar difficulties frequently arose when the Countess leased buildings. The Mulberry Gardens chapel in Wapping began about 1773, when

[10] The chapels themselves have left few eighteenth-century records. However we know that the plans for Bath and Hereford were drawn up by John Case (Cheshunt archives, F 1/626).

[11] Cheshunt archives, E 4/8, 6, J. Meldrum to Lady H., 12 February 1774.

[12] Cheshunt archives, F 1/1941, T. Wills, to Lady H., 12 October 1786; E 4/14, 1, Jernegan to Lady H., 29 May 1787. William Jernegan should not be confused with the better-known Edward Jerningham (cf. B. Little, *Selina Countess of Huntingdon* (Bath, 1989), 15). Cheshunt archives, F 1/850, E. Davis to Lady A. Erskine, 2 August 1787; E 4/14, 2, Jernegan to Lady H., 1 October 1787; E 4/14, 4, Jernegan to Lady H., 3 November 1787. JRL, Meth. Archives, Hunt. 119 probably relates to the laying of the foundation stone at Swansea (Lady H. to the Bath committee, n.d.).

[13] Cheshunt archives, E 4/14, 13 and 16, Jernegan to Lady H., 29 March and 19 May 1789.

[14] Cheshunt archives, F 1/2136, Dr J. Ford to Lady H., 5 July 1790; E 4/4, 17, Best to Lady H., 2 July 1789; E 4/14, 24, John Groves to Lady H., 7 September 1790.

she purchased the remainder of the lease of a building from the Revd Mr Richardson and spent almost £10 on cleaning up the property. In 1774 'a temporary building' was erected there for about £70. Two years later her students were still preaching in the temporary building. The delay was caused by the builders refusing to complete the work, probably because they had not been paid.[15] About 1789 it was proposed to have 'a Survey made of the Chapel which [was] thought to be in so bad a state as to render it improper for Lady Huntingdon to take a Lease of it'.[16] Holywell Mount in Shoreditch, the other London chapel, was held by an existing congregation, which applied to her for a minister in 1789. In return for their agreement to 'the rules observed in the Chapels belonging to the said Countess' she appointed William Francis Platt as their 'settled or stationed Minister'.[17] This was probably the more usual way in which chapels were added to the Connexion.

There was a more considerable trade in dissenters' meeting houses in the eighteenth century than is generally realized, and the Countess was often approached in this way. In 1780 she was offered the lease of a London chapel built as a speculation.[18] Moribund congregations were also sometimes willing to sell their building in order to pay their debts. About 1789 the Baptist church at the Adelphi had considered doing so: 'please to Inform her Ladyship, that we waited on Mr Hilton last night the 11 Inst, who gave us to understand that the Church are Come to a Resollution neither to Lett or sele the Chapel at present.'[19] 'Despite this letter, the Countess opened a chapel at the Adelphi in 1789, but very little is known of its history.[20] From 1770 there was considerable activity by the students in Kent. At Dover they found a Presbyterian chapel in Last Lane which was no longer in use, and obtained a lease from the trustees on condition that they rebuilt.[21] At Folkestone a chapel in Fenchurch Street

[15] Mallard, op. cit., 38; Cheshunt archives, A 2/9, vouchers, 1773–6; F 1/375, Glascott to Lady H., 8 January 1777.
[16] Cheshunt archives, F 1/1778, Thos Williams to Lady H., 15 August 1777; E 4/4, 17 and E 4/14, 23; T. Aveling, *Memorials of the Clayton Family* (London, 1867), 25; W. Wilson, *Dissenting Churches and Meeting Houses in London*, 1 (London 1808), 128.
[17] Cheshunt archives, E 4/15, 9, agreement with Holywell Mount trustees, 2 September 1789.
[18] Cheshunt archives, F 1/452, Brown to anon., 25 April 1780. There was a chapel at Bow by Stratford (London) which was available 'for any sect that will hire it' (Guildhall Lib., MS 9557).
[19] Cheshunt archives, F 1/824, anon., n.d.
[20] This chapel is not in Mallard's list. Cheshunt archives, F 1/810, John Ellis to Geo. Best, 31 January 1789; PRO, RG 4/ 4215.
[21] JRL, Meth. Archives, Hunt. 113, Lady H. to Benson, March 1770; T. Timpson, *Church History of Kent* (London, 1859), 417; PRO, RG 4/921, p. 1.

was taken over about 1801. It would appear to have been a mixed congregation of Baptists and Independents which joined the Connexion.[22] Only one meeting house of the Whitefield Connexion passed into Lady Huntingdon's hands, the Tabernacle at Norwich. This was in John Wesley's possession from 1758 until 1763, was rented by the Revd John Hook until 1775, and then it was leased by Lady Huntingdon and reopened.[23]

If nonconformist chapels and congregations entered the Connexion from time to time, they also left it with equal ease, though few clear examples have survived. In 1810 the Chichester congregation 'expressed a desire to dissolve the connection to which the Committee of management in London handsomely consented and resigned to the Congregation the present meeting'.[24] This church joined the Independents, but a move towards the Baptists was more usual. Also, after Lady Huntingdon's death, an attempt was made by the Baptist members of the Ely church to take it over by striking names out of the trust deed and eventually changing the locks on the chapel.[25] At the Cliffe chapel in Lewes, Baptist members of the congregation supported by Joseph Middleton, a student from Trefeca, tried to expel the paedobaptists.[26] Middleton arrived in the summer of 1780, and after a year refused to baptize children. Three years later, after many disputes, the local trustees took possession of the meeting house, and Middleton departed with the Baptist members to another building. It was also possible for the Countess to exclude a congregation from her Connexion. When she lost confidence in the Revd Adam Stumphousen in 1789 she notified the trustees of the Thame chapel that she no longer wished to be associated with it.[27]

Even when the Countess ceased to pay the entire cost of building, she was still expected to make a handsome contribution towards it. In 1783 Daniel Gray, a student sent to help the chapel at Kendal, wrote asking for her assistance, as he feared the chapel building would become private

[22] PRO, RG4/1006. Members' children were baptized as early as 1799.
[23] Mallard, op. cit., 42. Cheshunt archives, E 4/8, 16, W. Foster to Lady H., 19 April 1775; S. J. Wearing, *Georgian Norwich* (Norwich, 1926), 16; J. Browne, *History of Congregationalism in Norfolk and Suffolk* (London, 1877), 189–92.
[24] West Sussex RO, Add. MS 2459, p. 4.
[25] Ely church records, [history of the congregation], n.d.
[26] This information is taken from the Cliffe chapel records (East Sussex RO, NB 1/1/1A).
[27] SMU, Hunt. 107, Lady H. to Mr Cockayne, 6 March 1789. See E. B. Keeble, *These Hundred and Fifty Years* (Lewes, 1934); J. H. Pratt (ed.), *The Thought of the Evangelical Clergy* (Edinburgh, 1978), 178.

property.[28] 'Langatock people' were pressing her to pay 'the Remainder of the Bills' for work done there in 1788.[29] When she offered £100 towards the cost of a chapel in Dublin, she carefully stated the terms on which she would do so

> That there be a plan of the building – the Numbers it will contain, with proper estimate of the whole expences produced.
>
> That a proper plot of Ground be provided in a good scituation, upon such terms as shall not subject the Building to a ground rent of more than Ten pounds per Annum.
>
> That the whole money be raised and deposited in the hands of a Banker, under the direction of Trustees to be appointed by the majority of subscribers, previous to the taking one conclusive step relative to the Ground or Building...[30]

Probably wisely, the subscribers decided instead to rent a chapel. Henry Peckwell and others urged her to be cautious in opening new chapels, not only because of the difficulties of providing students, but also because of the cost of repairs and extensions.[31] However, she was still involved in leasing and building until her death. As she wrote about the Hereford chapel (opened in 1786), 'My Fingers has been so often in mortar for many years' that it was difficult not to continue.[32] Her intention was that Hereford people should pay the greater part of the cost, but by 1788 the builders had not been paid and the trustees had defaulted on her loan.[33]

The larger and more prosperous congregations in the Connexion were expected to maintain a school, to contribute towards the expenses of ministers and students and to engage in mission work in the surrounding countryside. Both Spa Fields and Bath are known to have had large schools. The Spa Fields school was supported entirely by subscriptions and money received from the chapel funds.[34] The teachers were the minister in residence and the organist (William Shrubsole jun.). No details are available for the Bath school, but a summary of the chapel accounts for 1788 gives details of the other chapel activities:[35]

[28] Cheshunt archives, F 1/579 and 594, Gray to Lady H., 4 December 1783 and 3 February 1784.
[29] Gloucs. RO, D 2538/8/1, 5, J. Williams to Lady H., 9 June 1788. Title deeds for Llangattwg Lingoed (Mon.) are in the Connexion archives.
[30] DWL, Cong. Lib., IIa 17/25, 10 February 1773.
[31] Cheshunt archives, F 1/288, H. Peckwell to Lady H., 5 May 1774.
[32] Hunt. Lib., HA 44039, Lady H. to anon., 30 December 1785.
[33] Cheshunt archives, F 1/626, Case to Lady H., 6 May 1787; F 1/1956, Thos Price to Lady H., 16 August 1787; F 1/2023, Henry Stone to Lady H., 19 June 1788.
[34] Cheshunt archives, D 1/2, fos. 9–24.
[35] Cheshunt archives, F 1/715, R. Carpenter to Lady H., 12 March 1788.

Moneys received for Quarterly Tickets, etc. ...	267	17	3
Cash Paid the Ministers for their services and Traveling Expences	127	11	6
The Revd Mr Watkins's Yearly Salary	20	0	0
The Organists Ditto	12	12	0
Mr Baileys Ditto	10	10	0
Mrs Hawkins's Ditto	10	10	0
Door Keepers Ditto	7	7	0
Interest of £400	20	0	0
Ground Rent	14	14	0
Candles	25	12	0
Servants Wages at the Chapel House	9	9	0
Sacrament Wine	6	4	6
Taxes, Insurance, Lamps, New Music and several small Bills	33	9	11
	297	9	11
Received	267	17	3
Balance	29	12	8

The travelling expenses were probably for visits to preach in towns and villages: the cost of travel for ministers when moving from one chapel to another was usually met by the Connexion's Travelling Fund, supported by collections made by all the congregations.[36]

The Countess appointed a committee to be responsible for the administration of each chapel. Its purpose was to relieve the ministers and students of all financial concerns.[37] Where she knew the local congregation well, the choice was a personal one; otherwise she was obliged to rely on the advice of a minister or student who had preached in the town. Only one set of early minutes of a committee (that for Spa Fields) has survived. In addition, a few of her letters to the Bath committee have been found together with the appointment of a new committee there.[38] The latter document appoints four local tradesmen as her attorneys 'to act, transact and Manage all Affairs relating to the said Chapel, and the carrying on the Worship of God in the same, and to receive all Sum and Sums of Money, Subscriptions, Donations, Dues ...' She reserved to herself the right to

[36] Travelling fund accounts for 1781–7 can be found in Cheshunt archives, E 4/15, 1. At that time it was administered by the Spa Fields secretary (Connexion archives, 4/8, Lady H. to W. Hodson, 9 June 1784).

[37] DWL, Cong. Lib., II c 7/16, Lady H. to T. Wills, 10 September 1782.

[38] The Spa Fields minutes have been printed in *Two Calv. Meth. Chapels*, 46–87, but other records of this chapel have disappeared since 1910 (D. E. Jenkins, *The Life of Rev. Thomas Charles* (Denbigh, 1910), 83, 460). The letters to Bath were sold after the congregation dissolved itself in 1922 and are now widely scattered. Cheshunt archives, F 1/533, agreement, 12 July 1783.

appoint and remove the ministers, and she closely supervised the committees. During the Gordon Riots, in which Spa Fields narrowly escaped plundering, she advised the Spa Fields committee to avoid the appearance of condoning treason even though they might approve Gordon's intentions.[39] She wrote twenty-one letters of advice to the Bath committee between November 1784 and March 1787. Most are concerned with the movement of ministers and internal problems, but she also told them of developments elsewhere, including the meeting of the Welsh Associations at Brecon and her son's visit to Trefeca.[40] She appreciated the work done by committee members, but was also ready to replace them if they defied her. In 1782 she replaced the entire committee at Bristol. When the Spa Fields committee defied her in 1789, all ten members signed the letter, and the secretary tactfully omitted the word 'obedient' from 'Your Ladyship's faithful and humble servants'.[41] They were not dismissed. Long after the Countess's death the committees began to assume more power, even though they were still appointed by the trustees and not elected by the congregation.[42]

Confirmation of the Countess's policy in appointing local committees can be found in the records of Sion Chapel at Ashbourne in Derbyshire. This was built by a member of Spa Fields chapel in 1801, after Lady Huntingdon's death, and he placed it in the hands of the College trustees. In a series of letters between Ashbourne and London the trustees justified their actions by an appeal to her rules.[43] All services were to be conducted according to the Anglican Book of Common Prayer; any tendency towards Independency was strongly discouraged; half-yearly chapel accounts had to be submitted to and audited by the trustees. The local committee had no powers of action: even such minor matters as the painting of the chapel windows or the behaviour of members of the congregation had to be decided by the trustees. It is clear from this that Lady Huntingdon controlled her congregations as strictly as John Wesley did his.

[39] Cheshunt archives, E 4/10, 15, copy of letter, 11 September 1781; W. J. Pinks, *The History of Clerkenwell* (London, 1880), 145.
[40] According to the endorsements, letter 7 (Univ. of Georgia) is dated 5 November 1784 and letter 27 (JRL, Meth. Archives, Hunt. 114) 17 February 1787. Emory Univ., letter 19 (14 October 1785) and JRL, Meth. Archives, Hunt. 118 (12 November 1784).
[41] Cheshunt archives, E 4/10, 9, Lady H. to Mr Derham, 18 January 1781; DWL, Cong. Lib., IIc 7/12, Lady H. to T. Wills, 12 February 1782; *Two Calv. Meth. Chapels*, 78.
[42] See Cheshunt archives, F 1/1096, Meffen to H. F. Stroud, 3 August 1821, about resignation of Hereford committee.
[43] Cheshunt archives, C 10/1 and 6. It was placed in the College trust as there was no Connexion trust deed.

Lewes is the only chapel for which eighteenth-century lists of members have been preserved. Unfortunately no other details are given, so it is impossible to deduce their social position or occupation. In 1776 it had thirty-seven men and twenty-two women, and in 1781 twenty-seven men signed a call to Mr Middleton.[44] However a number of early baptismal registers have survived for the Connexion. When the government imposed a stamp duty on every register entry in 1783, Lady Huntingdon supplied at least some of her chapels with blank registers.[45] Only a few of these registers record the father's occupation, but while Richard Freer was the minister at Norwich in 1788 and 1789 he carefully recorded occupations and parishes for the twelve baptisms he administered:

Baker
Bricklayer
Gauze-weaver
Haberdasher
Manufacturer
Mason
Staymaker
Weaver (two baptisms for same parents)
Woolcomber (two)
Worsted weaver[46]

Mulberry Gardens chapel register has seven such entries:

Glasscutter (1789, two)
Hatter (1790)
Linen draper (1790)
Sailor (1793)
Tallow chandler (1791)[47]

Later at Folkestone, between 1821 and 1825, the minister recorded the following eight occupations:

Bookseller
Bricklayer
Chemist
Farmer
Grocer
Printer

[44] East Sussex RO, NB 1/1/1A, pp. 2, 10, 29.
[45] See E. Welch, 'Nonconformist Registers', *Journal of Soc. of Archivists*, 2 (1964), 413.
[46] PRO, RG 4/3132. Any entries for ministers' or soldiers' children have not been included in these lists.
[47] PRO, RG 4/4165.

Sapper and Miner
Shoemaker[48]

All these entries confirm the impression already given by the Apostolic Society subscription list, that the majority of the members were drawn from the tradesmen and merchants of the town. However there are considerable discrepancies in the area from which they were drawn. Only two families out of forty-one entries for Brighton lived outside the parish, and a similar pattern can be found at Bath, Dover and Folkestone.[49] Tunbridge Wells, on the other hand, drew its support from an area seven miles around the town. Of seventy-one entries giving the parish between 1787 and 1798, only thirty are from 'Tunbridge' (i.e. Tonbridge or Tunbridge Wells). The two London chapels for which we have information also drew their hearers from a wide area. No comparable figures have been published for other Calvinist or Arminian Methodist congregations for the later eighteenth century. They can be compared only with those for Moravian churches. At Bedford the occupations given in the Moravian registers are very similar.[50]

It was the sermon, closely followed by hymn-singing, which attracted most people to the Connexion chapels. In the interior of the chapels at Spa Fields and Worcester the pulpit was the dominant feature.[51] Horace Walpole described the interior of the Bath chapel in similar terms:

> At the upper end is a broad *haut-pas* of four steps, advancing in the middle: at each end of the broadest part are two of *my* eagles with red cushions for the parson and clerk. Behind them rise three more steps, in the midst of which is a third eagle for a pulpit ... Behind the pit, in a dark niche is a plain table with rails.[52]

It was usual for the minister to confine his part of the service to the sermon and allow a student to read the prayers. Complaints about the way in which the service was read are rare: complaints and compliments about the sermons preached are frequent, showing that congregations shared the same values. The service was that to be found in the Book of Common

[48] PRO, RG 4/1006.
[49] PRO, RG 4/1416, 921 and 4165. The Moorfields Tabernacle register for 1795 and 1796 (RG 4/4523) shows a similar concentration of residence near the chapel.
[50] H. D. Rack (*Reasonable Enthusiast* (London, 1989), 366) believes that Wesleyan 'Methodism appealed to the industrious middling and artisan classes', but the list which he gives on p. 439 is not comparable with those given here. They are drawn from other sources which may emphasize the role of the more wealthy members. Beds. RO, MO 4.
[51] For the Spa Fields interior see Pinks, op. cit., 147, and for Worcester [C. F. Stell], *An Inventory of Nonconformist Chapels and Meeting-houses in Central England* (London, 1986), 258. For a contemporary description (probably of Mulberry Gardens interior) see Cheshunt archives, F 1/1602, Thomas Adams to Lady H., 5 May 1772.
[52] W. S. Lewis (ed.), *Horace Walpole's Miscellaneous Correspondence* (Yale, 1973), 119.

Prayer, but with certain amendments.[53] No revised service was ever published by the Connexion, though after the Countess's death unofficial versions appeared.[54] Lady Huntingdon's draft notes for a revision of the communion service and the Litany would have reduced their length considerably.[55] In the communion service the Lord's Prayer and the Commandments together with the exhortation and the absolution were to be omitted. In both, hymns were substituted for the psalms.[56]

There were so many editions of Connexion hymn books that it is impossible to compile a complete list.[57] It would appear that in later years new editions appeared almost every year, though they probably incorporated no important changes. The hymn books were very popular, and large numbers must have been printed. In 1774 Henry Peckwell ordered thirty dozen for Chichester, and thirty dozen for Brighton as soon as the new edition was published.[58] All the early copies which I have seen are small, and most are bound in red morocco with some gold tooling.[59] It was even found necessary to include in them a warning against 'spurious editions'. The authentic editions were printed by Hughes and Walsh of London, but in 1780 Mr Guy of Bath, produced an unauthorized edition. Five years later, when Mr Guy's hymn books were still in use at Bath, the Countess informed the Bath committee that 'the Printer of the Hymn Books has wrote about the hardship of Guys Books being publickly used in the school, and Could any thing be done as Mr Walch and Hughs are honest and respectable men in their Business, and you must know Guys was fraud and nothing better from the beginning.'[60]

Each edition states on the title page that the hymns were 'Collected by her Ladyship' and there seems no reason to doubt that these are her favourite hymns. The preface and advertisement, however, are almost certainly the production of another person. The 1765 edition is divided into three parts – 127 Society Hymns, thirteen Children's Hymns and ninety-one Congregation Hymns. There is no explanation of this

[53] The use of 'church prayers' was favoured by those who disliked extempore praying (G. Swann (ed.), *The Journals of Two Poor Dissenters* (London, 1970), 3–6).
[54] A. E. Peaston, *The Prayer Book Tradition in the Free Churches* (London, 1964), 66–9.
[55] Cheshunt archives, A 4/5, 25.
[56] Peaston, op. cit., 69. The church service continued to be used at Bath, Brighton, Tunbridge Wells and Worcester until the chapels closed.
[57] There is a very incomplete list with a reproduction of the title page of the 1780 edition (p. v) in R. A. Leaver, *Bibliotheca Hymnologica* (London, 1981). Another list, equally incomplete, can be found in J. Julian, *A Dictionary of Hymnology* (London, 1908), 543.
[58] Cheshunt archives, F 1/281, H. Peckwell to Lady H., 16 March 1774.
[59] E.g. Newberry Library editions of 1765 and 1788.
[60] Emory Univ., Lady H. to Bath, 14 October 1785; Cheshunt archives, F 1/463, Hughes and Walsh to Lady H., 18 July 1780.

arrangement and the hymns themselves provide no clue. The 1788 edition is only slightly less confusing. It has 248 hymns, each with a title, not grouped in any way. These are followed by fourteen hymns for the sacrament service and seven for funerals. A further twenty very short hymns are followed by seven doxologies and twenty-three choruses from the *Messiah*. There is an index of first lines, but not of subjects. No printed music has been found, but in 1781 Lady Huntingdon sent Lord Dartmouth 'the music of the Hymns'.[61] Many of the hymns could no doubt be traced to Charles Wesley or the Moravians, and the Countess owned a manuscript copy of Charles Wesley's hymns and the 1754 edition of the Brethren's hymn book. Her interest in Handel's works may be attributed to her daughter, Lady Selina.[62]

The reputation of the Bath chapel for fine musical services was well known. Horace Walpole described a service there in 1766: 'I have been at an opera, Mr Wesley's. They have boys and girls with charming voices, that sing hymns, in parts, to Scotch ballad tunes.'[63] His mistake about the ownership of the chapel can be attributed to the frequency with which Wesley preached there at that early period. The excellence of the music was the work of a local Methodist, Benjamin Milgrove, some of whose tunes are still in use. Walter Shirley described how he had put 'the most elegant tune' to the hymn which preceded the sermon in 1770.[64] Two years later there was a dispute between Milgrove and a Mr Shepherd about copying some of the music. Milgrove then complained to Lady Huntingdon that 'there is a division among the Singers, and that my Music is sadly mangled for want of their proper Attendance to learn.' A set of articles was drawn up for all the singers to sign, in which they promised to forget 'past little bickerings', 'harbour no Evil suspicions', and never give away copies of the composer's works. All ended happily when Milgrove again sang in chapel, though he refused to sit on the singers' bench.[65] The only other chapel where hymn-singing is known to have caused a dispute is Mulberry Gardens. Dr Henry Mayo, the minister of the Nightingale Lane Independent chapel in Wapping, complained to the

[61] Cheshunt archives, E 4/10, 7, copies of two letters of Lady H., November 1781.
[62] Cheshunt archives, B 5/6, Wesley's hymns, n.d.; *A Collection of Hymns of the Children of God in all Ages ... for the Use of the Congregations in Union with the Brethren's Church* (London, 1754) in Cheshunt College library; Cheshunt archives, B 5/10, Lady Selina's music book.
[63] *Walpole's Misc. Corr.*, op. cit., 118. John Wesley disapproved of musical services such as the one described by Walpole.
[64] Cheshunt archives, F 1/86, W. Shirley to Lady H., 27 January 1770.
[65] Cheshunt archives, F 1/1583, Lloyd to Lady H., 7 February 1772); E 4/1, 9, W. Shirley to Lady H., 21 February 1772; F 1/1577, Milgrove to Lady H., 15 January 1772; F 1/1296, Articles, n.d.; E 4/1, 9. For more information about Milgrove see *Wesley Hist. Soc. Proceedings*, vol. 44, 1983–4, p. 25.

Protestant Dissenting Deputies in 1778 about Mulberry Gardens chapel 'being built so very near that they could not go on, the singing being so loud that he could not be heard when preaching'.[66] The music in the Connexion chapels attracted such large congregations that they sometimes filled the chapels to overflowing. Thomas Haweis complained that the 'vitiated' air in the chapels caused the candles to burn dim, and he perspired so much as to rust the keys in his pocket.[67]

The supply of ministers and students to her chapels was organized by Lady Huntingdon herself until the day she died. This required her to write innumerable letters, both to the chapel committees and the preachers themselves. The usual pattern was for her ministers with no benefice or chapel to serve to be appointed to spend the winter at one of the larger chapels. In the summer they would itinerate, and their places would be taken by the beneficed clergy for whose parishes she would find a curate. The smaller chapels did not have a resident minister but were served by students, and received occasional summer visits from ministers.[68] This pattern was disrupted by a shortage of both ministers and students when the number of chapels began to grow, and frequent exceptions were made. Her organization of the moves was good. Difficulties arose only when someone was unable or unwilling to move at her request, or when a congregation tried to insist on retaining a popular preacher or on removing an unpopular one. A draft prepared by Lady Huntingdon for the summer of 1781 demonstrates the care which she took over these moves.[69] It begins with a list of ministers. This is followed by another arranged by chapels which they were to serve:

Bath–	June 11	Shepard
	July 2	Pentecross
	Aug. 2	John Jones
		Shepard
	till October	Students
Bristol–	June 11	Penty[cross]
	July 6	Jones [of] Langann succeeded by Students
Spafields–	June & July	Piercy
	Aug. & Sept.	Owen
	Oct.	Glascott

[66] Guildhall Lib., MS 3083/2, pp. 278, 280, Deputies' minute book. The minutes do not record the outcome.
[67] Mitchell Lib., B 1176, p. 125.
[68] Connexion archives, 4/2, T. Wills to Dickinson, 22 May 1783.
[69] Cheshunt archives, E 4/10, 16. It can be dated 1781 as it includes William Piercy's name.

Two accounts of the itinerating in 1781 have been preserved. Thomas Wills's journal of his progress through the West Country from 19 June to 1 September has been printed in his journal. The letters which Thomas Wills, Cradock Glascott and William Piercy sent to the Countess during the same period were edited by Thomas Pentycross and published in 1782.[70] In his introduction Pentycross stated Lady Huntingdon's intention 'that once at least every year, the voice of mercy, through a Savior's inexhaustible merits, should be sounded in the ears of millions, by Gospel-Ministers sent into every city, town, and larger village, throughout the kingdom. From these centers, it is presumed, Grace and Truth may be propagated to each surrounding vicinage.' Wills's journals for his itinerancies in 1784 (Wales and the West Midlands) and 1785 (Midlands and Northern England) have also been preserved, and the whole provides an illuminating account of the progress of Calvinistic Methodism in the provinces.[71]

Contrary to tradition, it does not appear that Lady Huntingdon travelled with her ministers. She attended sermons in her own house and in the chapels which she visited, but neither in her own letters describing her journeys, nor in those of others, is she said to be accompanied by a clergyman. There is one occasion on which she was accompanied by a student. She was sent to Teignmouth in Devon by her doctor in 1778 to recover from a fever brought on by Lady Fanny Shirley's death, and took the opportunity to evangelize 'this poor dark country'. She had with her 'little Davis the Student'. 'I made the student stand on the sands where never, never the Gospel had been preach'd and the last Sunday evening above two thousand attended – showers of [stones] about the ears of the preacher but three souls is awaken'd and Call'd in one family so that a Church is prepareing.'[72] However Lady Glenorchy, a friend of the Countess, did travel with a chaplain and arranged, often with difficulty,

---

[70] *Memoirs of the Life of the Rev. Thomas Wills* (London, 1804), 26–87; [T. Pentycross] (ed.), *Extracts of the Journals of Several Ministers of the Gospel ... In a Series of Letters to the Countess of Huntingdon* (London, 1782). All five letters of Glascott are now Cheshunt archives, E 4/11, 1, 2, 4–6.

[71] *Memoirs of Wills*, op. cit., 98–147, 149–97.

[72] JRL, Eng. MS 338, 4 and 5, Lady H. to T. Wills, 7 and 20 July 1778; SMU, Hunt. 99 and 100, Lady H. to T. Haweis, 8 August and Sept. 1778. In 1765 she hoped to find a minister to accompany her to Derbyshire (SMU, Hunt. 54, Lady H. to Mrs Wadsworth, 17 June 1765).

for him to preach in the towns which she visited.[73] This may be responsible for the tradition about the Countess.

For seven years after the secession the organization of the Connexion was the Countess's prerogative. It was probably never written down, or if it was, no copy has survived. It has to be reconstructed from her letters and papers. She provided the Connexion with a doctrinal standard, the Fifteen Articles, within a year of the secession.[74] Their author is unknown, but it is likely that Lady Huntingdon played an active part in their compilation. Her articles are drawn from the Thirty-nine Articles of the Church of England and quotes from them. The Anglican Articles 2, 7, 8, 14, 16, 18, 20–6 are omitted, and all the Articles from thirty onwards. Some were eliminated because they were no longer needed; others because they referred to matters rejected by the Connexion, and some of the phrases because they were not sufficiently Calvinist. The order of the Fifteen Articles is perhaps more logical for eighteenth-century hearers.

In 1789, soon after the Countess's eighty-second birthday, she was advised by her doctor that she should retire. During the past two years she had employed a secretary, George Best, for some of her correspondence. He and Lady Anne Erskine, her companion, had been able to relieve her of some of the labour of writing letters, but the volume of her work had not decreased since she was constantly undertaking new responsibilities. She now called a meeting at Spa Fields chapel which was 'to consider of forming an association to relieve her and take management of the whole Connection on themselves.'[75] The meeting, on 23 November, was attended by the whole of the Spa Fields committee, some members of the Holywell Mount and Mulberry Gardens committees, and five ministers. They resolved that

1. A state of all the chapels in the Connection be made out and laid before us.
2. To be informed what provision Lady H[untingdon] had made or intended to make for the discharge of the debts and incumbrances of the chapels.
3. That she should not enter into any new engagement without the consent and approbation of the association.
4. That the management, direction and controul of the whole Connexion

[73] Beds. RO, L 30/9/17/160, Lady Grey to Lord Breadalbane, 25 July 1771. For Lady Glenorchy, who also founded a number of churches, see T. S. Jones, *The Life of . . . Willielma Viscountess Glenorchy* (Edinburgh, 1822).

[74] The Fifteen Articles were first printed in *An Authentic Narrative of the Primary Ordination . . . On Sunday the 9th Day of March 1783* (London, 1784), 16–25. Earlier some use had been made of the Westminster Assembly's shorter catechism as a doctrinal standard.

[75] Cheshunt archives, D 1/1, fo. 30, printed in *Two Calv. Meth. Chapels*, 76.

should devolve on the association, whose view and intention was to keep it together and maintain it with energy after the decease of the Countess.

The meeting had some reason to fear the actions of the Countess. As we have already seen, the Apostolic Society was to do nothing but collect money for the College until she died. Although she now seemed willing to retire immediately, they may well have doubted whether she would cease from interference. She had admitted to Howell Harris in 1765 that her expenses were 'so vast' that she would be reduced to eating bread and cheese, and in 1779 she proposed to sell her house at Brighton in order to raise more money.[76] Nevertheless she continued to accept new congregations and more students. In 1788 she sent two students to New Brunswick, and she already had a congregation in Nova Scotia.[77] Her plan for the 'Indian nations' had still not been abandoned despite the lack of response from the United States Congress. She was planning to send students to the Pacific when the opportunity arose, and made enquiries of sailors about the practicability of doing so. Shortly before her death she was negotiating to buy the Haymarket Assembly Rooms in Leicester for £850. These activities were all extensions of her previous work, as were the chapels in 'five Country towns' in the Midlands 'all as Dark as Pagans'.[78] Her efforts extended to establishing churches in Europe. The attempt about 1785 to open a chapel in Brussels had been discovered to be a plot by a papist lord to assassinate her, or so Thomas Wills believed.[79] She now planned to take advantage of the French Revolution to begin a mission in Paris – 'France will be for the english prodistants if I succeed': 'my present Plan is to get my Friend Sir John Orter to go over (as he knows all the rules well) and applie from me to Neckor and agree for the finest Church in Paris, their Finances are so low that they will rejoice to have me

---

[76] NLW, Trev. letter 2608, Lady H. to Harris, 1 August 1765; DWL, Cong. Lib., IIc 7/7, Lady H. to T. Wills, 23 April 1779.

[77] Cheshunt archives, A 3/14, *An Address to the Inhabitants of New Brunswick* (1788); A 3/12, 13–15, Wm Furmage to Lady H., 9 May and 3 December 1785, 12 November 1786; SMU, Hunt. 108, Lady H. to T. Haweis, 27 February 1790.

[78] SMU, Hunt. 127, Lady H. to T. Haweis, 7 August 1790; Hunt. 121, Lady H. to Mr and Mrs Haweis, 8 April 1790. For this unsuccessful venture (which nevertheless led to the formation of the London Missionary Society) see Mitchell Lib., B 1176, pp. 185, 186 and C. S. Horne, *The Story of the L.M.S.* (London, 1908), 3; Cheshunt archives, F 1/2144 and 2148, Robt Hemington to Lady H., 6 and 27 September 1790; SMU, Hunt. 118, Lady H. to T. Haweis, 24 March 1790.

[79] Cheshunt archives, F 1/662, T. Wills to Lady H., 27 April 1787; *Memoirs of Wills*, op. cit., 204–. As late as 1787 Lady Huntingdon was still planning a visit to Brussels (Cheshunt archives, B 4/3, Lady H. to J. Bidwell, 10 April 1787).

Purchess it.'80 A few months later she sent an offer of £1,000 for a church there. Her college was to be enlarged to include the teaching of French and Flemish. Then she found 'an awaken'd man from Rouen' and sent him to College for training.[81] Her expectations of success were great: 'A Good and Glorious man sayes I shall not die untill I have a Chapel in Paris.'[82] She expected everyone to be as enthusiastic as she was, but a request to Spa Fields for more funds met with a polite refusal. They had too many expenses and insufficient income.[83]

When the meeting which Lady Huntingdon had called to consider her plan made its four demands she refused to agree. A second meeting held on 3 December to resolve the problem was attended only by four ministers, two members of the Holywell Mount committee and two members of Spa Fields committee, because notices of the meeting had been 'neglected or purposely omitted'.[84] Despite the small attendance, an association was formed and the members of the committee chosen. In answer to a protest from Spa Fields, it was agreed to enlarge the committee to include more of their number, but the entire committee of Spa Fields (except for the two who had attended the second meeting) declined to take part. They felt that the proposal was not 'calculated to promote the great and important ends' which they had contemplated.[85] No copy of this first plan of association has been found, but it is possible to deduce that one of the two members of Spa Fields was the chairman of the committee. Since the plan was so objectionable to the majority of the Spa Fields committee it is probable that the Countess planned to transfer the Connexion to six Anglican ministers – a proposal which Thomas Wills had earlier felt was dangerous.[86]

The dispute was resolved by 3 March 1790, when a *Plan of an Association for Uniting and Perpetuating the Connection* (probably drafted by the Countess) was printed over George Best's signature. It was not circulated to the congregations until May, when it was sent out with a letter signed by the Countess.[87] By this plan twenty-three districts were established. Each district was to have a committee of all the local ministers and two laymen

---

[80] SMU, Hunt. 118 and 122. Orter was the king's representative in Ostend; Necker was the French minister of finance.
[81] SMU, Hunt. 106, Lady H. to T. Haweis, 3 May 1790.
[82] SMU, Hunt. 112, Lady H. to T. Haweis, 29 January 1790.
[83] SMU, Hunt. 119, Lady H. to T. Haweis, 29 March 1790.
[84] SMU, Hunt. 117, Lady H. to T. Haweis, 15 March 1790.
[85] Cheshunt archives, F 1/794, W. Hodson to Lady H., 2 December 1788.
[86] Cheshunt archives, D 1/1, fo. 31.
[87] Cheshunt archives, D 1/1, fos. 31–4.

from each congregation. Each year a minister and two laymen from each district, together with the members of the 'London Acting Association' were to meet in the General Association. At all other times the London Association (the constitution of which is not given) would act on behalf of the General Association. A separate fund was to be established to carry on the work of the Connexion, and it was suggested that every member should contribute 'not less than a Penny a week'. In future no congregation was to incur any debt without the approval of the district committee, and no money from the fund was to be spent on building projects without the agreement of seven-eighths of the General Association. Thomas Charles of Bala, who was now the principal summer preacher at Spa Fields, approved the plan,[88] but Thomas Haweis, who had now resumed preaching for the Countess, did not. In February the Countess wrote to him that

> the longwish'd for time seems Comeing by the Plan of an Association of ministers and warm hearted men over the Connection to unite for the Carr[y]ing the Gospel forward abroad and at Home and to put it into such a line of General usefullness that when the Lord Calls for me my absence will not make more than an old shoe Cast aside.[89]

Haweis replied that he was unable to support her proposal because 'I should not chuse to be in Bondage to Laymen, or committees, and suppose the faithful Ministers themselves, would most zealously, and most profitably promote the work of God.'[90] The Countess tried to reassure him about the preponderance of laymen in the Association, and in one of her rare citations of the scriptures she quoted chapter 6 of Acts to support her view, but he refused to agree. Haweis had never entirely accepted the secession or the fact that the Connexion was now a body of dissenters, and warned her against the dangers of becoming a branch of the Independent churches.[91] It is clear from the Spa Fields records that little was done to implement the Plan.[92] Before the second plan had been drafted, Lady Huntingdon had made her last will, in which she bequeathed all her chapels to Thomas Haweis and his wife, Lady Anne Erskine and John Lloyd, and although she subsequently made two codicils, this was never revoked. Responsibility for the Connexion passed in 1791 to Lady Anne, and then in 1804 to other trustees. It would appear

[88] Cheshunt archives, F 1/1941, T. Wills to Lady H., 12 October 1786.
[89] Cheshunt archives, D 3/2, printed in *Two Calv. Meth. Chapels*, 92–5; NLW, MS 9231C, Lady H. to the Ely congregation, 19 May 1790.
[90] Cheshunt archives, F 1/890 and 908, Charles to Lady H., 8 March and 28 April 1790.
[91] SMU, Hunt. 108, Lady H. to T. Haweis, 27 February 1790.
[92] Cheshunt archives, F 1/2121, T. Haweis to Lady H., 27 February 1790.

that the Countess had abandoned her plan for an association, but felt unable to begin the process once more in the last year of her life.[93]

At the beginning of 1791 John Wesley was dying in London. He had probably not met Lady Huntingdon or corresponded with her for many years, but she could not help expressing her concern: 'Lady Huntingdon's Affectionate Compliments to Mrs Wesley and Mr Charles Wesley and hopes to hear they are both well. She has heard with concern of the dangerous illness of her old acquaintance Mr John Wesley, and this day a report of his death – She begs to hear from Mrs Wesley if it is true.'[94] Wesley had died that day at City Road, still 'fervent in spirit' and calling those present to prayer. Three months later Lady Huntingdon died in her house at Spa Fields, not far from the grave of her old acquaintance and former antagonist, but her deathbed was very different. For the past four years she had hardly left London. All her children, except Lady Moira in Dublin, were dead. Her son Frank, the tenth Earl, had died two years earlier. Although neither of her two eldest children shared her religious opinions, they retained a full share of her affection. Her letters to her son were often about business, but they are all addressed to her 'Dearest Son' and tell him of the success of her preachers.[95] He stayed with her from time to time, writing affectionate letters in his turn. 'I cannot refuse myself the pleasure of fulfilling my promise to you of a second visit at Bath. I shall therefore accompany Charles who longs to see you. We shall stop at lord Cravens near Newbury for a day or two and take a boiled chicken with you on Thursday night.' Her relations with her son-in-law and grandson were equally cordial.[96] Many of the Countess's closest friends, including Charles Wesley, were dead; others, such as Selina Wills, estranged. Those who attended her in the last few months were her constant companion, Lady Anne Erskine; her secretary, George Best; her assistant, Hannah Scutt; and Dr Lettsom, the last of a long line of medical advisers.

[93] SMU, Hunt. 116, Lady H. to T. Haweis, 6 March 1790; Cheshunt archives, F 1/2134 Haweis to Lady H., 12 June 1790; Mitchell Library, A 3023/131 and 132 draft letters from Haweis to Lady H., 12 June and 20 November 1790. Cheshunt archives, C 9/6, 9, 11 and 14; D 1/2. The Plan was adopted in 1821 after Haweis's death. For a summary account of the later history of the Connexion see E. Welch, 'Lady Huntingdon's Plans', *Guildhall Studies in London History*, 2 (1975), 31–40.

[94] Emory Univ., Lady H. to Mrs Wesley, 2 March 1791.

[95] *Gentleman's Magazine*, 59 (1789), 959.

[96] Drew Univ., Hunt. A 75–80, Lady H. to Lord H., 1769 and 21 May 1770, 10 and 28 September and 5 October 1775, 11 June 1776; Cheshunt archives, F 1/501, Lord H. to Lady H., 21 December 1782; E 4/8, 17, letter to Lord Moira used for notes by Lady H., n.d.; E 4/10, 7, copy of letter from Lady H. to Lord H., 20 November 1781; Hunt. Lib., HA Personal, box 34, 2, Lord Rawdon to Lady H., 26 April 1755.

There are two accounts of her last days. One, by Thomas Haweis, was printed; the other, by George Best, was not.[97] Each felt that his account was inadequate for such a death. Best explained that 'People in general expect wonderful dying experiences from eminent persons. Lady Huntingdons life was a continued testimony of what the Lord had done for her soul.' Therefore it was not to be expected that her deathbed should be a shining example to all sinners. Haweis, who wrote 'to confute the falsehood and silence the misrepresentations' already published, improved his narrative with pious remarks made before her illness. Her last days were concerned, as the whole of her life had been, with business. She discussed with Dr Lettsom the problem caused by her two South Seas missionaries who refused to leave England without episcopal ordination, and insisted that George Best should write a letter to Thomas Haweis about it. She worried about the supply of ministers at Spa Fields chapel. On the last day she wished to pay Jones of Llangan for his stay there, 'and said, I shall see Jones before he goes – I want to draw a Draft – the Doctor answered, you must not now have any thing to do with any Drafts but mine.'[98] Jones had been obliged to leave London early to attend an episcopal visitation, and Lady Huntingdon sent Thomas Charles 'the poor old widows importunate request' on 9 June to replace him on the 19th.[99] No reply had been received by the 17th: 'Three or 4 hours before her death ... she said to Lady Anne, Charles' Letter must be opened: I want to know if he comes – Lady Anne answered, I will go – My Lady replied, to know if he comes, that's the point.'[100]

After receiving Lady Anne's assurance that he was coming she died quietly:

> Forbear my Friends to weep,
> Since Death has lost its Sting,
> Those Christians that in Jesus sleep,
> Our God will with him bring.[101]

---

[97] T. Haweis, *A Short Account of the Last Days of ... Selina Countess Dowager of Huntingdon* (London, [1791]). Lady Moira thought that either this or Haweis's account of her mother in the *Impartial and Succinct History* was 'full of many lies' (Leics. RO, 26D53/2119, 2). NLW, Add. MS 894C, fos. 15–18, Geo. Best to David Griffiths, 20 June 1791. Griffiths was the evangelical vicar of Nevern (Pembs.).

[98] NLW, Add. MS 894C, fo. 18. A draft was a cheque on her bank, but Dr Lettsom referred to a draught (i.e. medicine).

[99] Bristol New Room, Lady H. to T. Charles, 9 June 1791.

[100] NLW, Add. MS 894C, fo. 18. Also in Haweis' *Account*, p. 11.

[101] Taken from a contemporary silk print in memory of the Countess, stored in Cheshunt archives.

Her coffin set out from Spa Fields on Monday, 27 June 1791, accompanied by four coaches containing three clergymen, John Lloyd, George Best and members of the Spa Fields and Sion chapel committees. At Highgate Dr Haweis, Dr Ford and John Lloyd returned, leaving one cleryman and the others to continue to Barnet where they dined together with a member of the Mulberry Gardens committee. From Barnet only three laymen went on to Ashby de la Zouch, where the Countess was buried, as she requested, 'as privately as decency will admit of' in an unmarked grave beside her husband.[102]

---

[102] Cheshunt archives, D1/1, f. 35. The quotation is taken from her will, printed in Cheshunt archives C16/3, p. 9.

Appendix

Seymour's *Life and Times*

There was no 'official' biography of Lady Huntingdon. In her will she directed 'that my Executors will not encourage, but will, so far as they can, prevent any publication of my life, or in any other way concerning me, nor publish, nor permit any of my letters, private correspondence, or other papers to be published'.[1] Thomas Haweis, who was the most suitable person to write a biography of his friend, observed her wishes, and contented himself with an account of her deathbed and a few pages in his book on the Christian Church.[2] One of the early students at Cheshunt College, the Revd Joshua Meffen, collected the materials in order to write a life, but nothing was ever published.[3] It was not until almost half a century later that a biography appeared, *The Life and Times of Selina Countess of Huntingdon*, which claimed to be written by 'A Member of the Houses of Shirley and Hastings.'[4]

For a century and a half writers have complained about this book. In 1841 E. P. Shirley, who called it 'a miserable work', stated that the assertion that it was written by a member of 'the families of Huntingdon and Ferrers' was untrue and that 'no member of the Shirley or Ferrers' family has given any assistance to the work in question.'[5] He endeavoured to trace the author, and was told at different times that it was the production of Lord Townshend, a minister in the Connexion and an illegitimate son of the Shirley family. The *Life and Times* was written by Aaron Crossley Hobart Seymour, whose claim to be related to either

---

[1] *Deeds of Trust and Like Documents relating to the Countess of Huntingdon's Connexion* (London, 1874), 9. A copy of this work is in the Cheshunt archives (C 16/3).
[2] *A Short Account of the Last Days of... Selina, Countess Dowager of Huntingdon* (London, [1791]; T. Haweis, *An Impartial and Succinct History* 3 (London, 1800), 239–57.
[3] Connexion archives, 4/11, John Clayton to J. Meffen, n.d.
[4] Originally issued in parts. The first edition, in two volumes, is dated 1839, and the second (with an index to each volume) 1844.
[5] *Stemmata Shirleiana* (1841), 148n.; M. Francis, 'Selina Countess of Huntingdon' (Oxford B. Litt. thesis, 1957).

family must have been very remote. Lady Huntingdon's daughter Elizabeth and her descendants were the only people who could establish a close link with both the Shirleys and the Hastings. Frequent complaints have also been made about the errors which appear in this work. Ronald Knox wrote that Seymour 'had no idea how to write a book, let alone a biography'. S. L. Ollard, writing about the expulsions from St Edmund Hall, noted the errors about that incident. J. S. Reynolds in his book on the Oxford Evangelicals refers to 'the notoriously confused testimony of Lady Huntingdon's biographer'. Canon Overton commented on the letter from Hester Gibbon to Lady Huntingdon which Seymour prints. He thought it a fabrication, but was unable to discern any motive for its concoction.[6] The general reaction of historians is that of Skevington Wood: 'This strange and often grossly inaccurate biography, is, nevertheless, packed with references',[7] which is echoed by Henry Rack's terse 'inaccurate, irritating, but indispensable'.[8]

However when the number of mistakes in Seymour's work is considered carefully, it would appear that his unreliability is sufficient to make anything that he wrote suspect. Skevington Wood's biography of Thomas Haweis has shown that Seymour's account of the Aldwinkle affair is wrong in almost all its details. His account of Lady Margaret's marriage to Benjamin Ingham is mistaken in everything but the date. His statement that Lady Huntingdon accompanied John Wesley when he left Fetter Lane in 1740 is not supported by the facts. Canon Overton's suspicions of fabricated letters has recently been confirmed by Dr Frances Harris, who has established that the two letters from the Duchess of Marlborough printed by Seymour are forgeries.[9] Yet all these authors, and many others, have continued to quote Seymour as an authority, and even on occasion to add to his errors.

A careful examination of the quotations printed by Seymour which can be identified by writer and date (many cannot) reveals that most of his sources were printed. His letters from John Wesley were almost all printed in the *Arminian Magazine* before 1839. His letters from Whitefield are taken from Gillies's collection (published in 1771) and his Doddridge letters from Humphreys's work (published in 1829). The only original manu-

[6] R. A. Knox, *Enthusiasm* (London, 1987), 486, 487; S. L. Ollard, *The Six Students* (London, 1911), 59; J. S. Reynolds, *The Evangelicals at Oxford* (Oxford, 1953), 24; J. H. Overton, *William Law, Nonjuror and Mystic* (London, 1881), 367, 368.

[7] A. S. Wood, *Thomas Haweis* (London, 1957), 23n.

[8] H. D. Rack, *Reasonable Enthusiast* (London, 1989), 559.

[9] I am indebted to Dr Frances Harris for supplying me with this information from her forthcoming biography of the Duchess of Marlborough.

scripts which he consulted are those in the Hawksworth collection (now divided between Cheshunt and the Congregational Library), and possibly the letters which Lady Huntingdon sent to her chapels which appear in his second volume, though for these no originals survive. In at least one of the Hawksworth letters he made additions to the text without indicating this.[10] His printed version would be suspect if the original had not survived. This alone makes the authenticity of any quotation in the *Life and Times* questionable. Seymour did have access to a number of transcripts of letters made about the beginning of the nineteenth century, and the letters of John Fletcher to the Countess which he prepared for publication in 1868 can be traced to this source.[11] This must be the basis for his claim that he had seen 'the documents and papers to which he alone perhaps was in a condition to have easy and continued access'.[12]

When Seymour returned from Italy towards the end of his life and settled in Bristol, Dr H. R. Reynolds, the President of Cheshunt College, made an attempt to obtain those of Seymour's 'manuscripts, pictures and books' which referred to the college. His efforts were unsuccessful, but the correspondence produced two useful references to Seymour's acquaintance with those who had known Lady Huntingdon. On 23 October 1869 he wrote: 'It was my privilege to have enjoyed the patronage and interest of Lady Huntingdon's only surviving daughter, the old Countess of Moira, who offered to support my application [to Cheshunt College].'[13] While it is quite possible that Seymour, who was born in Ireland in 1789, met Lady Moira at Dublin before she died in 1808, it is extremely unlikely that she knew anything at all of Cheshunt College, to which she did not even send an annual subscription. In a letter of July 1870 he claimed to have known Thomas Haweis well. This again is possible since Haweis spent the last years of his life at Bath, to which city Seymour removed after leaving Trinity College, Dublin. This claim is repeated in an anecdote preserved by Seymour, which he says he obtained from the 'late venerable Dr Haweis'.[14] However his acquaintance with Haweis does not appear to

[10] Cheshunt archives, G 2/ 1, 4, printed in vol.2, p.257n.
[11] This volume is now in the Methodist Archives at JRL. The letters are copied from the same transcript as those in a volume now in the Connexion archives. The original of that volume (now missing) cannot be later than 1824.
[12] *Life and Times*, vol.1, p.v. It is possible that these transcripts were made by Joshua Meffen and later passed to Seymour.
[13] The file of correspondence from which these quotations are taken is in Cheshunt archives C 9/ 6/ 63. See Leics. RO, 26D53/ 2119, 2 for Lady Moira's lack of interest in both College and Connexion.
[14] Cheshunt archives G 2/ 4.

have extended to asking him for a correct account of the Aldwinkle affair, which he might easily have done.

An examination of an earlier work published by Seymour reveals a similar pattern of duplicity. In 1811 he published in Dublin an edition of Gillies's *Memoirs of George Whitefield* 'Revised and corrected with large Additions and Improvements by Aaron C. Seymour'.[15] A year later the Revd John Jones published another edition in London 'Revised and Corrected with Observations illustrative and justificatory'. A comparison of the original with these two revisions shows that Seymour omitted chapter 8, but numbered Gillies's two appendices to make it appear that the book had one extra chapter. His 'large additions and improvements' are confined to a number of footnotes describing individuals mentioned in the text and a few additional anecdotes taken from printed sources.[16] Jones's edition, on the other hand, contains sufficient extra material to justify his more modest title.

Since it seems unlikely that any statement made by Seymour which was not supported by a reliable source can be relied upon, it has been my practice to use nothing in his book which could not be confirmed by an independent source. If it was in print before 1839, or is established by reliable manuscript evidence, then these sources (and not Seymour) are given as references. As Seymour has been extensively used by later writers who do not always quote their sources, I have occasionally encountered the self-defeating argument that Seymour must be correct since X, who wrote at a later date, has the same story. It is possible that my decision to ignore Seymour's work may have resulted in the omission of a few of his anecdotes which are authentic, but this loss is greatly outweighed by the new anecdotes given here, which cannot be suspect and which give a more accurate and more attractive picture of the Countess than Seymour's book.

---

[15] The copy in Cheshunt College library is said to be the second edition. Four editions were published in the United States.

[16] I am greatly indebted to Dr Schlenther of the University College of Wales, Aberystwyth, who has supplied me with several of the examples quoted here and has discussed Seymour's literary works with me.

Note on Sources

Manuscript Sources

The manuscript sources for the life of Lady Huntingdon have suffered more fragmentation than is usual. The records of the Shirley family were dispersed as a result of their family quarrels. Some have even found their way into the Hastings family archives. The eighteenth-century Hastings papers were scattered by the sale of 1926.[1] Many of these letters did not go to the Huntington Library, and two other large groups can be found at Leicester and Madison, NJ. Lady Huntingdon's later correspondence was never with the family papers at Ashby de la Zouch, and is now in Cambridge. However there are still notable gaps, and a few letters from this source were found in a Gloucestershire church. It is possible that, despite a careful search, other letters in private hands may come to light.

The records of other Methodist leaders, where we might expect to find letters written by Lady Huntingdon, have often been equally unfortunate. The Victorian passion for collecting the autographs of Methodists and Evangelicals has had its advantages and disadvantages. Thomas Raffles's famous collection, now dispersed, has preserved two volumes of George Whitefield's archives when all else has disappeared, but his group of letters written by Lady Anne Erskine can no longer be found.[2] Even more objectionable was the practice by some collectors of autographs of removing the signature and last few lines of a letter. This has left letters without dates, and signatures without other information. There are even a few examples of letters and their enclosures being divided between two record offices.

---

[1] See *The Huntingdon Papers*, 2 vols. (Maggs Bros, 1926).
[2] *HMC 6th Rep.* (London, 1877), App., 468–75.

Quotations from MSS

Transcribing Lady Huntingdon's letters is made doubly difficult by the need to disentangle her meaning from an unpunctuated flow of thoughts. After a possible meaning has been discovered and the appropriate breaks added to her breathless progress, it is still necessary to decipher her words. Surprisingly, the Countess normally read through her letters, making additions and alterations. She apologizes when time does not permit her to do this. However the final result is often to confound further the original meaning. Only one Methodist, Howell Harris, is her equal in illegibility, and for eccentric spellings and lack of punctuation she has no rival.

All quotations from original manuscripts, whether written by the Countess or not, are the result of a compromise between an exact transcript and the requirements of intelligibility. Apostrophes have been added to such words as 'coud', 'dont' or 'dependd' to assist the reader. The minimum amount of punctuation consistent with understanding has been added. Where a word is completely legible it has been reproduced exactly, but where this is impossible modern spelling has been used. It is not always possible to tell if such initial consonants as 'S', 'M' and 'W' were intended to be lower or upper case. Once again modern usage has been adopted if there is doubt. Where a word is abbreviated it is expanded and the writer's spelling used if it is known. These conventions occasionally lead to discrepancies, but do not affect the sense.

References to MSS

Some of the manuscript sources listed in the bibliography have never been listed, and others have only been listed by file or bundle. Some collections of letters were under rearrangement while I was using them. Therefore every letter and similar document is given a sufficiently full description either in the text or in the reference in order to enable it to be identified easily. This is particularly important for uncatalogued collections, where the number given here refers only to the arrangement of my own file of photocopies. In many cases I have also indicated where the document has appeared in print, but if the manuscript reference comes first the quotation is taken from that source.

Printed Sources

For most of the printed material I have given the name of the author or editor, the short title of the work, and the place and date of publication. Where the location of an original manuscript source quoted in the book is known, this information has been added after the citation of the printed book. For a few works, such as John Wesley's *Journals*, the date of the entry is given since previous editions are about to be superseded by Professor Ward's volumes. Similarly for Wesley's letters, references to vols. 1 and 2 (1721–55) are to Dr Baker's new edition: all other references are to the old Telford edition. An abbreviated reference is given for all reports of the Royal Commission on Historical Manuscripts – these can easily be identified from the *Guide to Location of Collections* (London, 1982). No references are given to those invaluable works, the *Dictionary of National Biography*, the *Dictionary of American Biography*, and the *Dictionary of Welsh Biography*. Most of the works cited can be easily traced in the catalogues of the British Library, Dr Williams's (and the Congregational) Library, or the *National Union Catalog*. However, an exception has been made where the original seems exceptionally rare, or a copy associated with Lady Huntingdon has been used. Occasionally, because of the difficulties of research prosecuted both in Britain and North America, different editions are cited in different places.

Manuscript Sources

Manuscripts, Britain

Aberystwyth, National Library of Wales
  Correspondence of Howell Harris (Trevecka Letters), 1739–91
  Diaries of Howell Harris (Trevecka Diaries), 1714–73
  Diaries of the Revd Edmund Jones, 1729–89
  Diaries of Thomas Roberts, 1774–89
  Correspondence of the Revd Thomas Charles, 1790–1802
  Account of Lady Huntingdon's death, 1791

Bedford, Bedfordshire Record Office
  Bedford Moravian Church records:
    MO 342 Congregation diary, 1760–2
    MO 965 Benjamin Ingham's diary, 1747
  Grey Correspondence, 1767–75

Belfast, Public Record Office of Northern Ireland
  Letter to Lord Rawdon, 1760
  Shirley of Ettington papers, 1730–91
  Gracehill Moravian church diaries (microfilm), 1758–62

Birmingham, University Library
  Venn papers, 1757–91

Bristol, City Record Office
  Episcopal records
    Piddletown institution records, 1675–1763

Bristol, Methodist New Room
  Two letters of Lady Huntingdon, 1785 and 1791

Bristol, Special Collections, University Library
  Bristol Moravian Church diaries, 1756–91

Cambridge, Cheshunt College Foundation, Westminster College
  Correspondence of Lady Huntingdon, 1727–91
  Apostolic Society minutes, 1787–1800
  Spa Fields Chapel records, 1780–1810
  Correspondence with A. C. H. Seymour, 1869–70
  Prof. A. V. Murray's papers for a biography of Lady Huntingdon, 1960–7

Cardiff, Glamorgan Record Office
  Letters of Lady H., 1742 and 1753
  Correspondence of David Jones, 1787

Chelmsford, Essex Record Office
  Correspondence of the Revd William Piercy, 1769–83

Chichester, West Sussex Record Office
  Record of Chichester Connexion chapel, 1811

Ely, Connexion Church:
  Papers, 1785–1802

Fulneck (Yorks.), Moravian Archives
  Diaries, 1760–2
  Correspondence of Benjamin Ingham and others, 1738–49

Gloucester, Gloucestershire Record Office
  Ebley Connexion Church:
    Letters to Lady Huntingdon, 1767–89

Hull, University Library
  Hotham correspondence, 1743–80

Leeds, District Archives
  Ledston Hall papers, 1702–58
  Diary of the Revd Henry Crooke, 1759–69

Leeds, Yorkshire Archaeological Society
  Records of Lady Elizabeth Hastings' Charity, 1732–40
  Records of Rodhill Inghamite Chapel, 1754–58

Leicester, Leicestershire Record Office
  Hastings family letters, 1700–50
  Shirley family legal and other papers, eighteenth century Parish registers of Ashby de la Zouch, Breedon and Castle Donnington
  Leicester Archdeaconry records, 1745–54
  Deacon family papers, 1769–1800

Lewes, East Sussex Record Office
  Records of Cliffe Chapel, 1776–91

London, British Library
  Newcastle papers, 1725–60

London, Congregational Library, Dr Williams's Library
  Letters to Haweis and Wills, 1763–90
  The Revd Thomas Gibbons's diary, 1749–85

London, Dr Williams's Library
  Three letters to the Revd Philip Doddridge, 1750
  Poem on death of Lady Huntingdon, 1791

London, New College Library, Dr Williams's Library
  Correspondence of the Revd Philip Doddridge, 1748–51

London, Friends House Library
  Abiah Darby's diary, 1744–69

London, Greater London Record Office
  London Consistory Court records, 1778–80

London, Guildhall Library
  Dissenting Deputies' minutes, 1778

London, Hoare's Bank Archives
  Ledgers, 1721–45

London, House of Lords Record Office
  Journals, 1698–1760

London, Lambeth Palace Library
  Correspondence with Bishop Lavington, 1752
  Court of Arches records, 1780–1
  Registers of noblemen's chaplains, 1714–91

London, Moravian Church House
  Correspondence with James Hutton, 1740–63

London, Public Record Office
  Registers of Connexion Chapels from 1769
  Duchy of Lancaster, Enfield Chase timber, 1756

London, Society for the Promotion of Christian Knowledge
  Correspondence, 1728–39
  Account books, 1729–41

Manchester, John Rylands University Library
  Whitefield's appointment as chaplain, 1748
  Letters to the Revd Thomas Wills and others, 1774–84
  Eng. MSS 1057–1081, transcripts of Moravian records

Manchester, Methodist Archives, John Rylands University Library
  Letters to Charles and John Wesley, 1741–75
  Letters of Ingham, De Courcy, Berridge and others
  A. C. H. Seymour's transcripts of Fletcher letters, 1760–73

Matlock, Derbyshire Record Office
  Levinge pedigree, *c.* 1800

Northampton, Northamptonshire Record Office
  Aldwinkle presentation deed and bond, 1764

Olney (Bucks.), Cowper and Newton Museum
  Letter from the Revd John Berridge, n.d.

Oxford, Rhodes House Library
  SPG, annual reports, 1722–41

Rayleigh (Essex), Connexion archives
  Original letters to Lady Huntingdon, 1783–90
  Copies of letters to Lady Huntingdon, 1760–84
  Letter of administration, 1746
  Probate accounts, 1746 and 1758
  Title deeds, 1768–92

Stafford, Staffordshire Record Office
  Letters to Lord Dartmouth, 1768 and 1773

Warwick, Warwickshire Record Office
  Shirley family correspondence, 1718–42
  Case of Earl Ferrers, 1726

York, Borthwick Institute
  Records of Lady Elizabeth Hastings's Charity, 1737–40
  Parish registers of Ledsham and Aberford
  Marriage Licence Allegations, 1741

Manuscripts, United States

Athens, Hargrett Manuscript Library, University of Georgia
  Letter of Lady Huntingdon, 1784; and printed hymn

Atlanta, University Library, Emory University
  Correspondence of Lady Huntingdon, 1775–91

Atlanta, Georgia Dept of Archives
  Bethesda minute book, 1791–1809
  Chatham County Court minutes, 1797

Carlisle, PA, Dickinson College
  Letter of the Revd C. Nisbet, 1771 (copy at Cheshunt, G 2/ 3)

Dallas, Bridwell Library, Southern Methodist University
  Letters to Mrs Wadsworth and the Revd Thomas Haweis, 1765–90

Durham, NC, William R. Perkins Library, Duke University
  Three letters of Lady Huntingdon, 1752–71

Madison, NJ, Methodist Archives, Drew University
  Correspondence of Lady Huntingdon, 1739–55

Nashville, The Upper Room
  Letters to the Revd Mr Beale, 1779–84 (copies at Cheshunt, G2/2)

New Haven, Osborn Collection, Yale University Library
  Letters to the Revd P. Doddridge, 1744–51

New York, Columbia University Library
  Letters to Sir James Jay, 1783

New York, Pierpont Morgan Library
  Letters of Lady Huntingdon, 1784–5

San Marino, CA, Huntington Library
  Hastings family papers, eighteenth century
  Lady Huntingdon's commonplace book
  Miscellaneous letters, 1748–85

Santa Barbara, CA, University of California Library
  Letter of Lady Huntingdon, 1752

Savannah, GA, Georgia Historical Society
  Account of Bethesda, 1748
  Copies of Habersham correspondence, 1756–75
  Clay correspondence, 1776–93
  John Johnson papers, 1791–2

Washington DC, Library of Congress
  George Washington's papers, 1784–99

Letters to the Revd George Whitefield, 1737–69

Washington, DC, National Archives
  Continental Congress correspondence, 1784

Manuscripts – other countries

Australia, Sydney, Mitchell Library
  Letters and autobiography of the Revd Thomas Haweis, 1734–96

Germany, Herrnhut, Moravian Archives
  Letters of Anna Nitschmann, 1739–40

Ireland, Dublin, National Library of Ireland
  Ormonde letters, 1705–6

Manuscripts – in private hands

Records of the Wheler family, Yorks., eighteenth century
Four letters of Lady Huntingdon 1769–84 (Mr Peter Conlan, Kent)
One letter of Jonathan Parsons, 1770 (Mr Heard, Arlington, Virginia)
Seven letters of Lady Huntingdon and one of Lord Huntingdon,
  1746–1775 (Lord Granard, Castle Forbes, Ireland)

Index

In this index 'chapel' means a chapel associated with the Countess or her Connexion, and 'student' a member of Trefeca/Cheshunt College

Aberford (Yorks.) 47
Abingdon, Lord 9, 10
Akenside, Dr Mark 73
Aldridge, William, student 118
Aldwinkle (Northants.) 103
   advowson 102–10
   dilapidations 106
American Revolution 146, 147, 162
Anderson, Capt. 137, 138
Apostolic Society 185, 186, 190, 197
   founded 184
   subscribers 186–8
Arches, Court of 158
Argyle, Duke of 94
Arminian controversy 5, 51, 120–4
Arminian Magazine 212
Articles, Fifteen 161, 184, 204
Arundel (Sussex) 100
Ashbourne (Derby.) chapel 197
Ashby de la Zouch (Leics.) 2, 17, 18, 77, 93
   Ashby Place 46, 58, 68–71, 87, 90
   church 63, 64, 210
Astell, Mary 18, 34, 96
Astle, William 187
Astwell House (Northants.) 7, 9, 11
Austin, Mr 58
Awakening, The Great 37, 38

Baddeley, George 71, 87
Baillie, George 163
Baptists 50, 51, 194
Barber, Jonathan 132
Barham, Mr 82, 87
Barlow, Ann 80–5

Barnard, Thomas 28, 36, 41, 42, 47, 56
Bartlet, Mrs 67
Barton in the Beans (Leics.) 50
Bateman, Lord 27
Bath, Lord 69
Bath (Som.) 24, 33, 47, 60, 61, 64, 69, 71, 81, 85, 98, 154, 165,
   chapel 100, 101, 191, 192, 196, 199, 201
   committee 196, 197
   school 195
   services 196
   singers 199, 201
   hospital 93
   Irish bishops at 95
   waters 22–4, 60
Bedford Moravians 82, 83, 86–8, 199
Bencoolen (India) mission 126, 127
Bengeworth (Worcs.) 112
Benezet, Anthony 144, 145
Benson, Joseph, student 119, 128, 176
Benson, Joseph 119, 121
Benson, Martin, Bishop of Gloucester 19, 28
Berridge, John 98, 118
Best, George 181, 204, 206–9
Bethesda (Georgia) 131–47, 162–75, 186
   College 134
   damage to 142, 143, 175
   Orphan House 4, 124, 133
Bethesda, Rape of 175
Bexley (Kent) 53
Birmingham chapel 191
bishops, Irish 95
Blatch, Benjamin 112

Boehme, Jacob, *Works* 65–7
Bolingbroke, Lord 70
Book of Common Prayer 148, 197
  amended 200
Bosanquet, Mary 97, 98
Bowen, Hannah 114–16, 119
Bowes, Mr 59
Bowlling, Mrs 115
Bradford, John 186
Bradford on Avon (Wilts.) 82
Brainerd, David 39
Breaston (Derby.) 49
Brecon (Brecknock) 183, 197
Brewer, Samuel 104–8
Bridgen, Mr 167
Brighton (Sussex) 99, 154, 181, 191
  chapel 89, 96, 99, 101, 199, 200
Bristol 54, 61, 87, 93, 122, 181, 197
  Clifton 74, 79, 84, 90, 91
  waters 23, 24, 79, 179
Brown, William 156
Brussels (Belgium) 205
Bunker Hill, Battle described 162
Burton on Trent (Staffs.) 24
Bury (Lancs.) 39
Byng, John (Lord Torrington) 75
Byrom, John 67

Caen (France) 73
Calvinist controversy 5, 51, 69, 120–4
Cambridge, St John's College 89
Cambridgeshire 60
Cambuslang (Lanark) 39
Canada
  New Brunswick 205
  Newfoundland 102
  Nova Scotia 205
Carolina Indians 43
Carrickmacross (Monaghan) 11, 14
Cart, Elizabeth 52, 53
Castle Donnington (Leics.) 42, 45
  Quakers at 51
Cathedral cities, chapels in 191
Chancery, Court of 13, 15, 18, 30, 32
Chapman, Walter 83, 84, 94
Charles, Thomas, of Bala 182, 188, 207, 209
Charleston (South Carolina) 137–40, 142, 172
Charlestown (Mass.) 162
Chartley (Staffs.) 8, 31
Chelmsford (Essex) 93
Chelsea, London 61–63, 69, 78
Cheshunt (Herts.) 149, 177, 187, 189, 213
Chesterfield, Lord 69, 73–5

Cheyne, George 23–5, 29, 60, 61, 65, 66
Chichester (Sussex) chapel 102, 191, 194, 200
circuits, preaching 190, 202
Clarges, Anne 8
Classics taught at College 129
Clay, Joseph 172–4
Clayton, John, student 179, 180
clergy discipline 149
Clifton, *see* Bristol
Clunie, Alexander 107–10
coal mines 47, 48
Cobham (Surrey) 81
Coke, Lady Mary 76
College, *see* Apostolic Society
College Farm (Trefeca) 89, 114, 115
colliers 47, 48, 93
Compton, Lady Elizabeth 13
Conduit, Mr 60
Congregationalists 194, 197
Connexion 204
  chapels 190–9
  districts 206, 207
  Fifteen Articles 161, 184, 204
  funds 196, 207
  hymnbooks 199–201
  members 198, 199
  ministers 202, 203
  music 199, 201
  schools 195
  services 196
  students 191
  trusts 207
Conon, George 106
conversion, stages in 40
Conyers, Dr 114
Cook, Joseph, student 136–9
Cookham (Berks.) 71, 83
Coram's Hospital 35
Cork (Ireland) 95, 164
Cornwall, miners 68
Cosson, Elizabeth 116, 136–9, 141, 142, 163
Cosson, John, student 127, 136–9, 141, 142
Cotes, John 8
Coughlan, Laurence 102
Courtney, Lady Ann 9
Cowper, Fanny 4–5, 68
Cowper, William, of Enfield 69
Cowper, William, poet 107
Craven, William 153
Cresset, Mrs 82
Cromwell, Oliver, lawyer 167, 168, 172, 174, 192

Index

Cureton, John, student 181
Cutts, General 10

Darby, Abiah 114
Darracott, Risdon 84
Dartmouth, Lord 108, 134, 144, 174, 201
Davies, Mr 116, 126, 203
Davies, Edward 112, 113
Davies, Thomas, student 181
Davies, William, student 179
Day, Thomas 167
De Courcy, Richard 101
Delegates, Court of 158
Delitz, Countess 70, 82
Deptford, (Kent) 39
Derbyshire,
  estates 8, 12
  riots 4, 76, 77
Dixon, George 111
Dodd, William 78
Doddridge, Philip 38, 70–2
Donnington Park 4, 17, 20 23, 28, 29, 42–5, 49, 56, 57, 60, 62, 63, 67, 73–5
Dover (Kent) 137, 193, 199
Draycott (Derby.) 49
Dublin 11, 136, 154
  chapel 4, 195
Durrant, Mr 166

Eccles, C. S. 136, 139–42
Edwards, Jonathan 38
Edwin, Catherine 67, 70, 71, 80–5, 94
Edwin, Lady Charlotte 82
Elliott, Mr 104
Elliott, Richard 94
Ellis, Edward 48, 49, 68, 71
El Pardo debate 27
Elstob, Elizabeth 18, 34
Ely (Cambs.) chapel 194
Enfield (Middx.) 11, 25, 56, 57, 60, 61, 68
  Chase 25, 26, 45, 53, 55
England, Methodist periodicals 38
Erskine, Lady Anne 4, 185, 204, 207–9
Erskine, James 52–5
Essex, Earl of, portrait 31
Ettington (War.) 13
Evans, John 170
Exeter (Devon) chapel 190
Eyre, John, student 129

Faculties, Court of 151, 152
Fénèlon, Archbishop, *Works* 65
Ferrers, Elizabeth, Countess 8, 30, 169
Ferrers, Henry, 3rd Earl 30, 31, 59

Ferrers, Lawrence, 4th Earl 59, 77
  executed 77, 78
Ferrers, Mary, Countess Dowager 10, 15, 22, 32, 33
Ferrers, Robert, 1st Earl 7–10, 12
Ferrers, Selina, Countess Dowager 8, 12, 13, 29–32
Ferrers, Washington, 2nd Earl 7–10, 12–15, 21, 29, 30
  See also Shirley
Fifteen Articles 161, 184
Finch, Selina, *see* Ferrers, Countess Dowager
Finchley (Middx.) 104
Fleetwood Family 103, 104
Fletcher, John William 89, 113–23, 176
Fletcher, Mary, *see* Bosanquet
Florida, East 164
Folkestone (Kent) chapel 193, 198, 199
Foote, Samuel 110
Ford, Benjamin 187
Ford, John 210
Fore (West Meath) 10
Forty-five, The 62
Fountain, Mr 28
Fox, HMS, wrecked 10
Francke, A.H. 38, 132
Frederick, Prince of Wales 23, 54, 70
French taught at College 206
Frey, Andrew 87
Fulneck (Yorks.) 86

Gardiner, Col. James 72
Geary, Archdeacon 18
Georgia 41
  Assembly 174
  University 172, 174
Georgia Packet 137, 138, 141
Gibbons, Revd. Thomas 71
Gibbons, Thomas, lawyer 174
Gibbons, William, student 128
Gidding, Little (Hunts.) 85
Glamorgan, preaching in 180
Glascott, Cradock 100, 102, 117, 126, 147, 154, 156, 158, 159, 188, 203
Glazebrook, James, student 114, 118, 127, 178
Glen, John 164
Glenorchy, Lady Willielma 203
Gloucester 39
  chapel 191
Gordon Riots 197
Gracehill (Antrim) 87
Grand Tour 19, 64, 73

Gray, Daniel, student 194
Green, Mr, student 181
Grinfield, Ann 80–4, 87
Groom of Stole 76
Grove, Thomas, student 112
Groves, Mr 165, 166
Gumley, Col. John 70, 71
Gurney, Mr 57
Guy, Mr, printer 200
Guyon, Mme, *Works* 65

Habersham, James 131, 136, 138, 140–3, 147
Habersham, John 172
Hagen, John 43
Halifax (Yorks.), Vicar of 46, 47
Hall, Nathaniel 164
Halle (Germany) 38, 132
Hamilton, Lady Archibald 70
Handel, George Frederick 201
Harris, Mrs 114
Harris, Betty 89
Harris, Howell 38, 40, 55, 69, 70, 78, 205
   and College 112–21, 125, 126, 176
   and Lady Huntingdon 44, 54, 64, 88, 89, 131
Harris, Thomas 114
Hartley, Thomas 84
   Sermons 40, 67, 82
Hastings, Mr, claimant 94
Hastings, Lady Anne 18, 24, 28, 45, 46, 58, 90
Hastings, Lady Betty 7, 17–21, 23, 24, 28, 33, 65, 89, 99
   'Aspasia' 18
   charities 33, 41
   death 35, 36, 43, 45, 46, 56, 58
   library 34, 38
   pensioners 94
Hastings, Lady Catherine 59
   marriage 19
   See also Wheler
Hastings, Lady Elizabeth, 22, 29, 208
   marriage 64, 76
   See also Rawdon
Hastings, Ferdinando 18, 22, 28, 58, 61
Hastings, Lady Frances 18, 20, 22, 24, 35, 43, 46, 58
Hastings, George 22, 28, 29, 34, 36, 56, 57, 58, 61, 65
Hastings, Henry 22, 64, 76, 99
Hastings, Lady Margaret 18, 24, 42–4, 46
   marriage 45–7
   See also Ingham

Hastings, Lady Selina 22, 29, 64, 76, 84, 201
   See also Huntingdon
Hastings estates 16, 18
Hastings, Rape of (Sussex) 60
Hatherleigh (Devon) 102, 159
Haweis, Thomas 1, 102, 149, 188, 207, 210, 213
   at Aldwinkle 102–10
   at Countess's deathbed 5, 209
   at Spa Fields 156–9
   trustee 207
Hawes, R., printer 67
Hawksworth, James, student 126, 154
Hayes, John, student 178
Hemington, Robert 90
Henry, Governor Patrick 171
Hereford chapel 182, 191, 195
Hertford, Countess of 64
Hervey, James 88, 151
Hewer, William, student 126, 127
Higson, John 111
Hill, Miss 126
Hill, Sir Richard 1, 174
Hill, Rowland 1, 100
Hill, Thomas, student 136–8
historians, opinions of *Life & Times* 212
Hole, Mrs 46
Holland, Mr, student 181
Holmes, John, student 128
Holms, Mr & Mrs 46
Hook, John 194
Hooke, Nathanial 83
Hotham, Sir Charles 70, 86
Hotham, Lady Gertrude 70, 99
Houghton Park (Beds.) 54
Howell, Henry 182
Hughes, Mr 115
Hughes, Mr, of Tregunter 183
Hughes & Walsh, printers 200
Hughes, Elizabeth, *see* Cosson
Hull, Christopher, student 128
Hunting 20
Huntingdon, Frances, Countess 17, 18
Huntingdon, Francis, 9th Earl 22, 28, 58, 61, 85, 101, 146
   collections 74
   Grand Tour 64, 73
   Groom of Stole 76
   Master of Horse 75
   politics 147
   travels 73–5
   visits to mother 197, 208
Huntingdon, George, 7th Earl 16, 17

Index

Huntingdon, Selina, Countess 14, 15
  accident to 61
  Aldwinkle 102–10
  Bethesda 4, 124, 131–47, 162–75
  biographies 211–13
  birthplace 7, 9, 11
  chapels 190–9
  chaplains 151, 154–8
  children 35
  College 113–30, 177
  conversion 42, 43, 52, 53, 64
  death 5, 6, 174, 209, 210
  dowry 13, 21, 77, 78
  Howell Harris 44, 54, 64
  health 26, 57, 60, 61
  Theophilus Lindsey 89–93
  marriage 19, 21
  ministers 202, 203
  missions 41, 126, 127, 209
  Moravians 52
  secession 160
  secretary 181, 204, 206–9
  students 128
  tracts 66, 67
  George Washington 169–71
  Charles Wesley 44, 45, 54, 79
  John Wesley 45, 79
  George Whitefield 44
  will 2
Huntingdon, Theophilus, 6th Earl 16, 17
Huntingdon, Theophilus, 8th Earl 7, 16, 19, 23, 25, 27, 30, 31, 46, 89
  accident to 61
  death 16, 63
  Grand Tour 19
  health 56, 60, 62
  marriage 19, 20
  See also Hastings
Huntingdon, William, S.S. 96
Hutchinson, John 80
Hutton, James 41, 43, 44, 46, 50
hymnbooks, Connexion 199–201

Independents, *see* Congregationalists
independent chapels, preaching at 180
independency discouraged 180
Indians, missions to 169–71, 205
indigo plantation 140, 164
Ingham, Benjamin 41–3, 87
  marriage 45–7
Ireland 9, 10, 14
  Shirley estates 9, 12, 30–2
  student from 178

Jackson, James 174

Jacobite trials 62
Jamaica 164
Jansenists 65
Jay, Sir James 171
Jenkins, Mr, student 178
Jernegan, William 192
Johnson, Mr 28
Johnson Dr J. 35
Johnson, John, murdered 77
Johnson John, student 173–5
Jones, Mr 182, 192
Jones, David 129, 170, 202, 209
Jones, Edmund 125, 129
Jones, Herbert 153
Jones, Joan 183
Jones, John 94, 202
Jones, Theophilus, student 179
Jones, Thomas 111, 112
Jones, Thomas, student 136, 181
justification 65

Kay, Benjamin 112
Keen, Robert 135, 142, 146, 166
Ken, Bishop Thomas, *Sermons* 49
Kendal (Westmorland) chapel 194
Kent, William 25, 56
Kilmorey, Frances, Lady 17
Kilmorey, Mary, Lady 11, 15, 32, 44, 61, 113
Kilmorey, Thomas, Lord 11, 29, 31, 32, 60, 61, 77
  See also Needham
Kilsyth (Stirling) 39
Kimpton, John 103–10
King's Bench, Court of 158
Kingsbury, William 51
Kingswood, Bristol 48, 54, 119

Lancaster, Duchy of 25, 26
Lang, Mlle. 74
La Place, Mrs 28
Lasere, Mr 94
Latin and Greek taught at College 129
Latrobe, Benjamin 86
Laurens, Henry 167, 171, 172
Lavington, George, Bishop of Exeter 94
Law, William 38, 66, 85
  Works 3, 65–7, 83
Leake (Notts.) 59
'leaping' 179
Ledston Hall (Yorks.) 17, 24, 28, 42, 46, 57, 58
Leeds Grammar School 28, 56
Leicester 72, 205

Leicestershire, Baptists 47–51
  Hastings estates 17, 18
  Shirley estates 8, 12
  riots 4, 76
Leighton, Archbishop, *Works* 71
  Mrs 115
Leominster (Herefs.) 179
Lettsom, Dr 208
Levinge, Lawrence 32, 33
Levinge, Mary, marriage 8
Levinge, Sir Richard 9, 13, 21
Lewes (Sussex) chapel 194, 198
Lewis, Mr 181
Lewis, Elizabeth, marriage 16
Lewis, Sir John 16, 17
Lighcliffe (Yorks.) 46
Lindsey, Miss 90
Lindsey, Theophilus 89–92
Llangatwg Lingoed (Mon.) chapel 195
Llewelyn, William 179
Lloyd, John 127, 183, 207, 210
Lloyd, Mr, student 178
Lloyd, Samuel, student 178
London
  Adelphi chapel 193
  Castle & Falcon Inn 184
  Clarges St. 29
  Clerkenwell 152, 153
  Consistory Court 154–7
  Coram's Hospital 35
  Downing St. 56
  Exmouth St. 153
  Holywell Mount chapel 193, 204, 206
  Lock Hospital 89
  Magdalene Hospital 153
  Marylebone School 28
  Mulberry Gardens chapel 187, 188, 191–3, 198, 201, 204, 210
  Northampton chapel 152
  Pall Mall 12
  Pantheon 153
  Portman chapel 153
  St Andrews Holborn 153
  St Giles in the Fields 153
  Savile Row 25, 56, 58
  Sion chapel 184, 188, 191, 210
  Spa Fields chapel 155–61, 165, 186–8, 191, 197, 199, 204, 206, 210
  school 195
  ordination at 161
  Spa Fields burial ground 160
  Shoreditch 193
  Spital House Square 90
  Tabernacle 55, 136, 167
  Tottenham Court 147, 167
  Wapping 202
  Westminster chapel 102
  School 28, 56, 59, 61, 73
  Whitechapel 188
  Woolwich chapel 165, 166, 175
Looe (Cornwall) 180
Lords, House of 13, 17, 30, 77, 158
Loughborough (Leics.) 18
Loughrea (Galway) 101

Macaulay, Catherine 147
M'Culloch, William 38, 54
Madan, Martin 89, 105–10, 136
Madeley (Salop) 89, 113
Madrid (Spain) 74
Margrate, David 142
Markfield (Leics.) 43, 48–50, 68, 71, 100
Marlborough, Duchess of 212
Master of Horse 75
Mather, Cotton 39
Matthews, John, student 111, 112
Maxfield, Thomas 101, 102, 127, 131
Mead, Henry, student 128, 138
Meeting House Licences 99, 151
Meffen, Joshua 213
'Men', The 39
Meldrum, John, student 128, 180
Methodism
  in eighteenth cent. 37, 38, 40, 148
  in Wales 37
Middlesex election 76
Middleton, Dr 80
Middleton, Erasmus 111
Middleton, Joseph, student 194
Milgrove, Benjamin 201
Moira, *see* Hastings and Rawdon
Molinos, Miguel de, *Works* 67
Mons New Testament 65
Montague 138
Moody, William, student 180
Moravian Church 5, 39, 40, 42, 43, 47, 51, 81, 82, 84, 85, 87
  hymns 42
Moses, Evan 179
music in chapels 200–2

Needham, Mr 94; *see also* Kilmorey
Nelson, John 95
Newcastle, Duke of 62
Newcastle upon Tyne 48
New England, Methodist periodicals 38
Newman, Henry 34
Newmarket (Cambs.) 26

Index

Newton, John 107, 112
New York State 169
Nicol, Dr 28
Nicoll, James 177
Nightingale, J.C. 22, 31, 77
   marriage 11, 30
Nightingale, Lady Mary 11, 15
Nitschman, Anna 43
Northamptonshire, Shirley estates 9, 12
North Carolina 169
Nottingham 27, 68
Nottinghamshire, Shirley estates 8, 12
Norwich chapel 194, 198
Nyberg, L.T. 87, 88

Oakthorpe (Leics.) 47
Ockham (Surrey) 81
Oglethorpe, James E. 41
Okely, Francis 113
Oldham, James O. 187
Ollive, John 99, 151
Ordinations 161
Ormonde, Lord 10
Orphan House, *see* Bethesda
Orter, Sir John 205
Ossett (Yorks.) 41
Ote Hall (Sussex) 99, 151, 191
Otterden (Kent) 59
Oxford
   Christ Church 19, 73
   Queen's College 41
   St Edmund Hall 91, 102, 111, 112, 114
   University Court 111, 112

Pacific Islands, mission 205
Page, Mr 144
paintings and sculpture collected 74
Pantycelyn, son of 181
Paris 22, 74, 205
Parrott, Mrs 88
Peach, Mr, student 126
Peckwell, Henry 102, 124, 152, 176, 191, 195, 200
peeress's right to chaplains 151, 154–8
Pennsylvania 169
Pentycross, Thomas 102, 202, 203
Peterborough, Bishop of 104–8
Pewsey (Wilts.) 89, 96
Philipps, Sir John 41
Phillips, David, student 173
Phillips, Samuel, student 191
Pickering, Mrs 67
Piddletown (Dorset) 90
Piercy, Richard 140, 143, 163, 166, 167

Piercy, William 136–47, 160–8, 175, 202, 203
Platt, W.F., student 193
Plymouth (Devon) 51, 150, 191
Porter, Edward, student 178
Portsmouth (Hants.) 180
Potter, John, Archbishop of Canterbury 95
Powell, Averina 181–3
prayers read 148, 197
Predestination 123
Presbyterians 55, 100, 180, 193
Prevost, Gen. 163, 165
Priestley, Thomas 101
Pritchard, James, student 180
Protestant dissenting deputies 201

Quakers 5, 51, 53, 91, 97, 98, 144
Quietists 51, 65, 67, 83

Rant, Felicia 21
Ratby (Leics.) 50
Rawdon, Lord 86
   marriage 22
   See also Hastings
Reynolds, H.R. 213
rice plantations 164
Richards, Lewis, student 136–8
Richardson, Mr 192
Rimius, Henry 87
riots, 76, 77, 150
Roberts, Daniel, student 136–8, 143
Roberts, Evan 116, 183
Roberts, Thomas 125, 126, 179
Rogers, Jacob 43, 44
Rome (Italy) 32
Rottingdean (Sussex) 100
rounds, preaching 180
Rowland, Daniel, student 180
Ryland, John 153

St Agnes (Cornwall) 102, 183
St Columb (Cornwall) 190
St Gennys (Cornwall) 94
St Ives (Cornwall) 68
sanctification 65
Satchell, Robert, student 181
Savannah (Georgia) 137, 138, 140, 147, 174
Scarborough waters 24
Scotland 37, 39, 178
Scott, Mr 81
Scutt, Hannah 4, 208
secession 157–61, 204

Secker, Thomas, Archbishop of
    Canterbury 95
Sellon, Walter 95, 152
Sellon, William 152-4, 158-61
sermons 149, 199
Seymour, A.C.H. 2, 213, 214
'shaking' 179
Shipman, Joseph, student 111, 112, 118
Shirley family 7-16
    Lady Anna 10
    Lady Barbara 10, 12
    E.P. 214
    Lady Elizabeth 9, 10
    Lady Frances 70, 151, 203
    George 31
    Lawrence 8, 9, 12, 21, 30, 31, 59, 77
    Lady Mary 10, 29, 33
    Lord Robert 9
    Robert 9, 31
    Lady Selina 7
    Walter 101, 110, 122, 123, 201
Shirley estates 8, 9
Shrubsole, William jun. 195
Sidney, Edwin 1
simony 103-10
Skrine, Elizabeth 81, 84, 85
slaves 133, 139, 141, 142, 144, 145, 175
Sloane, Sir Hans 61, 62
Smisby (Derby.) 95
Smith, Roger 164
Society for Promoting Christian
    Knowledge 34, 35, 41
Society for Propagation of the Gospel 34,
    41
societies, religious 39, 40, 49, 54
soliders, conscripted 93
Somerset, Duchess of 90
    Duke of 90
Southampton 51
spas, chapels at 190, 191
Staffordshire, Shirley estates in 8
Stair, Lord 95
Stanhope, Mr 95
Staunton Harrold (Leics.) 8, 12, 20, 29, 60
Steele, Richard 18
Story, Thomas 51
Strafford, Lady 33
Strafford, Lord 27
students 40
    preaching 180
    reports on 178, 181
    senior 176
    Welsh 178
Stumphousen, Adam 194

Swansea (Glam.) 184
    chapel 100, 191, 192
    Corporation 192

Talgarth (Brecknock.) 114, 180
Tatnall, Joseph 164
Taylor, David 49, 50
Taylor, John 50
Taylor, William 154-9, 186
Teignmouth (Devon) 203
Telfair, William 146, 163
Thame (Oxon.) chapel 194
Thirty-nine Articles 90
Thomas, Elizabeth 128
Thomson, George 94
Thoresby, Ralph 34
Thornton, John 108-11
tickets, admission 156, 157
tobacco 26
Toleration Act 150
Toplady, Augustus M. 63, 126
Townsend, Joseph 89
Townshend, Lord 211
Tranquebar (India) 35
Trancker, George 86
Travelling Fund 196
Tredustan Court (Brecknock.) 183
Trefeca (Brecknock.) 40, 78, 92, 141, 144,
    197
Trefeca College 89, 112-20, 124, 176-89
    Apostolic Soc. 184, 185
    anniversaries 116, 125
    curriculum 119, 185
    description 117
    housekeepers 116, 181
    library 128, 129
    moved 184
    opened 116
    presidents 113-23, 125, 176
    revival at 117, 118
    students 120, 128, 161, 177-82, 184,
        185
    tutors 116
    Welsh spoken 185
Trefeca Family 112-21, 130
Trefeca Isaf 114, 115
Trelawny, Sir Harry 180
Trevecka, see Trefeca
Truro (Cornwall) 106
Trust deeds 207
Tunbridge Wells (Kent) chapel 100, 116,
    181, 191, 199
Twickenham (Middx.) 10, 12

Unitas Fratrum, see Moravians

Vanhorne, David 144
Vaughan, Gwen 179
Venn, Henry 89
Virginia 52, 169, 171

Walford, Richard 156, 157
Walker, Samuel 106
Walkinshaw, Mrs 27
Wallingford (Berks.) 102
Walmesley, Magdalen 62
Walpole, Horace 75, 199, 201
Walpole, Sir Robert 23
Warburton, William, Bishop of Gloucester 95
Warcopp, John 151
Warrington (Lancs.) 67
Warwick 180
Warwickshire, Shirley estates 8, 12, 30
Washington, George 169–71
Washington, Lawrence 8
Watkins, Thomas 196
Watts, Isaac 70
Welsh Association 197
Welsh language 185
Wesley, Charles 41, 44, 45, 49, 50, 52–4, 66, 68, 69, 78, 79, 83, 85, 88, 117, 208
  hymns 201
  letters 68
Wesley, John 37, 38, 40, 45, 48, 50, 52, 53, 66, 69, 78, 79, 116, 119, 147, 192
  complaints 89, 101, 120, 123
  death 208
Wesley, Mrs Sally 79, 88, 182, 208
Wesleyan Conference 120
West, Daniel 108, 135, 146
Weston, Mr, student 181
Wheatley, Phyllis 131, 144

Wheler, Lady Catherine 18, 21, 27, 35
Wheler, Sir George 19
Wheler, Granville 34, 59, 90
  marriage 19
Wheler, Selina 98, 102, 208
Whitaker, Nathaniel 144
White, William, student 136, 137
Whitefield, George 34, 38, 41, 43–5, 52, 55, 68, 69, 109, 132–5, 214
  chaplain 152
  death 124, 131
Wigan (Lancs.) chapel 173
Wilkes, John 76
Williams, Mr 118, 119
Williams, Mr, student 118
Williams, John 125, 181, 182
Williams, Peter 179, 181
Williams, William 120, 127, 181
Wills, Thomas 98, 102, 154, 157, 160, 170, 186, 187, 203, 205
  marriage 102
  secedes 157–9
Wilmot, Eardley 62
Wilson, Dr 147
Wiltshire, Shirley estates 12, 13
Winchester College (Hants.) 57
Winchmore Hill (Middx.) 96
Winter, Cornelius 134
Winwick (Northants.) 67
Wivelsfield (Sussex), *see* Ote Hall
women, public role of 96
  preachers 98
Woolwich (Kent) 136
Worcester chapel 191, 192, 199
Wright, Sir James 162, 163, 165
Wright, Mr 140

Zinzendorf, Count 39, 42, 52, 78, 86